The Romance Writer's
Pink Pages

How to Order:

Single copies may be ordered from Prima Publishing, P.O. Box 1260BK, Rocklin, CA 95677; telephone (916) 786-0426. Quantity discounts are also available. On your letterhead, include information concerning the intended use of the books and the number of books you wish to purchase.

The Romance Writer's Pink Pages

The Insider's Guide to Getting Your Romance Novel Published

Eve Paludan

Prima Publishing
P.O. Box 1260BK
Rocklin, CA 95677
(916) 786-0426

Production: Robin Lockwood, Bookman Productions
Copyediting: Toby Wraye
Typography: WESType
Interior design: Paula Goldstein, Bookman Productions
Cover design: The Dunlavey Studio, Sacramento

Library of Congress Cataloging-in-Publication Data

Paludan, Eve.

    Romance writer's pink pages : the insider's guide to getting your romance novel published / Eve Paludan.

      p. cm.

      Includes index.

      ISBN 1-55958-349-5

      1. Love stories—Authorship.   2. Love stories—Marketing.

I. Title.

PN3377.5.L68P34   1993

808´.066813—dc20   93-4319

                                                    CIP

94 95 96 97 98 RRD 10 9 8 7 6 5 4 3 2 1

Printed in the United States of America

Contents

*I dedicate this book to every romance writer
who has ever breathed two lovers to life
across a blank sheet of paper.*

Acknowledgments

$\mathcal{I}$ would like to express my deep appreciation to literary agent Evan Fogelman for his enthusiasm, encouragement and advice, as well as for writing the candid lead article about agents.

All the staff at Prima Publishing including:

Jennifer Basye, who voiced her enthusiasm for this book to Ben Dominitz.

Ben Dominitz, for trusting his gut instincts (and Jennifer) when he said yes.

And especially to Andi Reese Brady, my developmental editor, who patiently coached me through the entire publishing process.

Thanks to all agents, publishers, and editors who filled out my pink questionnaires and granted permission to reprint their copyrighted guidelines.

A special thanks to all the authors from Desert Rose RWA (Phoenix, AZ) who generously shared insider info, especially Connie Flynn Alexander (her Harlequin pseudonym is Casey Roberts). Connie, who teaches romance novel classes at Mesa (AZ) Community College, taught me everything from writing the hook to the synopsis, to running a writer's critique group.

Also, thanks to my critique partners for their helpful criticism and encouragement: Linda Style, Walt Ellsworth, John Hetherington and Cher Menefee.

To Kristine Hughes and Jacki Whitford, historical reference authors and columnists at *Romantic Times* magazine, who lent their moral support and friendship.

Most of all, I want to express my gratitude to my husband, Ron Paludan, who showed me a self-published directory of who's who in the software development industry, then commented, "Why isn't there a career directory for aspiring romance writers?"

For the next year he didn't say a negative word about the astronomical postage expenses and phone bills! Well, how could he? This book was his idea!

Introduction

*W*elcome to the premiere edition of *The Romance Writer's Pink Pages*. This directory, which is planned to be an annual publication, was conceived as a solution to the frustration of romance writers trying to connect with agents and publishers.

While 40 percent of the paperback trade is in romance, little information is available in standard publisher's directories. The romance publishing industry is a specialized one, and a sort of "Yellow Pages" was needed, just for romance authors.

The agent's section is not just listings, but also includes specific information about agent's fees and commissions, types of romance manuscripts handled, method of contact, and much more.

In the publisher's section, some of the editors have given *The Romance Writer's Pink Pages* permission to reprint their exact guidelines, as well as their tips and comments. This section will save writers the expense and trouble of sending a self-addressed stamped envelope to each publisher for their individual "tip sheets."

If you are in the business of selling or buying romance manuscripts, and are not listed in this edition, you are invited to contact us for details about inclusion in the next edition of *The Romance Writer's Pink Pages*. There is no charge for a listing. However, advertising copy is not accepted, and listings are at the discretion of the editor.

This directory is as complete and accurate as possible, but if there is an error in your listing, please contact us, so we can correct it in the next edition.

Publishers, please notify us of editorial or other changes, such as adding or discontinuing a line, or new tip sheets. Agents, please send your new address and phone number, if you move your office.

Efforts have been made to make sure that everyone listed is reputable, but *The Romance Writer's Pink Pages* does not necessarily endorse them, nor accept liability for the results obtained from contacting anyone in this directory.

So, approach each agent or publisher in a professional manner, and don't be afraid to ask questions about contracts, fees, and pay rates. If you have a word of praise or a complaint about someone listed in *The Romance Writer's Pink Pages*, please write. We'd like to know.

Whether you are a writer, an agent, an editor, or another professional involved in the romance publishing industry, I hope you will find this book to be an invaluable reference.

Eve Paludan
P.O. Box 24739
Tempe, AZ 85285-4739

1

Using Good Sense to Find the Right Literary Agent

Evan M. Fogelman

*O*nce you've completed that first manuscript, your focus should shift from the lives of your characters to the commercial realities of publishing that exist outside the book's cover. Of course in publishing, as in most businesses, you won't have to go it alone. There will be those for whom your talent is lifeblood, the very element without which they could not exist. Yes, you guessed it: the agents.

Give some thought to what you want—besides that first sale—from the author-agent relationship. With the exception of situations where publishers require agented submissions, begin with the premise that agents aren't really necessary. We're not. If you're the type of person who prefers to do everything yourself, you may not want to associate with a literary representative. If, however, you want to delegate some of your responsibility to a qualified professional, you'll need to explore your goals for the three areas in which agents work.

The first area is *editorial contact*. I often say this is the most overrated aspect of an agent's work. This may be especially true among the Romance Writers of America (RWA) where there are a manageable number of acquisitions editors and even the most novice of unpublished authors can meet editors at a conference. Moreover, in category genre fiction there are a limited number of editors to begin with, and it certainly does not take great professional acumen to determine which editor acquires for a certain line. You could probably hunt down the range of editors yourself and not be out the 15 percent agent's commission.

Now, the more complicated the area of editorial contacts becomes, the more you'll want to explore what an agent can do for you. For example, if you're writing for several lines or across genre boundaries, you may want someone to help manage your different obligations. Also, you'll need to consider the larger concerns of publishing programs. If you write more mainstream, single title books, you'll have to consider which publishers might really foster your talent and move you up the list. An agent might help you quite a bit in locating those editors whose sensibilities accord with your writing.

You might also consider the value of an agent's endeavors to your own relationship with an editor. Many editors like working with agents because it's clear then who handles the business details and who handles the creative aspects. Thus, the author-editor relationship is freed from the encumbrances of commerce and can exist on a nurturing-of-talent level.

Once you're comfortable with evaluating the propriety of an agent's benefit in terms of editorial contacts, you'll want to explore a second area, *business management.* Business management is much more than advances and royalty rates. It's the area where agents can really earn their commissions. Yes, in some cases an agent can get you some more money up front and a better royalty for a first book than you could get on your own, yet that alone might not be enough to justify the relationship. Particularly in the case of category works, the little extra money the agent might get for you could be more than eaten up by the agency commission you'll have to pay. Thus, I encourage you to think of business management not only as a contract negotiation, but also as contract maintenance. Signing the contract is only the very beginning. From there, the accounting starts.

Perhaps the most important part of contract maintenance is subsidiary rights action. These include TV and feature film options, foreign rights, reprints, audio, serializations, book club sales, and other sources of potential income that should be exploited throughout the life of the title. Depending upon the publishing contract, it is often the publisher who takes primary responsibility for garnering subrights income. In the case of author-retained rights, though, it is the author's agent who should seek the subrights deals.

There is also a business management side to the author-editor relationship. Happily, once your book is acquired, the agent will be the liaison between you and your editor for any pre-press information the publisher requires.

When you understand the necessity of good business management, you're able to move on to the last area you'll need to evaluate in your decision about an agent, *career development*. This is the most underrated, yet perhaps the most important aspect of your decision. The right agent can help your career development by associating your talent with future deals. Though I hope your first book is a runaway bestseller, I know most publishers look at authors as incremental commercial propositions. That is, your second book should be more successful than your first, your third more than your second, and so forth. Imagine how much more productive you might be along that route if someone were guiding you along the way.

This area of career development leads us naturally to perhaps the best criterion for measuring agents: *communication*. You must feel your potential agent expresses an understanding of your work and your goals to be a truly effective representative. Thus, I encourage you to learn as much as you can about the agents you are considering. Make an effort to find out their backgrounds, who they represent, and what sales they've recently made. Don't just blindly send your manuscript to a list of agents who may or may not be receptive to your work. Look for the ones who accept unpublished authors, for those who have a good reputation in the romance genre, and for those about whom you feel generally confident.

Like most things in book publishing, finding the right agent is not nearly so easy as it sounds. Many agents do not accept unpublished authors. Yet take heart: many do. Since there are no particular qualifications needed to become an agent— and no certifications of any sort required—you should approach the matter cautiously. I think you'll find, though, most agents don't run scam operations. There simply is not enough money in publishing to attract the professionally unscrupulous. All businesses have some measure of individuals who are dishonest, yet there's no reason to assume that in book publishing there are any more than in other places.

All agents have different policies about submission. Please follow them. We design them to help us find the best writers and writing available. As a general rule, we don't appreciate gimmicks. Some agents require a formal query letter before you send any manuscript. Others are perfectly amenable to seeing sample chapters right off the bat. Some of us like pre-submission phone calls. Some frown on multiple submissions. Most do not charge reading fees. The best thing you can do for yourself is to follow the procedures in a professional and courteous manner.

When you and an agent are ready to come to terms, I recommend you use a written agreement. It's not that you shouldn't trust your agent. It's not that the law requires a written agreement. It's not that it even matters to potential publishers. *It is that you have a right to know how your intellectual and emotional property is being handled.* It makes good business sense.

To help ensure a smoother, happier, clearer road to publication, authors are well-served to look for the following in writing:

1. A definition of the represented property. Are all genre or types included? What, if anything, is to be excluded?

2. An acknowledgement of the agent's commission. What about the rate for subsidiary rights and sales?

3. A clear statement of the accounting practices involved. Will the agent promptly forward to the writer all funds and statements? When? Will the agency provide accounting documentation separate from the publisher's?

4. An unequivocal obligation to the author that the author will be informed about all offers relating to publication and licensing.

5. A clear statement of what expenses the agency will be responsible for, and for which ones the author will pay. For example, what if five copies of the manuscript are needed to submit to various publishers?

6. An obligation for the agency to send to the writer copies of all correspondence related to the manuscript, and a similar requirement that the agent notify the author about all conversations concerning the book.

7. A delineation of how the author-agent relationship can be terminated by either of the people involved.

Many other provisions are perfectly acceptable and indeed may even be necessary. Yet the main objective should be fairness to the author. In publishing, fairness and clarity are often related. One should beware of excessive legal jargon or gobbledygook. The framers of our Constitution granted intellectual property protection, and authors and agents should underpin the business of handling that property with the same good sense.

Now you are ready. Supplied with creative property and business information, you can make the good decisions about your career. When it's all said and done, there's one piece of advice which may be more important than anything else in these pages: Finish your book. The starters never really succeeded at anything—only those who finish their dreams can make them come true.

Good luck.

Evan M. Fogelman, member of the Association of Author's Representatives and the American Bar Association Forum on Entertainment Law, owns the literary agency which bears his name.

2

Directory of Agents

PAMELA G. AHEARN

The Ahearn Agency
2021 Pine Street
New Orleans, LA 70118
(504) 861-8395
FAX: (504) 866-6434

Professional Affiliations: Romance Writers of America.

Office Hours: 8:30–4:30

Fees: Charges reading fees to previously unpublished authors and to authors writing in areas other than those of previous publication. Fee based on manuscript's length.

Terms: 15 percent on domestic rights, 20 percent on foreign and dramatic rights.

Recent Sales
Lions and Lace by Meagan McKinney
The Rose of Blacksword by Rexanne Becnal
Deadly Currents by Caroline Burnes
Moonlight Enchantment by Deborah Martin
Passion's Deep Spell by Lynette Vinet
To Kiss a Thief by Kate Moore
Where Magic Dwells by Rexanne Becnal
Christmas Wish by Rexanne Becnal
Cheyenne series by Judd Cole, Leisure Books

Submissions: Query first with SASE.

Seeking

Long Contemporary	70,000–85,000 words
Short Contemporary	50,000–65,000 words
Historical	any time period, 100,000+ words
Mystery	60,000+ words
Mainstream Romance	100,000+ words
Regency	length not specified

Comments: Would prefer to work with published contemporary romance authors rather than new authors.

Editor's Note: Pamela Ahearn is a romance author, a former agent at Southern Writers, and a former editor at Bantam. Ms. Ahearn started her own agency in 1992.

MARCIA AMSTERDAM
Marcia Amsterdam Agency
41 West 82nd Street, Suite 9A
New York, NY 10024
(212) 873-4945

Professional Affiliations: Writers Guild of America, Signatory Writer's Guild.

Office Hours: 9:30–5:30

Fees: 15 percent domestic publishing, 10 percent TV and feature scripts. No reading fee.

Recent Sales
Client list and sales are confidential.

Submissions: Query first with SASE.

Seeking

Long Contemporary	100,000 words
Historical	Civil War, 100,000 words
Mystery	70,000–80,000 words

MEREDITH BERNSTEIN
Meredith Bernstein Literary Agency
2112 Broadway
New York, NY 10023
(212) 799-1007
FAX: (212) 799-1145

Office Hours: 9:30–5:30

Fees: Query first.

Terms: 15 percent domestic sales, 20 percent foreign sales.

Recent Sales

Shirl Henke	5 book deal with Leisure
Ashland Price	Viking trilogy with Zebra
Georgina Gentry	multi-book deal with Zebra

Submissions: Query first with SASE.

Seeking

Long Contemporary	out of the genre à la mainstream
Historical	Any time period, 95,000–125,000 words
Ethnic	depends on story
Mystery	word length depends on line and story
Fantasy	sometimes need fantasy, query first
Mainstream Romance	"YES!" word length open

Futuristic and psychological suspense are also needed

PAM BERNSTEIN

Pam Bernstein and Associates
790 Madison Avenue, Suite 310
New York, NY 10021
(212) 288-1700

Office Hours: 9:00–5:00

Fees: No reading fee. Please send a letter of inquiry first, since unsolicited manuscripts are not accepted.

Terms: 15 percent commission.

Submissions: Query first with SASE.

Seeking

Long Contemporary	Word length is varied
Historical	Time period is varied
Mainstream Romance	Word length is varied

Editor's Note: Pam Bernstein had a successful fourteen year career at the William Morris Agency. In May of 1992, her husband swept her away on a once-in-a-lifetime adventure. For six months they traveled to Bangkok, Thailand, Hong Kong, and England. When Pam came back to New York, she knew that she wanted to open her own agency. And she did, in March of 1993. Unfortunately, she had to leave behind her contracted clients at William Morris. Some past clients include: Susan Johnson, Georgia Bockoven, Sandra Kitt, Brooke Hastings, Maureen Dean, Camille Archer, Tina Ansa, Nancy Price, Ivana Trump, and more. An experienced agent who is just beginning her own agency provides a timely opportunity for new writers.

ANDREA BROWN
Andrea Brown Literary Agency, Inc.
P.O. Box 429
El Granada, CA 94018
(415) 726-1783

Professional Affiliations: Association of Author's Representatives, Women's National Book Association, National Association of Female Executives.

Office Hours: 9:00–5:00 Monday–Friday

Fees: No reading fees or other fees.

Terms: 15 percent commission.

Submissions: Query letters only with SASE.

Recent Sales
Harlequin and HarperCollins Paperbacks.
The client list is confidential.

Seeking
Historical   any time period, word length unspecified

Young Adult

JANE JORDAN BROWNE

Multimedia Product Development, Inc.
410 S. Michigan Avenue, Suite 724
Chicago, IL 60605
(312) 922-3063
FAX: (312) 922-1905

Office Hours: 9:00–5:00 Monday–Friday

Fees: No reading fee. Clients are charged for overseas calls, FAXes, postage, and for copying manuscript.

Terms: 15 percent domestic, 20 percent foreign.

Recent Sales

Fire! by Jo Horne Schmidt, Berkley (lead book in Great Lakes Series)
The Trouble with Terry by Jackie Hyman, Harlequin
The Summer Rose by Bonnie K. Wynn, Berkley Wildflower (lead launch)
Serpent Beguiled by Betina Lindsay, Pocket
Rubies by L. J. Bingham, Pocket
Silken Promises by L. J. Bingham, Pocket
Red Sky by Linda Sandifer, Zebra
Mountain Ecstacy and Midnight Hearts by Linda Sandifer, Zebra
The Last Goodbye and *Defy the Night* by Lynn Leslie aka Sherrill Bodine/Elaine Sima, Harlequin
Redeeming Love by Francine Rivers, Bantam
3 book contract to Harlequin for Elaine Sima/Sherrill Bodine
Contract to Berkley Historical for Bonnie K. Wynn

Submissions: No unsolicited material. Will read 1–2 page query letters with SASE. Highly selective. Prefers personal recommendation from editors or clients, since this agency receives around 300 queries a week. Seeking very talented writers only.

Seeking
Contemporary only for Harlequin, Silhouette, and Loveswept,
 to fit their guidelines.

Historical	to 1885, 90,000–100,000 words
Mystery	75,000–85,000 words
Mainstream lead title	85,000–90,000 words

PEMA BROWNE
Pema Browne Ltd.
Pine Road HCR, Box 104B
Neversink, NY 12765
(914) 985-2936
FAX: (914) 985-7635

Professional Affiliations: Signatory Writer's Guild.

Office Hours: 9:00–6:00 Monday–Friday

Fees: 15 percent standard commission. No reading fees for romance manuscripts.

Terms: After first book is sold, a three year letter of agreement.

Recent Sales
Sweet Fire by Jo Goodman, Zebra
Defiant Angel by Stephanie Stevens, Avon
Keeping Up with the Joneses by Patricia Ellis, Harlequin
Tollin's Daughter by Elizabeth Michaels, Harlequin
Highland Rivalry by Lucy Muir, Harlequin
A Twist of Evil by Kaye Walton, Harlequin Superromance
Miss Ware's Refusal by Caitlin Power, NAL
Mirror Games by Karen Rhodes, Lucky in Love
Tournament of Hearts by Catherine Toothman, Avon

Earth Angel by Eileen Hehl, Zebra
Calypso Wind by Sandra Dark, Lucky in Love
Luckenbooth Lady by Rebecca Robins, Avon
The Spinster & The Rake by Catherine Nickens, Harlequin
Dream Strings by Karen Rhodes, Lucky in Love

Submissions: Query first with SASE.

Seeking

Long Contemporary	100,000–125,000 words
Short Contemporary	60,000–80,000 words
Historical	before 1900, 100,000+ words
Mystery	70,000 words
Mainstream Romance	100,000 words
Women-In-Jeopardy genre	100,000 words
Regency	short/long, 60,000–100,000 words

Comments: Also handles juvenile, picture books, middle grade, young adult, non-fiction, scholarly, horror, men's adventure, and illustration. "Really, any good manuscript."

PERRY BROWNE
Pema Browne Ltd.
Pine Road HCR, Box 104B
Neversink, NY 12765
(914) 985-2936
FAX: (914) 985-7635

Professional Affiliations: Signatory Writers Guild.

Office Hours: 9:00–6:00 Monday–Friday

Fees: 15 percent standard commission. No reading fees for romance manuscripts.

Terms: After first book is sold, a three year letter of agreement.

Recent Sales
Sweet Fire by Jo Goodman, Zebra
Defiant Angel by Stephanie Stevens, Avon
Keeping Up with the Joneses by Patricia Ellis, Harlequin
Tollin's Daughter by Elizabeth Michaels, Harlequin
Highland Rivalry by Lucy Muir, Harlequin
A Twist of Evil by Kaye Walton, Harlequin Superromance
Miss Ware's Refusal by Caitlin Power, NAL
Mirror Games by Karen Rhodes, Lucky in Love
Tournament of Hearts by Catherine Toothman, Avon
Earth Angel by Eileen Hehl, Zebra
Calypso Wind by Sandra Dark, Lucky in Love
Luckenbooth Lady by Rebecca Robins, Avon
The Spinster & The Rake by Catherine Nickens, Harlequin
Dream Strings by Karen Rhodes, Lucky in Love

Submissions: Query first with SASE.

Seeking
Long Contemporary	100,000–125,000 words
Short Contemporary	60,000–80,000 words
Historical	before 1900, 100,000+ words
Mystery	70,000 words
Mainstream Romance	100,000 words
Women-In-Jeopardy genre	100,000 words
Regency	short/long 60,000–100,000 words

Comments: Also handles juvenile, picture books, middle grade, young adult, non-fiction, scholarly, horror, men's adventure, and illustration. "Really, any good manuscript."

Editor's Note: Perry says to slant your manuscript towards a specific line and write to guideline specs, making sure your manuscript fits their length, plotline, and content requirements. For example, if you want to submit to Harlequin Presents or Harlequin Romance you should be ready with the first ten pages plus a short synopsis. He reminds authors that St. Martin's and Walker are no longer doing regencies. He also says to avoid show biz plots where actors, actresses, artists, or models are the main characters. These are difficult to sell right now. For more info on this agency, send an SASE for a brochure.

ANDREA CIRILLO
Jane Rotrosen Agency
318 East 51st Street
New York, NY 10022
(212) 593-4330
FAX: (212) 935-6985

Professional Affiliations: Association of Author's Representatives.

Office Hours: 9:30–5:30 Monday–Friday

Fees: No reading fee.

Terms: 15 percent commission on sales in U.S. and Canada.

Recent Sales
Client list is confidential.

Submissions: Query first with SASE.

Seeking
Long Contemporary
Short Contemporary
Historical   All time periods

Mystery
Mainstream Romance
(Lengths were unspecified. Check publisher's guidelines for
    the line you are writing for.)

RUTH COHEN
Ruth Cohen Inc., Literary Agent
Box 7626
Menlo Park, CA 94025
(415) 854-2054

Professional Affiliations: Association of Author's Representatives.

Office Hours: 8:00–5:00 Monday–Friday

Fees: Only for photocopying manuscripts, FAX charges to foreign agents, or mailing charges to foreign agents. No reading fee.

Terms: 15 percent on all gross sums.

Recent Sales
Prefers not to list.

Submissions: Query first with ten opening pages of manuscript and don't forget to enclose your SASE. PLEASE, NO MULTIPLE SUBMISSIONS TO THIS AGENCY!

Seeking

Long Contemporary	125,000–150,000 words
Historical	before 1900, 125,000 words
Mystery	"Cozy with female protagonist preferred, although will read a male protagonist if it's not drugs or mob crime oriented." 65,000–75,000 words.

Comments: "I really do want manuscripts that are well written and carefully plotted. See my agent's article in RWR (Romance Writers Report) for Nov/Dec 1991."

ELAINE DAVIE
Elaine Davie Literary Agency
Village Gate Square
274 North Goodman Street
Rochester, NY 14607
(716) 442-0830

Office Hours: 9:00–5:00 Monday–Friday

Fees: No reading or other fees. Authors must provide copies of manuscript for purposes of submission.

Terms: No contracts. 15 percent commission when book sells (20 percent on foreign and film rights).

Recent Sales
The Ruby by Christina Skye
Guardian Spirit by Marcia Evanick
Passion's Fever by Jane Kidder

Submissions: Prefers query letter with synopsis and first three chapters, and SASE, of course. Speedy replies are given to queries, partials are responded to within a month. No telephone queries, please. No fax queries. (Does NOT represent short stories, poetry, novellas, or children's books.)

Seeking
Long Contemporary
Short Contemporary
Historical
All genre romances, especially category
Mystery
Fantasy
Westerns (a few)
Women's fiction (Word lengths not specified)
Also handles well-written non-fiction

Editor's Note: Well-known and respected in the industry since 1986, Elaine Davie and her five agents specialize in books "by and for" women, particularly genre fiction, category romance and historical romance. Manuscript should be exciting, fast-paced and unique. No typos.

ANITA DIAMANT

Anita Diamant Literary Agency
310 Madison Avenue #1508
New York, NY 10017
(212) 687-1122

Professional Affiliations: Association of Author's Representatives.

Office Hours: 9:30–5:30 Monday–Friday

Fees: None.

Terms: 15 percent domestic sales.

Recent Sales
Twilight's Child by V. C. Andrews, Pocket Books
Midnight Whispers by V. C. Andrews, Pocket Books
Midnight Rainbow by Linda Howard
The Solomon Organization by Linda Howard, Putnam

Submissions: Query first with SASE.

Seeking:
Long Contemporary   75,000–100,000 words
Short Contemporary   50,000 words

Historical
Mystery
Mainstream Romance

LINDA M. DIEHL
Fogelman Literary Agency
7515 Greenville Avenue, Suite 712
Dallas, TX 75231
(214) 361-9956
FAX: (214) 361-9553

Professional Affiliations: Association of Author's
Representatives.

Office Hours: 8:30–5:30 Monday–Friday

Fees: None.

Terms: 15 percent domestic; 10 percent foreign.

Recent Sales
(See recent sales for Evan Fogelman.)

Submissions: Please call before querying.

Seeking
All types of romance
Regency
Historicals
Young Adult
Women's non-fiction

Comments: We do not accept unsolicited manuscripts of any
sort. There is no slush pile here, though we are receptive to
unpublished authors. Please contact Linda M. Diehl at the
above phone number for more information.

ETHAN ELLENBERG
The Ethan Ellenberg Literary Agency
548 Broadway, #5E
New York, NY 10012
(212) 431-4554
FAX: (212) 941-4652

Professional Affiliations: Romance Writers of America,
Western Writers of America, Mystery Writers of America, others

Office Hours: 9:00–5:00 Monday–Friday

Fees: No reading fee whatsoever.

Terms: Normally receive 15 percent commission.

Recent Sales
Ascent to the Stars by Sharry Michels, Leisure Books
Mabuhay by Peggy Fielding, Zebra Books

Submissions: Queries are preferred.

Seeking
Long Contemporary
Short Contemporary
Historical
Mystery
Fantasy
Mainstream
(Any word length for all of the above)

Comments: "I am interested in all areas of romance fiction.
My chief concerns are good writing, strong character development, solid plotting, and not externals like word length or time
period. Actively taking clients. Editorial help without charge for
clients we're excited about. Strong track record in commercial

fiction and anxious to grow in romance area. Agency's ninth year in business. Previously held positions of Contracts Manager for Berkley/Jove and Associate Contracts Manager of Bantam. Fifteen years in professional publishing here in New York."

JANICE FISHBEIN
Freida Fishbein Ltd.
2556 Hubbard Street
Brooklyn, NY 11235
(212) 247-4398

Office Hours: 10:00–6:00 Monday–Thursday

Fees: New writers $75.00 first 50,000 words, $1 per thousand thereafter for analysis and critique of *requested* manuscripts only after query letter.

Terms: If manuscript is marketed and sold, 10 percent agent's fee on all royalties.

Recent Sales
Queen's War
Doublecross
Fat Is Not a Four Letter Word

Submissions: Query first with SASE.

Seeking
Long Contemporary
Short Contemporary
Ethnic
Fantasy
Mainstream Romance

JOYCE A. FLAHERTY
Joyce A. Flaherty, Literary Agent
816 Lynda Court
St. Louis, MO 63122
(314) 966-3057

Professional Affiliations: Association of Author's Representatives, Romance Writers of America, Mystery Writers of America, Western Writers of America, Authors' Guild.

Office Hours: 9:00–5:00 Monday–Friday

Fees: No reading fee. Marketing fee of $50.00 for unpublished authors.

Terms: 15 percent commission domestic; 25–30 percent foreign translation rights when co-agents are used.

Recent Sales
South of Paradise by Marica Martin, Berkley-Jove
Wild Conquest by Hannah Howell, Avon
Cheyenne Dreams by Peggy Hanchar, Fawcett
Tarnished Silver by Patt Bucheister, Bantam Loveswept
The Founders, Book One of the Gairden Legacy by Coleen L.
    Johnston, St. Martin's Press
Fortune's Mistress by Judith E. French, Avon

Submissions: Query with SASE only.

Seeking
Long Contemporary from RWA Finalists or published
    authors only
Short Contemporary from RWA Finalists or published
    authors only
Historical from RWA Finalists or published authors only
Ethnic from RWA Finalists or published authors only
Mystery from published mystery authors only

Fantasy from published fantasy authors only
Mainstream Romance from published authors only
Time travel from RWA Finalists or published authors only
Paranormal from RWA Finalists or published authors only

Comments: Always be sure to include your phone number on a query and SASE. Also be sure to include the information that the query is a simultaneous submission, if that is the case.

EVAN M. FOGELMAN
The Fogelman Literary Agency
7515 Greenville Avenue, Suite 712
Dallas, TX 75231
(214) 361-9956
FAX: (214) 361-9553

Professional Affiliations: Association of Author's Representatives, American Bar Association–Committee on Literary Publishing.

Office Hours: 8:30–5:30 Monday–Friday

Fees: None.

Terms: 15 percent domestic; 10 percent foreign.

Recent Sales
Four untitled historical romances by Elizabeth Leigh to Zebra
Romance Writer's Pink Pages by Eve Paludan to Prima
    Publishing

Submissions: Call before querying.

Seeking
Short Contemporary   to 70,000 words
Historical   before 1700, to 125,000 words

Mainstream Romance (Glitz)   to 110,000 words

Women's Non-fiction

Comments: We do not accept unsolicited manuscripts of any sort. There is no slush pile here, though we are receptive to unpublished authors. Please contact Linda M. Diehl at the above phone number for more information.

JAY GARON
Jay Garon-Brooke Associates
101 W. 55th Street
New York, NY 10019
(212) 581-8300
FAX: (212) 581-8397

Professional Affiliations: Association of Author's Representatives.

Fees: None.

Terms: 15 percent domestic; 30 percent foreign.

Recent Sales
The Client by John Grisham, Doubleday
Blue Truth by Cherokee Paul Macdonald
Taboo by Elizabeth Gage, Pocket
Carpool by Mary Cahill, Random House
Trial of a Thousand Years by Eric L. Harry, Simon and
    Schuster

Submissions: Query by mail only. Please do not send unsolicited manuscripts. A query should describe the work and also include a bio and SASE.

Seeking

Mystery	100,000–120,000 words
Romantic Thrillers	all types 100,000–120,000 words

Comments: Mainstream only with thorough characterization, thoroughly textured. Hardcovers and/or paperback leads. We will reject any unrequested proposals or sample chapters.

IRENE GOODMAN
Irene Goodman Literary Agency
521 Fifth Avenue, 17th Floor
New York, NY 10175
(212) 682-1978
FAX: (212) 573-6355

Professional Affiliations: Association of Author's Representatives.

Office Hours: 9:30–5:30 Monday–Friday

Fees: None.

Terms: 15 percent commission.

Recent Sales
Garters by Pamela Morsi, Berkley
A Christman Short Story by Linda Lael Miller, Avon
The Man You'll Marry by Debbie Macomber, Harlequin

Submissions: Query first with SASE.

Seeking

Long Contemporary	75,000 words
Short Contemporary	55,000–65,000 words

Historical	Viking to 1900, 100,000 words
Mystery	65,000 words
Mainstream Romance	125,000 words

LINDA HAYES

Columbia Literary Associates, Inc.
7902 Nottingham Way
Ellicott City, MD 21043
(410) 465-1595
Call for FAX number and permission to FAX

Professional Affiliations: Association of Author's Representatives, Washington Romance Writers.

Office Hours: 10:00–5:00 Monday–Friday

Submissions: Query first with SASE (a must!), credits, narrative synopsis, first few chapters, manuscript submission history, and manuscript word count. For category romances, note the line the manuscript is geared to.

Fees: No reading or marketing fees.

Terms: 15 percent domestic commission.

Clients: Ruth Glick, Eileen Buckholtz, Mary Tate Engels, Louise Titchener, Binnie Syril Braunstein, Wendy Corsi Staub, Chassie West, Jean Favors, Kathryn Jensen and others.

Recent Sales

Forty-Three Light Street Series (Books 7, 8, & 9) by Rebecca York, Harlequin
Homebody by Louise Titchener, HarperCollins
Everywhere That Mary Went by Lisa Scottoline, Harper Paperbacks

Seeking

Long Contemporary	variable length
Short Contemporary	variable length
Ethnic, Category and Mainstream	variable length
Suspense	variable length
Mainstream Romance	variable length

Young Adult
(NO Historical, NO Fantasy)
Also handles contemporary mainstream fiction and commercial
nonfiction.

Comments: While we're open to unpublished authors, due to
the highly competitive market, manuscripts must be top notch!
Due to high activity level, we're taking on very few new clients
right now.

Editor's Note: Linda Hayes has been a literary agent for 14
years. She has packaged several series with her authors. She accepts new clients who are either published authors or talented
newcomers.

YVONNE HUBBS
Yvonne Trudeau Hubbs Agency
32371 Alipaz #101
San Juan Capistrano, CA 92675
(714) 496-1970
FAX: (714) 240-1213 (call before faxing)

Professional Affiliations: Romance Writers of America.

Office Hours: 9:00–5:00 Monday–Friday. Closed holidays.

Fees: $75.00 reading fee for unpublished writers. Refunded if
a sale is made within one year.

Terms: 15 percent–20 percent standard.

Submissions: Please query first with SASE.

Seeking
Long Contemporary
Short Contemporary
Historical
Mystery
Fantasy
Mainstream Romance
Writers should follow the publishers' guidelines regarding manuscript length.

Comments: "I was featured in the 1987 Fiction Writers Market. I've lectured at various conferences and colleges. I've helped unpublished writers become published."

NATASHA KERN
Natasha Kern Literary Agency
Box 2908
Portland, OR 97208-2908
(503) 297-6190
FAX: (503) 297-8241

Professional Affiliations: Association of Author's Representatives, Romance Writers of America, Mystery Writers of America, Western Writers of America.

Office Hours: 8:00–6:00

Fees: $45.00 Reading Fee for unpublished writers, reimbursed upon sale. (Please do not send a check unless it is specifically requested.) Overseas phone and FAX billed.

Terms: Commission 15 percent; foreign 10 percent (after sub-agent); film 15–20 percent, no marketing fees.

Clients: Veronica Blake, Robin Lee Hatcher, Connie Mason, Vella Munn, Jane Peart, Joan Overfield, Leigh Greenwood, Diane Levitt, Pat Kennedy, Linda Guss, Pat Simpson, Penny Richards, Kathleen Morgan, Irene Brown.

Recent Sales

Rose by Leigh Greenwood (First in a series of "The Randolph
     Brides")
Love Everlasting by Moeth Allison (Mollie Adghadjian),
     Silhouette
Dangerous Company by Susan Anderson, Zebra
Love on Strike by Jan Boies, Bantam Sweet Dreams
Twenty-five titles by Jane Peart to HarperCollins, Bantam
     and others
Whisper of Midnight by Pat Simpson, HarperCollins
The Legacy by Pat Simpson, HarperCollins
Private Sins by Diane Levitt, Pinnacle
The Night Lily by Pat Simpson
Briar Rose by Pat Simpson, Silhouette
The River's Daughter by Vela Munn, St. Martin's
Brides of Monclair Series by Jane Peart, Harper
Orphan Train Series by Jane Peart, Harper
Two titles by Laura Sonnemark, Scholastic
Four titles by Robin Weite, Penguin USA
(Many more recent sales, but unable to list them all!)

Submissions: Query first with SASE. Do not send reading fee unless it is requested after querying.

Seeking

Futuristic and fantasy
Historical   all time periods, 100,000–125,000 words

Mystery
Mainstream Romance
Gothic

Glitz & Glamour
Occult/Paranormal/Time Travel
Serious women's fiction with romance elements

Comments: Fiction specializations include mainstream women's fiction, romance, historicals, mysteries, young adult, action/adventure, and thrillers. Also see above.

DANIEL P. KING
Daniel P. King, Literary Agent
5125 N. Cumberland Boulevard
Whitefish Bay, WI 53217
(414) 964-2903
FAX: (414) 964-6860
TELEX: 724389

Office Hours: 9:00–5:00

Fees: No fee to read query and sample chapters. Consultation fee may be required if (1) author has no credits and (2) editorial work must be done.

Terms: 10 percent on U.S. sales; 20 percent on foreign sales.

Recent Sales
Confidential.

Submissions: Query first with SASE.

Seeking
Long Contemporary   50,000–75,000 words
Historical   50,000–75,000 words
Mystery   50,000–75,000 words
Fantasy   50,000–75,000 words
Mainstream Romance   50,000–75,000 words

FRAN LEBOWITZ
Writers House
21 W. 26th Street
New York, NY 10010
(212) 685-4701
FAX: (212) 685-1781

Professional Affiliations: Women in Publishing.

Office Hours: 9:30–6:00

Fees: None.

Terms: 10 percent commission.

Recent Sales
Two first time category authors to mainstream houses.

Submissions: Query first with SASE.

Seeking
Long Contemporary
Historical (pre World War II)
Mainstream Romance

Comments: "I am especially interested in witty repartee and women-in-jeopardy."

LETTIE LEE
Ann Elmo Agency
60 E. 42nd Street
New York, NY 10165

(212) 661-2880
FAX: (212) 661-2883

Office Hours: 9:30–5:00

Fees: Usually no reading fee. Sometimes charges a $25 handling fee. Please query first.

Terms: 15 percent commission.

Recent Sales
Confidential list.

Submissions: Query first with SASE.

Seeking
Open to different types of romance fiction.

RICIA MAINHARDT
Ricia Mainhardt Literary Agency
612 Argyle Road #L5
Brooklyn, NY 11230
(718) 434-1893
FAX: (718) 434-2157

Professional Affiliations: Association of Author's Representatives.

Office Hours: 9:00–6:00 Monday–Friday.

Fees: $20.00 reading and evaluation fee.

Terms: 15 percent commission on sales.

Recent Sales
To Harlequin, Avon, Berkley, and Zebra

Submissions: Query first with SASE.

Seeking
Long Contemporary
Short Contemporary
Historical
Ethnic
Mystery
Fantasy
Mainstream Romance
Children's Fiction and Non-fiction

Comments: Word length is not specified, for that often varies. See the genre specifications already established by publishers in the publisher's guidelines section of this directory.

DENISE MARCIL
Denise Marcil Literary Agency
685 West End Avenue Suite 9C
New York, NY 10025
(212) 932-3110
FAX: (212) 932-3113

Professional Affiliations: Literary Vice President, Association of Author's Representatives.

Office Hours: 9:30–6:00 Monday–Friday.

Fees: $45.00 for three chapters, ONLY if we request the fee at that time. Do not send checks with unsolicited materials.

Terms: Discussed with prospective clients privately.

Recent Sales

Category romances were sold to Loveswept, Harlequin and Silhouette.

Mainstream romances and women's fiction were sold to Pocket Books, Dell, Bantam, Zebra.

Also have done some mainstream sales.

Submissions: A one page query letter with SASE only. No unsolicited manuscripts. Please do not send any chapters unless they are specifically requested.

Seeking

Contemporary   55,000 or 75,000 words

Mainstream Romance   100,000–120,000 words

Comments: "I've been one of the top romance agents since 1977. I've launched the careers of many romance writers, and built the careers of many others. I'm always looking for great new category romance authors."

EVAN MARSHALL

The Evan Marshall Agency
22 South Park Street, Suite 216
Montclair, NJ 07042-2744
(201) 744-1661
FAX: (201) 744-6312

Professional Affiliations: Associaton of Author's Representatives, Romance Writers of America.

Office Hours: 9:00–5:00 Monday–Friday

Fees: Small handling fee for unpublished writers who are not referred by an editor or by a client of this agency.

Terms: 15 percent commission on domestic deals; 20 percent on foreign sales.

Submissions: Query first with SASE.

Recent Sales
Confidential.

Seeking
Long Contemporary
Short Contemporary
Historical, all time periods
Ethnic
Mystery
Fantasy
Mainstream Romance

ALLISON MULLEN
Howard Morhaim Literary Agency
175 Fifth Avenue, Suite 709
New York, NY 10010
(212) 529-4433
FAX: (212) 995-1112

Professional Affiliations: Association of Author's Representatives.

Office Hours: 9:30–5:30 Monday–Friday

Fees: No reading fee. Charges clients for photocopying and unusual expenses only.

Terms: 15 percent commission on domestic deals; 20 percent on foreign sales (10 percent of this goes to our co-agent).

Submissions: Query first with SASE.

Seeking

Long Contemporary	approximately 85,000–90,000 words
Historical	any time period, approximately 95,000–115,000 words
Mystery	any length
Mainstream Romance	any length

Comments: "Although I have specified my preferences, I will gladly consider any category of romance novel as long as authors query first with a synopsis."

EDWARD NOVAK

Edward A. Novak III Literary Representation
711 North 2nd Street
Harrisburg, PA 17102
(717) 232-8081
FAX: (717) 232-7020

Office Hours: Irregular.

Fees: 15 percent commission. No reading fee.

Recent Sales

Daggers of Gold by Katherine Deauxville
Savage Dreams by Nicole Jordan
Tame the Wind by Katherine Kilgore

Submissions: Query first with SASE.

Seeking

Long Contemporary	100,000–150,000 words
Historical	18th-19th Century, 100,000–150,000 words
Mainstream Romance	any length

ALICE ORR
Alice Orr Agency, Inc.
305 Madison Avenue, Suite 1166
New York, NY 10165
(718) 204-6673
FAX: (718) 204-6023

Fees: None specified. In addition to the usual client services, special services include editorial guidance, manuscript critique, and career strategy advisement.

Terms: 15 percent on domestic sales, 20 percent on foreign sales and film.

Submissions: Cover letter with 2–5 page summary plus SASE. Send SASE for *How to Write the Fiction Book Synopsis*. Also send SASE for *How to Write the Non-Fiction Book Proposal*. Currently not accepting new clients, but that could change. Make sure to query first.

Seeking
Contemporary Women's Fiction
Mystery/Suspense
Occasional Non-fiction

Comments: No juvenile, young adult, literary, short stories or poetry.

JOHN K. PAYNE
John K. Payne Literary Agency
P.O. Box 1003

New York, NY 10276
(212) 475-6447

Office Hours: 9:00–5:00 Monday–Friday

Fees: $75.00 evaluation fee, until two published books.

Terms: 15 percent first book, 10 percent subsequent books.

Recent Sales
Cloud Dancer by Peggy Bechko, Harlequin

Seeking

Historical	19th century, 100,000 words
Mystery/Contemporary	50,000 words
Mainstream Contemporary Romance	50,000 words

ELIZABETH POMADA
Larsen/Pomada Literary Agents
1029 Jones Street
San Francisco, CA 94109
(415) 673-0939

Professional Affiliations: Association of Author's Representatives, Women's National Book Association, Author's Guild, American Society of Journalists and Authors.

Office Hours: 9:00–5:00 Monday–Friday

Fees: 15 percent on U.S. sales; 20 percent on foreign sales. No reading fee.

Terms: Exclusive, with 60 days cancellation notice.

Recent Sales
The Last Innocent Hour by Margot Abbott, St. Martin's
Sweet Vengeance by June Lund Shiplett
Priceless by Christina Dodd, HarperCollins
Days of Blood and Fire by Katharine Kerr

Submissions: Send the first 30 pages and a synopsis. Allow
6–8 weeks plus mailing time for the reading and include an
SASE. Multiple queries are accepted.

Seeking
Long Contemporary
Short Contemporary
Historical
Mystery
Fantasy
Mainstream Romance
Literary Fiction

Comments: "Love is a primary moving force in the world and
one of the real reasons people read. From *War and Peace* to
Gone With the Wind to Harlequin #24, stories of romance are
what I read and what I enjoy working on."

Editor's Note: Please send a long SASE to request a brochure.

RAY POWERS
Marje Fields Agency
165 W. 46th Street, Suite 909
New York, NY 10036
(212) 764-5740

Office Hours: 10:00–6:00

Fees: No reading fee. 15 percent commission.

Submissions: Query first with SASE.

Seeking
Historical Romance only.

PESHA RUBINSTEIN
Pesha Rubinstein, Literary Agent
37 Overlook Terrace #1D
New York, NY 10033
(212) 781-7845

Professional Affiliations: Romance Writers of America, Society of Children's Book Writers, Association of Author's Representatives.

Office Hours: 8:30 a.m.–2:30 p.m. and 8:00 p.m.–10:00 p.m.

Fees: Manuscript photocopying. No reading fee. Only enclose SASE to cover return of all material.

Terms: 15 percent commission on sales.

Recent Sales
Angel of Fire by Tanya Crosby
A book by Amy Littlesugar to Simon and Schuster
Pirate in My Arms by Danelle Harmon
Historical romances for Penelope Neri
Virgin Star by Jennifer Horsman, Avon
Romantic Suspense for Jayne Manus (aka Sheryl Lynn)
A children's book by Katherine Kincaid

A book by Jane Kurtz to Simon and Schuster
An artist's work to Harcourt Brace

Submissions: Query first with SASE.

Seeking

Long Contemporary	85,000+ words
Historical	after 1100 A.D. of 95,000+ words
Ethnic	60,000+ words
Mystery	60,000+ words

Romantic Suspense/Woman-in-Jeopardy
Mainstream

Comments: "Of all genre fiction, I like romance and mystery best. I think these are the most fun to read, and have the most fans, and also have the most sanguine outlook in today's market. I want books that will appeal most to women. I am willing to work with new and experienced authors."

MEG RULEY
Jane Rotrosen Agency
318 East 51st Street
New York, NY 10022
(212) 593-4330
FAX: (212) 935-6985

Professional Affiliations: Association of Author's Representatives.

Office Hours: 9:30–5:30

Fees: No reading fee.

Terms: 15 percent commission on sales in U.S. and Canada.

Recent Sales
Client list is confidential.

Submissions: Query first with SASE.

Seeking
Long Contemporary
Short Contemporary
Historical—All time periods
Mystery
Mainstream Romance

Comments: Word lengths are specific to the line you are writing for. Check the publisher's guidelines section of this directory.

VICKI LYNN WATSON
Rising Sun Literary Agency
1507 Oakmont Drive
Acworth, GA 30101
(404) 591-3397
FAX: (404) 591-0369

Professional Affiliations: Romance Writers of America, Optimist's Club.

Office Hours: 8:00–5:00 Monday–Friday

Fees: $125.00 reading fee.

Terms: One year exclusive.

Recent Sales
The Falcon Rises by Michael Staudinger
Dialogue on the Path of Initiation by Goettmann
Prayer of Jesus Prayer of the Heart by Alphonso and Rachel
    Goettmann

Submissions: Query first with SASE or call.

Seeking
Long Contemporary
Short Contemporary
Historical—any time period
Ethnic
Mystery
Fantasy
Mainstream Romance

Comments: Accepts all type of romance. Specializes in new authors, romance of any type, and especially, futuristic romance.

NANCY YOST
Lowenstein Associates
121 W. 27th Street, Suite 601
New York, NY 10001
(212) 206-1630
FAX: (212) 727-0280

Professional Affiliations: Association of Author's Representatives, Mystery Writers of America, Sisters in Crime.

Office Hours: 9:00–5:00

Fees: No reading fee or other fees.

Terms: 15 percent agency commission.

Recent Sales
Three female sleuth mysteries by Jan Burke to S & S
Two historicals by Emily Bradshaw to Dell

Two historicals by Rebecca Paisley
Shattered Echoes by Barbara Shapiro to Avon (lead title)

Submissions: Query first with SASE.

Seeking

Historicals	ancient/pre-history and 1100–1900 A.D., 90,000–150,000 words.
Mystery	Usually female sleuths (except hard-boiled), 50,000–80,000 words.
Mainstream Romance	80,000–120,000 words

Also interested in medical thrillers, psychological suspense, true crime, and Jean Auel-like historicals. No fantasy please!

Comments: "I love a sense of humor, and I am also looking for very sexy romances. Please be sure to send a very detailed query letter and include your phone number."

SUE P. YUEN
Susan Herner Rights Agency
10 Oxford Road
Scarsdale, NY 10583
(914) 725-8967
FAX: (914) 725-8969

Office Hours: 9:00–6:00

Fees: No reading fee.

Terms: 15 percent domestic.

Recent Sales
The Lion's Angel by Libby Sydes, Dell
A Suitable Suitor by Alicia Farraday, Harlequin
Mayfield by Joy Chambers

Submissions: Prefers query with first 1–3 chapters and out-line/synopsis. (Don't forget the SASE.)

Seeking

Long Contemporary	100,000 words minimum
Short Contemporary	65,000 words minimum
Historical	100,000 words minimum
Mystery	90,000 words minimum
Fantasy	90,000 words minimum
Mainstream Romance	100,000 words minimum

No children's or young adult books.

ALBERT ZUCKERMAN
Writers House, Inc.
21 West 26th Street
New York, NY 10010
(212) 685-2400
FAX: (212) 685-1781
TELEX: 620103 WRITERS

Office Hours: 10:00–6:00

Fees: None. 15 percent commission.

Recent Sales
Major titles by Nora Roberts, Barbara Delinsky, Betty
    Receveux and Eileen Goudge.

Submissions: Query first with SASE.

Comments: "We are interested in experienced, published nov-elists who feel that they are now ready to move from paperback into hardcover."

Agents Who Do Not Charge Reading Fees

Compiled from the previous listings, here are the names of agents who, to the best of our knowledge, do *not* charge reading fees:

Marcia Amsterdam, Pam Bernstein, Andrea Brown, Jane Jordan Browne, Pema Browne, Perry Browne, Andrea Cirillo, Ruth Cohen, Elaine Davie, Anita Diamant, Linda M. Diehl, Evan M. Fogelman, Jay Garon, Irene Goodman, Linda Hayes, Daniel P. King, Fran Lebowitz, Allison Mullen, Edward Novak, Alice Orr, Elizabeth Pomada, Ray Powers, Pesha Rubinstein, Meg Ruley, Nancy Yost, Sue Yuen, Albert Zuckerman.

Compiled from all the agent listings, here are the names of agents, categorized by their subject interests:

Long Contemporary
Pamela G. Ahearn, Marcia Amsterdam, Meredith Bernstein, Pam Bernstein, Jane Jordan Browne, Pema Browne, Perry Browne, Andrea Cirillo, Ruth Cohen, Elaine Davie, Anita Diamant, Linda M. Diehl, Janice Fishbein, Joyce A. Flaherty, Evan M. Fogelman, Irene Goodman, Linda Hayes, Daniel P. King, Fran Lebowitz, Lettie Lee, Ricia Mainhardt, Evan Marshall, Allison Mullen, Edward Novak, Alice Orr, Elizabeth Pomada, Pesha Rubinstein, Meg Ruley, Vicki Lynn Watson, Sue Yuen.

Short Contemporary
Pamela G. Ahearn, Jane Jordan Browne, Pema Browne, Perry Browne, Andrea Cirillo, Elaine Davie, Anita Diamant, Linda M. Diehl, Janice Fishbein, Joyce A. Flaherty, Evan M. Fogelman, Irene Goodman, Linda Hayes, Lettie Lee, Ricia Mainhardt, Denice Marcil, Evan Marshall, Allison Mullen, Alice Orr, Elizabeth Pomada, Meg Ruley, Vicki Lynn Watson, Sue Yuen.

Hardcover Titles
Albert Zuckerman.

Historical
Pamela G. Ahearn, Marcia Amsterdam, Meredith Bernstein, Pam Bernstein, Andrea Brown, Jane Jordan Browne, Pema Browne, Perry Browne, Andrea Cirillo, Ruth Cohen, Elaine Davie, Anita Diamant, Linda M. Diehl, Joyce A. Flaherty, Evan M. Fogelman, Irene Goodman, Natasha Kern, Daniel P. King, Fran Lebowitz, Lettie Lee, Ricia Mainhardt, Evan Marshall, Allison Mullen, Edward Novak, John Payne, Elizabeth Pomada, Ray Powers, Pesha Rubinstein, Meg Ruley, Vicki Lynn Watson, Nancy Yost, Sue Yuen.

Ethnic
Meredith Bernstein, Janice Fishbein, Joyce A. Flaherty, Linda Hayes, Lettie Lee, Ricia Mainhardt, Evan Marshall, Allison Mullen, Pesha Rubinstein, Vicki Lynn Watson.

Fantasy
Meredith Bernstein, Elaine Davie, Janice Fishbein, Joyce A. Flaherty, Daniel P. King, Lettie Lee, Ricia Mainhardt, Evan Marshall, Allison Mullen, Elizabeth Pomada, Vicki Lynn Watson, Sue Yuen.

Glitz & Glamour
Linda M. Diehl, Evan M. Fogelman, Natasha Kern, Allison Mullen.

Gothic
Natasha Kern, Allison Mullen.

Mainstream Romance
Pamela G. Ahearn, Meredith Bernstein, Pam Bernstein, Jane Jordan Browne, Pema Browne, Perry Browne, Andrea Cirillo, Anita Diamant, Linda M. Diehl, Janice Fishbein, Joyce A. Flaherty, Jay Garon, Irene Goodman, Linda Hayes, Natasha Kern, Daniel P. King, Fran Lebowitz, Lettie Lee, Ricia Mainhardt, Denice Marcil, Evan Marshall, Allison Mullen, Edward Novak, John K. Payne, Elizabeth Pomada, Meg Ruley, Vicki Lynn Watson, Nancy Yost, Sue Yuen.

Thriller
Jay Garon, Allison Mullen, Nancy Yost.

Mystery/Suspense
Pamela G. Ahearn, Marcia Amsterdam, Meredith Bernstein, Jane Jordan Browne, Andrea Cirillo, Ruth Cohen, Elaine Davie, Anita Diamant, Linda M. Diehl, Joyce A. Flaherty, Evan M. Fogelman, Irene Goodman, Natasha Kern, Daniel P. King, Lettie Lee, Ricia Mainhardt, Allison Mullen, Alice Orr, John Payne, Elizabeth Pomada, Pesha Rubinstein, Meg Ruley, Vicki Lynn Watson, Nancy Yost, Sue Yuen.

Regency
Pamela G. Ahearn, Pema Browne, Linda M. Diehl, Allison Mullen.

True Crime
Nancy Yost.

Westerns
Elaine Davie.

Women's Fiction
Elaine Davie, Linda M. Diehl, Evan M. Fogelman, Allison Mullen, Pesha Rubinstein.

Women-In-Jeopardy
Pema Browne, Perry Browne, Fran Lebowitz, Allison Mullen.

Young Adult
Andrea Brown, Pema Browne, Perry Browne, Linda M. Diehl, Linda Hayes.

Children's Fiction
Ricia Mainhardt.

Non-fiction
Elaine Davie, Linda M. Diehl, Evan M. Fogelman, Linda Hayes, Ricia Mainhardt, Alice Orr.

Literary
Elizabeth Pomada.

3

Harlequin's Inside Track

$\mathcal{D}$o you have a desire to write a super romance? Or is temptation leading your women-who-dare into the shadows? Can you present intrigue and intimate moments in a very special way? If you read lots of category romances, you know that Desire, Superromance, Temptation, Women Who Dare, Shadows, Presents, Intrigue, Intimate Moments, and Special Edition are the names of some of the romance lines published by Harlequin Enterprises Limited, under the Harlequin and Silhouette imprints. (Women Who Dare was a special short series.)

But Harlequin Enterprises Limited, like most romance publishers, didn't start out this big. It all began a few years after World War II, when pulp magazines no longer provided enough entertainment for women readers.

The first title published by Harlequin was *The Manatee* by Nancy Bruff. In 1951, Harlequin's first romance novel was a reprint of *Beyond the Blue Mountains* by Jean Plaidy (#113). Thus began a satisfying series of novels, created especially for twentieth century women readers. Today, with the incredible release of over 700 titles per year, they are the largest and most prolific publisher of romance novels in the world. Harlequin Enterprises Limited, under the Harlequin and Silhouette imprints, sells 200 million books annually in more than 100 international markets. Printed in over 25 languages, because 'Love speaks all languages' (from *A Global Success Story*, 1992), the name "Harlequin" has become synonymous with quality paperback romance in Germany, France, South America, Greece, Bulgaria, and the list goes on and on. Poland is one of the many countries that has opened the door to Harlequin for distribution and sales to bookstores and newsstands. Harlequin's Polish translations are delivered twice a month, but the 700,000 copies have been known to sell out in just one day! (*Romantic Times*, March 1992.) These are pretty impressive sales figures, considering Poland is a country with a population of only thirty-eight million, and whose steep price increases in 1991 had a serious effect on their economy.

No matter what country readers live in, the continued popularity of ten monthly series of Harlequin releases assures that there is a Harlequin romance to fit every woman's (or man's) reading taste. From sweet, short romances, to romantic suspense stories, to sizzling contemporaries with complex plots, to historicals with authentic detail, plus occasional special interest releases like the Crystal Creek and the Tyler series, Harlequin offers a cornucopia of delicious entertainment to delight and enthrall even the pickiest of romance readers.

What's Harlequin's equation for their incomparable success? Reader satisfaction seems to be the primary factor that generates repeat customers. And reader satisfaction added to affordability, availability, new monthly releases, clever marketing and promotions, plus phenomenal distribution methods equals success.

Many romance readers get initiated via an impulse item added to the supermarket cart. This is one of the distribution strategies that skyrocketed Harlequin to the top, despite the economic woes of many shoppers. At about the same price as a box of Cheerios, a romance novel can be absorbed into the weekly grocery budget without much problem. Attractive displays of new monthly releases at grocery stores, discount stores, train and bus stations, car washes, airports, drug stores, and even convenience stores like 7-Eleven, mean that practically no potential reader is overlooked.

The Harlequin logo, which graces every cover and book spine, has become a familiar trademark. The slender man in diamond-patterned tights is an historic character from Italian popular comedy, the "commedia dell'arte." The harlequin, a masked character improvising from a plot outline, could build stock characters and situations into fresh, new entertainment. A Harlequin novel also provides this continuity with basic story elements, but the stories are fresh and new each month.

Each line of books follows the basic Harlequin story: hero and heroine meet, the emotional intensity level of their relationship develops, the obstacles to their permanent togetherness are overcome, and the happy ending leaves the reader satisfied. This is not "formula" writing. The manner in which this drama is staged and performed is left up to each individual author, and there are infinite ways to create romance novels without ever repeating a plot or character.

Romance writers contribute their unique 'what if' ideas that fit the needs of the line and tell a story. Each story makes the word 'love' fresh and appealing as the characters and situations propel the reader toward the inevitable happy ending.

Romance writers love Harlequin editors, who are even easy to work with during the manuscript revision stage of a book. They provide detailed suggestions for changes and explain the hows and whys. Harlequin editors encourage and promote new authors. They are always looking for new talent and will read unsolicited, agented, and unagented manuscripts. Despite the large volume of submissions, authors who send manuscripts to Harlequin say the editors usually respond within six to eight weeks, often giving personal comments.

Advances and royalty rates for first time Harlequin authors remain confidential. This is not unusual in the industry. In fact, it is poor etiquette and also unprofessional to ask other romance writers about the dollar amount of their advances. Publishers negotiate these individually and keep the information privileged.

You do not need a literary agent to break into the Harlequin market. However, an agent may be better equipped to negotiate contract details and provide career guidance for the new novelist.

Speaking of guidance, when submitting a manuscript to Harlequin Enterprises Limited, remember that the Canadian office keeps a strong eye on foreign sales. Some of the manuscripts they acquire will be translated for the overseas market. Some book themes acceptable to a native New Yorker might be inappropriate for a native European, so keep each line's guidelines firmly in mind and stay focused on the story's goals. Maintain this focus while you write your manuscript and when you choose which office, New York or Toronto, to submit to. Consider which would be most receptive to the themes, characters, and plot devices of your manuscript. Above all, pay close attention to the specific guidelines of the line you are writing for. Make certain that you have a firm idea of what *that line's reader* has grown to expect. Match the pattern set by previous books in each series.

There is one important thing the guidelines don't tell you, something you should consider before sending your manuscript: In Harlequin's rose garden there is a small thorn. Though this requirement is nearly across the board with romance publishers, Harlequin "strongly prefers" that authors use pseudonyms. They also own the author's pen name and say they will not use it on books not written by the author. You should talk to your agent or editor about any legal questions regarding the use of pen names BEFORE signing that contract.

Although it may be difficult for some authors to keep a following if and when they move from one publishing house to another, if romance readers want to find an author's books, they can and will. They may inquire through romance bookstores, old or new publishers, *Romantic Times* magazine, or directories of contemporary authors that list all pseudonyms and works. Some diligent readers look for the novelist's real name on the copyright page to reveal the true identity of the author. Other die-hard *Romantic Times* readers keep a log of nom de plumes.

Pseudonyms aside, the editorial 'personal touch' and the way Harlequin treats both unpublished and published authors makes this mega-publisher one of the best places for aspiring romance authors to send a manuscript. In fact, *The Romance Writer's Pink Pages* attempted to find out any negative comments about Harlequin but could not locate ONE author who was uncomplimentary about the editorial staff. One Harlequin author, who is very happy writing for Harlequin, did report that a single fan letter had somehow fallen through the cracks, but added that the editor was a real sweetheart.

When asked 'What makes a manuscript fit your wish list?', Harlequin Enterprises Ltd. (in Canada) responded:

> *"See guidelines. Editors look for good, well-told stories with engaging, believable characters. Well-constructed, well-paced plots with plausible, resolvable conflicts.*
>
> *"Read. Read. Read. Read the most recent titles to get a clear idea of the kinds of stories we are currently publishing. Write for the series you most enjoy reading. If you don't have empathy for a particular series, it is unlikely that you can write successfully for that series."*

So if you desire to break into romance as a Harlequin author, do read and analyze every recent Harlequin title you can lay your hands on. If you have several romance pals, you can each buy books in a different line and then swap after reading! Make your own list of tips and hints that you pick up while reading Harlequin's and Silhouette's monthly offerings.

Here are a few tips about writing romance novels to fit a

Harlequin or Silhouette line:

> *Learn to dissect a romance from the first sentence on, so that the inner anatomy is revealed. Look at examples of each line's hook (the very first sentence).*
>
> *What is the main conflict (also known as the "terrible trouble") that the main characters face?*
>
> *What prompts the protagonists' first eye contact, touch, or kiss? Who initiates it?*
>
> *Consider the house style: How many pages and how many chapters are there? How long are the chapters? Do the chapters end with cliffhangers, which lead into the next chapter, or on a low note?*
>
> *Given the fixed word count of each line, how many sub-plots and secondary characters are usual?*
>
> *What do you feel is the "reality quotient" of each line?*
>
> *When does the couple make love: when they are first attracted, when they are still uncertain about their relationship, when they are emotionally committed, or perhaps, not at all?*
>
> *Don't limit your manuscript's creation to characters and plot ideas that you have already seen. Create a unique story that still fits the line's current voice.*

Keeping all this advice in mind, write your characters' own original story about their triumphs over adversity. Tell how they found that one true love of a lifetime and made a commitment to it. For above all else, Harlequin editors keep a sharp eye out for an enthralling love story, one their line's faithful readers will buy, enjoy, and remember for years to come.

(Thanks to Karin Stoecker, Editorial Director of

Harlequin Enterprises Ltd., for contributing historical and statistical information for this article.

Thanks also to Casey Roberts, who, besides writing Harlequin romances and being active in Romance Writers of America, is dedicated to sharing her knowledge of the genre with her students at Mesa Community College in Arizona. Some of the writing tips are paraphrased from, or influenced by, her lectures.)

4

Avoid Rejection —
Write Within
Romance Guidelines

$\mathscr{D}$id you know that Danielle Steel's *Messages From Nam* is NOT a romance?

It's called women's fiction, because the heroine has more than one lover, more than two lovers, more than—OK, well you get the idea! Multiple lovers are a big no-no in true romance novels, but are often a plot element of women's fiction.

Romantic fiction is as different from women's fiction as LaVyrle Spencer is from Erica Jong. You wouldn't catch LaVyrle writing about the "zipless" you-know-what any more than you would catch Erica writing about that once-in-a-life-time man who lays bouquets of sweet clover between the pillows! This contrast between Erica Jong and LaVyrle Spencer, that is, between women's fiction and romance, will help you discern what is a romance and what isn't.

Each genre—romance and women's fiction—has its own unwritten rules, characteristics, and plot devices. Stepping over the line into another genre can result in agents and publishers rejecting your manuscript. After all, one of the key unwritten rules is that both publishers and readers have certain expectations of a romance novel, and you, as the creative director, need to tailor your manuscript to meet those expectations. You must know what elements are acceptable, even necessary, in your story, but you must also know what is taboo. As you read, read, read, to study and analyze the genre, take special note of the demarkation lines that separate romance novels from women's fiction.

Women's fiction includes storylines that often mirror the real-life disappointments of spousal cheating, divorce, death, serious illness, alcoholism, drug addiction, incompatibility, sexual difficulties, and other relationship-oriented issues. Romance novels usually downplay these issues and zoom in on a happy ending with one true love in about half the wordage.

Women's fiction may also contain unemotional or "married-for-the-money" relationships, topics of special interest to women, male or multiple viewpoints, unwholesome characters, or taboo events like rape. These usually do not fit in with a romance publisher's requirements.

So, then, what is a romance novel? At the risk of seeming simplistic, let's make a mental flow chart: Heroine in terrible trouble has cute meet with hero; they are physically attracted, but there's a serious conflict between them; sparks fly (both good and bad); they get together because they are emotionally and intellectually attracted; they break up or they remain unsure of their relationship until a big event or situation throws them together in an exciting climax (no pun intended); they find out they really DO love each other and are willing to make it work: they resolve their conflict and live happily ever after in a beautiful place where nobody ever says the "F" word. And what is not romance? Well, here are some of the riskiest taboos:

A bitchy or mean-spirited heroine.

Promiscuity or infidelity by one of the protagonists.

Excessive violence by the hero, especially against the heroine.

The unhappy ending is the "horror of horrors" that makes romance novel editors throw up their hands in disgust.

Sometimes, because story elements of both may be present, it is difficult to tell whether you are reading romance or women's fiction. Romance readers call them cross-over books—editors call them "breaking-into-hardcover" books.

Cross-over authors make the distinctions between romance and women's fiction even more confusing, but as aspiring writers, keep your writing focused on the romance novel genre. Opportunities to write cross-over books and then women's fiction may come later, when hardcover publishers start a bidding war over your manuscripts.

Agents and editors also agree that it's nearly impossible for first-time authors to break into the women's fiction hardcover market. Aspiring authors have a much better chance of breaking into romantic fiction. Nora Roberts and LaVyrle Spencer wrote many, many romances before the doors to women's hardcover fiction were opened to them.

Each book you sell is a stepping stone to greater things, but concentrate on one goal at a time. Make every manuscript the best work you've ever written. Study editors' listings and publishers' guidelines seriously, and keep your romance manuscript elements within the boundaries of the genre.

5

Directory of Publishers

AMERICAN AUDIO LITERATURE, INC.

P.O. Box 1392
Cicero, NY 13039
(315) 676-7026

President: Joan Basile

Media Type: Audio Cassette

Titles Published Per Year: Will be 20

Submissions Policies

Send complete manuscripts with SASE. New authors are encouraged. Unsolicited manuscripts are OK. Unagented manuscripts are OK. No simultaneous submissions or electronic submissions. Agents may call after manuscripts is approved. Usual response time is one month.

Pay Rate

Average advance is $1,000–$500. Average royalty is .65 after the first 2500 copies are sold. Normal publishing schedule is about 4 months after acceptance.

Actively Seeking

Contemporary	25,000–30,000 words
Women's Fiction	25,000–30,000 words
Mystery/Suspense	25,000–30,000 words
New Age	25,000–30,000 words

Tips

Romances are conservative stories read aloud and are three hours in length. Good writing makes manuscripts fit the editor's wish list. Violence is unacceptable. Audio cassettes are not adaptations of published books. They are original works of fiction. This concept sets American Audio Literature apart from other audio cassette companies that buy rights to already published material. See guidelines section for more information.

AVALON BOOKS (THOMAS BOUREGY CO.)

401 Lafayette Street, 2nd Floor
New York, NY 10003
(212) 598-0222

Vice President/Publisher: Marcia Markland

Media Type: Hardback

Titles Published Per Year: 60

Submissions Policies

Send first chapter and 2–3 page synopsis. Send complete manuscripts if you are sure it fits our guidelines. New authors are encouraged. We publish many first novels. Unsolicited or unagented manuscripts are OK. Please, no simultaneous submissions. No electronic submissions. Agents may call. Response time is about three months, sometimes longer.

Actively Seeking

Non-formula Contemporary	40,000-50,000 words
Mystery/Suspense	40,000-50,000 words
Western/Historicals	40,000-50,000 words

Career romances with plot centered around heroine's job.
    (Research well!)

Tips

Conservative to sweet romances. No explicit sex, no profanity. Also see guidelines section.

AVON

1350 Avenue of the Americas
New York, NY 10019
(212) 261-6800
FAX: (212) 261-6895

Editor: Ellen Edwards

Media Type: Paperback

Titles Published Per Year: 48–62 romance titles

Submissions Policies

Agents may call. A query will get you the quickest response, but you may send a synopsis and sample chapters or the entire manuscripts plus a 1–2 page synopsis. New authors are always encouraged. Avon is constantly on the lookout for new talent. Unsolicited manuscripts are OK. All submissions, unsolicited and agented, are given fair consideration. Simultaneous submissions are OK. No electronic submissions. The usual response time for agented submissions is 6–8 weeks. Usual response time for unsolicited and unagented submissions is about 3 months.

Pay Rate

Books are normally published about 12 months after acceptance. Average advance varies.

Actively Seeking
Historical 1100–1899	100,000 words
Contemporary	100,000 words
Women's fiction	100,000 words
Mystery/Suspense	60,000 words, Psychological suspense; Women in jeopardy, straight mysteries, cozies

Tips

Read current Avon novels. Endings are always happy. Also see guidelines section.

Turn-offs/Taboos

Avon novels are sexy. No rape, except in rare instances, when handled with extreme sensitivity. No category romances.

BALLANTINE/DEL REY/FAWCETT/IVY
A Division of Random House
201 E. 50th Street
New York, NY 10022
(212) 751-2600

Editor: Barbara Dicks

Media Type: Paperback

Submissions Policies

Unagented manuscripts are OK. Submit complete manuscripts (preferred) or partials (synopsis and first three chapters) with SASE. Manuscripts should be double-spaced with no blank lines between paragraphs except scene breaks. Paragraphs are indented five spaces. Don't bind manuscript. Response time is several months. Reads all manuscripts. Printed form rejections are usual due to volume of submissions.

Pay Rate

Competitive advances and royalties. Contracts are individually negotiated.

Actively Seeking
Editor Barbara Dicks is actively seeking:

Historicals	100,000–125,000 words
Regencies for Fawcett/Ballantine	70,000–75,000 words
Adult Fantasy (and Science Fiction) for DelRey	60,000–100,000+ words

Tips

Fantasy plots and characters are propelled by magic and the supernatural. No UFO or occult works. No coincidence solutions. Read McCaffrey, Foster and Chalker to see what kind of fantasy is published. Romance is usually light and sweet when it is a plot element.

BANTAM/DOUBLEDAY/DELL BOOKS

1540 Broadway
New York, NY 10036
(212) 782-9187

Administrative Editor: David Underwood

Media Type: Paperback

Titles Published Per Year: 48

Submissions Policies

Send partials or completed manuscripts, agents may call. Unpublished authors, please query first. No unsolicited manuscripts, except from agents. No unagented manuscripts, unless requested after query. No simultaneous submissions. No electronic submissions. Response time is 6–8 weeks. Please specify Senior Editor's or Associate Publisher's name and the name of the line on outside of envelope:

Editors

Dell: Damaris Rowland, Associate Publisher Loveswept: Nita Taublib, Associate Publisher
Contemporary/Historical/Fanfare/Women's Fiction: Wendy McCurdy
Loveswept/Women's Fiction: Beth deGuzman

Pay Rate

Confidential advances and royalties. Books are normally published 16 months after acceptance.

Actively Seeking

Bantam Historical any time period	100,000-150,000 words
Bantam Fanfare (Contemporary Romance)	100,000-150,000 words
Bantam Women's Fiction	100,000-150,000 words
Loveswept contemporary Romance	up to 60,000 words

Tips

Bantam and Loveswept books range from sensual to sexy. See guidelines section for more information.

HARCOURT BRACE JANOVICH

Odyssey and Voyager Paperbacks
1250 Sixth Avenue
San Diego, CA 92101
(619) 699-6810 FAX: (619) 699-6777

Attention: Manuscripts Submissions

Media Type: Paperback

Titles Published Per Year: 75+

Submissions Policies

Query first with SASE. Double-spaced manuscripts are preferred. No simultaneous or multiple submissions are allowed. Response time on queries is 4–8 weeks. No phone calls, please.

Tips

Read current Young Adult Odyssey and Voyager paperbacks to determine what editors are buying.

HARLEQUIN AMERICAN ROMANCE

300 E. 42nd Street, 6th Floor
New York, NY 10017
PHONE: (212) 682-6080 FAX: (212) 682-4539

Senior Editorial Coordinator: Debra Matteucci

Media Type: Paperback

Titles Published Per Year: 48

Submissions Policies

Query first. If we think it's appropriate, we'll ask for complete
manuscripts from unpublished authors, partial from published.
New authors are encouraged. Query before sending unsolicited manuscripts. Unagented manuscripts are OK. No simultaneous or electronic submissions. No phone calls from agents.
Usual response time to a query is two weeks, a manuscripts six
weeks.

Pay Rate

Advances will be discussed at the contract offer. Books are normally published about 12 months after acceptance.

Actively Seeking
Contemporary sensual romance   70,000 words.

Editor's Wish List

Fast paced.
Adventure (i.e., new experience).
Emphasis on hero, who happens to be sexy.
Strong romance.

HARLEQUIN HISTORICALS

300 E. 42nd Street, 6th Floor
New York, NY 10017
PHONE: (212) 682-6080 FAX: (212) 682-4539

Senior Editor: Tracy Farrell

Media Type: Paperback

Titles Published Per Year: 48

Submissions Policies

Query first or query and full manuscript. Prefers full manuscripts. New authors are encouraged. Unagented manuscripts
are OK. No simultaneous or electronic submissions. Agents
may call. Usual response time to a query is 6–8 weeks on
queries (if possible), 4–6 months on manuscripts.

Pay Rate

Advances are variable. Royalties are standard. Books are normally published about 24 months after acceptance.

Actively Seeking
Historicals, primarily 1700 to 1900,
   occasionally before 1770,
   rarely after 1900   95,000–105,000 words

Tips

Write from the heart.

Editor's Wish List

A great story.

HARLEQUIN INTRIGUE
300 E. 42nd Street., 6th Floor
New York, NY 10017
(212) 682-6080 FAX: (212) 682-4539

Associate Editor: Julianne Moore

Senior Editor and Editorial Coordinator: Debra Matteucci

Media Type: Paperback

Titles Published Per Year: 48

Submissions Policies

Query first or query and full manuscript. New authors are encouraged. Unagented manuscripts are OK. No simultaneous or electronic submissions. Agents may call. Usual response time to a query is 6–8 weeks on queries (if possible), 4–6 months on manuscripts.

Pay Rate

Advances are variable. Royalties are standard. Books are normally published about 24 months after acceptance.

Actively Seeking
Contemporary romantic danger
   and suspense   70,000–75,000 words

Tips

Read current Intrigue to see what the editor is buying.

HARLEQUIN REGENCY

225 Duncan Mill Road
Don Mills, Ontario, Canada
M3B 3K9
(416) 445-5860 FAX: (416) 445-8655

Regency Editor: Paula Eykelhof

Media Type: Paperback

Submissions Policies

Unpublished authors should query first. Don't forget Canadian
postage on SASE, or enclose International Reply Coupons.
Published authors may send synopsis and three chapters or
query and full manuscript. New authors are encouraged.
Unagented manuscripts are OK. No simultaneous or electronic
submissions. Agents may call. Usual response time to a query is
6–8 weeks on queries (if possible), 4–6 months on manuscripts.

Pay Rate

Advances are variable. Royalties are standard. Books are normally published about 24 months after acceptance.

Actively Seeking
Regency romances in 1811–1820
England, Scotland, etc.   50,000–60,000 words

Tips

Read current Regency to see what the editor is buying.

HARLEQUIN, HARLEQUIN PRESENTS, AND HARLEQUIN ROMANCE

225 Duncan Mill Road
Don Mills, Ontario, Canada
M3B 3K9
(416) 445-5860 FAX: (416) 445-8655

Senior Editor: Dianne Moggy

Acquisitions Editor: Paula Eykelhof

Media Type: Paperback

Submissions Policies

HARLEQUIN ROMANCE and HARLEQUIN PRESENTS
are accepting queries.

Tips

See HARLEQUIN's guidelines section for a complete description of a new line of long, contemporary dramas set against a backdrop of "glitz and glamour." For all Please see the guidelines section for detailed submissions information and tips.

HARLEQUIN SUPERROMANCE

225 Duncan Mill Road
Don Mills, Ontario, Canada
M3B 3K9
(416) 445-5860 FAX: (416) 445-8655

Senior Editor: Marsha Zinberg

Media Type: Paperback

Submissions Policies

Query first or query and full manuscript. SASE must have Canadian postage or International Reply Coupons. New authors are encouraged. Unagented manuscripts are OK. No simultaneous or electronic submissions. Agents may call. Usual response time to a query is 6–8 weeks on queries (if possible), 4–6 months on manuscripts.

Pay Rate

Advances are variable. Royalties are standard. Books are normally published about 24 months after acceptance.

Actively Seeking
Contemporary mainstream-type romance   85,000 words

Tips

Read current Superromance to see what the editor is buying.

HARLEQUIN TEMPTATION
225 Duncan Mill Road
Don Mills, Ontario, Canada
M3B 3K9
(416) 445-5860 FAX: (416) 445-8655

Senior Editor: Birgit Davis-Todd

Media Type: Paperback

Submissions Policies

Query first with SASE (Canadian stamps or IRC's) or query and full manuscript. New authors are encouraged. Unagented manuscripts are OK. No simultaneous or electronic submissions. Agents may call. Usual response time to a query is 6–8 weeks on queries (if possible), 4–6 months on manuscripts.

Pay Rate

Advances are variable. Royalties are standard. Books are normally published about 24 months after acceptance.

Actively Seeking
Contemporary sensuous
    page-turner romance   60,000 words

Tips

Hero is always super sexy! Read current Temptation to see what the editors are buying.

HARPERCOLLINS/HARPER PERENNIAL
10 E. 53rd Street
New York, NY 10022
(212) 207-7000

Editorial Manager: Tracy Behar

Media Type: Paperback, Hardback

Titles Published Per Year: 600

Submissions Policies

Agents must query first. Do not send unsolicited manuscripts. Agents may not call. No electronic submissions. Simultaneous submissions are OK. New authors are encouraged, but only through agents. Usual response time is 6–8 weeks.

Pay Rate

Advances and royalty figures are confidential. Books are normally published about 9-12 months after acceptance.

Actively Seeking
Women's Fiction
Ethnic
Gothic
Mystery/Suspense

Tips

"For best results, submit only through an established, qualified literary agent."

Editor's Wish List

Women's fiction that is 'literary fiction' not genre-type romances.

HARPER PAPERBACKS
10 E. 53rd Street
New York, NY 10022
(212) 207-7752 FAX: (212) 207-7759

Senior Editor: Carolyn Marino

Media Type: Paperback

Titles Published Per Year: 48–60

Submissions Policies

Authors must QUERY first. Do not send unsolicited or unagented manuscripts. Agents may call. No electronic submissions. Simultaneous submissions are OK, if that is explained in the query letter. New authors are encouraged. Usual response time is 2 months.

Pay Rate

Varies from book to book. Books are normally published about 12 months after acceptance.

Actively Seeking

Historical	100,000–115,000 words
Contemporary	
Women's Fiction	
Mystery/Suspense	

Tips

"Our books are very individual; we do not have guidelines."

Wish List

"I look for stories that are well-written and that hold my interest. Highly emotional stories generally work well, as do stories that are fairly complex."

LEISURE BOOKS/DORCHESTER PUBLISHING
276 Fifth Avenue, Room 1008
New York, NY 10001
(212) 725-8811 FAX: (212) 532-1054 TELEX: 238198

Executive Editor: Alicia Condon

Media Type: Paperback

Titles Published Per Year: 140

Submissions Policies

Query first OR send synopsis and first three chapters. SASE a must. Don't send complete manuscript, unless it is requested. New authors are encouraged and unsolicited manuscripts are OK. Unagented manuscripts are OK. No simultaneous submissions or electronic submissions. Agents may call. Usual response time is 6–8 weeks.

Pay Rate

Average advance varies, as does average royalty. Books are normally published about 12 months after acceptance.

Actively Seeking:

Sensual Historicals	in various time periods	115,000 words
Futuristic romances	in "lavish lands on distant worlds"	90,000 words
Time travel romances	credibility between the two times	90,000 words

Tips

In time travel romances the hero or heroine falls in love with someone from another era. No undue violence. See guidelines section for more information. NOT accepting Gothic Romances at this time. Free catalog of Leisure Books for #10 SASE.

THE NAIAD PRESS, INC.

P.O. Box 10543
Tallahassee, FL 32302
(904) 539-5965 FAX: (904) 539-9731

CEO: Barbara Grier

Editor: Katherine V. Forrest

Media Type: Paperback

Titles Published Per Year: 24

Submissions Policies

Always query first. No exceptions. Send synopsis or precis; no sample chapters. Never send complete, unsolicited manuscripts. We have readers around the U.S. and we delegate. New authors receive much encouragement. No simultaneous submissions. No discussions of manuscripts with agented authors. Electronic submissions are OK. Usual response time to queries is seven days maximum. Often 48 hours is enough. SASE is a must.

Pay Rate

Advances are very flexible. We use standard 15 percent recovery contract 99 percent of the time. Books are normally published 18–24 months after acceptance.

Actively Seeking

Historical	time period is variable	52,000 words
Contemporary	various topics	52,000 words
Women's Fiction	all topics	52,000 words
Mystery/Suspense	variable topics	52,000 words

Tips

"All of our books are lesbian. Romances range from conservative to sweet to spicy to sensual to sexy. Books by, for, and about lesbians, but we work in every sub-genre. Self-serving authors win the prize. Know the books already done by the company. Think slim and well-done books. Our advantages are that we keep books in print permanently and we market to a very hungry and fast growing audience. Reader loyalty to name of author is incredible and increases rapidly with each book. We like to publish a new book by an author every 18–22 months, sometimes more often than that. See guidelines section for more information."

Editor's Wish List

"As is probably true of all publishers, we work towards getting a book to do as well as some of our historical best sellers. Books like *Curious Wine* by Katherine V. Forrest (my favorite), *Horizon of the Heart* by Shelly Smith, *Cherished Love* and *To Love Again* by Evelyn Kennedy. All of these are contemporary love stories."

Turn-offs/Taboos

"Any and all sado masochistic involvement is a definite no-no. Our readers tend to be conservative at least in terms of adventurous sexuality. All of them tend to be very conservative in terms of sexual extension, i.e., no menage a trois, no multiple girlfriends. Everyone needs to end up happily 'wed' to the girl of her dreams. The same requirements apply to lesbian romances as apply to heterosexual romances."

NAL/DUTTON PUBLISHING

A Division of Penguin USA
375 Hudson Street
New York, NY 10014-3757
(212) 366-2525

Senior Editor: Audrey LaFehr

Topaz Editor: Hillary Ross

Imprints: Dutton, Signet, Onyx, Topaz.

Media Type: Paperback, Hardback

Submissions Policies

Agents, please query first by phone. Send complete manuscripts after query. New authors are encouraged. Unsolicited manuscripts are not OK, nor are unagented MS, unless an unagented author is approached by editor. Simultaneous submissions are permitted. No electronic submissions. Agents may call editor. Usual response time is 4 weeks.

Pay Rate

No average advance. Books are normally published about 12 months after acceptance.

Actively Seeking

Historicals set before 1900	100,000 words
Contemporaries	100,000 words
Women's fiction	90,000+ words
Ethnic fiction with Black, Hispanic and Asian topics	Varied length
Mystery series	80,000 words
Medical thrillers	80,000 words

EDITORIAL NOTE: Although the editor did not provides specific pay rate information, research revealed that well-known Signet Regency author April Kihlstrom receives about $5,000 as an advance, plus royalties above a certain minimum, plus foreign rights for each book. (Woman's Day Magazine, 2/18/92, page 36.)

NEW VICTORIA PUBLISHERS
P.O. Box 27
Norwich, VT 05055
(802) 649-5297

Editor: Claudia Lamperti

Vice President: Beth Dingman

Media Type: Paperback

Titles Published Per Year: 6

Submissions Policies

Query first. If requested, send synopsis and sample chapters. Do not send complete manuscripts. New authors are encouraged. Unsolicited manuscripts are OK. Unagented manuscripts are preferred. Simultaneous submissions are OK, if the editor is made aware of the other submissions. Claudia Lamperti prefers to read hard copy, but is happy if it is on disk as well. Prefers letter queries from agents. Usual response time is 2–3 weeks.

Pay Rate

Usually no advance. Average royalty is 10 percent. Books are normally published 12–18 months after acceptance.

Actively Seeking
Historical
Contemporary
Women's Fiction
Ethnic
Mystery
(Word counts not specified)

Tips

New Victoria Romances are sensual. No heterosexual sex. Be sure to enclose SASE or we will not respond. See guidelines section for more information.

Wish List

Strong female protagonists, preferably lesbian.
Complex, exciting plot.
Intelligent writing.

Turn-offs/Taboos

"We are not interested in heterosexual sex. Not interested in pornography. Not interested in typical, cliche-ridden romances (even if it is lesbian)."

POCKET/POCKETSTAR
Simon & Schuster Consumer Group
1230 Avenue of the Americas
New York, NY 10020
(212) 698-7000

Executive Editor: Claire Zion

Senior Editor, YA novels: Ruth Ashby

Historical Romance Editor: Carolyn Tolley

Titles Published Per Year: 300+

Submissions Policies

Agents: Query first to appropriate editor with detailed synopsis and sample chapters. SASE for return of material.

Actively Seeking
Contemporary Romance
Historical Romance
Archway—Young adult novels   35,000 words or 160 pages

Tips

For young adult novels, looking especially for romantic comedies and suspense/thrillers.

PUBLISHERS SYNDICATION INT'L.
1377 K St., N.W. Suite 856
Washington, D.C. 20005

Editor: A. P. Samuels

Media Type: Paperback, Hardback

Novelettes Bought Per Year: 12 romances, 12 mysteries, and 12 miscellaneous subjects.

Submissions Policies

Send complete manuscripts, including word count and SASE. Unsolicited and unagented manuscripts are OK. New authors are encouraged. No simultaneous submissions. No phone calls from agents. Specify computer type, disk size and density, and word processing program used in case a disk copy of the story is requested. Usual response time is 4–6 weeks.

Pay Rate

Upon acceptance; up to 3 cents a word.

Actively Seeking
Romance	30,000 words
Mystery	30,000 words
Miscellaneous Subjects novels	30,000 words

Tips

Romances should not contain explicit sex, as they are for a general audience. Mysteries should be similar to Sherlock Holmes. No blood and guts violence.

ST. MARTIN'S PRESS
Mass Market Division
175 Fifth Avenue
New York, NY 10010
(212) 674-5151 FAX: (212) 677-7456

Senior Editor: Jennifer Weis

Media Type: Paperback

Submissions Policies

Query or send synopsis and sample chapters. Send completed manuscripts if available. Agents may call. New authors are encouraged. Unagented and unsolicited manuscripts are OK. No electronic submissions. Usual response time is 3 months.

Submit synopsis and sample chapters of contemporaries to Editor Christey Bahn.

Pay Rate

Advances and royalties are confidential. Books are normally published about 9 months after the acceptance of a full manuscript.

Actively Seeking
Contemporary   75,000–100,000 words.
Historical
Women's Fiction
Suspense
Woman-in-Jeopardy

SILHOUETTE DESIRE

300 East 42nd Street
New York, NY 10017
(212) 682-6080

Senior Editor: Lucia Macro

Media Type: Paperback

Titles Published Per Year: 72

Submissions Policies

Authors, send query letter first. Only send synopsis, sample
chapters or complete manuscripts if requested. Agents may call.
No unsolicited manuscripts. Unagented manuscripts are OK,
but query first. No simultaneous submissions. No electronic
submissions. Usual response time is 3 months for an unagented
completed manuscript. New authors are encouraged.

Pay Rate

Books are normally published about 12–18 months after acceptance. Average advance is $2,000–$4,000 for a first time author,
depending on the amount of work the manuscripts needs.
Standard royalty starts at 6 percent.

Actively Seeking
Contemporary   55,000–60,000 words.

Tips

"Read recent books to get an idea of what I'm looking for. Our
romances are sensual to sexy. When I say 'write from the heart'
I mean write with an obvious love and respect for the genre. As
an author, you need to sell your book, and sometimes that
means creating a saleable story. After you've developed your

name you can write me that ballet dancer hero you've been trying to sell me on! But again, look at the Desire line to see what types of stories I've been 'going for.' My favorite romance novel is *Through a Glass Darkly* by Kathleen Koen. (I know it's depressing but it's so vivid!)"

Editor's Wish List

"I want to see manuscripts where the author has developed a unique voice within the obvious boundaries of the category romance genre. Stories should have strong emotional conflicts or—in the case of what I call "plotless wonders"—a great deal of sassy verve to carry the story along. In addition, the love scenes should enhance the story and somehow move the romance forward."

Turn-offs/Taboos

"It's up to the author to study the market and get an idea of what readers seem to like (an obviously what editors are buying)! However I have this pet peeve against land development stories."

SILHOUETTE INTIMATE MOMENTS
300 East 42nd Street
New York, NY 10017
(212) 682-6080

Senior Editor/Editorial Coordinator: Leslie Wainger

Media Type: Paperback

Titles Published Per Year: 72

Submissions Policies

Unsolicited authors, send query letter first. Only send synopsis and sample chapters if requested. No unsolicited manuscripts. Unagented manuscripts are OK if we have requested them. No simultaneous submissions. No electronic submissions. Usual response time on a query is several weeks. Usual response time on a complete manuscripts is about 3 months. New authors are encouraged. Agents may call. Not necessary for agents to send a query. Agents only may send synopsis and sample chapters, or complete manuscript.

Pay Rate:

Books are normally published about 12–24 months after acceptance. Average advance is $2,000–$4,000 for a FIRST TIME author; negotiable otherwise. Standard royalty starts at 6 percent.

Actively Seeking
Contemporary category   80,000–85,000 words

Topics are varied. Suspense is OK.

Tips

"Our romances are sensual. Write from your heart as well as your head. If you truly feel an emotional connection with your work, it's far more likely that the reader (and the editor) will feel it, too. My favorite romance novel is *Summer of the Red Wolf* by Morris West. (I may be alone in classifying this as a romance!)"

Editor's Wish List

Strong characters who will appeal to readers; an interesting, generally complex plot with tension that grows naturally from the characters; a strong focus on romance; good writing.

"I try never to say never, and we've done successful books with such difficult subjects as alcoholism, drug addiction and prostitution. We will and want to do works with ethnic heros and heroines."

SILHOUETTE ROMANCE

300 East 42nd Street 6th Floor
New York, NY 10017
(212) 682-6080 Fax: (212) 682-4539

Senior Editor: Anne Canadeo

Media Type: Paperback

Titles Published Per Year: 72

Submissions Policies

Authors, send query letter first. Agents may call. New authors
are encouraged. No unsolicited manuscripts. Unagented manuscripts are OK, but query first. No simultaneous submissions.
No electronic submissions. Usual response time is 6–12 weeks.

Pay Rate

Books are normally published about 12–24 months after acceptance. Average advance is variable. Standard royalty starts at 6
percent.

Actively Seeking
Contemporary Romance   53,000–58,000 words

Tips

"Our romances are conservative. SILHOUETTE
ROMANCES are contemporary, warm, and dynamic with a
solid base of traditional, family values. Stories can be powerful-
ly emotional or humorous and charming, but all must be
believable, compelling love stories at heart."

Editor's Wish List

Strong, believable characters and conflict. Emotional, believable ROMANCE. Stories must be fresh, contemporary even
when using classic storylines such as marriage of convenience.

SILHOUETTE SHADOWS
300 EAST 42nd Street
New York, NY 10017
(212) 682-6080

Senior Editor/Editorial Coordinator: Leslie Wainger

Media Type: Paperback

Titles Published Per Year: 4 per month.

Submissions Policies

Authors, send query letter OR send synopsis and sample
chapters OR send complete manuscript. Agents may call. New
authors are encouraged. Unsolicited manuscripts are OK.
Unagented manuscripts are OK. No simultaneous submissions.
No electronic submissions. Usual response time is several
weeks for a query, 3 months for a complete manuscript.

Pay Rate

Average advance is $2,000–$4,000 for a FIRST TIME author;
negotiable otherwise. Standard royalty starts at 6 percent.

Actively Seeking
Dark romance/"spooky" romance   70,000–75,000 words

Gothic
Paranormal
Soft Horror

Tips

"Our romances are sensual. This line represents a new direction for category romance, so writers trying for it need to be
willing to take a few chances. If you play it too safe and conser-
vatively, you'll fall short. And never forget that at heart, these
are still romances. My favorite romance novel of this type is
Airs Above the Ground by Mary Stewart."

Editor's Wish List

"It must scare me, thrill me, developing both the romance and a dark spooky atmosphere simultaneously."

Turn-offs/Taboos

"Nothing should be too bloody or gross, but nothing too tame and 'usual' will fit either."

SILHOUETTE SPECIAL EDITION
300 East 42nd Street, 6th Floor
New York, NY 10017
(212) 682-6080

Senior Editor: Tara Gavin

Media Type: Paperback

Titles Published Per Year: 72

Submissions Policies

Authors, send query letter first plus outline of story. Send synopsis and sample chapters only at editor's request after query letter. Agents may call. New authors are encouraged. No unsolicited manuscripts. Unagented manuscripts are OK, but query first. No simultaneous submissions. No electronic submissions. Uusual response time is 6–8 weeks.

Pay Rate

Book publishing schedule varies. Average advance is variable. Standard royalty starts at 6 percent.

Actively Seeking

Contemporary with a strong focus
on romance   75,000 words

Tips

A SILHOUETTE Special Edition has a broad range—sensuality depends on the author and what works for the story. Read the line and study the market! Keep in mind who you are writing for and what subjects will be meaningful and entertaining to them.

Wish List

"Our readers look to us for stories with a strong focus on the developing romance as well as an awareness of what satisfies the romance reader. The longer length of the SILHOUETTE Special Editions offers authors the opportunity to create more in-depth characterizations. The broader concept necesary for the length offers the challenge to connect with the reader in a unique and meaningful way."

Turn-offs/Taboos

"Too much reliance on contrivance, misunderstanding—or the other woman/other man chestnut."

SINGER MEDIA CORPORATION

Seaview Business Park
1030 Calle Cordillera, Unit #106
San Clemente, CA 92672
(714) 498-7227 FAX: (714) 498-2162

President: Kurt Singer

Media Type: We are a newspaper syndicate with a very active book department. 300 publications worldwide.

Submissions Policies

Query first by brief letter. Do not send synopses or sample chapters. Unagented queries are OK. Published articles are OK. Average response time is 2–4 weeks.

Pay Rate

"Standard." Pays on sale. Publishing schedule varies.

Actively Seeking

Contemporaries	50,000–70,000 words
Romantic Suspense	50,000–70,000 words
Mainstream with romance elements	50,000–70,000 words
Mysteries	
Biographies	
Non-fiction	

Tips

Especially interested in reprints of previously published books for which the author holds foreign rights. Also, anything new, different, and not run of the mill. See guidelines section for more information.

TOR BOOKS

175 Fifth Avenue, 14th Floor
New York, NY 10010
(212) 388-0100

Senior Editor: Melissa Ann Singer

Assistant Editor: Natalia Aponte

Media Type: Paperback, Hardback

Submissions Policies

Don't query. Send a 1 page synoposis and sample chapters or complete manuscript with SASE. Agents are invited to call. New authors are encouraged. TOR accepts unsolicited and unagented manuscripts. Simultaneous submissions will not be considered. No electronic submissions (paper only). Please do not fax anything! Usual response time is 2–3 months.

Pay Rate

Books are normally published about 12 months after acceptance. Average advances and standard royalty rates remain confidential.

Actively Seeking

Historial	any time period	60,000 words minimum
Contemporary	wide range of topics	60,000 words minimum
Women's fiction	wide range of topics	60,000 words minimum
Mystery/Suspense	hard-boiled featuring a woman; cozies	60,000 words minimum

Wish List

"We don't really do too much in the way of category-type romances. We are looking for more women's fiction and will consider almost any plot. Writing must be strong, plot handled in a fresh way, and the heroine must be strong."

WALKER AND COMPANY

720 Fifth Avenue
New York, NY 10019
(212) 265-3632 FAX: (212) 307-1764

Mystery Editor: Michael Seidman

Media Type: Hardback

Titles Per Year: 12–18

Submissions Policies

Send (up to) 5 page synopsis and three sample chapters. Only
send complete manuscripts if requested. New authors are
encouraged. Unagented manuscripts are also OK, but please
query first. Simultaneous submissions are OK only at the query
letter stage. No electronic submissions. Agents may call the
WALKER phone number (718) 802-9487 if Editorial Director
is not at WALKER. Usual response time is six weeks to three
months.

Pay Rate

Average advance and royalty rate was not filled out on the
questionnaire. Books are normally published 12–15 months
after acceptance.

Actively Seeking
Mysteries with romance elements   60,000–70,000 words

Tips

Read our books. No longer publishing regency romances. You
can order our books by calling 1-800-AT-WALKER. Authors
should do this for any line they want to write for. See guidelines section.

Mystery Editor Michael Seidman Speaks: "Walker Mysteries may indeed have an element of romance in them; they do not though, fulfill any of the usual guidelines or marketing needs of category romance houses. My primary focus is on the mystery: the clues, the red herrings, rounding up the usual suspects, the rational deductive process leading to the apprehension and—we assume—legal prosecution of a crimnal. Romantic suspense, with its threats both real and imagined, and its almost coincidental capture (or explanation) of the 'evil' as the hero and heroine come together, would be out of place for my readers."

WARNER BOOKS

Time-Life Building
1271 Avenue of the Americas
New York, NY 10020
(212) 522-5054 FAX: (212) 522-7990 or (212) 522-7989

Senior Editor: Jeanne Tiedge

Media Type: Paperback, Hardback

Titles Per Year: approximately 250

Submissions Policies

New authors are encouraged. Query first. May send synopsis with query, but please do not send unsolicited manuscripts. Do not send complete manuscripts or sample chapters unless requested by editor. Agents may call. Simultaneous submissions are acceptable from agents only. No electronic submissions. Present a professional appearance–clean typewritten queries, and SASE enclosed. Usual response time is 4–6 weeks.

Pay Rate

Advances and royalties vary. Books are normally published about 12–18 months after acceptance.

Actively Seeking

Historical	any time period	100,000–125,000 words
Contemporary (but not category)	U.S. settings	100–125,000 words
Mystery/Suspense	Woman-in jeopardy	80,000–100,000 words

Tips

Warner Books are sensual to sexy. Warner does not have tip sheets. Read *Forbidden* by Pat Warren ('94 release) to get an idea of the type of woman-in-jeopardy themes these editors acquire.

Wish List

Originality, tension between hero and heroine, great writing, strong subsidiary characters.

Turn-offs/Taboos

Standard category plots; pirate/castaway, abduction, forced marriage, sold in a card game, etc.

ZEBRA/PINNACLE PUBLISHING CORP.

475 Park Avenue South
New York, NY 10016
(212) 889-2299 FAX: (212) 779-8073

Senior Editor: Beth Lieberman

Senior Editor: Alice Alfonsi

Senior Editor: Ann LaFarge

Media Type: Paperback, Hardback

Titles Per Year: 500

Submissions Policies

Don't query. Send synopsis and complete manuscripts with
SASE. Stamps must be attached, not loose. New authors are
encouraged. Unsolicited manuscripts are OK. Simultaneous
submissions are OK, as are unagented manuscripts. For the
Regency line query first with cover letter, 3-5 page synopsis
and sample chapters. For the Sleuth Series send complete
manuscript with synopsis and short proposals of books planned
for a series. Agents may call. The usual response time varies.

Actively Seeking

After-fifty Line (heroines over aged fifty)	Contemporary romance	100,000 words
Glitz and Glamour (life and love of the rich and beautiful)	Contemporary romance	100,000 words
Gothic (Spooky settings, compelling mysteries set before 1920)	written in the first person	100,000+ words
Heartfire	Historicals (any time period)	107,000– 130,000 sensual words
Horror	Scary tales, especially vampire fiction, for both Zebra and Pinnacle	100,000 words

Magnolia Road (Setting is real or fictional plantation.	Antebellum South historicals	120,000 words
Regency	Seeking completed Regencies in an English setting.	60,000–75,000 words or 120,000+
Romantic Suspense/ Woman-in-Jeopardy	Modern-day gothics which feature the heroine in terrible danger.	100,000 words
Saga	A fictional family's lives and loves	100,000+ words
Sleuth Series	Female amateur detective teams up with the hero to solve mysteries in all time periods.	
Women's Fiction	Contemporary stories	100,000+ words

Tips

Read the line you plan to write for, for instance, for the Magnolia Road line read *Southern Fire* by Ashley Snow to see what Zebra is buying.

The following publishers/imprints are listed by subject:

Antebellum South (See also Historical)
Zebra Magnolia Road

Biographies
Singer

Career Romance
Avalon

Contemporary
American Audio Literature
Avalon
Avon
Bantam/Loveswept
Harlequin American
Harlequin Superromance
Harlequin Temptation
Harper
NAL/Dutton
Publisher's Syndication Int'l.
St. Martin's Press
Silhouette Desire
Silhouette Intimate Moments
Silhouette Romance
Silhouette Special Edition
Singer
Tor
Warner
Zebra Lovegram

Ethnic
HarperCollins
NAL/Dutton

Fantasy
Ballantine/Del Rey

Futuristic
Leisure

Glitz and Glamor
Harlequin
Zebra

Gothic
Silhouette Shadows
Zebra

Historical
Avon
Ballantine
Bantam Historical
Harlequin Historical
Harper
Leisure
NAL/Dutton
St. Martin's Press
Tor
Warner
Zebra Heartfires

Horror/Soft Horror
Silhouette Shadows
Zebra

Lesbian
The Naiad Press
New Victoria

Mainstream
Harlequin Superromance
Singer

Medical Thriller
NAL/Dutton

Mystery/Cozies/Suspense/Woman in Jeopardy
American Audio Literature
Avalon
Avon
Harlequin Intrigue
HarperCollins
Harper

NAL/Dutton
Pocket/Pocketstar (Young Adult)
Publisher's Syndication International
St. Martin's Press
Singer
Tor
Walker
Warner
Zebra

New Age
American Audio Literature

Older Heroines & Heroes
Zebra After Fifty Line

Paranormal
Silhouette Shadows

Regency
Ballantine/Fawcett
Harlequin Regency
Zebra

Romantic Comedy
Pocket/Pocketstar (Archway YA Books)

Saga
Zebra

Science Fiction
Ballantine/Del Rey

Sleuth
Zebra

Time Travel
Leisure

Western
Avalon

Women's Fiction
American Audio Literature
Avon
Bantam
HarperCollins
Harper
NAL/Dutton
St. Martin's Press
Tor
Zebra

Young Adult
Harcourt Brace Janovich (Odyssey/Voyager)
Pocket/Pocketstar (Archway)

6

"Romancing" the Sale — With Professional Etiquette

Although there is really no right or wrong when asking an editor or agent a sincere question after you've established a working relationship, first impressions are important. A few phone calls to an editor on deadline, ones that could easily be answered by reading their tip sheet, or even a clear breach of publishing etiquette, like setting deadlines for an agent to read and comment on your manuscript, are things that will make you seem very unprofessional. Though your actions are innocent and not done out of rudeness, your lack of understanding about what goes on in the publishing business could well cause your manuscript to be shoved to the bottom of the pile. This is not out of contrariness on the part of the editor or agent. It is because that person is too busy to hold your hand through the process of getting your manuscript read and evaluated. It is easier to deal with a manuscript based on its own merits, without unnecessary interference from the author.

You can avoid unnecessary phone calls to an editor or agent if you enclose a self-addressed stamped postcard with your manuscript. One that says something like, "Harlequin Temptation received your manuscript entitled Hearts On Fire on _____. (Editor fills in the date.) Editor's name or initials here: _____." This simple addition to your submission envelope is almost never ignored by the editor or agent who knows this returned postcard will help to lessen phone calls from anxious authors. This postcard buys them time, because they know that YOU know when your submission arrived and which editor or agent is reading it.

An agent has to be more discriminating than an editor when choosing a manuscript, because an agent puts a reputation on the line with every submission to an editor. Agents (who do not charge reading fees) only make their livings on commissions from sales and the royalties off of those sales.

Agents cannot afford to waste any time, money, or effort on any manuscript that will not sell within a month or two, sometimes three. If agents took on every manuscript that was good, without knowing which line would be likely to acquire it, their agency would soon go out of business.

So, let's define professionalism and find out how to treat agents and editors with the proper etiquette. If an editor or agent knows you understand what goes on behind the scenes, they will appreciate your writing efforts that much more.

Here are some quick and easy-to-remember tips that will help you to always present a professional image to an editor or agent.

> *Don't call an editor to ask about the manuscript your agent has submitted for you. Only call your agent to ask about the status of your manuscript if you don't hear anything in a reasonable amount of time, say about three or four weeks. Your agent should be providing you with photocopies of cover letters to the editor, as well as photocopies of any rejections received. The agent should tell you what editors were called about your manuscript, even if the editors didn't want to look at it.*

Do ask your agent to inform you of rejections, and ask to see copies of rejection letters. It's sometimes discouraging, sometimes enlightening, but part of the painful process of growing as a professional author.

Don't ask your agent how much money he or she can get for your book until your first manuscript is accepted by a publisher, and a verbal offer has set a contract into motion. Before this point, it would be unprofessional for an agent to speculate on your possible income from writing. Agents deal in concrete integers based on written contracts from publishers.

Likewise, if you are unpublished don't expect an agent to sign you on as a client until your book is finished, polished, and ready for submission to a publisher. A query letter and the first three chapters may be enough to make a sale for an experienced author, but first-time authors must usually go the entire distance before being taken seriously by either an agent or editor. There are exceptions of course, but it's wise to be prepared with a completed or almost completed manuscript.

Agents have a little more leeway about simultaneous submissions than do authors, and editors expect that the agent will be lining up other publishers to look at the manuscript, almost the minute the agent hears of a rejection. That's the agent's job. An agent's business demands that he or she "sell, sell, sell," and without those sales commissions, the agency will not survive. But, if it is against the house policy, don't YOU send an editor a simultaneous submission. Editors know editors at other publishing houses too, and a description of your manuscript just might come up over lunch or at a convention!

If you're unagented and you don't get a reply within the usual response time listed in this directory, write a polite letter to the editor inquiring about your manuscript. It helps the editor if you enclose a copy of your original cover letter with your inquiry.

Always include a self addressed stamped envelope of sufficient size and postage to cover the return of your manuscript. The only exception to this is if the publisher does not respond to rejected manuscripts. Good Housekeeping magazine is one of the publishers who requests NO SASE.

When submitting a manuscript to a Canadian address, make sure the postage is correct. Letters marked 'postage due' may be refused by the recipient. Also, in lieu of hard-to-get Canadian stamps for the SASE, enclose an International Reply Coupon (IRC) for the proper amount. Contract postal stations (such as those in grocery stores) do not sell IRC's. They must be purchased at a regular post office.

Also, when mailing manuscripts to Canadian addresses, the author must fill out a postal receipt for Customs. The value of the package should be declared at $10.00 or less, to expedite the package through Canadian Customs. (Thanks for that tip, Harlequin!)

Never fax anything unless you are asked to do so by an editor or agent. If you do have permission, make sure to fax a cover sheet with your letter. This helps direct the fax to the right person, especially at a large publishing house.

Don't type copyright notices on your manuscript. Always submit a manuscript that is typed, double-spaced, and free of typos, coffee rings, and margin notes. Use wide margins and white bond paper only (20 lb.), not onion skin. Don't staple or bind the manuscript unless asked to do so. Make sure the title of the book (or a keyword from it), your last name, and the page number is on EVERY page!

Agree to make revisions if an editor asks you to do so. You'll establish yourself as an author who is easy to work with.

When you're rich and famous, you can play prima donna, but for now, ego must take a back seat to professionalism.

Never send your only copy of anything. It could get lost! Keep backup disks or copies of manuscripts in a safe place that is both cool and dry, like a safety deposit box at a bank (for 3½" disks). Don't forget, 5¼" floppy disks must not be stored in or near metal.

Backup your work on a daily basis, including correspondence to agents and editors, cooperate with editors who request revisions, and let your agent wheel, deal, and worry.

Historical accuracy is a must in historical romances. Check your facts carefully and keep your notes and a bibliography to back your facts. There is nothing more embarrassing than the hero using a sword of steel before the metal was invented, or the heroine wearing a bustle thirty years after they were out of fashion!

Contemporary authors must also do research on locales, hobbies, occupations, psychology and motivation, murder weapons, police procedure, single lifestyles, and much more.

Make a habit of using the library's computer to do research. Besides the electronic book and periodical listings, some libraries have access to entire information networks, such as Infotrack. Use the print screen button on the keyboard to retain evidence of your electronic research.

Just keep submitting tidy, completed manuscripts, use your spellcheck, don't forget SASE, and hopefully, you'll never have to say you're sorry!

(Thanks to all the acquisition editors and agents who candidly shared their tips for this section. You will remain anonymous as you requested!)

7

Directory of Publishers' Guidelines

The following publishers' guidelines are being printed in *The Romance Writer's Pink Pages* with written permission from the editors.

These guidelines are the most recent "tip sheets" provided by the publishers, and every effort has been made to assure the accuracy of the stated requirements, editor's names and so forth.

There are many books that can instruct in the art of writing the romance novel. But the following guidelines are the romance writer's blueprint for slanting their novel toward a specific publisher. The chances of being published are greater if you are familiar with the individual guidelines.

AMERICAN AUDIO LITERATURE, INC.

American Audio Literature, Inc.
Box 1392
Cicero, NY 13039

American Audio Literature is a company that produces audio tapes of original literature.

There are at the present time several very successful companies recording previously published books. The tapes are adaptations of that published material. These include self-improvement tapes, instructional tapes, inspirational tapes, and fiction/non-fiction tapes.

Our intention is to deal primarily in fiction. However, there are two major differences between our concept and the recycled, pre-published books that are now on the market.

Our material is specifically designed by the author for the three hour listening format, which has proven successful. We do not pay major publishing houses for the rights to use their material, and we do not pay for a book that would take several hours to read aloud to be scaled down to three hours of reading time. These two items save thousands of dollars and allow us to be highly competitive.

You should design your stories to be read aloud in three hours, (approximately 23,000–28,000 words.) They should be designed to capture the attention of adults in situations that are normally considered boring (e.g., driving, jogging).

Interested writers should submit manuscripts for review. Our cash offering will be a maximum of $1,000. Royalties will be paid after the first 2,500 copies are sold. Be assured that those writers who come with us initially will be highly rewarded as the company grows and expands.

Please notify us if you intend to begin work on a manuscript and give us an idea of the expected completion date.

The success of the audio business is irrefutable. The ten year manager of one of the largest nationally known booksellers in the Syracuse area tells us that five years ago they carried less that a dozen audio tapes. Today it is in excess of 1,000 titles! There is a tremendous demand for more. The market is definitely there and expanding at breathtaking speed!

We feel that with this concept we will establish a whole

new and exciting art form for the 21st century. We hope you
will be a part of it with us.

Send manuscripts and SASE to Joan Basile, President

AVON BOOKS
The Hearst Book Group
1350 Avenue of the Americas
New York, NY 10019
(212) 261-6800 FAX: (212) 261-6895

Historical Romance and Regency Guidelines

Have you ever dreamed of being a published romance writer?
If so, now may be a good time to put your pen to paper—or
your fingers to the typewriter keys.

If you love romances, have an active imagination, enjoy
writing, and are willing to work hard to become a published
writer, we encourage you to try your hand at writing a historical
romance for Avon Books, THE Number One publisher of romances. Here are some helpful hints to get you started:

Avon Romances are 100,000–125,000 words long
(400–500 manuscript pages) and take place in any time period
from the Middle Ages to the end of the 19th century
(1100–1900).

"Hook" the reader with a strong opening that makes her
want to keep reading.

The hero and heroine should meet early in the book (by
page 30 at the latest), and once they've met, they should not be
separated for lengthy periods.

Do careful research. Historical accuracy is a must.

Try to capture the special flavor of the particular time and
place you're writing about.

Start by creating an appealing and memorable hero and heroine who interact in exciting, original, sexy and romantic ways.

Know your characters thoroughly. Know why, besides sexual attraction, they're drawn to each other and fall in love.

The hero and heroine should make love in sensual, tastefully described love scenes, but NOT before you've established a degree of emotional intimacy between them.

The heroine shouldn't make love with anyone but the hero. (I'm afraid the double standard still applies; it's OK for the hero to make love to other women, but preferably NOT after he makes love with the heroine.)

Make sure the focus of your book is the romantic relationship between the hero and heroine. Everything you include should contribute to the development of that relationship in some ways.

Be original. Read other historical romances to know what story ideas have been overused. Do something different; find variations on the tried and true themes.

Master the technique of writing well. A good story will only come alive for the reader if you tell it skillfully and energetically.

Be critical of your work. Make sure it's your very best work.

Keep asking yourself, "Will a "jaded" romance reader who's read dozens of historical romances find my manuscript entertaining?"

Keep in mind who your audience is and why they read historical romances.

Make sure your book ends "happily ever after."

Neatly type your manuscript on plain bond paper, double-spaced with generous margins, and send it with a letter briefly describing who you are, what your book is about, and your background as a writer. Include a stamped, self- addressed envelope big enough to contain your manuscript, should it be returned to you.

Have fun writing your historical romance! And send it to Ellen Edwards, Senior Editor or Marjorie Braman, Senior Editor.

Regency Romances:

Manuscripts should be 60,000 words.

Emphasis should be on romance, with lots of interactions between the hero and heroine. The hero and heroine should woo each other with words.

Accurate period detail. It should include the wit and sparkle that makes the Regency period so popular.

Please submit Regency romances to Marjorie Braman, Senior Editor or Ellen Edwards, Senior Editor.

BANTAM DOUBLEDAY DELL
Publishing Group, Inc.
1540 Broadway
New York, NY 10036
(212) 354-6500

Loveswept

Dear Author:

Thanks for your interest in our Loveswept line. Here are some pertinent facts about our romances:

Loveswepts run about 55,000 words and are set in the present. The books are wonderfully written and feature sparkling dialogue rather than long narrative. Quickly paced, our Loveswepts are page turners!

The characters are deftly crafted, well-rounded people whom readers care about and root for. They should meet as close to page one as possible and never be apart for more than 8–10 manuscript pages. The sexual tension and attraction between the hero and heroine should be apparent from their first encounter on, but their love for each other should be based on emotions and feelings, not simply on sexual attraction.

We expect mystery/intrigue/adventure/paranormal and other elements to be kept to a minimum, and that the romance remain the focus of the story at all times. Secondary characters should also be limited in number and in importance. More valuable than any "tip sheet" or "guideline," the books themselves are your best tools for learning what we're looking for in a Loveswept. Read as many as possible before you submit to us.

Send us a query letter if you don't have an agent. The query should be no more than two or three pages, but it should cover the basics of who your characters are, what the conflict is that they face, and how your plot develops. It usually takes 4–8 weeks to receive a response from us. Please don't submit sample chapters or a complete manuscript until we request them. Unfortunately, we cannot give comments on any submissions.

For further assistance in preparing your work, we suggest you consult The Writer's Survival Manual: The Complete Guide to Getting Your Work Published Right by Carol Meyer (Bantam), which is available at your local bookstore, or The Literary Market or The Writer's Market, which can be found at your local library.

We're constantly searching for the stars of tomorrow, the new authors who are the genre's life blood. Write a great book, and we'll buy it!

Sincerely,

The Loveswept Editors

BANTAM DOUBLEDAY DELL
Publishing Group, Inc.
1540 Broadway
New York, NY 10036
(212) 354-6500

Fanfare

Dear Author,

Thank you so much for your inquiry about the FANFARE imprint. Here are a few pertinent facts about FANFARE romances.

Fanfare is the showcase for Bantam's popular women's fiction. With spectacular covers and even more spectacular stories. Fanfare presents three novels each month—ranging from historical to contemporary—all with great human emotion, all with great love stories at their heart, and all by the finest authors writing in any genre. Fanfare authors include such favorites as Amanda Quick, Nora Roberts, Iris Johansen, Beverly Byrne, and Rosanne Bittner.

Because the stories and styles of Fanfare books cover the entire spectrum of women's fiction we have no guidelines for Fanfare. If you wish to submit your work for consideration under the Fanfare imprint and do not have an agent, send us a query letter. The query letter should be no more than two or three pages, covering the basics of who your characters are, what the conflict is that they face, and how your plot develops. It usually takes 4–8 weeks to receive a response from us. Please don't submit sample chapters or a complete manuscript until we request them. Unfortunately, we cannot give comments on any submissions.

For further assistance in preparing your work, we suggest you consult The Writer's Survival Manual: The Complete Guide to Getting Your Work Published Right by Carol Meyer (Bantam), which is available at your local bookstore, or The Literary Marketplace or The Writer's Market, which can be found at your local library.

We're constantly searching for the stars of tomorrow, the new authors who are the genre's life blood. Write a great book, and we'll buy it!

Sincerely,

The Fanfare Editors

THOMAS BOUREGY & COMPANY, INC.

Avalon Books/Airmont Classics
401 Lafayette Street
New York, NY 10003 (212) 598-0222 (800) 223-5231 FAX:
(212) 979-1862
Vice President/Publisher: Marcia Markland

Under its Avalon Books imprint, Thomas Bouregy & Co., Inc., publishes hardcover secular romances and westerns for the library market. Our books are wholesome adult fiction. No profanity or graphic sex.

We publish sixty books a year in bimonthly cycles of ten. A cycle consists of two career romances, two mystery romances, four general romances, and two westerns. All the romances are contemporary; all the westerns are historical. Books range in length from a minimum of 40,000 words to a maximum of 50,000 words (usually about 160–210 manuscript pages).

ROMANCES

General Information: We do not want old-fashioned, predictable, formulaic books. We are looking for contemporary characters and fresh contemporary plots and storylines. Supporting characters and subplots should be interesting and realistic, and they should add an extra and interesting dimension to the book.

Heroines: Every Avalon heroine should be an independent young woman with an interesting profession or career. She is equal to the stresses of today's world and can take care of herself.

Heroes: Avalon heroes should be warm, likable, realistic, sympathetic, understanding men who treat the heroine as an equal with respect for her intelligence and individuality.

Mysteries: The heroine does not have to be the protagonist in a mystery. It doesn't even have to be a romance. (Just keep in mind that we do not publish explicit sex or violence.) We are interested in how the mystery is unraveled, that is, through clues, red herrings, and logical deductions from the evidence.

Career Romances: The only difference between a romance and a career romance is that the plot of the career romance is centered around the heroine's job. We want these novels to explore the many exciting professionals open to women today. They must be carefully researched so that all the background information is authentic. It is all right for a career romance to straddle categories and have a mystery plot.

Westerns

General Information: All westerns are historical novels, and it is important that they be accurately placed in time and that the background be carefully researched. Avoid using words and phrases that were not part of the language at the time your western is set. Plots should be suspenseful and action packed, but vivid descriptions of gory, violent details are to be avoided.

Submissions: We prefer to see the first chapter and a brief summary of the rest of the book; however, if you have a complete manuscript that you are positive fits all our requirements, you may send it in. If you are submitting a complete manuscript, please include a one-page summary of the story with it. Please be sure to include a self-addressed stamped envelope for the return of your material if it is not suited to our needs. Because of the vast number of manuscripts and proposals we receive, we DO accept simultaneous submissions.

Suggested Reading

Romances:

Yesterday's Dreams	Alice Sharp
In Love's Own Sweet Time	Audrey Lazier

The Runaway Heart	Anne Ladley
This Time for Always	Jane Shore
Dreams of Joy	Holly S. McClure

Career Romances:

Prescription for Love	Anne Ladley
Love on Trial	Wendy Martin
Programmed for Danger	Karen G. McCullough
Harvest of Love	Nancy Sheehan
Where the Heart Seeks Shelter	Anne Ladley
A Storybook Love	Alice Sharp

Mystery Romances:

Dangerous Odyssey	Jane Edwards
The Night Prowlers	Karen G. McCullough
The Vanishing Bridegroom	Alice Sharpe
The Dark Side of Paradise	Alma Blair
Secrets of Echo Moon	Jill Giencke

Westerns:

Dead Man's Walk	Lee Martin
Devil's Raiders	Clifford Blair
Trail of the Long Riders	Lee Martin
Raid at Black Persimmon Bluff	Howard Pelham
The Ruination of Dan Becker	Robin Gibson

HARLEQUIN ENTERPRISES LIMITED
225 Duncan Mill Road
Don Mills, Ontario, Canada M3B 3K9
TEL (416) 445-5860/FAX (416) 445-8655/TELEX 06-966697

To the romance author:

Enclosed are editorial guidelines for Harlequin's various romance lines. Please keep in mind that these pages will give you some tips but no easy answers. There is no "formula" to writing a publishable romance novel.

Remember that if you hope to write romance fiction, it's important to enjoy reading it. If you are already a fan, your appreciation will be apparent in your writing. If you have not done so already, we encourage you to read many books in each series available on the market. The line that emerges as your favorite is probably where you should submit your manuscript.

Remember too, that reading is an emotional experience. We hope you write from the heart, that you will let us feel touched by what you have to say. When you put pen to paper, do so because you indeed have something to share with other readers.

On the last page of this package you will find answers to some frequently asked questions. Should you wish further information, don't hesitate to get in touch with me.

Sincerely,

Karin Stoecker, Editorial Director

HARLEQUIN ENTERPRISES LIMITED
225 Duncan Mill Road
Don Mills, Ontario, Canada
M3B 3K9

"Let me tell you about the rich. They are different from you and me."

—F. Scott Fitzgerald, *The Rich Boy*

Wealth. Power. Privilege. Acclaim. Ambitious women and men who want it all and who are driven to turn their dreams into reality. Their arena: great urban meccas, centers of fashion, finance, film, culture, and government—anywhere opportunities exist to succeed big, play hard, and live and love to the fullest. Their stories: larger-than-life, sensuous, contemporary dramas set against a backdrop of "glitz and glamour."

Harlequin's new program will be a glittering showcase for the rich and famous—and the want-to-be rich and famous. Two novels of at least 100,000 words will be published each month with striking, sophisticated covers and story lines that range from intense drama to intrigue, romantic suspense, and family sagas. Anything goes—as long as there is a strong love story with a satisfying conclusion.

Please submit first two chapters and detailed plot synopsis to Dianne Moggy, Senior Editor of Privileges.

"I have been poor and I have been rich. Rich is better."
                                        —Sophie Tucker

HARLEQUIN AMERICAN ROMANCE

American Romance
Harlequin Enterprises Ltd.
300 East 42nd Street, Sixth Floor
New York, NY 10017
USA

These novels are bold, brash, exciting romantic adventures that tap the pulse of America. The stories capture the *spirit* of America, a place where anything is possible and where dreams come true. These contemporary romances feature dynamic, aggressive men and women who take on new experiences—where they encounter the unexpected and where, through determination and luck, they realize their version of the

American dream and find true love. Each story captures the challenges, the opportunities, the spunk that characterizes America and its people.

Plot

Lively, fast-paced and upbeat stories that are action-packed. *Not* problem based or introspective. The stories are American fairy tales. The characters conquer the odds and win their every heart's desire. The stories aim for fictional credibility, not realism. Instead of everyday experience, look to your imagination and dreams for inspiration.

The developing romantic relationship between the hero and heroine is the focus. The stories are told from both the hero and the heroine's point of view, and may be "hero-led," where the hero (not the heroine) is the central character.

Hero

He is the bold, brash, and brave American man. Rugged around the edges, or earthy, or slick and sophisticated; he is the sexiest man in the world. A real take-charge modern man, he embodies the lost qualities of the frontiersman: a lust for adventure, a hunger for challenge, and a thirst for daring. He is not the average American boy-next-door!

Heroine

She, too, is sassy, strong, and full of spunk. A contemporary American woman with a confident self-image. She never wimps out to the dynamic hero.

Setting

The action unfolds itself in the United States, though the characters may travel to other locales during the course of the book. Each novel is grounded in the ambience of a particular American locale and of the people and spirit who characterize that locale. (There's a difference between a Texas man and a New York man!) The sense of place is essential but should not dominate.

Sensuality

These are intense, passionate stories filled with sexual tension, lovemaking and all the emotions of falling in love.

Length

70,000 words or approximately 280 manuscript pages.

Submission

Query first! All query letters should include a complete 2- page synopsis.

Please mark "Harlequin American Romance" on all submissions and direct them to Debra Matteucci, Senior Editor and Editorial Coordinator.

HARLEQUIN HISTORICALS

Harlequin Enterprises Limited
300 East 42nd Street, Sixth Floor
New York, NY 10017
USA

The primary element of the Harlequin Historical novel is romance. The story should focus on the heroine and how her love for one man changes her life forever. For this reason, it is important that you have an appealing and believable hero and heroine, and that the relationship that builds between them be a compelling one. The conflicts they must overcome and the situations they face can be as varied as the setting, but there must be romantic tension, some spark between your hero and heroine that keeps your reader interested.

Heroine

The reader's main identification is with the heroine. Therefore, it is imperative that she be a sympathetic character. She should be strong willed, independent, and intelligent, but she should also be emotionally vulnerable. Though she is in circumstances unfamiliar to readers, she should react in a familiar and believable way.

Hero

The hero must be appealing. He should be strong, both physically and emotionally, though he should not be physically dominating or abusive.

Plot

The historical setting—time period, place, culture, and events—is vital and should be well developed and authentic. But it is your characters who must make history come alive. Your writing should be rich and evocative. Be sure to avoid textbook and travelogue descriptions. Your story will be much more meaningful if your readers see your historical setting as it is seen and experienced by the characters about whom they care.

We're looking for stories with depth and complexity; subplots and secondary characters are important. The overall tone may vary. Some stories may be more humorous and entertaining; some more adventurous; others more dramatic or emotional.

Sex

Your story should be sensual, though the level of sensuality will be determined by your characters. The emphasis should not only be on the sensual, but on the emotional aspect of your hero and heroine's relationship.

Setting—Time Frame

We rarely accept books set after 1900. We are looking primarily for books set in North America, England, and France between 1700 and 1900 A.D. We are, however, flexible, and will *consider* most periods and settings.

Length

95,000—105,000 words.

Submissions

We prefer to review complete manuscripts, but we will also look at the first three chapters and a synopsis if the entire manuscript is not available. Be sure to send a query letter, which should include word length, a brief synopsis (a paragraph or two, even if you're submitting a formal proposal), and pertinent information about your writing experience. Please include a self-addressed mailer with sufficient postage for return.

Please mark your submissions "Historical" and send it to Tracy Farrell Senior Editor, Historicals.

HARLEQUIN INTRIGUE

Harlequin Enterprises Limited
300 East 42nd Street, Sixth Floor
New York, NY 10017
USA

Harlequin Intrigue is an exciting blend of contemporary romance and mystery, suspense and adventure. To maintain the unique character of this series, we encourage writers to focus the plot of their story on the mystery element rather than relegating it to a subplot.

Harlequin Intrigue encourages variety. Subject matter may range from everyday occurrences with unusual twists, to murder mysteries, whodunits, psychological suspense, thriller, espionage, adventure, and puzzles. Essential ingredients are sustained suspense and/or mystery, constant interaction between the protagonists, a threat of danger, and of course, a strong romance. There should always be a satisfying resolution to the intrigue and a happy ending to the romance.

Please mark "Intrigue" on queries or submissions and direct them to: Debra Matteucci Senior Editor and Editorial Coordinator, Intrigue.

Heroine

She is a mature woman of any nationality. She must be active in the mystery and work toward solving it. And she must contribute some knowledge or skill that is necessary to resolve the situation.

Hero

He is a mature man of an age compatible with that of the heroine. He, too, may be of any nationality. He must be active in the mystery and possess skills that complement the heroine's, so that together they can resolve the situation that neither of them could have resolved alone.

The hero and heroine do not have to be on opposite sides working against each other, though such "seeds of doubt" are acceptable.

Plot

Stories may be either action-oriented or psychological intrigue. The plot must always be complex, realistic, and quickly paced. Provide enough twists and turns of plot and red herrings to avoid a predictable ending. The intrigue or mystery should present itself early in the book and be maintained throughout. Any clues planted during the course of the book must be tied up at the end.

The romance should be continually interwoven, so that the romantic relationship grows and develops as the plot develops. As the protagonists work together, their shared dangers lead to shared passions.

Sex

Love scenes are acceptable, provided they do not detract from the tension and pacing. Since this is a romance, it is essential to show the sexual tension.

Setting

The story may take place anywhere in the world. It is imperative that the setting be presented accurately. An interesting setting can serve to enhance the mystery/suspense.

Length

70,000-75,000 words. Approximately 275–300 manuscript pages.

HARLEQUIN PRESENTS

Mills & Boon, Ltd.
Eton House
18-24 Paradise Road
Richmond, Surrey, TW91SR
United Kingdom

Harlequin Presents is the best-selling romance series in the world. These are intense, exciting, and dramatic stories, often set in exotic locales, featuring strong, passionate men and women.

Heroine

A Presents heroine should be contemporary, interesting, and individual. Her age and professional status may vary according to the demands of the plot, and she may or may not be career-oriented, according to need. She may or may not be sexually experienced but never promiscuous. She should definitely be intelligent, should show integrity, and develop as a character during the course of the story.

Hero

Often older and usually (but not necessarily) more worldly and sexually experienced than the heroine. He should be attractive, compelling, and powerful—should have real *presence.* The author must ensure that the reader will fall in love with him as deeply as the heroine does.

Plot

Obviously, the books should deal with the love between a man and woman, a love that is happily resolved by the story's end. The emphasis should be on the shattering power of that love to change lives, to develop character, to transform perception. It should be treated as a once-in-a-lifetime happening, and its repercussions should be clear throughout the book. Any situation may be used—from those that confront such contemporary concerns as divorce, single parenthood, or career conflicts to those bordering on fantasy.

Strong characters in conflict are part of the appeal of Presents. If hero and heroine are immediately compatible, the story loses tension and excitement.

Sex

Readers have come to expect a high degree of sensuality and sexual tension from this series. But the art of sexual description depends on what is appropriate for the characters and situation.

Again, although Presents can be more sexually explicit than Romance, the emphasis should be on emotion, not clinical detail.

Setting

Anywhere in the world. Bear in mind that Presents are truly *romantic* novels, so the setting should be integral to the mood and story.

Style

The style should convey the intensity and acute sensitivity of emotion that accompanies falling in love. Writing should be clear, natural, and exciting—not pedestrian but not over-wrought either.

Length

50,000–55,000 words.

Submission Format

We will consider *queries* only. Your query letter should include a 1–2 page synopsis; if you wish, you may also submit the *first 10 pages* of your manuscript.

Please address any correspondence to Frances Whitehead, Editorial Director.

HARLEQUIN ROMANCE
Mills & Boon, Ltd.
Eton House
18-24 Paradise Road
Richmond, Surrey, TW91SR
United Kingdom

Harlequin Romance, our original and longest-running series, is the traditional romance for today's woman.

Heroine

She's often a little younger than the hero (but doesn't have to be) and can be sexually inexperienced. She should hold traditional (not to be equated with old-fashioned) moral values. The heroine may be a career woman, whether in an unusual occupation or in a more typical job; she can be self-employed, a full-time mother, etc.—it's up to the author. Most essential, she must be portrayed with depth and affection. She must be a likable, interesting, and sympathetic character—one with whom readers will want to identify.

Hero

He can be older than the heroine (probably mid-twenties to late thirties but try to avoid excessive age difference between them). He should be very attractive, worldly and successful (on his own terms of course). Above all, he must have a compelling, dynamic personality. He needs to balance strength with gentleness. And he should exude confidence and natural authority. In other words, the Harlequin hero is a little larger than life, yet strongly true to life.

Plot

Plots can be relatively simple, though there must be enough complexity to maintain interest for the length of the book. Subplots that add elements of mystery, suspense, or adventure are fine as long as the emphasis remains on the central relationship. Plots can certainly be traditional but must be approached with freshness and individuality. A legitimate, sustained and resolvable conflict is essential. The plot should not be too grounded in harsh realities. Traditional romances need an edge of fantasy, of dream fulfillment, yet they must be plausible.

Sex

Explicit sexual description does not belong in a Harlequin Romance; the emphasis should always be on the emotional, not the physical.

Setting

Anywhere in the world, from a small American town to the Australian outback. A sense of place is an important element in most Harlequin Romance novels. That place should be one the writer is familiar with and can convey with authenticity. Background detail must be naturally integrated into the story and not allowed to overwhelm it.

Style

Often light, always natural; humorous only if the author has a bent for humor and humor fits the story. Style should be clear, direct, individual—never obscure, imitative, or pretentious. Dialogue should reflect the way people actually speak (with profane language and provocative, sensual comment kept to a minimum).

Length

50,000–55,000 words

Submission Format

We will consider *queries* only. Your query letter should include a 1–2 page synopsis; if you wish, you may also submit the *first 10 pages* of your manuscript.

Please address any correspondence to Frances Whitehead, Editorial Director.

HARLEQUIN SUPERROMANCE

Harlequin Enterprises Limited
225 Duncan Mill Road
Don Mills, Ontario, Canada
M3B 3K9

Provocative, passionate, contemporary stories that celebrate life and love!

The only requirements for today's Superromance novels are page-turning stories of 85,000 words strongly focused on believable heroines and heroes. Their quest to find love and to shape their lives must take place in a dynamic plot and conclude with a satisfying resolution.

Character is action . . .

The characters should define and drive the plot through their actions and reactions. The heroines are intelligent, warm, and motivated women with a clear idea of their own strengths. Whether they desire to make their mark in the world or in the fabric of the family, their values reflect their dreams of true partnership. The heroes are sexy, passionate men. Their strengths may emanate from their knowledge of who they are and what they want from life.

For the rest, let your imagination be your guide . . .

The choice of components can be diverse, as can the level of sensuality and scope of time frame... And the locale? Anywhere from Paris, Texas to Paris, France. The tone is up to you. It can range from comic to intense, provocative to emotional. You can choose multiple or central points of view. Whatever the story elements and issues, they should be explored within the context of the central romance. The range of possibilities is endless: fun, moving, exciting, heartwarming, sensuous, imaginative, humorous, innovative, suspenseful, or adventurous.

In dreams begin responsibilities . . .

Your responsibility is to summon your own distinctive voice to harness the kind of story that only you can tell.

The ESSENCE of Superromance . . . lies in emotionally compelling characterization.

The EXCITEMENT of Superromance . . . vibrates in the scope, variety, and complexity of the story *you* want to tell.

The EXCELLENCE of Superromance . . . IS ITS AUTHORS.

Please submit first three chapters and a detailed plot synopsis to Marsha Zinberg, Senior Editor, Superromance.

HARLEQUIN TEMPTATION

Harlequin Enterprises Limited
225 Duncan Mill Road
Don Mills, Ontario, Canada
M3B 3K9

Sensuous, bold, sometimes controversial, Harlequin Temptation stories focus on contemporary relationships between adults. These fast-paced books may be humorous, topical, adventurous, or glitzy, but at heart, they are pure romantic fantasy.

Please mark "Temptation" on queries or submissions and direct them to Birgit Davis-Todd, Senior Editor, Temptation.

Heroine

She is an attractive North American woman aged 23 or older, who may be single, divorced, or married. A contemporary woman of the Nineties, the heroine is involved with a career she cares about and has a strong sense of her own individuality.

She'd like to meet the right partner in order to fulfill herself emotionally and sexually and to make a lifetime commitment.

Hero

He is compatible in age to the heroine and may or may not be North American. Handsome, successful at his job, he's sexier than any man has a right to be! The Temptation hero should be strong, compelling, larger than life, and play an active role in the story. Beyond that, he may be characterized as the most self-assured, strong-willed, new alpha man, the unpredictable bad boy, or the highly appealing and sometimes humorous Nineties man.

Plot

In a Harlequin Temptation novel, the plot is the developing romance between the hero and heroine. The plot must be fresh, original, complex enough to sustain 60,000 words, and action-oriented rather than introspective. A good blend of sparkling dialogue and minimal narrative is important. Strong, believable conflicts are also essential in a Temptation. Secondary characters and minor subplots may be included to enrich the plot. Temptation books cover a range of plots: humorous, fantasy (both romantic and sexual fantasy), topical, adventurous, emotional, glitz and glamour. Truly innovative stories may be designated "Editor's Choice."

Sex

Temptation is Harlequin's boldest, most sensuous series, mirroring the lives of contemporary women. A high level of sexual tension is required throughout the story in order to maintain the necessary edge and arousing feel. The hero and heroine should have several sensuous encounters and should consummate their relationship at a point appropriate to the plot. Love scenes should be highly erotic, realistic and fun, but above all, emotional. Let your imagination be your guide!

Setting

The stories are written from a North American viewpoint, but may take place anywhere in the world. A feeling for the setting should be subtly evoked without overwhelming the romance.

Length

60,000 words or approximately 235 manuscript pages.

GENERAL INFORMATION FROM HARLEQUIN ENTERPRISES LIMITED

Submission Format: For unagented and unsolicited submissions, please send a query letter. State the length of your manuscript and enclose a brief synopsis as well as any pertinent information about yourself, including publishing credits and professional affiliations.

Agents: We give equal consideration to manuscripts sent by authors and agents. We do not give recommendations.

Return Postage: Please include sufficient return postage, preferably a money order or international reply coupons.

Customs Value: The declared value of a manuscript copy should be a maximum of $10.00 to expedite processing through Canadian customs. This does not apply to manuscripts mailed in the U.S. to our New York office.

Simultaneous Submissions: We will not consider any submission that has been sent simultaneously to another publisher.

Financial Arrangements: We enter into discussions about payments only when we are going to contract. This information is confidential.

Copyright: Under the United States copyright law, copyright for any work is secured when the work is created; i.e. an author has copyright protection the moment the work is put on paper and can be visually perceived. When a manuscript is published by Harlequin, every copy bears a copyright notice that entitles the copyright holder to certain additional rights. Harlequin registers all copyrights with the United States Copyright Office; this registration, although not a requirement for protection, establishes a public record of the copyright claim. For more information regarding copyright, write to Copyright Office, Library of Congress, Washington, DC 20559.

Manuscript Tips

Here are tips on the professional presentation of any manuscript:

Title Page should state the author's real name and address, the title, and the approximate number of words. Also indicate pseudonym if applicable.

Manuscripts should be typewritten, error-free, double-spaced, and on one side of the paper only. Leave a 1¼-inch margin around the entire page, and be sure to use a good grade of white bond.

In the upper right-hand corner of each manuscript page, include the author's last name and the page number (e.g. Smith–12, Smith–13, and so on).

If you use a computer printer, the print must be letter-quality. Dot matrix is unacceptable.

Be sure to make a complete copy for your files.

Do not bind or staple your manuscript. Use an envelope or box large enough to contain your manuscript flat.

LEISURE BOOKS

A Division of Dorchester Publishing
276 Fifth Avenue
New York, NY 10001
(212) 725-8811 FAX: (212) 532-1054 TELEX: 238198

Historical Romance

Sensual romances with strong plots and carefully thought-out characterizations. Spunky heroine whose love for the hero never wavers; he's the only one she makes love with and she's as passionate as he, although he may have to instruct her in the ways of love, since she's almost invariably untouched before she falls in love with the hero. Hero is often arrogant, overbearing; heroine often can't stand him at first, but discovers that beneath the surface lies a tender, virile, and experienced lover. It helps if both the heroine and hero have a sense of humor—a certain amount of wit leavens the heavy-breathing passion. Hero and heroine are constantly separated by misunderstandings, jealousy, Acts of God, war, etc., but in the end they overcome the barriers between them and live happily ever after.

We don't want a heroine who sleeps around, or a hero who's sadistic, although if there's a villain or villainess, he or she can be as nasty as possible.

Historical background, details of costume, etc., should be accurate; however, we don't want endless descriptions of battles, the political climate of the period, or a treatise on contemporary social history. Our readers are more interested in the trials, tribulations, and love life of the heroine than in how many men Napoleon lost at the battle of Waterloo.

Historical Romances should be approximately 115,000 words.

Gothic Romance

The traditional Gothic Romance includes a beautiful, virginal, 18–25 year old heroine and a dark, brooding hero who fall in love, separate due to some conflict, and reconcile, against the backdrop of a foreboding, gloomy setting. Gothic Romances contain a suspense or mystery element that always puts the heroine in danger. American and foreign settings are acceptable as well as the first-person and third-person narrative. The most important guidelines to remember are that the atmosphere is very important in these romances and that clichés should be avoided.

Complete manuscripts should be 90,000 words.

Futuristic Romance

Futuristic Romances contain all the elements of Historical Romances—beautiful heroine, dashing hero, some conflict that separates them, a happy ending, etc.—but they are set in lavish lands on distant worlds. Avoid science-fiction-type hardware, technology, and the like.

Finished manuscripts should be 90,000 words.

Time Travel Romance

A modern-day hero or heroine goes back in time and falls in love. Traditional guidelines for Historical Romances apply. The challenge here is to maintain credibility during the transition between the present and the past. The fun is seeing history and another way of life through the eyes of someone from our own time. The conflict and resolution of the romance arise from the fact that the hero and heroine are from different eras.

Beware of a lot of philosophizing about fate, the meaning of time, and how the past affects the present.

Finished manuscripts should be 90,000 words.

Submissions

Please query or submit synopsis and first three chapters *only*—no complete manuscripts unless specifically requested. Include a stamped, self-addressed envelope (of sufficient size) for possible return of proposal or manuscript. *No material will be returned without SASE.*

Synopsis and sample chapters (manuscript if requested) must be typed and double-spaced. Word processors are OK, but letter quality only. Please retain a copy of all material sent, in case the original gets lost in the mail.

For a free catalogue of Leisure Books, please send a self-addressed stamped number 10 envelope to the above address.

The best way to learn to write a Leisure romance is to read a Leisure romance.

NAIAD PRESS

P.O. Box 10543
Tallahassee, FL 32302
(904) 539-9322 (904) 539-5965 FAX: (904) 539-9731

Submissions

As you read this please consider that we receive about 750 inquiries and/or wholly unsolicited novel length manuscripts each year. Following the suggestions below is your only chance of consideration or acceptance.

Any unsolicited manuscript received without a stamped return mailer will be discarded. There are no exceptions.

Write (type) a single page letter on 8½ × 11 inch paper. Ask permission to submit a manuscript by identifying it by type, that is, novel, nonfiction, etc. Give a single brief statement that includes your name, your address, your day and evening telephone number, and the times you can best be reached. Please do not include any personal information that is not directly related to your ability to create a book suitable for publication. (A possible exception to this would be your movement status.) Always include all publication information.

We accept no simultaneous query letters or submissions. If you are interested in being published by the oldest, largest, and by far the most successful of the lesbian publishing companies, please direct your query to us. If not, please do not include us in a list of possible publishers.

Do not submit poetry or poetry queries. Do not submit queries on autobiography unless your name is a household word in the lesbian movement.

Include a one page precis of the plot. No testimonials about its quality from your friends, your family, or any famous writer are helpful to your cause, and may in fact be damaging. Include the word count of the book (the best way to do this is to count the words on ten pages, divide by ten, and multiply by the number of pages in the manuscript). Be sure your precis includes the conclusion of your book, as well as what happens, why, when, where, and how. We will not read any novel in excess of 60,000 words. There are no exceptions. Manuscripts in the 52,000 word length range are considered ideal.

Be very sure, before you begin the process, that you have completed your end of the book. You have written it (and rewritten and revised and rewritten), neatly typed it (consult many writing manuals in any public library), and you have edited it to the limit of your ability. It is a finished product from your point of view.

Know our works. Be sure you understand that you are submitting a manuscript to The Naiad Press and that our publishing program is unique. We do books, by, for, and about lesbians, and we emphasize popular fiction sub-genres, such as romances, mysteries, spy novels, ghost stories, fantasy and science fiction, erotica, westerns, regencies . . . Know that we feel that being a lesbian means being superior at once and that our books reflect that philosophy.

If your book is to be read, you will be instructed on how and to whom it is to be sent. Good luck.

Barbara Grier

NEW VICTORIA PUBLISHERS

P.O. Box 27
Norwich, VT 05055

Submissions

New Victoria is interested in fiction with a clear narrative story line. We are primarily looking for well-written novels using mystery, adventure, romance, science fiction (speculative fiction), or fantasy as a vehicle to discuss important issues in lesbian and feminist lifestyles and relationships, stories which contain strong, active protagonists and transformation in the characters. Humor and passion are always vital ingredients.

We will consider stories with strong feminist heroines, "woman-identified" journeys into and out of the self, as long as the material investigates real alternatives or models for living.

In addition, we are interested in well-researched lesbian and feminist history or biography that would appeal to a general as well as an academic audience.

Please send your inquiry with an outline and a sample chapter. If you would like it returned, enclose a self-addressed stamped envelope.

Yours,

Claudia Lamperti

POCKET BOOKS

Simon and Schuster Consumer Group
1230 Avenue of the Americas
New York, NY 10020

Pocket Books author's guidelines are free with an SASE sent to the above address.

PUBLISHERS SYNDICATION INT'L
1377 K Street N.W. Suite 856
Washington, D.C. 20005

For free author's guidelines from Publishers Syndication Int'l, send a SASE to A. P. Samuels, Editor.

SILHOUETTE
300 East 42nd Street, Sixth Floor
New York, NY 10017
(212) 682-6080 FAX (212) 682-4539

Submissions

Thank you for your interest in Silhouette Books. We do not accept unsolicited complete or partial manuscripts, but ask instead that you submit a query letter. Please indicate what Silhouette series you think your project is appropriate for, if it is completed, what you think makes it special, and previous publishing experience (if any). Also include a synopsis of your story that gives a clear idea of both your plot and characters and is no more than two single-spaced pages. A self-addressed envelope (SASE) will ensure a reply. Should your manuscript be requested, please note the following information:

We publish only category romances! Please do not submit any other type of fiction or non-fiction. Your manuscript should take place in the present and be told in the third person, primarily from the heroine's point of view. However, the hero's perspective may be used to enhance tension, plot, or character development.

All material should be the author's own original work. Stories that contain scenes or plot lines that bear a striking resemblance to previously published work are in breach of copyright law and are not acceptable.

All material must be typewritten, double-spaced, and on 8½ × 11 inch paper. No disk submissions. Computer generated material is acceptable but must be letter quality and pages must be separated. Any material received on computer reams will be returned without evaluation.

DO NOT submit your material bound in binders or placed in boxes or containers of any kind. Secure material with rubber bands. You may enclose a postcard if you wish acknowledgement of receipt. Cover sheets must have your complete name, address, and phone number. Each page should be numbered sequentially thereafter. Please type your name and title in the upper left-hand corner of each page. If we ask to see your manuscript, please include a complete synopsis.

All material will be evaluated in as timely a fashion as volume allows. Please do not call regarding the status of your manuscript. You will be notified by mail as soon as your work has been reviewed.

DO NOT SEND ANY MATERIAL THAT IS BEING CONSIDERED BY ANOTHER PUBLISHER. "Multiple submissions" are not acceptable. A literary agent is not required in order to submit.

You must enclose a SASE with all material you send in. This will ensure the return of your material. Please send an envelope large enough to accommodate your work and adequate postage.

This sheet is designed as a guide to aid you in understanding our requirements and standards. However, there is no better way to determine what we are looking for than reading our books.

Copyright 1992 Silhouette Books

SILHOUETTE
300 East 42nd Street, Sixth Floor
New York, NY 10017
(212) 682-6080 FAX: (212) 682-4539

Write to: Isabel Swift, Editorial Director

Silhouette Romance:

53,000–58,000 words
Senior Editor: Anne Canadeo

Silhouette Romance requires talented authors able to portray modern relationships in the context of romantic love. Although the hero and heroine don't actually make love unless married, sexual tension is a vitally important element. Writers are encouraged to try new twists and creative approaches to this winning formula. Our ultimate goal is to give readers a romance with heightened emotional impact—books that make them laugh or cry, books that touch their hearts.

Silhouette Desire

55,000–60,000 words
Senior Editor: Lucia Macro

Sensual, believable, compelling, these books are written for today's woman. Innocent or experienced, the heroine is someone we identify with—the hero irresistible. The conflict should be an emotional one, springing naturally from the unique characters you've chosen. The focus is on the developing relationship, set in a believable plot. The characters don't have to be married to make love, but lovemaking is never taken lightly. Secondary characters and subplots must blend with the core story. Innovative new directions in storytelling and fresh approaches to classic romantic plots are welcome.

Silhouette Special Edition

75,000–80,000 words
Senior Editor: Tara Gavin

Sophisticated, substantial, and packed with emotion, Special Edition demands writers eager to probe characters deeply, to explore issues that heighten the drama of living and loving, to create compelling romantic plots. Whether the sensuality is sizzling or subtle, whether the plot is wildly innovative or satisfyingly traditional, the novel's emotional vividness, its depth and dimension, should clearly label it a very special contemporary romance. Subplots are welcome but must further or parallel the developing romantic relationship in a meaningful way.

Silhouette Intimate Moments

80,000–85,000 words
Senior Editor & Editorial Coordinator: Leslie Wainger

Believable characters swept into a world of larger-than-life romance, such is the magic of Silhouette Intimate Moments. These books offer you the freedom to combine the universally appealing elements of a category romance with the flash and excitement of mainstream fiction. Adventure, suspense, melodrama, glamour—let your imagination be your guide as you blend old and new to create a novel of emotional depth and tantalizing complexity, a novel that explores new directions in romantic fiction, a novel that is quintessentially Intimate Moments.

Copyright 1992 Silhouette Books

SILHOUETTE SHADOWS

A Division of Harlequin Enterprises Limited
300 East 42nd Street, Sixth Floor
New York, NY 10017
(212) 682-6080 FAX: (212) 682-4539

In an empty house, the air thick with darkness, a woman waits
alone. Her heart beats faster as she hears the creaking of the
front door, and then a man's voice, soft with menace, calls out,
asking if anyone is there. Is the threat in his voice for her? Or
will the danger turn to passion when he finds her waiting for
him? Her heart begins to pound, and the blood runs hot
through her veins as she prepares to confront her fate . . .

And now, we at Silhouette Books invite you to join us as
we embark on an exciting new publishing venture, the creation
of Silhouette Shadows. These are tales from the dark side of
love, designed to keep the reader on the edge of her seat as
she, like the heroine, steps into the unknown, risking everything in a search that can lead to the fulfillment of love or the
edge of madness, even the possibility of death. Behind every
door lies danger, down every curving corridor the embodiment
of fear, and even the heart of the man she loves may hide a fatal
passion in place of the enduring romance she craves. The possibilities, like your imagination, are limitless.

The heroine is a strong, contemporary woman, capable of
confronting and conquering the dangers that threaten her,
whether physical or psychological, of the world as we know it or
from beyond. She is always a match for the hero as they play out a
compelling romance in the midst of a plot that may range from
Gothic in tone to a woman-in-jeopardy story, even incorporating
elements of the paranormal and moving into soft horror. The hero
may represent—even personify—the dangers she faces, or he
may provide support and comfort in the midst of a dark and men-
acing world. Always, though, their ending must be a happy one,
with lasting romance her reward for triumphing over darkness.

Silhouette Shadows novels are contemporary romances that explore the dark side of love, send shivers up the spine, and make the heart beat faster—from passion *and* from fear. These novels are atmospheric, dark, sensuous (in the fullest sense of the word), and always frightening. Black humor and occasional comic relief may play a role, but these are not ghostly romps or spoofs of the genre.

Classic examples that capture the tone and types of stories we envision, even if not the contemporary setting, include Mary Stewart's *Nine Coaches Waiting,* Victoria Holt's *Menfreya in the Morning* and Daphne DuMaurier's *Rebecca.*

When complete, these contemporary romance manuscripts should be 70,000–75,000 words in length and generally written in the third person, though first person is acceptable.

We are accepting submissions of query letters, partial manuscripts, and complete manuscripts.

Leslie Wainger: Senior Editor and Editorial Coordinator of Silhouette Books.

SINGER MEDIA CORPORATION
1030 Calle Cordillera #106
San Clemente, CA 92672
(714) 498-7227 FAX: (714) 498-2162

Singer Media Corporation is an internationally oriented syndicate, and as such, we must produce multiple sales by reaching as many places as possible. Forty to fifty percent of our income comes from foreign countries where television is limited and people read more. We have been on the international scene for decades and many of our staff have been actively watching the needs and changes for over forty years.

The problem we face as we review incoming submissions is that the bulk of the material—features, comics, books and manuscripts—is the product of tunnel vision. That is, the author, interviewer or artist is concerned primarily with his/her locale with its problems, interests, and uniqueness. From our standpoint, the story, article, cartoon may be stunning and well presented, but it is of no value to us unless it will hold the readers' interests in such places as Stockholm, Hong Kong, Cape Town, or Sydney. From the standpoint of those who submit material to us, it is clear that the greater the global appeal, the greater the number of sales and remuneration.

It is wise for those who wish us to look at material to realize the process we must go through. First we must process the material in an attractive form. It is then sent to our representative in each paying country in the Free World. They in turn, must find markets in their countries. The material must then be translated into the language which is most prevalent in that country. It is a laborious sequence before any material is selected and published.

It is obvious we must reject material which:

1. Relies on U.S. statistics.
2. Is filled with local terms or vernacular.
3. Relies on products that are not available in other countries.
4. Has words that rhyme or statements that have no meaning if translated from English, such as riddles and poetry.

Because of the time gap between our acceptance of material and its publication abroad, we look for a timeless approach to writing. For instance, John Doe may be 35 at the time the author writes about him, but he may be 40 by the time the piece is released or re-released a second time. Therefore if his birthdate is given rather than his age, the material is still correct and not out-dated.

We are especially interested in seeing reprints of previously published books and features. They are easier for us to process and are more impressive to foreign editors. We insist however, on written assurance that the author control his/her reprint rights for legal reasons.

When submitting manuscripts of any length, we encourage the author to include a short synopsis of the book, on-going column, comic strip, etc.

We also prefer a letter of query from those who wish to submit. If we see a possibility, we answer immediately asking to see the material. If not, we frankly say so, thus saving postage money, time, and inconvenience for all concerned.

In keeping with professional etiquette, we expect all submissions and queries to be accompanied by addressed stamped envelope or proper return postage.

At the present we are in search of:

1. Published books for which you hold foreign rights, both fiction and non-fiction.
2. Interviews with people in the international public eye, preferably with accompanying photographs.
3. Published short stories or feature articles. Published cartoons, comic strips, and juvenile activity features, puzzles, and games.
4. Anything new, different, and not run-of-the-mill.
5. Columns and cartoons to run for at least 52 weeks.

Write for the world, and not only for home consumption. Milk your good old literary properties for a new run. We like out-of-print books, and features published by leading magazines for second, foreign, and subsidiary rights sales.

These Guidelines are not meant to infer that we concentrate only on foreign markets. To the contrary, we have a business that is healthy and growing in the United States, but because so few people look no farther than their own local or national boundaries, we have emphasized our hints on how to search for global sales in an effort to broaden their scopes.

We look forward to hearing from you.

Distributed by the Singer Media Corporation, San Clemente, California

(We take every possible care in handling of your material, but are not responsible in case of loss or damage.)

***Pink Pages* Editor Note:** According to Publisher's Weekly (August 30, 1991) Kurt Singer has placed over 100 romance titles in the foreign market, through contacts in Italy and Germany. The novels are marketed through newsstands.

For more information on foreign rights, send a SASE to Singer. Request a copy of the article *Foreign Rights* by Marcy Goodfleisch.

WALKER AND COMPANY

720 Fifth Avenue
New York, NY 10019
(212) 265-3632 FAX: (212) 307-1764
CABLE: REKLAWSAM

Walker Mysteries

We prefer receiving three chapters and a brief outline or synopsis (no more than five pages). If you can't tell your story in that amount of space, how can a publisher reduce it even further for copy purposes? The chapters (and the complete manuscript) should be double-spaced and, if you are using a word processor, printed in letter quality. Do not use fancy fonts, mixed typefaces, or true italics, nor should the manuscript be printed in justified right format.

All pages should have a page number, your name, and the manuscript title.

Remember, neatness counts!

Walker Mysteries are written in all the major subcategories of the genre: cozy (or amateur detective), private investigator, police procedural, and general suspense. There is always a puzzle to be solved (by both the detective and the reader), clues are fairly presented (and red herrings unfairly so), and detective and villain evenly matched. Genre conventions are respected and acknowledged though not necessarily adhered to; if you can come up with a new twist, we'd be more than happy to consider it.

There are no restrictions as to story line, plot devices, characters, or anything else you, as the author, feel is necessary to your story. The editors will, however, make the final decision as to whether something is either in bad taste or flat out boring; both of these "reviews" will work against acceptance.

We are not interested in seeing gothics, horror or mysteries resolved through supernatural means. Our novels are rooted in the real world and depend on the detective's ability to deduce facts from clues and arrive at a solution through rational processes.

Some storylines are getting tired: drugs, drug running, drug cartels, and the entire Miami Vice school of mystery has been done to death, if you'll excuse the expression. So has the Middle East, Latin America, Vietnam and other headline-oriented topics. This doesn't mean we won't consider them; it does mean that the novels have to be brilliantly written to catch our attention. If you're up to the challenge, feel free to intrigue us.

Length is generally between 60,000 and 70,000 words. We will, of course, make exceptions to that rule as necessary.

If you have further questions, or wish to explore some area more fully, please feel free to get in touch with us. Your query should be addressed to Michael Seidman, Mystery Editor.

Finally, it is possible that your manuscript or proposal will be rejected. Unfortunately, the volume of material received makes it impossible for the editors to send personal letters explaining the reasons or offering editorial guidance. We hope that you understand that a form rejection does not reflect on the quality of your writing or ideas; it simply means that the book was not right for us at this time.

Thank you for thinking of Walker and Company and we look forward to considering your manuscript.

ZEBRA/PINNACLE PUBLISHING CORP.
475 Park Avenue South
New York, NY 10016

ZEBRA tipsheets can be obtained free by sending an SASE to the above address.

8

My Sizzling Secret: I'm Addicted to Confession Magazines!

I confess! They thrill me, titillate me, sadden me, shock me, make me laugh, and even banish writer's block!

Being only twelve when I typed out my first confession story, I fabricated most of it from tales of woe that I recalled my former gossipy neighbor repeating into the black telephone receiver that was ever-present against her left ear. I addressed my "manuscript" to the confession magazine and left it in our mailbox for the mail carrier. I didn't count on my brother retrieving the envelope, reading my story, adding some really sick stuff, and readdressing it to *Life* magazine.

It wasn't as funny then as it is now that I look back on it. But you won't laugh when I tell you that confession stories are a hot romance market that can put dollars in your pocketbook. According to Cari Spivak, associate editor at *True Love* magazine, their circulation is 250,000. And that's only one magazine. Put this address on a bunch of labels, because 233 Park Avenue South, NY, NY 10003 is THE place to send your best heartfelt, sizzling, shocking and traumatic "true" romance stories.

Whose offices are at 233 Park Avenue? It's Macfadden Women's Group, a successful publisher of magazines. In 1899, an eccentric genius named Bernarr Macfadden began publishing a fitness magazine, followed by *True Story* and twenty other periodicals, which he built into a thirty million dollar empire during his lifetime.

Macfadden also publishes *True Love, True Confessions, True Romance, Modern Romances,* and *Secrets.* These magazines are 90 percent to 100 percent freelance written. At least ten romance stories are published per month, per magazine. That's a lot of confessing, and a lot of opportunity for romance writers to get their foot in the door.

What's the catch? There are several. First of all you have to learn to write the most intimate stories in the first person, as in, "How Could I Tell My Sister That I Was Going to Have Her Husband's Baby?" or, "I Paid My Husband to Marry Me!" or, "I Saw My Fiance with Another Man!" or even the amnesiac, "I Forgot Where I Left My Baby!" or one of my favorites, "The Day I Found Out My Husband Was Cheating on Me, Was the Day He Found Out I Was Cheating on Him, Too!"

When writing for the confession market, authors do not get bylines. This is positive or negative news, depending on your perception of confession magazines. Another disadvantage is that the pay is a only few cents per word. Usually the magazine buys all rights.

Now for the good news: romance writers can send out a bunch of short romances and love poems that have been sitting in their file cabinets for ages. It's worth the effort. Those little checks could add up!

Something that may surprise you is that most of the writing published in confession magazines is really very good, and you can add the names of these magazines to your credit sheet with pride. Writing for confession magazines is an excellent way to break into the romance fiction industry.

By the way, male romance writers, men buy these magazines too. On page 31 of the December 1991 issue of *True*

Confessions is a romance written from the man's point of view. Check it out.

They say confession is good for the soul, so why shouldn't it be good for the pocketbook?

What do you mean those stories aren't true?

Of course they are!

Magazine Markets

AFFAIRE DE COEUR
1555 Washington Avenue
San Leandro, CA 94577
(510) 357-5665 FAX: (510) 357-1337

Owner: Barbara Keenan

Fiction Editor: Louise Snead

Circulation: 150,000

Submissions

Queries only. Do not send unsolicited manuscripts. No un-agented queries. Don't forget SASE. Average response time is one month.

Pay Rate

$5–$25 per non-fiction article. Pay is on acceptance. Publishing schedule is about one month after acceptance.

Actively Seeking

Confessional	2,000 words
Contemporary	2,000 words
Ethnic	2,000 words
Romantic Suspense	2,000 words
Mainstream with Romance Elements	2,000 words
Inspirational Romance	2,000 words

Tips

We are looking for articles about writing and authors, publishing, and author's bios. We would like manuscripts that are for (book) review only. Ads are also accepted. No unpublished manuscripts.

AMELIA
329 "E" St.
Bakersfield, CA 93304
(805) 323-4064

Editor: Frederick A. Raborg Jr.

Circulation: 1,250 quarterly

Submissions

Queries are not necessary. Send synopsis and sample chapters for novel excerpts. It is preferred that the complete manuscript be sent. Unagented and unsolicited manuscripts are OK. Average response time is 2 weeks to 3 months.

Pay Rate

$35 per story over 2,000 words.
$10 per 1,000 for short material.

Pay is on acceptance. Publishing schedule is about 12 months after acceptance.

Actively Seeking

Contemporary Romance	1,000–4,500 words
Ethnic Romance	1,000–4,500 words
Romantic Suspense	1,000–4,500 words
Mainstream with Romance Elements	1,000–4,500 words
Inspirational (if not religious)	1,000–4,500 words
Science Fiction and Fantasy	1,000–4,500 words

Tips

Be professional and always include SASE.

BLACK CONFESSIONS/BLACK SECRETS/BRONZE THRILLS/JIVE

Lexington Library, Inc.
355 Lexington Ave.
New York, NY 10017
(212) 949-6850

D. Boyd, the editor for these Afro-American confession magazines, did not respond to the letters and questionnaires sent by *The Romance Writer's Pink Pages.* However, markets for Black romances were too important to exclude from this directory.

Black romance and confession stories are bought from freelancers for these magazines. Don't stereotype Black characters. Use timely social themes, like AIDS, safe sex, and single moms.

Read current issues of each magazine. Write to each magazine separately to request sample copies, writer's guidelines, and tip sheets. Enclose a 9 × 12 inch SASE with five first class stamps for each request.

FIFTY-SOMETHING MAGAZINE
Media Trends Publications
8250 Tyler Blvd., Unit E
Mentor, OH 44060
(216) 974-9594

Editor: Linda L. Lindeman

Circulation: 25,000 Bi-Monthly

Submissions

No queries. Send synopsis and sample chapters or complete manuscript of 500–1,000 words. Unsolicited manuscripts are OK. Average response time is 6–8 months.

Pay Rate

Negotiable pay rate. Payment is upon publication. Publication is about 6 months after acceptance.

Actively Seeking

Confessional	about 500–1,000 words
Contemporary Romance	500–1,000 words
Ethnic Romance	500–1,000 words
Romantic Suspense	500–1,000 words
Mainstream with Romance Elements	500–1,000 words
Inspirational	500–1,000 words

Tips

Looking for stories related to the 50+ population. See guidelines section.

FIRST FOR WOMEN

270 Sylvan Avenue
Englewood Cliffs, NJ 07632
(no phone calls or faxes accepted from writers)

Managing Editor: Theresa Hagan

Circulation: 1.6 million, 16 issues per year

Submissions

No queries. Send complete manuscript to 2,000 words. Address to Fiction Department. Unagented and unsolicited manuscripts are OK. Average response time is 1–2 months.

Pay Rate

$1,000 on acceptance. Publishes about 6 months after acceptance.

Actively Seeking
Mainstream with romance elements   about 2,000 words

Tips

No foreign settings. No mysteries or New York settings. SASE a must. Send one story at a time. See guidelines section for more information.

GOOD HOUSEKEEPING
959 Eighth Avenue
New York, New York 10019
(212) 649-2202 FAX: (212) 265-3307

Fiction Editor: Lee Quarfoot

Circulation: 5 million per month

Submissions

No queries necessary for short fiction. Send complete manuscript. No SASE please. Rejections are not returned or acknowledged. Unagented and unsolicited manuscripts are OK.

Pay Rate

Pays "market rates" on acceptance. Publication schedule varies.

Actively Seeking
Contemporary Romance   1,000–3,000 words
Mainstream with Romance Elements   1,000–3,000 words
Short fiction   Emotional interest
                                          to women

Tips

We purchase first serial rights only on about-to-be-published novels. We do not accept submission of unpublished novels; therefore, there is no reason to send sample chapters or synopses. We do welcome short story submissions. See guidelines section for more information.

MAHOGANY & MOLASSES FAMILY READER
6712 Bywood Road
Orlando, FL 32810

Managing Editor: Laurie Thoroman

Circulation: Bi-monthly

Submissions

Wholesome romance, other fiction and poetry is purchased from freelancers. Send complete manuscript with SASE.

Pay Rate

$2–$15 for short stories of 100–4,000 words
$1–$3 for poetry of 1–50 lines
Pays on acceptance. Publishes about 6 months after acceptance.

Actively Seeking
Romance
Historicals
Humor
Western
Sci-fi

Tips

100% freelance written. No violence or erotic scenes.

MODERN ROMANCES

Macfadden Women's Group, Inc.
233 Park Ave., South
New York, NY 10003

Editor: Cherie Clark King

This editor did not respond to the letters and questionnaires sent by *The Romance Writer's Pink Pages*. This magazine is owned by Macfadden Women's Group, who also publishes other confession magazines, such as *True Love, True Romance* and *True Confessions*. Request guidelines for *Modern Romances* and enclose a number 10 SASE.

PUBLISHERS SYNDICATION INT'L.

1377 K St. N.W., Suite 856
Washington, D.C. 20005

Editor: A. P. Samuels

Media Type: Paperback, Hardback, The *Post*.

Short Fiction Bought Per Year: 12 romantic adventure, 12 mystery/suspense.

Submissions

Send complete manuscripts, including word count and SASE. (Sleuth Editor is Mary Straub.) Unsolicited and unagented manuscripts are OK. New authors are encouraged. No simultaneous submissions. No phone calls from agents. Specify computer type, disk size and density, and word processing program used, in case a disk copy of the story is requested. Usual response time is 4–6 weeks.

Pay Rate

Upon acceptance; 1–4 cents a word, plus royalty. (Sleuth novelettes pay .75–3 cents a word)

Actively Seeking
Romance Adventures	9,000–10,000 words
Mystery/Suspense	9,000–10,000 words
"Sleuth" novelettes	10,000 words

Tips

Romances should not contain explicit sex, as they are for a general audience. Mysteries should be similar to Sherlock Holmes. No blood and guts violence.

"Sleuth" novelettes are solved by the reader, who has a choice of multiple suspects. Solution and justification for solution should be typed on a separate page. Include pencil sketches of floor plans or street maps that will involve the reader.

RADIANCE, THE MAGAZINE FOR LARGE WOMEN
Box 30246
Oakland, CA 94604
(510) 482-0680

Editor: Alice Ansfield

Circulation: 10,000 quarterly

Submission

Authors may query first, or send synopsis and sample chapters or send complete manuscripts. Unagented and unsolicited manuscripts are OK. Average response time is 6 weeks.

Pay Rate

$50–$100. Payment is on publication at this time.

Actively Seeking

Contemporary Romance	800–2,000 words
Ethnic Romance	800–2,000 words
Romantic Suspense	800–2,000 words
Mainstream with Romance Elements	800–2,000 words
Inspirational	800–2,000 words

Tips

Other Topics are woman coming into her own awareness of her own strength, career, self-awareness, standing up for herself. Read a copy of *Radiance* to get our point of view before sending us your story. We like stories about women as intelligent, thoughtful, sensitive, strong, vulnerable, sensual beings. We want more than woman hates self, woman meets man, woman likes self stories! We welcome writers as yet unpublished. We want stories about women from all walks of life, of all ethnic groups, ages and sizes. Stories from women and men desired. See the guidelines section.

SECRETS

MacFadden Women's Group, Inc.
233 Park Ave., South
New York, NY 10003
(212) 979-4898

Editor Pat Byrdsong did not respond. However, this magazine is a good market for Black women's true stories and light romances written in the first person. Write to *Secrets* for guidelines. Enclose a number 10 SASE.

SINGER MEDIA CORPORATION
Seaview Business Park
1030 Calle Cordillera, Unit #106
San Clemente, CA 92672
(714) 498-7227 FAX: (714) 498-2162

President: Kurt Singer

Circulation: 300 publications worldwide

Actively Seeking
Kurt D. Singer buys reprint rights to short romance stories, historical and romance novels, gothics, westerns, and mysteries published in the last 25 years. Pays a percentage or purchases outright. See Singer's listing under Publishers.

TRUE CONFESSIONS
Macfadden Women's Group, Inc.
233 Park Avenue, South
New York, NY 10003
(212) 979-4800 FAX: (212) 979-7342

Editor: Jean Sharbel

Monthly Circulation: 300,000

Submissions

Queries are not necessary. Please do not send synopsis and partials. Send the complete manuscript. Unagented and unsolicited are OK. Usual response time is up to 6 months.

Pay Rate

Five cents a word. Pays on last day of publication date. Publishes about 1–6 months after acceptance.

Actively Seeking

Confessional stories	1,500–8,000 words
Contemporary romances	1,500–8,000 words
Mainstream with romance elements	1,500–8,000 words
Inspirational stories	length depends on whether it's a story or an article.

Tips

All stories are based on true incidents. No fiction. If you don't have a typewriter or the money to pay a typist, this market is one that will accept neatly hand printed stories! See magazine guidelines for details.

TRUE EXPERIENCE

Macfadden Women's Group, Inc.
233 Park Avenue, South
New York, NY 10003
(212) 979-4903

Fiction Editor: Jean Press Silberg (212) 979-4896 (direct line)

Associate Editor: Cynthia Di Martino

Publication: Monthly

Submissions

All stories are written in first person, past tense. Submit the complete, typed, doublespaced manuscript with SASE. Unsolicited and unagented manuscripts are OK. Average response time is 1–2 months.

Pay Rate

Three cents a word, upon publication. Publishes about 3 months after acceptance. No byline, buys all rights.

Actively Seeking
Confessional   7,000–20,000 words

Tips

Cynthia Di Martino reports, "We're looking for true-to-life stories about current topics women are interested in, although we're glad to accept a good love story."

TRUE LOVE

Macfadden Women's Group, Inc.
233 Park Avenue, South
New York, NY 10003
(212) 979-4800 FAX: (212) 979-7342

Fiction Editor: Mary Lou Lang

Circulation: 250,000 year

Submissions

All stories are written in first person, past tense. Submit the complete manuscript of 2,000–10,000 words with a large

SASE. Unsolicited and unagented manuscripts are OK. Average response time is 3 months.

Pay Rate

Three cents a word, upon publication. Publishes about 2-4 months after acceptance. No byline, buys all rights.

Actively Seeking

Confessional	2,000–10,000 words
Contemporary Romance	2,000–10,000 words
Ethnic Romance	2,000–10,000 words
Romantic Suspense	2,000–10,000 words
Mainstream with Romance Elements	2,000–10,000 words
Inspirational	2,000–10,000 words

Tips

Sample copy for $2. See magazine guidelines.

TRUE ROMANCE

Macfadden Women's Group, Inc.
233 Park Avenue, South
New York, NY 10016
(212) 979-4800

Editor Pat Byrdsong did not respond. However, this magazine is a good market for women's confessionals and light romances written in the first person. Write to *True Romance* for guidelines. Enclose a number 10 SASE.

TRUE STORY

Macfadden Women's Group, Inc.
233 Park Avenue, South
New York, NY 10003
(212) 979-4800

Non-fiction Editorial Director: Sue Weiner

Circulation: 1 million

Publication: Monthly

Submissions

No query letters. Prefers to see entire manuscript with large
SASE. Unsolicited and/or unagented manuscripts are OK.
Average response time is 6 months. Stories are written in first
person, past tense.

Pay Rate

Five cents a word. Publishes about 3 months after acceptance.
Pays one month after publication.

Actively Seeking
True Confessional
Contemporary Romance
Romantic Suspense
Mainstream with Romance Elements
Inspirational

Tips

Editorial Director Sue Weiner says, "We publish only true stories, no fiction."

WOMAN'S WORLD
270 Sylvan Avenue
Englewood Cliffs, NJ 07632
(201) 569-0006 FAX: (201) 569-3584, (201) 569-6699

Fiction Editor: Jeanne Muchnick

Circulation: 1.5 million per week

Submissions

Send the complete manuscript. Unagented and unsolicited manuscripts are OK. Average response time is 6–8 weeks.

Pay Rate

$500 mini-mystery. $1,000 romance. Payment is on acceptance. Publishes about 3 months after acceptance.

Actively Seeking
Contemporary Romance   1,900 words
Mini-mystery   900 words.

Tips

No phone queries. No faxes. No response without SASE. No excerpts from novels. No foreign locales in stories. See magazine guidelines section.

WRITER TO WRITER NEWSLETTER
P.O. Box 1003
Wickenburg, AZ 85358

Editor/Publisher: Laraine McDaniel Bell

Circulation: 200+ Quarterly

Submissions

Published by an award-winning Harlequin author, *Writer to Writer* is a non-profit newsletter with a goal to further the careers of writers, at a minimum, by a collective effort to share informative articles, grammar tips, and market news. Query first with SASE.

Pay Rate

Since this is a non-profit newsletter, there is no payment, except the satisfaction of sharing knowledge and news with other romance and suspense writers. Articles should be sent pro bono publico. Publication is about one to three months after acceptance.

Actively Seeking

Unique ideas to aid writers; feature articles; conference and contest news; first sales—share your good news; comments and opinions from a writer's slant; and anything unusual you think would benefit writers and the pursuit of literacy.

Tips

Send SASE with a request for a copy of the newsletter.

ADDITIONAL INFO ON MAGAZINE MARKETS

AMERICAN DANE does not publish romance fiction, as reported in 1991 *Writer's Market*.

BRIDE'S left a message on my answering machine, saying they're not interested in romance. (I laughed too.)

COSMOPOLITAN at 224 West 57th Street, New York, NY 10019 did not respond. But if you're determined, we recommend you query first with SASE and be prepared to wait for a response. Buys short stories (some are romance) from 750–3,000 words. Pays top dollar, but the competition is stiff due to the volume of submissions.

LADIES' HOME JOURNAL, 100 Park Avenue, New York, NY 10017 only accepts fiction submissions from agents or publishers.

MADEMOISELLE wrote "Don't send *anything* to Eileen Schurr!" As of March 1992, they no longer publish fiction. Their annual fiction contest has been cancelled.

NEW WOMAN does not consider fiction for publication.

REDBOOK receives about 40,000 unsolicited manuscripts per year, from which they buy 36 stories. Good pay, but the chances of acceptance are slim for unknowns.

SPECTRUM PRESS editor Dan Agia responded that romance is not the prime interest of this publication.

'TEEN's Fiction Editor, Roxanne Camron at 8490 Sunset Blvd., Hollywood, California 90069 prefers published writers. She buys teen-aged love stories of wholesome kids with happy endings only.

TQ's Editorial Assistant, Michele Jeffres (P.O. Box 82808, Lincoln, NE 68501), writes that TQ does not publish women's fiction. It is a Christian youth magazine whose fiction stories center around the lives and problems common to teens.

WOMAN'S DAY sent a form letter stating that they are unable to consider unsolicited fiction.

10

Directory of Magazine Market Guidelines

*T*he following magazine guidelines are being reprinted with written permission. Thank you, magazine editors!

FIFTY SOMETHING MAGAZINE

8250 Tyler Blvd. Unit E
Mentor, OH 44060
(216) 975-0455 (Cleveland) (216) 974-9594 (Lake County)
or (216) 974-1004 (FAX)

Dear Writer:

Thank you for your inquiry regarding writing for *Fifty Something Magazine*. Our publication is directed toward the 50+ mature reader. We focus on departments such as travel, finance, retirement, romance, health and fitness, employment and family matters. Historical editorial essays are always welcome, as well as major achievements of individuals in this age group.

Artwork or photographs are also encouraged to accompany editorials. If you have set fees, please include them with your submission. Otherwise, payments will be negotiated upon the decision to publish. Authors will be credited and materials will remain the property of the authors. Submissions will be kept on file indefinitely and cross-referenced for future use. *Fifty Something Magazine* assumes no responsibility or liability for return of the materials submitted.

To receive a sample copy of the magazine please include a 9 × 12 inch self-addressed envelope with $1.25 in postage.

I look forward to reviewing your work.

Sincerely,

Linda L. Lindeman, Managing Editor

FIRST FOR WOMEN
Bauer Publishing Company
270 Sylvan Avenue
Englewood Cliffs, NJ 07632
(201) 569-6699 or (201) 569-0006

Fiction Guidelines

First is looking for quality fiction that will appeal to intelligent, thoughtful women in all walks of life. Many of our readers are working mothers between the ages of 24 and 45 with some college education; some have limited education and hold blue collar jobs. We believe they enjoy serious, sensitively told stories that leave the reader feeling she has been enriched as well as entertained.

The stories we publish will have memorable images, a style that expresses the writer's personal voice, and vivid realistic settings that provide a strong sense of place. They offer insights into relationships and suggest a positive movement in the lives of the characters, through changes in circumstance or in perception. At the core of these stories is a vividly rendered female protagonist who is grappling with the important issues in her life.

We prefer dramatic narratives with a strong sense of emotional resolution, but the rich story that doesn't quite form a neatly tied package, if it leaves the reader with something to consider, has a chance here.

We do not publish mysteries, tales of the rich and famous, or stories with foreign settings or pat, moralistic messages. A strong regional flavor is okay as long as our readers can easily identify with the characters and situations. We use very few stories set in New York City. We may publish an occasional story from a male viewpoint if female characters are the true focus of the story.

SASE is essential; no queries; please send one story at a time unless we have asked to see more of your work. Thanks.

Length: About 2,000 words

Pay Rate: $1,000

GOOD HOUSEKEEPING
Fiction Department
959 Eighth Avenue
New York, NY 10019
(212) 649-2202 FAX: (212) 265-3307

We welcome short fiction submissions (1,000–3,000 words). We look for stories with strong emotional interest—stories revolving around courtship, romance, marriage, family, friendships, personal growth, coming of age, etc. The best way to gauge whether your story might be appropriate for us is to read the fiction in several of our recent issues. (We are sorry, but we cannot furnish sample copies of the magazine.)

Owing to the huge volume of submissions, those manuscripts not accepted for publication cannot be returned, so please DON'T include a self addressed stamped envelope. We do assure you, however, that every submission is read. If in our judgement a story has possibilities for *Good Housekeeping*, you will hear from us within a month's time.

We prefer double-spaced typewritten (or keyboarded) manuscripts, accompanied by a short cover letter listing any previous writing credits. Make sure your name and address appear on the manuscript and that you retain a copy for yourself.

Good Housekeeping pays current market prices on acceptance, with prices varying, according to the length and merit of the material.

We hope this information is helpful to you and thank you for your interest.

MAHOGANY & MOLASSES MAGAZINE
6712 Bywood Road
Orlando, FL 32810

When sending your original work for consideration, please follow these guidelines:

Can be poetry, fiction, or non-fiction stories up to 2,500 words (1,500 for children's stories). We may occasionally buy an essay, particularly humor, but we generally give preference to fiction stories.

Remember, this is a family publication. Avoid offensive language and excessive violence.

Manuscripts should be typed, double-spaced, on white paper.

Be sure to include your name and address, and remember to enclose a self-addressed, stamped envelope (SASE) for return of your manuscript.

We publish mainstream, juvenile, romance, historical, western, humor, and adventure stories.

We buy one-time rights and reprint rights and pay token amounts on acceptance: $3–$5 per poem, and $5–$15 per story, depending on length, quality, and availability of funds.

Sample copies available—$2.00 postpaid.

Subscription information: Check or money order payable to Mahogany & Molasses; 6 months (3-bi-monthly issues)—$4.00 or 12 months (6-bi-monthly issues)—$7.50.

RADIANCE
The Magazine for Large Women
Box 30246
Oakland, CA 94604
(510) 482-0680

Radiance is a quarterly magazine now celebrating its seventh year in print with more than 100,000 readers worldwide. Its target audience is the one woman in four who wears a size sixteen or over—an estimated 30 million women in America alone. *Radiance* brings a fresh, vital new voice to women all sizes of large with our positive images, profiles of dynamic large women from all walks of life, and our compelling articles on health, media, fashion, and politics. We urge women to feel good about themselves now—whatever their body size. *Radiance* is one of the leading resources in the "size acceptance movement," linking large women to the network of products, services, and information just for them.

Departments

Up Front and Personal: Interviews or first person accounts relating to life as a large woman from all walks of life. We like strong, intimate, in-depth profiles about a person's life and philosophy.

Health and Well-Being: Articles on health, fitness, emotional well-being related to women in general and large women in particular. Also profiles of healthcare professionals sensitive to the needs of large women.

Perspectives: Cultural/historical/social views of body size and female beauty attitudes worldwide.

Expressions: Interviews with artists who are either large themselves or whose work features large-sized women.

Getaways: Articles on vacation spots, getaways of all types anywhere in the world. Prefer if article somehow includes ideas or special tips for the woman of size.

Women on the Move: Articles about plus-sized women who are involved in some sort of sport or physical activity.

Images: Interviews with designers or manufacturers of plus-sized clothing or accessories. Prefer if the store/designer caters to women all sizes of large, i.e., includes "supersize" women. Can also be an article on color, style, and wardrobe planning.

Inner Journeys: Articles on personal growth and inner-directed approaches to feeling better about oneself. Can be profiles of people doing this work or general info.

Book Reviews: Books relating to women, body image, health, eating, politics, psychology, media, fashion, cultural attitudes, and so on.

Short Stories & Poetry: Related to body size, self-acceptance. Especially want fiction or poetry that is more than the "woman hates self until meets man to love her" type writing.

Deadlines

Winter: July 1; Spring: Oct 1; Summer: Jan 1; Fall: April 1.

To Writers

We recommend you read at least one issue of Radiance prior to writing anything for us. Query us far in advance of the deadline if you want assurance that your articles will be considered for a particular issue. Our usual response is 1½–2 months. Include your name, address and phone number on the title page and type your name and phone number on subsequent pages. Keep a copy of anything you submit to us. Remember to indicate availability of photos, artwork, illustrations (or ideas for them) in your query or with your article. Pertinent, high-quality photos or art can greatly enhance an article's desirability. If you do send photos, please make sure they are marked with a caption and the photographer's name, phone, and address.

At this time, payment is made on publication. We intend to pay upon acceptance in the near future. And as we grow, we will continue to increase payment to writers, photographers, illustrators, etc. We appreciate and value your work.

Payment

Book reviews	$35–$100
Features/Profiles	$50–$100
Fiction	$50–$100
Poetry, Short Articles	$15–$50
Color Cover Photos	$50–$200
B & W Inside Photos	$15–$25
Illustrations/Artwork:	$25–$100

Once we develop a working relationship with the writer, artist, or photographer and we can count on their professionalism, service, quality, and reliability, payment can increase. We will always send the contributor a copy of the magazine she/he is in. The contributor needs to send us an invoice after the work is completed with details of the service. To get a "feel" for the magazine, writers may request a sample copy for $3.50.

Editorial Staff

Publisher/Editor: Alice Ansfield
Senior Editor: Catherine Taylor
Editorial Assistant: Carol Squires
Proofreader: Kathy Kaiser

TRUE CONFESSIONS

Macfadden Women's Group
233 Park Avenue South
New York, NY 10003
(212) 979-4800

Dear Reader,

All the stories in *True Confessions* are true.

If you would like to send us your story on speculation, we would be happy to read it. Write it in the first person, as you would tell it to a friend, and type it on one side of each sheet of paper, leaving double spaces between the lines. If you do not have a typewriter, please *print* neatly on one side of each sheet of lined paper.

If we publish your story, we will buy all world rights and pay you at our regular rate—five cents a word. Payment is made during the last week of the month of issue. For example, checks for stories printed in our June issue are mailed out during the last week of June.

Please include a stamped self-addressed envelope with your story, so we can return it to you if it does not meet our needs. If we decide not to publish your story, you should expect to hear from us only if you have enclosed a return envelope and sufficient postage. It is advisable for you to keep a copy of your story in case anything should happen to the original.

Because of the vast number of stories we receive, it usually takes at least six months for us to give you a report about your story.

Please enclose a self-addressed stamped envelope with any correspondence to *True Confessions.* Otherwise, we cannot guarantee a reply.

Sincerely,

The Editors

(Note: MacFadden Women's Group also publishes *True Story, Photoplay, Modern Romances, True Experience, True Love, True Romance* and *Secrets!*)

TRUE LOVE MAGAZINE
233 Park Avenue South
New York, NY 10003
(212) 979-4800 FAX: (212) 979-7342

True Love is a romance magazine. Most of our readers are female. Each month we print an average of 10 true-to-life stories and several poems.

The best way to learn about our editorial style is to read the magazine itself and study the range of possibilities within the "romance" category.

We look for well-written stories that involve real people and real emotions. Subject matter ranges from light romance to current social concerns. Some aspect of love or romance will usually figure in but need not be the primary focus. Characters will often face a conflict or solve a problem in their lives.

All stories should be written in the first person, past tense, typed, double-spaced, and can range from 2,000 to 10,000 words. Our current rate of pay is three cents a word, and payment is made on publication. No byline is offered. We buy all rights. A large envelope with sufficient postage must be included for the manuscript to be returned.

If you wish to purchase a sample copy of *True Love,* send a check or money order for $2 to our address. Thank you for your interest in *True Love.*

The Editors

WOMAN'S WORLD, THE WOMAN'S WEEKLY MAGAZINE

Bauer Publishing Company
270 Sylvan Avenue
Englewood Cliffs, NJ 07632
(201) 569-6699 (201) 569-0006

Short Story

Our feature fiction each week is a short story with a light romantic theme, at a length of approximately 1,900 words. The stories can be written from either a female or male point of view. Women characters may be single, married, divorced, or widowed. I like to see strong interesting characters. Plots must be fast-moving, emphasizing vivid dialogue and plenty of action. The problems and dilemmas should be contemporary and realistic, handled with warmth and a sense of humor. The stories must have a positive resolution.

We are not interested in science fiction, fantasy, historical romance, or foreign locales. We do not want explicit sex (although a strong attraction between the main characters should be apparent, early on), no graphic language or steamy settings. Stories slanted for a particular holiday should be sent at least 6 months in advance.

Please specify "short story" on the outside of your submission envelope. And always enclose a stamped, self-addressed envelope. We purchase North American rights for 6 months at a standard rate of $1,000 paid on acceptance.

Mini Mystery

The mini mysteries, at a length of 900 words, may feature either a whodunnit or howdunnit theme. The mystery may revolve around anything from a theft to a murder. However, we are not interested in sordid or grotesque crimes. Emphasis should be on the intricacies of the plot rather than gratuitous violence. We don't print horror or ghost stories, science fiction, fantasy, or foreign settings. Stories slanted for a particular holiday should be sent at least 6 months in advance.

We purchase North American rights for 6 months at a standard rate of $500 paid on acceptance. Sorry, no manuscripts will be returned without SASE or International Postal Coupons. Label the submission envelope "mini mystery."

Send fiction manuscripts to: Jeanne Muchnick, Fiction Editor.

I strongly encourage you to examine a sample copy before submitting your manuscript. Please allow six to eight weeks for a reply. No phone queries, please.

11

Networking Through Romance Writers of America

*R*omance Writers of America (RWA) is a national organization offering both the unpublished writer and the published author the chance to meet and network with others who have the same interests and goals of publication. The continuous benefits of current market news, conferences, contests and more, assure that the aspiring romance author receives lots of support in return for affordable yearly dues.

Over 100 local chapters of RWA, some of which are listed here, also offer opportunities to meet others who are interested in writing romance and getting it published. Besides writers, related professionals—agents, editors, and bookstore owners— are welcome to join this helpful professional organization.

Local chapter affiliations of RWA welcome visitors at meetings. Besides informative guest speakers, educational workshops, monthly newsletters, and meetings, RWA chapters (in medium to large cities) often host annual local conferences featuring the expertise of successful romance authors, round table discussions with editors, and private appointments with agents. Tuition for these conferences and workshops is worth the expense and may be tax deductible.

At these annual RWA conferences you can meet, network with, and shamelessly pick the brains of editors, literary agents, and other romance authors, both published and unpublished. (Hopefully you will provide information to them of equal value!) Editors are very informative about what they like and what they don't like. They are compassionate, caring, and have a great respect for the romance genre. Agents are helpful too, whether or not you are their clients. They are generally free with advice and will tell you when an idea "works" for them, when it doesn't, and why not. (You can squeeze a lot of "brain-probing" into a ten-minute agent or editor appointment!)

I urge you to seek out your local RWA chapter, as well as joining nationally. The benefits are invaluable. Through education, networking, market information, conferences, contests, and moral support, RWA members have helped other RWA members to become published authors.

12

Directory of Networks

Canada

**GREATER VANCOUVER CHAPTER OF
ROMANCE WRITERS OF AMERICA**
(GVCRWA)
22412 Morse Crescent
Maple Ridge, B.C., V2X 9G6, Canada

Advisor: Barbara Briggs

Annual Dues: $25

Benefits of Membership

Monthly meetings and speakers; critique service; monthly
newsletter; daylong workshops; networking; and support from
fellow writers.

Other

Affiliated with Romance Writers of America. No annual conference or contest. Instead GVCRWA hosts daylong workshops twice a year.

RWA ONTARIO
P.O. Box 2221, 5334 Yonge St.
North York, Ontario, M2N 6M2, Canada

Annual Dues: $35 Canadian.

Benefits of Membership

Lectures by published authors and editors; workshops; tape library; reference library; market news.

Other

Affiliated with Romance Writers of America. No annual conference is planned at this writing. Annual contest.

WINNIPEG RWA CHAPTER
4-468 Carpathia Rd.
Winnipeg, Manitoba, R3N 1Y5, Canada
(204) 488-6370

Contact Person: Shirley Alton

Annual Dues: None

Benefits of Membership

Free; critique each other's work; offer support and a friendly ear. Group is very small and members become good friends.

USA–National and Regional Associations

ASSOCIATION OF AUTHOR'S REPRESENTATIVES (AAR)
10 Astor Place, Third Floor
New York, NY 10003
(212) 353-3709

Formerly ILAA and SAR, this new, merged association is for literary agents. For $5, AAR will send a brochure, a list of members, and a "Code of Ethics." Enclose SASE with 52 cents postage.

THE AUTHORS GUILD
330 W. 42nd St.
New York, NY 10036-6902
(212) 563-5904

Annual Dues: First year is $90. Thereafter, dues are based on income from writing on a graduated scale.

Benefits of Membership

Over 6,500 members have a collective power to voice opinions on professional issues. Members receive a copy of *Recommended Trade Book Publishing Contract and Guide*. The Guild issues reports and even offers call-in help for members who need guidance with contract negotiations and other issues related to the business of writing. Periodic symposia provide opportunities to get expert answers to questions on libel, publicity, editors, book reviews, and more. Transcripts are circulated. The Guild publishes the *Authors Guild Bulletin*, a periodical. Health insurance may be obtained through the Guild (at an extra charge).

Requirements for Membership

Active (voting) membership requires publication of one book within the last seven years by an established American publisher, OR three magazine works within the last eighteen months, OR approval by the membership committee for authors who otherwise have professional standing. Associate (non-voting) memberships are available for contracted authors who have not yet met the above requirements, and member-at-large status is available for persons interested in supporting the Guild and its services. Write for an informative précis regarding membership requirements and benefits.

Other

Not affiliated with Romance Writers of America. The Authors Guild and The Dramatists Guild are component organizations of The Authors League of America, representing American writers in the battle to reform copyright laws, which resulted in the 1976 Copyright Revision Act. The Authors Guild has an active lobbying campaign to protect the interests of all writers. *The Authors Guild Bulletin* keeps members up-to-date on professional writer's topics like contracts and royalty statements, libel, taxes, Guild activities, and more.

NATIONAL WRITER'S CLUB

1450 S. Havana, Suite 620
Aurora, CO 80012
(303) 751-7844 FAX: (303) 751-8593

Executive Director: Sandy Whelchel

Annual Dues: $50 Regular members, $60 Professional members.

Benefits of Membership

Critiques; editing; manuscript review service; agenting; marketing assistance; bi-monthly Authorship magazine; complaint service; reports on various phases of writing; yearly novel contests; confidential information on editors, agents and publications; writing course for beginners and professionals through the National Writers School; yearly conferences beginning in 1993.

Other

Not affiliated with Romance Writers of America. Write for conference and contest rules.

ROMANCE WRITERS OF AMERICA (RWA NATIONAL)

13700 Veterans Memorial, Suite 315
Houston, TX 77014
(713) 440-6885 FAX: (713) 440-7510

Annual Dues: $55 the first year, $45 per year renewals.

Benefits of Membership

Networking with other romance writers; subscription to bi-monthly magazine *Romance Writer's Report* (RWR); may join local RWA chapters; eligible to enter RWA contests; may attend annual RWA National conference; and the RWA Hotline (recorded messages of current market news).

Other

RWA National has over one hundred regional, local, and outreach chapter affiliates. Outreach chapters support romance writers who live in remote areas or who cannot attend meetings. RWA holds an annual national conference in June or July and sponsors contests for members. Please call or write for conference brochures.

Conferences

1994: New York City
1995: Hawaii

Agent and Editor Appointments, Banquet, Book Fair, Hands-On Classes, Social Gatherings and much more. Contact RWA for complete details on events and workshops for annual conference.

Annual Contests

Details of Golden Heart Contest and the RITA awards are available to RWA members through RWA National or their local chapter.

1994 ANNUAL ROMANTIC TIMES BOOKLOVERS CONVENTION

When: April 28–May 2, 1994

Where: Nashville, TN

Cost: Check the latest issue of *Romantic Times* for details or call the magazine at (718) 237-1097.

Agents', authors', and editors' panels discuss all types of romantic fiction. Also offered will be a screenwriting workshop, book promotion advice, and special "New Age" lectures. Social events are scheduled, as well as seminars and book sales.

Travel: American Airlines will offer discounts to convention attendees.

1995 Convention: Europe (tentative).

WOMEN'S NATIONAL BOOK ASSOCIATION
160 5th Avenue
New York, NY 10010
(212) 675-7805

Contact Person: Carolyn Wilson

Annual Dues: Varies by chapter

Benefits of Membership

This national network of women and men wants to promote women and books.

Other

Not affiliated with Romance Writers of America. No annual conferences or contests at this writing.

WRITER'S GUILD OF AMERICA, EAST
555 W. 57th St. #1230
New York, NY 10019
(212) 550-1000

WRITER'S GUILD OF AMERICA, WEST
8955 Beverly Blvd.
Los Angeles. CA 90048

Write to the closest Guild for free membership information.

LOCAL NETWORKS

Included below are many of the local chapters of Romance
Writers of America. Many others, including some from
Australia and Canada did not respond in time to meet press
deadlines. Contact the Romance Writers of America (National)
for information on the local chapter or outreach chapter in
your area.

Arizona

PHOENIX DESERT ROSE CHAPTER—RWA #60
Laraine McDaniel Bell
PO Box 1003
Wickenburg, AZ 85358

Co-Presidents: Beverly Cohoon and Laraine McDaniel Bell

Annual Dues: $15 plus membership in National RWA.

Benefits of Membership

Exposure to published writers, professional workshops, editors and agents. Updates information on publishing industry, current trends, requirements, etc. Members attend monthly meetings, receive a monthly market newsletter, and learn from guest speakers.

Other

Affiliated with Romance Writers of America. No annual contest. Annual conference with big name authors, editors, agents, and more.

1993 Seventh Annual Desert Dreams Conference

When: September 1993

Where: Tempe, Arizona, Mission Palms Hotel

Cost: about $120 for non-members, Desert Rose members about $100. Fees for individual events are also available.

Guests and speakers include Catherine Coulter, Nan Ryan, Pat Warren, and Casey Roberts. Agents will be taking appointments and leading roundtables. Editors will talk about their lines and scout out new talent. The don't-miss workshops have topics such as Synopsis, Sensuality, Humor in Historicals, Characterization and Motivation, and more. Events include a no-host cocktail party (Friday night), a Continental breakfast (Saturday morning), Saturday lunch, Sunday Hospitality Room, and a Sunday brunch with editors and agents. Call or write for a brochure. If conference is past, request to be mailed a brochure for the 1994 conference.

SOCIETY OF SOUTHWESTERN AUTHORS
P.O. Box 41897
Tucson, AZ 85717

Write for information on membership, conferences
and events.

TUCSON RWA #58
13460 East Wetstones Rd.
Vail, AZ 85641
(602) 623-0727

Contact Person: Evelyn Marie Snover

Annual Dues: $15.

Benefits of Membership

Networking; workshops; updates on market news; and lots of
inspiration.

Other

Affiliated with Romance Writers of America. No annual conferences or contests at this writing.

California

AFFAIRE DE COEUR MAGAZINE'S ANNUAL ROM CON

Annual Romance Writer's Conference in California
(510) 357-5665 FAX: (510) 357-1337

GOLD COAST CHAPTER RWA

P.O. Box 6118
Santa Barbara, CA 93160
(805) 683-6340

Contact Person: Margaret Dear

Annual Dues: $15 plus membership in National RWA.

Benefits of Membership

Monthly newsletter; monthly meetings with interesting speakers; critique groups available; networking.

Other

Affiliated with Romance Writers of America. No annual conferences or contests are planned as of this writing.

RWA/MONTEREY BAY CHAPTER

137 Rustic Lane
Santa Cruz, CA 95060
(408)427-2275 (evenings and weekends)

President: Suzanne J. Barrett

Annual Dues: $20 plus National RWA membership fee.

Benefits of Membership

Hands-on programs on varied writing topics; published authors network; critique groups; reference library; tapes on all aspects of writing and publishing.

Other

Affiliated with Romance Writers of America. No annual conferences are planned at this writing.

Annual Contest

Silver Heart Competition. Entries consist of synopsis (10 page maximum) and first chapter, not to exceed 30 pages. Call the chapter for more info on this annual contest.

SACRAMENTO CHAPTER RWA

P.O. Box 215884
Sacramento, CA 95821
(916) 624-1469 or 924-3598

Advisor: Constance Cullivan

Annual Dues: $20

Benefits of Membership

Newsletter; conferences; and workshops.

Other

Affiliated with Romance Writers of America.

Annual One-Two-Three Step Synopsis Workshop and Context

Send SASE or call for more information.

RWA SAN DIEGO CHAPTER

P.O. Box 22805
San Diego, CA 92192
(619) 464-6340

Advisor: Teresa Carpenter

Annual Dues: $25 plus $45 RWA National dues.

Benefits of Membership

We feature a hands-on workshop every month focusing on a specific writing skill, i.e., setting, characterization, dialogue, etc. Every meeting includes a program speaker qualified in his/her field of expertise.

Other

Affiliated with Romance Writers of America. No annual conferences at this writing, although we do host all day special event workshops. There are several during the year, one usually in the fall. Call or write for exact location and cost.

Annual Content

ChEMistry Test, focusing on Conflict, Emotion and Motivation. ChEMistry Workbook is available for sale. The deadline is in November and results are returned in February. Contest is a 10-page scene incorporating the three elements indicated. Send long SASE for info to:
ChEMistry Test
c/o Beverly Lane
4928 Vista Arroyo
La Mesa, CA 91941

WOMEN WRITERS WEST
P.O. Box 1637
Santa Monica, CA 90406
(818) 841-1193

President: Betty Payton

Annual Dues: $25

Benefits of Membership

Monthly newsletter lists events, contests, and other information of interest to writers. Monthly meetings feature excellent speakers. There are opportunities to read work in progress or to present published work. Our monthly meetings are rich and not costly. They've almost replaced the need for a conference. We have not had a conference for the last six years. It will be a while before we do.

Other

Not affiliated with Romance Writers of America.

Colorado

PIKE'S PEAK ROMANCE WRITERS

P.O. Box 310
Monument, CO 80132-0310
(719) 481-4418

President: Betty Duran

Annual Dues: $21.

Benefits of Membership

PPRW is dedicated to support, networking, education, market news, and getting published in romantic fiction. PPRW offers a monthly meeting, monthly newsletter and workshops.

Other

Affiliated with Romance Writers of America. No annual conferences or contests at this writing, although "Back to the Basics" workshops are held 3–4 times per year for genre fiction writers.

Florida

FLORIDA ROMANCE WRITERS, INC.

1092 NW 10 Ct.
Boynton Beach, FL
(407) 734-5569

Conference Chair: Gail DeYoung

Annual Dues: $20

Benefits of Membership

Newsletter; writing programs; monthly luncheons; summer seminar.

Other

Affiliated with Romance Writers of America. No annual contests at this writing.

Annual Conference

Usually held in February, the annual conference features: romance editors; agents; keynote speaker; Friday orientation sessions; all-day Saturday workshops and seminars; Sunday breakfast with editors and agents; plus a manuscript evaluation service. Please write for information.

SARASOTA FICTION WRITERS
Sarasota, FL
(813) 923-3047

Contact Person: Deanne C. Miller

Annual Dues: $12.

Benefits of Membership

Latest market and agent news; published author networking; how-to classes; guest speakers; and critiques.

Other

Not affiliated with Romance Writers of America, although several members also belong to RWA. No annual conferences or contests at this writing, but there are future plans.

SOUTHWEST FLORIDA ROMANCE WRITERS
P.O. Box 10104
Naples, FL 33941
(813) 434-2509

President: Kristine Hughes

Annual Dues: $20

Benefits of Membership

Writer's support and meetings with guest speakers (whenever possible) with time allotted for question and answers, followed by critique group sessions, and idea exchange. This chapter has planned annual "Joint Chapter Luncheons" with other writers groups. Contact this RWA chapter for info on membership or current events.

Other

Affiliated with Romance Writers of America. No annual conferences or contests are planned.

Editor's Note

Kristine Hughes has a regular column in *Romantic Times* magazine, called "The Writer's Question Corner." Questions for her monthly column should be addressed to her at *Romantic*

Times. An Anglophile, Kris is also the author of three refer-
ences for historical romance writers: *Ticket to Tyburn, A
Writer's Guide to Researching Historic Great Britain* and
England: 1066–1901, A Research Bibliography.

Georgia

GEORGIA ROMANCE WRITERS
P.O. Box 142
Acworth, GA 30101
(404) 974-6678

Contact Person: Marian Oaks

Current President: Sandra Chastain
4128 Manson Avenue
Smyrna, GA 30082
(404) 432-4860

Annual Dues: $15.

Benefits of Membership

Access to writing/marketing information; informative newsletter; monthly meetings and networking with other writers;
reduced rates for annual conference.

Other

Affiliated with Romance Writers of America.

Moonlight and Magnolias Eleventh Annual Conference

When: Fall 1993.

Where: Atlanta.

Cost: Approximately $60 for members, $80 for non-members (1991 rate).

Editor/Agent appointments; published author suite; assorted workshops and panels for all levels of writing skill; unique programs. Agents and editors are from the major publishing houses.

Annual Published and Unpublished Division Contest

For rules write to:
Ann White
440 Dogleg Court
Roswell, GA 30076

Idaho

COEUR DU BOIS ROMANCE WRITERS
P.O. Box 4722
Boise, ID 83711-4722
(208) 338-1005 FAX: (208) 338-1005

Contact Person: Robin Lee Hatcher

Annual Dues: $15.

Benefits of Membership

Monthly workshops; critique groups; monthly newsletter.

Other

Affiliated with Romance Writers of America. No annual contests at this writing.

Annual Conference

Where: Boise, Idaho.

Cost: approximately $75 for all workshops, lunch, and autograph session.

Authors-in-attendance will be speaking on subjects related to writing romance. Contact Robin Lee Hatcher for more information.

Illinois

CHICAGO NORTH CHAPTER RWA

411 E. Roosevelt Rd.
Wheaton, IL 60187
(708) 668-3316

Contact Person: Susan Donahue

Annual Dues: $25.

Benefits of Membership

Monthly newsletter; group critique; networking.

Other

Affiliated with Romance Writers of America. No annual conferences or contests at this time.

LOVE DESIGNERS WRITERS CLUB, INC.

1507 Burnham Avenue
Calumet City, IL 60409
(708) 862-9797

Advisor: Nancy McCann

Annual Dues: $20.

Benefits of Membership

Support group—we encourage each other and share our knowledge with each other.

Other

Affiliated with Romance Writers of America. No annual contest at this time. Nancy Mc Cann writes " . . . we do publish *Rendezvous,* a monthly review magazine of contemporary and historical romances, mysteries, and women's fiction. We are currently in our eighth year of publication and are extremely proud of the reviews that have appeared on novels and ad material." (See magazine section for more info on *Rendezvous.*)

1993/1994 Conference: Autumn Authors Affair XI

When: Usually held in October

PRAIRIE HEARTS

607 W. Park
Thomasboro, IL 61878
(217) 643-2592 (6–10 P.M.)

Advisor: HiDee J. Eckstrom

Annual Dues: $12.

Benefits of Membership

Prairie Hearts holds monthly meetings and offers critique and support for romance writers.

Other

Affiliated with Romance Writers of America. No annual conferences yet.

Annual Contest

Dark and Stormy Night Contest. Send SASE for more info.

Maryland

MARYLAND ROMANCE WRITERS

3101 E. Northern Parkway
Baltimore, MD 21214
(410) 254-3946

Advisor: Shannon E. Katona

Annual Dues: $17.50.

Benefits of Membership

Monthly meetings; monthly newsletter; networking.

Other

Affiliated with Romance Writers of America. No annual conferences or contests at this writing.

Massachusetts

NEW ENGLAND CHAPTER, INC. RWA #2

P.O. Box 1000
Attleboro, MA 02703
(508) 226-8205

Contact Person: Linda Murphy

Annual Dues: $20—Must also be a member of RWA National.

Benefits of Membership

Education; support; access to critique service; information/marketing news about publishers and agents; conferences/seminars.

Other

Affiliated with Romance Writers of America. Conference information is not available at this time. This chapter holds an annual contest.

Annual First Kiss Contest

The "First Kiss Contest" is for authors unpublished in book length fiction. Finalists will be judged by an editor. Please write for details and entry form.

Michigan

MID-MICHIGAN RWA #2

930 Lincoln Lake
Lowell, MI 49331
(616) 897-5500

Contact Person: Laurie Kuna

Annual Dues: $15.

Benefits of Membership

Monthly meetings; speakers; monthly newsletter containing market news; annual spring retreat with outside speakers.

Other

Affiliated with Romance Writers of America. No annual contest at this writing. Holds annual retreat.

Annual retreat

When: Usually held in May.

Where: Kalamazoo area.

Cost: about $15. Does not include meals or overnight accommodations. Call or write for information.

Authors will speak on romance writing topics. This is an informal, very laid-back, "kick off your shoes" type of thing, with ample time to talk about the writing industry.

UPPER MICHIGAN CHAPTER RWA

425 Summit
Marquette, MI 49855
(906) 226-8493

Advisor: Carol Anne Smith

Annual Dues: $15.

Benefits of Membership

Bi-monthly meetings; bi-monthly newsletter—the two alternate. Meeting programs; critique sessions; and chapter critique-by-mail.

Other

Affiliated with Romance Writers of America. No annual conferences or contests are planned yet.

Minnesota

MIDWEST FICTION WRITERS

16101 125th Avenue North
Dayton, MN 55327
(612) 422-9639

Advisor: Lois Greiman

Annual Dues: $20.

Benefits of Membership

Informative monthly meetings; interaction with many well-known published authors; monthly newsletter.

Other

Affiliated with Romance Writers of America. Annual conferences are held. Contact the Midwest Fiction Writers for further information on the conference or current contests.

Missouri

OZARKS ROMANCE AUTHORS
P.O. Box 412
Purdy, MO 65734
(417) 442-3692

Advisor: Karen Gautney

Annual Dues: $12 plus membership in National RWA.

Benefits of Membership

Members receive support, information, education, encouragement and opportunities to meet with authors, editors, agents, and other related professionals.

Other

Affiliated with Romance Writers of America. Holds conference, but no annual contest.

Annual Conference

Contact this chapter for location, dates and cost.

Authors, editors and agents network in a professional and educational atmosphere.

Nebraska

ROMANCE AUTHORS OF THE HEARTLAND
11218 Leavenworth
Omaha, NE 68154
(402) 330-3025

Contact Person: Pam Hart

Annual Dues: $15.

Benefits of Membership

Newsletter; discounts.

Other

Affiliated with Romance Writers of America. No annual conference at this writing, although occasional conferences are held. Contact the chapter for information on current events.

Annual Hot Stuff Contest

Five-page scene of sexual tension. Send SASE to Pam Hart for info.

New Jersey

NEW JERSEY RWA #34

P.O Box 646
Old Bridge, NJ 08857

Write for membership, meetings, and conference information.

New York State

HUDSON VALLEY CHAPTER RWA #80

224 South Broadway
South Nyack, NY 10960
(914) 358-7141

Advisor: Janet Walters

Annual Dues: $15 plus National Membership dues.

Benefits of Membership

The group offers critiques, support, specialized knowledge of members (e.g. medicine, astrology) and more.

Other

Affiliated with Romance Writers of America. No annual conferences at this writing.

1993/1994 Annual Contest

"Hook, Line and Sinker" is the first three pages of a novel. The contest runs from June to the deadline, October 31. There is a $10 entry fee for each entry. SASE is required. Write or call for information.

ROMANCE WRITERS OF AMERICA/NEW YORK CITY, INC.
Bowling Green Station, P.O. Box 1719
New York, NY 10274-1133
(718) 441-5214

Contact Person: Maria C. Ferrer

Annual Dues: $20 (plus required membership fee to RWA National).

Benefits of Membership

Support! Monthly meetings featuring editors, agents, and more. Monthly newsletter. Discount to annual writing workshop and wine and cheese party for editors. Chapter library access. Outings. Publicity campaign and book signings for published members.

Other

Affiliated with Romance Writers of America.

Annual Workshop

Call or write for details of this intensive writing workshop usually held in February.

Annual Love and Laughter Contest

Open to unpublished writers. $10 entry fee. Writers must submit 3 copies of a humorous scene between the protagonists, plus a synopsis. The grand prize is a critique by an editor of a major publishing house and a subscription to the writer's magazine of the winner's choice. Write for deadlines. Winner will be announced at the annual workshop.

WESTERN NEW YORK ROMANCE WRITERS INC.

135 Colony Street
Depew, NY 14043
(716) 685-1425

Contact Person: Vera M. Hodge

Annual Dues: $25. Also available are annual $15 auxiliary memberships for long distance members, which includes 2 free meetings of choice, plus all newsletters.

Benefits of Membership

Attendance at all meetings, workshops and other chapter functions plus a bi-monthly newsletter.

First Annual Conference

When: October 23, 1993

Where: Buffalo, N.Y.

Cost: $40 for members includes luncheon.

The one day event features romance authors Rainy Kirkland, JoAnn Ferguson, and others. A Harlequin editor will attend. Autograph party. Send SASE to Vera for further information.

Other

Affiliated with Romance Writers of America, Chapter #99.

Ohio

CENTRAL OHIO FICTION WRITERS #48
Cincinnati, OH

NORTHEAST OHIO ROMANCE WRITERS OF AMERICA
16508 Westdale Avenue
Cleveland, OH 44135
(216) 476-1477

Contact Person: Teresa Warfield

Annual Dues: $15 Chapter dues plus $55 National dues.

Benefits of Membership

Chapter has monthly meetings with speakers published and unpublished in romance genre and a monthly newsletter with market updates, chapter news, and how-to articles. National benefits include a bi-monthly national magazine called *Romance Writer's Report* featuring articles from romance authors and others. The RWR magazine also offers the latest romance publishing industry updates.

Other

Affiliated with Romance Writers of America. Chapter conferences are held every other year. Call or write for information on membership, the contest, or the conference.

1993/1994 Conference

When: Fall of 1993, exact date to be announced.

Where: Northeast Ohio area, exact location to be announced.

Cost: Approximately $40 to $50.

Plans are in the works. We hope to draw both authors published in the romance and mainstream genres, as well as romance editors to lecture on various aspects of getting published.

1993/1994 Annual Romancing The Novel Contest

For a $15 entry fee, two judges, one published in romance fiction, will judge the first thirty pages of a novel in progress in four categories: short contemporary; long contemporary; regency; historical. If points earned differ by 30 or more, a third judge will be judging the manuscripts.

WOMEN FICTION WRITERS ASSOCIATION
715 San Moritz Drive
Akron, OH 44333
(216) 867-5786

Contact Person: Debra Moser

Annual Dues: $15 (Must also belong to National RWA).

Benefits of Membership

This chapter offers support, critiques, accessibility to workshops, seminars, conferences, contests, and networking.

Other

Affiliated with Romance Writers of America.

Annual Great Beginnings Contest

RWA members only may enter the first ten pages of an unpublished manuscript. The pages will be judged and scored for $10 and critiqued for an additional $5. Write for exact contest rules and details.

Oregon

CASCADE CHAPTER RWA #59
7218 NE Sandy #3
Portland, OR 97213
(503) 284-2021

Contact Person: Janet L. Brayson

Annual Dues: $20.

Benefits of Membership

An active chapter of 70+ members. We have monthly meetings, workshops, reference library, and a friendly group of writers who are always willing to help.

Other

Affiliated with Romance Writers of America. Annual contest and annual conference.

Annual Romance & Roses Writer's Conference

Brings together authors, aspiring writers, agents, and editors in a relaxed country setting. We bring out at least one New York editor (often more) and some very knowledgable speakers. Topics are aimed to provide help and encouragement to beginning and advanced writers. Call or write for exact dates and other information.

1993/1994 Contest

Our contest is open ONLY to members and those attending our annual conference. This year's contest is a synopsis and a pivotal scene. Call or write for more information.

HEART OF OREGON RWA

1140 Waverly St.
Eugene, OR 97401-5235
(503) 485-0583

President and Publicist: Ann Simas

Annual Dues: $15.

Benefits of Membership

Includes monthly educational/informational meetings, monthly newsletter (awarded 1992 best by RWA), annual writing contest, annual writing conference, and periodic writing workshops.

Other

Affiliated with Romance Writers of America.

1994 Conference

Where: Eugene, Oregon.

Cost: approximately $120–$135.

Editors, authors, and agents gather to exchange information and discuss "breaking in." There will be a focus on general writing with emphasis on theme topics, as well as other published and unpublished authors to "network with."

Annual Contest

Twilight Shadows is the theme. Send query letters (up to 2 pages), prologue/first chapter (up to 25 pages), and synopsis (up to 5 pages). There will be five finalists with final judging to be done by an editor. Contest guidelines are available with SASE. Contest entry fee is $15 for RWA members or $20 for non-members. Critiquing will be done and score sheets and entries will be returned.

MID-WILLAMETTE VALLEY RWA

490 Lochmoor Place
Eugene, OR 97405
(503) 687-8879

Advisor: Sharon Morris

Annual Dues: $12.

Benefits of Membership

We not only have wonderful speakers at our meetings, but every three to four months we bring our manuscripts for a group critique—putting into practice what we have learned.

Other

Affiliated with Romance Writers of America. No annual contests at this writing.

Annual Conference

When: Usually held in April.

Cost: About $30.

Write for details about this one day workshop.

Pennsylvania

CENTRAL PENNSYLVANIA ROMANCE WRITERS (CPRW)

R.D. #1 Box 303
Port Royal, PA 17082
(717) 527-2510

or
Janice Costello, Secretary
24 E. Manor Avenue
Enola, PA 17025
(717) 732-2454

President: Judy C. Kiner

Annual Dues: $15.

Benefits of Membership

As a newly formed organization, CPRW is establishing goals,
both long term and short term, at this point. Members will
be able to benefit from lectures, guest speakers, group
and/or individual critiquing—all associated with romance
writing. CPRW is planning a conference for the group early
in 1994. Members will be able to participate in the preparation, carrying out, and any such benefits (meeting contact
persons, other writers, gaining valuable insight from workshops) a local conference will be able to provide, especially
when financial realities limit members from traveling to
many other state conferences.

Other

Affiliated with Romance Writers of America.

1994 Conference

We are hoping to have one main speaker at our conference.
We also have a 3–4 time published author who is currently
serving as CPRW's Vice President, who will, most likely, be
giving a seminar. We are hoping to include agents and editors.
Write or call Janice Costello during the day for additional
information.

Tennessee

RIVER CITY ROMANCE WRITERS RWA #23

4513 Ernie
Memphis, TN 38116
(901) 346-2859

Advisor: Debra B. Dixon

Annual Dues: $15.

Benefits of Membership

Education, camaraderie, and networking with others involved in the romance industry.

Other

Affiliated with Romance Writers of America.

Annual One Day Workshop

When: Usually held in November.

Where: Memphis, Tennessee.

Cost: $20 for RCRW members, $25 for non-members.

This one-day gathering features morning and afternoon "workshop" discussions with at least three published authors (TBA). The RCRW goal for this workshop is to reach all romance authors within 150 miles and provide them with an affordable workshop. Lunch is included. Contact the chapter for more details.

Annual River City Showdown Writing Contest

Deadline: High Noon on October 1.

Entry Fee: $10.

Prizes: Overall Winner $50
                Best Bad Boy $10
                Best Good Guy $10

For more information, please write to Barbara Christopher, 6055 Halstead, Memphis, TN 38134 or call her at (901) 386-6137.

Texas

GREATER DALLAS WRITERS' ASSOCIATION
4201 Nightfall
Plano, TX 75075

Not affiliated with Romance Writers of America. (214) 596-5335 or call the University of Texas at Dallas Center for Continuing Education at (214) 690-2204.

NORTH TEXAS ROMANCE WRITERS OF AMERICA
5425 Stanley-Keller Road
Ft. Worth, TX 76117
(817) 498-4313

Advisor: Paula Oates

Annual Dues: $18.

Benefits of Membership

Founded in 1983, the NTRWA has about 120 members, offering opportunities to veteran authors as well as novice writers. The monthly *Heart to Heart* newsletter has a news exchange and features editors and agents. The PARTners program (for published authors) offers support, market news, and discussions. Awards are presented for service, first sales, scholarships, etc. Also available is an audio/video library, monthly programs, hands-on workshops, and more.

Other

Affiliated with Romance Writers of America. No annual conference.

Annual Great Expectations Contest

(Call or send for complete rules)

Eligibility: RWA members must be unpublished and uncontracted in fiction. Limited to the first 50 entries per category. Previous first place winners may enter another work.

Format of Entry: LARGE SASE is a must (no metered mail, stamped only). May enter up to 2 entries per category.

Cover Sheet: contains the title, author's name, address, phone number and entry category. The cover sheet is the only place where the author's name can appear!

Entry: 4 copies of the first chapter (up to 30 pages), must be double-spaced with one-inch margins. Near letter-quality dot matrix and photocopies are OK. Manuscript headers must include the title and page number only.

Query Letter: targeted to an agent or editor, must be single-spaced, not more than 2 pages, with one-inch margins. Query should mention book title, but remember, NOT the author's name!

Deadline: Call for deadline date.

NORTHWEST HOUSTON ROMANCE WRITERS OF AMERICA

2507 Woodvale
Kingwood, TX 77345
(713) 361-3603

Advisor: Laura Powell

Annual Dues: $15.

Benefits of Membership

This chapter has a monthly newsletter, monthly meetings with informative speakers, yearly one-day workshop, and manuscript critiquing.

Other

Affiliated with Romance Writers of America. Annual conference but no contest.

1993/1994 Conference

The speakers will be Candace Camp, Sally Hawkes, Penny Richards, Erica Spindler and Gina Wilkins. Contact:

Mica Kelch
4426 Algernon Drive
Spring, TX 77373
(713) 350-2844

ROMANCE WRITERS OF THE TEXAS PANHANDLE

P.O. Box 1343
Amarillo, TX 79105-1343
(806) 372-2447 (day) or 655-1675 (evening) FAX: (806) 345-2299

Contact Person: Vanessa Reeves

Annual Dues: $15.

Benefits of Membership

Monthly meetings, monthly newsletter, fellowship, support and understanding, as well as contact with published writers and the chance to hear interesting speakers.

Other

Affiliated with Romance Writers of America.

1993/1994 Conference

Call or write for more information.

Annual Contest

"Take It to the Limit": 5 pages of sexual tension. Call or write for more information.

WEST HOUSTON RWA #28

P.O. Box 430577
Houston, TX 77243
(713) 932-6368

Contact Person: Victoria Simmons (President)

Annual Dues: $20 local West Houston dues/$55 National RWA dues.

Benefit of Membership

Sixteen-page newsletter; networking; education; support; motivation; annual local conference; annual contest; special members only workshops; National RWA conference every July (in different cities); National RWA Golden Heart and RITA contests; group discounts; market information; sharing information.

Other

Affiliated with Romance Writers of America. Holds annual chapter conference and contest. For the 1994 Foundations of Fiction Conference information/brochure send SASE to:

M. J. Selle
6807 Cedar Street
Katy, TX 77493

Utah

ROMANCE WRITERS OF AMERICA, UTAH CHAPTER

416 E. 3075 N.
Ogden, UT 84414
(801) 782-8336

Treasurer and Conference Chair: Isolde Carlsen

Annual Dues: $20.

Benefits of Membership

Informative programs on writing skills; critique of work; Annual Golden Pen contest; conference; and plain old support.

Other

Affiliated with Romance Writers of America.

Annual Tricks of the Trade Conference

When: Usually held in October.

Where: Salt Lake City.

Cost: $45 includes lunch, all sessions and autograph party.

In attendance will be children's and Young Adult's author Lane Ferguson, Region IV Advisor Debbie Bedford, Region IV Representative Pat Collinge, and local Harlequin authors Rebecca Winters, Danise Allen a.k.a. Emily Dalton, and Betina Lindsay. Sessions will be on creativity, what to do before you start writing, characterization, synopsis preparation, and more!

Annual Golden Pen Contest

Obtain rules from Isolde Carlsen.

Virginia

VIRGINIA ROMANCE WRITERS

P.O. Box 35
Midlothian, VA 23112

Contact: Chapter Advisor

Annual Dues: $20

Benefits of Membership

Monthly newsletter; monthly programs on writing.

Other

Affiliated with Romance Writers of America. Holds annual conference and contests.

Annual Conference

When: Usually held in April.

Where: Williamsburg, Virginia.

Cost: Members $90, Non-members $110.

We will feature editors from major romance houses. Keynote speakers are bestselling authors Sandra Brown and Karen Robards.

Annual Contests

"Fool for Love Contest"   One chapter
"One Liner Contest   Opening line for a novel

Contact VRW for more info on either the conference or the contests.

Washington

SEATTLE CHAPTER ROMANCE WRITERS OF AMERICA
P.O. Box 5845
Bellevue, WA 98006
(206) 643-7737

Contact Person: Angela Butterworth

Annual Dues: $20 local (plus national).

Benefits of Membership

This chapter offers monthly meetings, a newsletter, market news, support, and networking with fellow writers.

Other

Affiliated with Romance Writers of America. Holds annual conference and contests.

Annual Conference

When: October 9–10, 1993.

Where: Bellevue, Washington at the Bellevue Hilton.

Cost: $135 ($69 per night lodging single/double).
The theme is "The Hidden Story." The keynote speaker is Jayne Anne Krentz. Also speaking are Robin Lee Hatcher and Katherine Stone. Editors, agents, and other authors will also attend. Large bookfair. Contact Nancy Radke at (206) 823-2044 for more details.

Annual Emerald City Opener Contest

The first five pages of a manuscript may be entered for a $10 fee. Contact this chapter for more information on rules and eligibility.

TACOMA CHAPTER RWA
18210 SE 121st Place
Renton, WA 98059
(206) 228-6004

Advisor: Darcy Carson

Annual Dues: $10.

Benefits of Membership

RWA networking; programs; workshops; monthly newsletters; and monthly meetings.

Other

Affiliated with Romance Writers of America. No annual conferences or contests at this writing.

Wisconsin

WISCONSIN ROMANCE WRITERS OF AMERICA
4546 Sundance Court
Cottage Grove, WI 53527
(608) 839-4275

Contact Person: Pamela E. Johnson

Annual Dues: $15 plus $45 in National RWA.

Benefits of Membership

Wisconsin RWA offers critique groups, networking and support for published and unpublished writers, bi-monthly newsletter, local contest, workshop and conference.

Other

Affiliated with Romance Writers of America.

Annual Romance Writer's Workshop

When: Usually held in September

Where: Oshkosh, Wisconsin

Cost: Write to this chapter for further information on cost and exact location.

Don't miss this hands-on critique workshop with a special guest!

Annual Write Touch Conference and Writing Contest

Write to this chapter for further information on cost, and exact location of the conference as well as cost and rules for the contest.

13

Promoting Your Romance Novel in Romantic Times Magazine

*S*o you've landed your book contract, finished the revisions, mailed the final corrections, and sent your editor a balloon bouquet to celebrate. You've photocopied the advance check, had Wal-Mart enlarge it into a poster, and plastered it on the wall of your office as incentive. Now all that's left to do is rest on your laurels while you think about drafting the next book—NOT!

If you have a romance novel about to be released, the best time to launch your publicity campaign is yesterday! And the best promotional vehicle is *Romantic Times* magazine, with 100,000+ subscribers plus 50,000 newsstand buyers who use the information in *Romantic Times* to prepare their monthly book shopping list.

Romantic Times is an inexpensive and effective promotional opportunity for romance authors to help their romance novel become a "sell-through." There are exceptions, but in most cases, because of limited publicity budgets, first time authors need to develop a unique and inexpensive way of promoting their blossoming career. And the staff of *Romantic Times* is there to help.

There are at least four ways to promote your romance novel in *Romantic Times* magazine. Three are free: the book review, the author profile, and a brief mention in one of the regular columns.

Melinda Helfer, who has been a *Romantic Times* reviewer for many years, reads and reviews novels because she loves getting a sneak peek at all the new releases. Although her review specialties include science fiction and fantasy, romance is her primary interest and she thoroughly enjoys reviewing series romances.

Melinda is eager to receive galleys or unbound copyedited pages, which she will accept from either romance authors or their publishers. She advises checking with your publisher to ensure they've already sent a review copy to *Romantic Times*. She urges authors not to wait until their books are released to send a review copy. *Romantic Times* needs to have review materials about three months ahead of the issue month; sooner if possible. For example, for a September release, the reviewer would like to have the "pages" before July 1.

The review format consists of an objective plot and character summary as well as the reviewer's concise opinions on the book's level of reader satisfaction and whether the book's premise seemed plausible. Comments range from "full of adventure, with many twists and turns," to "poignant, sensual and wonderful," or even "fans of the genre will find nothing new." But, unlike some book review magazines, *Romantic Times* does not stoop to the cutting witticisms that other magazines sometimes use to malign a book or make a reviewer seem oh-so-clever.

Romantic Times reviews also have numbered ratings, which are symbolized by a line of hearts. For example, four hearts followed by a plus sign is a 4+, an "exceptional" numerical rating by the book reviewer. A historical reviewer may go as high as a five heart rating, which means the book is a "classic," but fives are rare.

Profiles are the author's second option for promotion in *Romantic Times* magazine. The in-depth author capsules offer romance readers an opportunity to meet new authors.

The authors of single titles have a good chance of having their profiles grace the beginning pages of *Romantic Times,* because their books will be easily available to romance readers months and months after the magazine is printed. This makes the majority of the information in the magazine useful to readers for a very long time. The profiles are more useful to the single title authors than to series/category authors, whose interviews would soon be old news. Interviews of single title authors give these authors ample time to interact with their reader audience regarding those books.

Authors interact with readers? Definitely.

Many romance readers delight in writing to the authors of their "keeper" novels. The majority of authors respond to fan letters by sending free bookmarks, autographed postcards, or bookplates (an SASE is customarily provided by the requestor).

Responding to fan letters and offering readers promotional newsletters or bookmarks helps romance authors develop an interactive and consistent audience—and a mailing list. Fan mail is important to romance authors, so they can find out what readers liked about their books and what turned them off!

What should you include in your profile?

The author's profile is a marketing tool that can make your book stand uniquely apart from all the other new releases—if you make it so. The staff at the magazine can help with "angles" and suggestions for writing your author's profile. Readers are often motivated to buy a book because of an exciting excerpt from your upcoming novel (get permission from your publisher first!), an author's funny or mysterious anecdote, a story-behind-the-scenes, or retelling the event that sparked the idea to write the book.

How does an author get chosen for a profile? Ask a reviewer for assistance when you call the magazine for a review. The reviewer will likely ask you to send a press kit, which should contain an uncopyrighted black and white photo, your bio, a fact sheet, maybe even a profile ready-to-go with importable text on disk.

The third opportunity to get your name and your book's name in print in *Romantic Times* is the regular columns where you and your book may be mentioned if space allows. One column called "Under the Covers" usually has one or two paragraph "scoops," such as news of an author who is setting out on an African safari, another whose husband put a sign in their front yard to let the neighborhood know his wife's book made #1 on Waldenbooks' bestseller list.

Another column called "Tete à Tete" features teasing hints about upcoming books from veteran romance authors, and author news.

There are other types of columns where romance authors and their upcoming novels may get a line or two of promo copy—sometimes a whole page.

The monthly "Agent News" column talks about one agent of the month, the type of romance novels handled, and a list of clients, sometimes even some of their book titles. This is a good opportunity for your agent to get your name (and his or hers) in *Romantic Times*.

The monthly "Bookstore News" column details the fun and promotional ingenuity connected with author appearances and book signings.

"Market News" is often written by authors to help other authors break into the publishing market. For example, Patricia Simpson, author of *The Legacy*, gave some excellent tips on writing occult romances in the March '93 issue.

"Industry News" contains such diverse advice as an author's tips on preparing your book for a movie "treatment," to how to get an agent, to the proper length for a script.

There are also regular how-to columns for writers, which are expanding to fit the needs of romance readers who have become romance writers. If you have an interesting idea for a column, call the magazine and let them know about it. A column or feature article is a great way to promote yourself and share helpful information with other romance writers.

The fourth way to promote your novel through *Romantic Times* magazine is the paid ad. Now wait, don't go away. Advertising advice is important, especially for those authors who can't afford a paid publicist.

Carol Stacy, the associate publisher, is a helpful and savvy professional who is willing to help romance authors with their ad campaigns in *Romantic Times*. She can help tailor sizes and types of ads for upcoming romance novels, especially for authors who have a very small advertising budget from their publishers or are even considering paying for their own promotion. Classified ads and small display ads are reasonably priced for a magazine with such a large readership.

By the way, publishers can help by providing the author with half-toned book cover art and some ad copy. Don't be afraid to ask your publisher's publicity department for assistance. They want your book to be a "sell-through" too!

A quick word about ad costs: Compare these two rates for a similar "spread." *Publisher's Weekly* magazine charges $3,960 for a black and white camera-ready full page ad for one insertion, which translates to one week of exposure. *Romantic Times*, a monthly, charges only $880 for the same size and type of ad (March 1993 price quotes from both magazines).

Unless the romance author is a big name, an ad in *Publisher's Weekly* may be skimmed over by book distributors, who often ignore the fact that romance comprises about half of all paperback sales. But, the romance readership of *Romantic Times* assures that the author is aiming the promotional package at the correct audience. You can bet that romance readers faithfully devour *Romantic Times* magazines from cover to cover, marking up the pages with highlighting pens as they read, deciding from the book reviews which are "must-reads," which are "maybes," and which are "probably nots."

Is there a writing formula that will assure a glowing book review in *Romantic Times?*

Melinda says, "Romances are about triumphing over life's difficulties. A romance author creates something beautiful between two people . . . It's a story about the good guy's winning, the right way . . . Romances are about values, about things we dream of, and I believe that romance writers are the keepers of those dreams."

Many thanks to Romantic Times reviewer Melinda Helfer for much of this insider information about the publishing business, which she shared in a speech to the Desert Rose Chapter of Romance Writers of America at their annual Author Appreciation Luncheon in March 1993.

Thanks too, to Jacki Whitford, a Romantic Times book reviewer, columnist, and romance research expert who also provided information and assisted with fact-checking for this chapter.

14

*Directory of
Writer's Publications*

AFFAIRE DE COEUR
1555 Washington Avenue
San Leandro, CA 94577
(510) 357-5665

Affaire de Coeur is a magazine for writers of romance fiction.
Dedicated to presenting all eras of romance including regency,
historical, and contemporary. *Affaire de Coeur* contains articles
about writing romance fiction, publishing news, author bios, and
reviews. A subscription is $30 per year for first class mail delivery.

FACTS FOR FICTION
CMB PUBLICATIONS
4101 Green Oaks Blvd, W. Suite 138
Arlington, TX 76016

Facts for Fiction is an 8–10 page newsletter for historical writers. A one-year subscription is $15 for 12 issues. Samples are $3. *Facts for Fiction* is a historical cornucopia of facts for historical writers with book reviews of historical nonfiction, descriptions of historical clothing and hairstyles, an on-going dictionary of sailor's jargon, a classified page, and a list of historical book releases for the following month.

GOTHIC JOURNAL

9757 Janero Ct., North
St. Paul, MN 55115-1339
(612) 426-8826

Publisher: Kristi Lyn Glass

Gothic Journal reviews gothic, romantic suspense, women in jeopardy, ghost romance, and romantic mysteries. There are author bios, market news, articles, readers' letters, forthcoming release news, and more. $18 per year for 6 issues. Sample copy for $4.00 plus long SASE.

HEART TO HEART

Heart to Heart is a bi-monthly romance newsletter with book reviews, author interviews, and a check-off shopping list of new titles. It's available free at B. Dalton Bookstores.

HOUSEWIFE-WRITER'S FORUM
P.O. Box 780 Dept R
Lyman, WY 82937

$15 year for 6 issues ($4 Sample Copy).

JACKI WHITFORD'S TIME AFTER TIME
P.O. Box 3068
Falls Church, VA 22043

This 16-page monthly newsletter is $3 for a sample issue or $36 per year (12 issues). *Time After Time,* praised by authors Carole Nelson Douglas and Raine Cantrell, is a cornucopia of historical trivia, quotes, publicity hints, a historical calendar, bibliographies, and much more.

MANDERLEY
P.O. Box 880
Boonville, CA 95415-0880
(800) 722-0726 for questions or book orders

Call for a book catalog, which features many book reviews of classic, historical, regency, fantasy, contemporary, gothic, and suspense romances. Also sells nonfiction of interest to romance writers, audiocassettes, romantic film classics, and gifts.

THE MEDIEVAL CHRONICLE
P.O. BOX 1663
CARLSBAD, CA 92018-1663

Six issues for $10 a year. This newsletter contains articles relating to life in the Dark Ages, Middle Ages, and Tudor period. It also has information on upcoming Medieval romances.

OLD TIMES CHRONICLE
P.O. Box 247
Dedham, MA 02026

$24 a year for 12 issues or $3 for a sample copy of this publication devoted to history, as told by those who actually lived it, through the words they left behind.

PAPERBACK PREVIEWS MAGAZINE
P.O. Box 6781-RT
Albuquerque, NM 87197
(800) 872-4461

Monthly newsletter/book catalog listing new releases with mini-"blurbs." Several longer reviews. Not a book club; no purchase is required. Write to request a free sample copy. A subscription is $15.00 per year.

POETS & WRITERS MAGAZINE
72 Spring Street
New York, NY 10012
(212) 226-3586

Published six times a year, this magazine has interesting interviews with poets and literary writers, grants and awards information, news about legislation that affects authors, etc. A literary/arts focused magazine that is helpful to all types of writers. $18.00 a year by subscription.

PSYCHIC WRITER'S NETWORK
119 Cregar Road
High Bridge, NJ 08829
(908) 638-4426

Contact: Christina Lynn Whited

Bi-monthly newsletter focusing on paranormal, time-travel, and fantasy. Network of writers who like to weave astrology, numerology, palmistry, and other esoteric themes into their romances (and other fiction). $15 for 6 issues.

PUBLISHER'S WEEKLY
P.O. Box 1979
Marion, OH 43302
(800) 842-1669 inside the continental U.S. or (614) 382-3322

51 issues for $97.00. Most large libraries subscribe to this magazine. *Publishers Weekly* is the info-track magazine of the entire publishing industry.

THE READER'S VOICE
2646 Wyoming Ave., SW
Wyoming, MI 49509-2370

Editor: Jean Riva

This 12-page bimonthly publication is $14 per year (6 issues) or a sample issue is $3. By and for romance readers, this newsletter is an open forum for romance readers who enjoy exchanging personal opinions about romance novels, book reviews, profiles, and all things related to reading romance books.

THE REGENCY PLUME NEWSLETTER
Box 870049
Mesquite, TX 75150

Contact: Marilyn Clay

$8 for 6 issues, this 8–10 page indexed newsletter is for Regency devotees, readers, and writers. Articles range from subjects like divorce in Regency Times to what songs were popular at Covent Gardens during this period, to bonnets, a recipe for Twelfth Night cake, description of a Regency garden, currency information, and more. Marilyn Clay also sells reproductions of authentic historical maps, Fleet Marriage certificates, and more. Write her for a complete list of Regency information for sale or for a newsletter subscription.

RENDEZVOUS
1507 Burnham Avenue
Calumet City, IL 60409
(708) 862-9797

This monthly is published by the Love Designers Writer's Club. It is 32 pages of very candid reviews of current romance, fantasy, gothic, mystery, and women's fiction. There is also a market news column by Nancy McCann. Rendezvous has no slick ad copy to clutter the pages or motivate reviewers to lie about a book's readability. A subscription is six months for $18 or one year for $36. Single copies are $3.

ROMANCE READERS
3402 Edgemont Avenue, Suite 331
Brookhaven, PA 19015-2804

A $15 membership fee includes a quarterly newsletter containing romance industry news briefs, invitations to lectures with authors and publishers, book reviews, reduced admission to *Romance Reader* events, and assistance in setting up local discussion groups. *Romance Readers* is an advocate for the rights and privileges of romance authors.

ROMANCE WRITER'S REPORT (RWR)
Romance Writers of America
13700 Veterans Memorial Drive, Suite 315
Houston, TX 77014
(713) 440-6885

A bi-monthly publication of Romance Writers of America for members.

ROMANTIC READER
This free bi-monthly newsletter is distributed next to the cash registers at Waldenbooks chain stores. They run out quickly, so find out when they are usually delivered.

ROMANTIC TIMES
Romantic Times Publishing Group
55 Bergen Street
Brooklyn Heights, NY 11201
(718) 237-1097

Now a monthly publication, *Romantic Times* magazine is filled with current information on the ever-changing world of the romance publishing industry. Besides profiles of romance authors, helpful articles on romance writing, convention news, industry gossip, and current trends, new books are previewed and reviewed in-depth and rated for readers' shopping convenience. U.S. subscription fees are $21.00 for 6 issues by Third Class Mail, or $30.00 for 6 issues by First Class Mail.

ROSE PETALS AND PEARLS
PO Box 7082
Jackson, TN 38303

Contact: Deborah Britt at (901) 424-4665 or Diane Kirk at (901) 422-6223

The monthly newsletter of this new non-profit charter organization is dedicated to the preservation of the romance genre. Members can be readers or writers. Newsletter has information on events and articles by romance authors. $20 fee includes membership and newsletter subscription.

TRUDY'S TIME PERIODS
PO Box 70388
Richmond, VA 23255
(804) 264-1325

Editor: Trudy Bateman

Trudy Bateman publishes a quarterly reference guide that categorizes historical romances by their time periods. Index lists author, title, time period, and, so you can read them in order, if a book is part of a series. An annual subscription is $20 for one category or $32 for all categories.

WGA JOURNAL
8955 Beverly Blvd.
Los Angeles, CA 90048

Published by Writers Guild of America, this $5.00 monthly magazine gives an up-to-date list of television series in current production and names and phone numbers of contact people accepting submissions.

WRITER'S DIGEST
1507 Dana Avenue
Cincinnati, OH 45207

All types of writing and markets are discussed in how-to articles. Monthly market information is usually related to non-fiction articles needed for magazine markets. Subscription rates: $21.00 per year or $3.00 per single copy at newsstands.

WRITER'S JOURNAL
Minnesota Ink, Inc.
27 Empire Drive
St. Paul, MN 55103

How-to articles are combined with quality gems of fiction, poetry, book reviews, contests, columns, and more. Format and tone of magazine is somewhere between the literary-type *Poets and Writers* magazine, and the slick commercial presentation of *Writer's Digest* magazine. Subscription rate: $18.00 per year for 6 issues bi-monthly.

WRITER'S YEARBOOK
1507 Dana Avenue
Cincinnati, OH 45207

This annual publication rates the top hundred magazine markets of the year. Also, famous authors give advice on getting published.

WRITER TO WRITER NEWSLETTER
P.O. Box 1003
Wickenburg, AZ 85358

Editor: Laraine McDaniel Bell

This quarterly non-profit publication for romance writers is free with a SASE. Award-winning Harlequin author Laraine McDaniel shares her professional tips and secrets for writing romance and suspense. She keeps other romance authors informed of conferences, contests and market news, results of surveys about readers, and more. Submissions from other writers who want to share their news and articles about romance writing are always welcome, but please query first with a SASE. Since this is a non-profit publication, there is no payment.

Index

About the Author

Eve and her husband Ron live with their two children in Arizona. She became interested in the romance genre at age eight, when she watched Christopher Plummer kiss Julie Andrews in "The Sound of Music." Her own version of happily-ever-after occurred when she answered a personals ad in 1987. She and Ron were married within the year.

A full-time writer, Eve has been published in *Writer's Journal* and *Kumquat Meringue* literary magazine. She also finds time for travel and patent research for her inventions and is an active member of Romance Writers of America.

MORE BOOKS FOR THE
FREELANCER'S LIBRARY
FROM PRIMA PUBLISHING

Insider's Guide to Book Editors, Publishers,
and Literary Agents by Jeff Herman $19.95
Offers detailed information about every aspect of getting published,
whatever your field—children's, young adult, suspense, new age, and
more. Includes a comprehensive section on who's who among literary
agents and those in other key areas of the publishing industry.
Updated yearly, *Insider's Guide* has become a standard in the field.

How to Make $50,000 a Year or More As
a Freelance Business Writer by Paul D. Davis $14.95
The business of business writing is a well-kept secret, and the unknown group of writers who make big sums of money doing it would
certainly prefer it stay that way! Fortunately, successful freelance
business writer Paul Davis is willing to share the secrets with writers
everywhere. Learn how to find business, keep clients happy, effectively plan your time, market your services and charge accordingly,
and bill your clients.

How to Sell More than 75% of Your Freelance Writing $12.95
by Gordon Burgett
Amateurs write, then try to sell. Professionals sell, then write. Most
beginners think that 90% of publishing success comes from having
talent as a writer. Burgett's step-by-step guide teaches you how to
avoid the most common mistakes beginners make; how to receive
positive replies from editors before you write a single word; and how
to spin one article idea into several well-paying articles.

The Travel Writer's Guide by Gordon Burgett $14.95
Travel writing is the simplest and most lucrative way to start a writing
career. The public's fascination with travel keeps growing, and numerous kinds of publications seek articles on exciting domestic and
international destinations. Areas covered include: what editors look
for; how to brainstorm ideas for travel articles; how to document and
deduct your travel expenses; and how to write query letters.

FILL IN AND MAIL . . . TODAY

PRIMA PUBLISHING
P.O. BOX 1260BK
ROCKLIN, CA 95677

USE YOUR VISA/MC AND ORDER BY PHONE
(916) 786-0426 (Mon-Fri 9-4 p.m. PST)

Please send me the following titles:

Quantity	Title	Amount
_____	_____	_____
_____	_____	_____
_____	_____	_____
_____	_____	_____
_____	_____	_____

	Subtotal	$_____
	Postage & Handling	$ _3.95_
	CA Sales Tax if applicable (7.25%)	$_____
	TOTAL (U.S. funds only)	$_____

Check enclosed for $ _____(payable to Prima Publishing)

OR

Charge my MasterCard ☐   Visa ☐

Account No. _____ Exp. Date _____
Signature _____
Your Printed Name _____
Address _____
City/State/Zip _____
Daytime Phone   (   ) _____

Satisfaction is guaranteed—or your money back!
Please allow three to four weeks for delivery.

THANK YOU FOR YOUR ORDER

THE
RIVER
ROSE

GILBERT MORRIS

THE RIVER ROSE

A WATER WHEEL NOVEL

NASHVILLE, TENNESSEE

Published by B&H Publishing Group,
Nashville, Tennessee

Dewey Decimal Classification: F
Subject Heading: BOATS AND BOATING—FICTION \
LOVE STORIES \ STEAMBOATS—FICTION

1 2 3 4 5 6 7 8 • 16 15 14 13 12

CHAPTER ONE

The Gayoso House Hotel in Memphis, Tennessee, gleamed like Mount Olympus on the bluff high above the Mississippi River. Its six fifty-foot-high Doric columns topped by the grand, white marble pediment had become a sure landmark to the lesser beings on the river. A pallid December sun rose behind the hotel, its weak light still making the grand edifice seem to glow.

Jeanne Bettencourt's eyes watered a little as she stared up at the hotel. The wind was keening off the river, and as she hurried along Front Street she adjusted her woolen muffler to cover her mouth and nose. Above the plain gray wool were wide-set velvet brown eyes, odd because they had a perfect almond shape that was more East Indies than red-blooded American. The searching bitter wind teased out several thick chestnut-brown curls from her mobcap and hood, and impatiently she tucked them back in.

1

She went around to the back of the hotel to the servant's entrance, of course, because she was a chambermaid, not a guest. Sometimes Jeanne dreamed of having enough money to stay at Gayoso House. It was a luxurious place, with real brass room keys and fobs, daintily wrapped guest soaps, satiny bed linens, eiderdown comforters, fireplaces, and velvet chairs and cherry tables in each room. And most elegant and desired—marble tubs, silver faucets, hot and cold running water, and even flush toilets. Indoor plumbing was grandiose indeed.

A crowd of maids, porters, waiters, and wood boys were gathered at the service entrance, and just as Jeanne reached the bottom step the great Gothic bells of St. Peter's church began to ring the hour of 7:00 a.m. The door was opened by Mrs. Wiedemann, the stern German housekeeper, who stood frowning as the servants filed in. Jeanne was last, on the final stroke of seven, and Mrs. Wiedemann frowned. "You are almost late, Jeanne."

"Yes, ma'am," she said submissively, following the woman's heavy tread into the housekeeping supply room. She wasn't late, of course. But Jeanne was lucky to have this job, and she never crossed Mrs. Wiedemann. Under the circumstances, the two got along very well.

The housekeeping supply room was something like a long railroad car. Along one wall was a row of hooks, each with a neatly printed white card above it. Jeanne hung her cape and muffler on the hook labeled *J.Bettencourt*, gave another quick pat-push to the hair escaping from her mobcap, and checked her white apron to make sure it was spotless. At the Gayoso one was not required to have a uniform as such, though they required that the maids wear gray skirts and plain white blouses. The hotel supplied each maid with two aprons and two mobcaps, and if you came to work at the Gayoso with your apron dirty you did not work at the Gayoso on that day. Satisfied that she presented a neat and clean appearance, Jeanne began to gather her cleaning supplies. They were all stored in a long row of closets across from the hooks, kept locked to deter stealing. Mrs. Wiedemann had a very impressive bunch of keys hanging at her waist. She stood watching suspiciously as the maids gathered their supplies.

When they were all ready with their five-gallon buckets full, they started filing up the back staircase to begin the day. Mrs. Wiedemann called out, "Jeanne, I would speak with you for a moment."

Jeanne kept her face expressionless, though she was dismayed. She never knew what Mrs. Wiedemann was going to say to her when she asked to speak to her. Sometimes she berated her for some imaginary wrong, or chided her for the faults of other maids assigned to her. Sometimes she asked polite questions of Jeanne, as to how so-and-so new maid was adjusting, how Mr. Such-and-Such was enjoying his stay, was Jeanne happy with her supplies, did she feel anything useful may be added to the cleaning materials?

Jeanne hurried back to her and asked politely, "Yes, Mrs. Wiedemann?"

"Yes, Jeanne. This week we have some soaps barely used from overnight guests. Also we have pillow slip turnover. You may buy ten soaps for one penny, and five pillow slips for one penny, if you wish."

Jeanne's dark winged eyebrows rose with surprise. All such perquisites belonged to the housekeeper, and in four years this was the first time she had ever known Mrs. Wiedemann to let anyone have a chance to buy any castoff supplies. And the price she quoted was excellent; the swift thought went through Jeanne's mind, *she could sell them to the secondhands five for a penny, one for a penny . . .*

"Yes, ma'am, I would very much like to buy some soaps and pillow slips," Jeanne said gratefully. "Ten soaps for one cent and five pillow slips for one cent is very generous. Thank you, ma'am."

To Jeanne's surprise, Mrs. Wiedemann seemed slightly uncomfortable. "The pillow slips are very thin. Perhaps we make it six for one penny. Yes. I will have them for you tonight, when you leave."

"Oh, I am so sorry, Mrs. Wiedemann, I have no money with me at all," Jeanne said in embarrassment. "Please, hold them for me until tomorrow. I'll bring the money then."

"No. You take them tonight. I know you will bring the money, Jeanne. Now get to work, please." She turned and marched away.

Jeanne was ecstatic as she flew up the three flights of stairs to the top floor. It was December 18, 1854, two days before her daughter's birthday and seven days until Christmas morning. She would have time to sew a soft long-sleeved chemise from the pillow slips in the next week, so Marvel would have two birthday presents and two Christmas presents.

Jeanne began, as always, with the first room, #301. All of the rooms at the Gayoso were alike, but the wealthiest and most prestigious patrons preferred the top floor. In winter it was warm, and in summer the cool breezes off the river kept them bearable. The third floor was, of course, the most difficult one for the chambermaids because they had to travel up and down three flights of stairs to resupply or to take their twenty-minute lunch break. Mrs. Wiedemann had started giving Jeanne the top floor every day she worked, and at first Jeanne had thought that the woman was deliberately making it difficult for her. But then she realized that the third floor patrons tipped generously, as a rule. Too, Mrs. Wiedemann had started assigning all the newest maids to work with Jeanne, and over time she had stopped coming up to the top floor to check the maids' work. Jeanne slowly started training the maids, and then supervising them.

Jeanne was very happy to see that her first guest was a regular, an older man named Mr. Borden. She knew that he was a very prominent man, for she had overheard snippets of conversations and she knew that when he was in town he saw the mayor, city council members, judges, presidents of companies, insurance executives, and the sheriffs and marshals. He was no salesman.

She knocked twice on the door and said, "Chambermaid to attend the room, sir?"

"Yes, yes, come in, come in," he called. She opened the door, stepped in, and curtseyed. At the Gayoso the chambermaids always curtseyed.

He was sitting at the tea table by the window wearing a maroon satin dressing gown over his clothes, for the fire had not yet caught well and the room was chilly. His tea table was littered with newspapers. A fat cigar was lit and smoldered in an ashtray next to a silver coffee service. Mr. Borden was a round, jovial man, bald with a thick silver fringe and sideburns, and bright blue eyes. "Jeanne! Oh, I am glad to see you, Jeanne. Come in, come in, girl!"

"Good morning, Mr. Borden," Jeanne said with real pleasure. She went to the fireplace, noting that the wood boy had cleaned the mantel and hearth well, and stirred the coals and added another log. The flames leapt up and the fire began crackling comfortably. Then Jeanne picked up her bucket and started toward the bathroom.

"Just a minute, Jeanne. Come here, I have something for you," he called after her. "Besides, I'm too lazy to pour my own coffee. Sad, isn't it? Would you do me the honor?"

"Of course, sir," she said, returning to pour out a steaming cup of coffee with three sugars and heavy cream, just as he liked it.

"Mmm, you fix it better than I do anyway," he said appreciatively. "Now, I've got some things here—oh, where is the blasted—there it is. *Frank Leslie's Illustrated Weekly*. From last week, but I thought that you might not have seen it yet," he said tactfully.

"No, I have not," Jeanne said. "That's very kind of you, Mr. Borden. Thank you."

He waved dismissively. "And there's some other papers, the *New York Herald*, the *Arkansas Gazette*, the local *Appeal*. I believe you'll find them underneath the night table."

Jeanne found the newspapers and looked up at him questioningly. "You brought all these for me, sir?" Mr. Borden always left her his newspapers when he stayed, but this was a stack of about a dozen current papers.

"Of course," he replied with a smile. "Ever since I caught you sneaking a read of my *Herald*, I've thought about it. You see, Jeanne, I've never thought twice about buying half-a-dozen newspapers every morning, skimming the headlines, then throwing them away. But you can't do that, can you?"

"No, sir," Jeanne said, slowly rising. "But I never meant to—"

"I know," he interrupted her hastily. "No, you wouldn't. I just think you should be able to read the newspapers if you want." Very busily he re-lit his cigar, sipped his coffee, shuffled newspapers, and finally began reading.

Jeanne put the newspapers outside the door and began cleaning. She scrubbed the bathroom, polished the faucets, cleaned the toilet, then went into the room to shake out the sheets and plump the comforter, change the pillow slips, remake the bed, sweep the carpet, and clean the windows. As she was gathering her supplies to leave, he looked up from his newspaper and said, "Jeanne, don't forget your *Leslie's*."

She had not forgotten it—far from it—but she was too embarrassed to intrude upon him to greedily shuffle through the untidy pile of newspapers on the table to find it again. She went back to the table, and it was lying to the side, with a five-dollar bill on top of it. Eyes wide, she stared at him.

"Merry Christmas, Jeanne!" he said as jovially as Santa Claus himself.

"Oh, thank you, sir," she breathed. "It's—it's—very generous, sir."

"Not really," he said lightly, then cocked his head, as alert as a bird. "Jeanne, may I be extremely impertinent and ask you a personal question? Dunno why you'd object, you see, I'm already rude enough to call you by your given name and smoke cigars in front of you."

"I don't object to any of that, sir," she said with a small smile, "and you may ask me a question."

"Hmm. Are you married, Jeanne?"

"I am a widow, Mr. Borden."

"And do you have children?"

"Yes, sir. A daughter."

"And how old is she?"

"She will be six years old in two days, sir," Jeanne replied, now thoroughly surprised. In her experience even the kindest guests had no interest in a chambermaid's life, unless it was one of the men who took a great deal of interest, generally in a chambermaid's person. When Mr. Borden had asked the first question, she had had a moment of discomfort, but it had swiftly passed. She knew he wasn't that type of man. She had always known. Still, his questioning was curious.

"And what is her name, if you please?" he continued.

"Marvel Bettencourt. No middle name, sir."

He nodded. "I have two sons and two daughters. They're all grown now, of course. And I have a grandson that is possibly the most intelligent, the most wondrous child that has ever been born."

Deadpan, Jeanne said, "I'm sorry to tell you this, sir, but my daughter is quite the cleverest and most wonderful child ever."

He laughed, a delightful boyish sound. "So she is clever, is she? Must take after her mother. Thank you for indulging my boorish questions. I've just wondered about you, you see. I'd like for you and your daughter to have a good Christmas."

"Mr. Borden, with this money, I can assure you that my daughter and I will have a glorious Christmas. Thank you again, sir." She gathered up her things, gave him a final curtsey and a smile, and left.

As soon as she pulled the door closed behind her she stretched out the five-dollar bill and stared at it in wonder. In the previous Christmases, she had made some one-dollar tips but never five dollars. Happily tucking it into her ankle boot, she checked her list for the occupant of the next room. She was the only chambermaid that could read. The other girls had lists with the room numbers carefully drawn the exact same way as the brass numerals on the doors.

With some trepidation she knocked on Room #302, for her cleaning list told her that this was J. B. Cunningham. "Chambermaid to attend the room, sir?" she called.

"Come on in."

She entered the room, which was deliciously heated by the roaring fire. On the air was the sharp mentholated scent of shaving lather. The bathroom door was open and delicate wisps of steam wafted out of it. A young man peered around the door, his face half smothered with big dollops of shaving cream. He held a straight razor in his hand. "Hello, Beautiful! Just give me a minute, I'm finishing up."

It's not like I'm calling on you, Jeanne thought grimly with an angry bob to pass for a curtsey. "No, Mr. Cunningham, since you are still at your morning toilette I will return later."

She turned, but too late. He popped into the room. He had trousers on—for which Jeanne was excessively grateful—but he was in his sock feet, and he wasn't wearing a shirt. His face still had shaving cream on it, but he seemed unaware as he came and put both hands on her waist. "Who says toilette? You're not like any chambermaid I ever saw, Jeanne." He tried to draw her closer. "And you're so beautiful—"

With deliberation Jeanne grabbed his hands and lifted them away from her as if they were some loathsome rodents, and said icily, "Didn't you know? I learned it at Chambermaid School. It's very exclusive; they all look like me at Chambermaid School."

He laughed. "Wish I knew where that school was! Aw, c'mon, Jeanne, I'm sorry I'm—er—"

"Half naked?" she supplied. "I know that word, too. I'll be back after I do the next two rooms, Mr. Cunningham. Please be clothed by then."

Without waiting for his comment, she flung the door open and stalked out. J. B. Cunningham pawed all of the maids. The first time she had cleaned his room, he had lightly laid his hands on her shoulders, turned her around to give her a jolly hug, and then tried to kiss her. She had been new, and frightened, and awkward, and she had barely managed to keep darting away from him until finally she had managed to complete her work. Since then he had tried again and again, but as Jeanne gained more experience she had become quite adept at keeping men at arm's length. This was the first time, however, that he had been half-clothed—or half-naked, as she saw it—and she had been sharper with him than ever before. *Lost that tip*, she thought dryly as she went to the next room.

The guest wasn't in the room, so Jeanne unlocked it with her master key and went in. After automatically checking the hearth she went into the bathroom and paused before the big gilt-edged mirror over the sink to study her reflection. In her opinion, J. B. Cunningham always told her she was beautiful because he was trying to seduce her. She was not beautiful; she was pretty. Her eyes were dark and fringed with heavy, dark lashes, and above them her eyebrows made perfect arched wings. Her face was a small oval, with a delicate nose and wide mouth. Her hair was rich, dark brown, luxuriously thick and curly, reaching almost to her waist. She was of average height but her frame was slender, almost boyish. She looked much younger than her age; she was twenty-five but she knew that she barely looked eighteen. That, she reflected, was something that women usually desired, but to her it was a nuisance. Men would have been more respectful of her, surely, if they knew she was a widow with a young daughter.

Efficiently she finished the room and went on to the next, noting that it was another frequent guest, Mr. George Masters. He responded to her knock and bid her to come in. She opened the door, stepped inside, and curtseyed.

"Good morning, Jeanne," he said with pleasure. "How are you today?" George Masters was thirty years old, with wavy yellow hair, blue eyes, and a classic Greek profile. He was a wealthy planter, and in the last six months his stays at the Gayoso had become much more frequent and of longer duration. He always looked at Jeanne with admiration, she had seen, but he was never forward or insinuating. He did talk to her, much like Mr. Borden did, with particular cordiality, though he didn't ask personal questions. He seemed to be truly interested in what she had to say.

"I am doing very well, thank you, Mr. Masters," she replied.

"And are you looking forward to Christmas?" he asked. He was standing in front of the fireplace, his hands behind his back. His tailoring was always elegant, his frock coats perfectly fitted, his double-breasted waistcoats of satin, with a fine gold watch chain suspended from the pocket and hooking onto the middle button. His hair was perfectly styled. Jeanne could not imagine him allowing her into the room in such a coarse state of undress as Cunningham had done.

"Yes, sir, thank you, sir," she replied politely. She picked up her bucket and started toward the bathroom.

"I'm glad to hear it," he said, and Jeanne stopped, put her bucket down, and turned to face him. When a guest wished to converse with you, you stopped what you were doing until they were finished with you. He went on, "I came into town particularly for the Christmas Regale. I was wondering if you were planning on attending?"

This year, for the first time, the City of Memphis was sponsoring a public Christmas fair. The playbills posted all over the city promised a lavish party at Court Square on Christmas Eve.

"Yes, sir, I do plan to attend," Jeanne said with pleasure. "It sounds like it's going to be quite a fête."

One of his smooth eyebrows arched. "Yes, a fête. How do you know—er, pardon me. Perhaps I may see you there, Jeanne?"

"Perhaps, sir," she said evenly, and waited.

He looked as if he wanted to say more, but finally he went to the armoire and pulled out a heavy, dark blue double-breasted topcoat and a fine beaver top hat. "If you'll excuse me, I have people waiting for me. There is an envelope on the mantel, it's for you. I hope you have a good day. I'll see you in the morning, Jeanne."

She curtsied as he went out the door, and then hurried to open the envelope. He had left her two dollars. She smiled a little. He never handed her a tip; he always left it for her. Jeanne marveled at his delicacy. Most of the guests—who were males, of course—made a show of tipping her, with the obvious expectation of gratitude, and sometimes more. George Masters had always shown her unusual respect.

When she finished with George Masters' room she returned to Cunningham's. He was shaved and clothed, to her relief. He gave her a dollar tip, and then tried to envelope her in a hug. But Jeanne was not going to give anyone a hug for a dollar, or even for a lot of dollars, and she slipped away from him.

Each floor of the hotel had fifty rooms, and normally all one hundred and fifty rooms were occupied. This close to Christmas, however, the hotel had only eighty occupied rooms, and many of them were checking out today. Twenty-two rooms had to be cleaned on the third floor, and Jeanne had two other maids working with her. They interrupted her several times so that she could let them into a room when the guest wasn't there. As far as she knew, she was the only person that Mrs. Weidemann ever gave a master key to. She did her seven rooms, and the extra. She then checked all the other girls' rooms to make certain they were thoroughly cleaned. It was about five o'clock, and close to full dark, when she left the Gayoso.

She carried her newspapers, her soaps, her pillow slips, and eight dollars and forty cents in cash. It usually took her over seventeen days of work to earn that much money. *Thank you, Lord!* she exulted to the bitter east wind. *Thank You for taking such good care of us!*

Because of the Christmas season, the shops along Main Street were staying open late, and the streets were still busy. Men in heavy wool topcoats and tall beaver hats, arm-in-arm with fur-clad women, mingled with the rivermen, the clerks, the charwomen, the coal scuttlers, the woodcutters, the couriers, the tradesmen, and all of the different kinds and shapes of people that made up a relatively cosmopolitan city such as Memphis. Jeanne was charmed by Main Street at Christmastime. Every shop window was framed with holly and evergreens, and the lanterns cast an angelic golden glow over the boardwalk. She would have liked to linger and look at some of the shops that she could never go into, like Madame Chasseur's Cosmetics and Perfumery, but she was in a hurry to get home to Marvel. And it was still harshly cold, though the wind had died down.

Quickly she made her way down Main to Anderton's Grocery and Butchery. The store was busy, with women crowding around the fresh vegetables that Mr. Anderton had just gotten in that very day. Jeanne looked at the bins with a jaundiced eye. She disliked the most common winter vegetables—beets, collard greens, turnips, and particularly brussels sprouts. Her long mouth twisted as she looked at the little, round green balls and thought how very good they would be for Marvel, but she had never been able to bring herself to buy them, she loathed them so. She didn't think she could take a bite of a brussels sprout, not even for Marvel. The kale did look freshly green, and cabbage cooked with a ham hock would be very good. Picking through the bundles of kale carefully, she finally chose one that seemed full and without blemish and went up to the long counter, where Mr. and Mrs. Anderton were busy waiting on customers. Mrs. Anderton finally looked up at her with a flushed plump face and said, "Oh, Mrs. Bettencourt, I see you found the nice kale we got in today. Did you see the brussels sprouts?"

"Yes, ma'am, they look very—green," Jeanne said politely. "May I please have a quart of milk, and would you happen to have any ham hocks at a good price this evening?"

Mrs. Overton frowned. "Hmm, I'll check for you, Mrs. Bettencourt. We did this afternoon, but we've been this busy all the day long . . ." She bustled off toward the butchered meats in the back. Jeanne leaned over to look behind the counter, for there were two large bins of the plumpest, reddest apples she had ever seen. Her mouth watered. Mrs. Overton returned, still a-bustling, holding a ham hock in brown paper and a glass quart of milk. "This is the smallest ham hock we have, Mrs. Bettencourt, but it still has some good meat and fat to it. That would be seven cents a pound, and this is about two pounds."

"That's fine, Mrs. Overton, I'll take it. Those apples, they are very fresh, aren't they?"

"Oh, yes, fresh-picked in Pennsylvania, I understand, and shipped downriver. We just got them today. I apologize, but we had to put them back here, people were stealing them, and they're a nickel apiece. Would you like to come around and look at them?"

"No, thank you, ma'am, if you would—"

But suddenly the kind, warm Mrs. Overton turned into a termagant. She leaned over to look behind Jeanne, her face red with outrage. "Here, you! D'ye think I'm blind? Plain as plain, I saw you poking holes in that there cabbage! Y'ain't gittin' no deals, neither! Plain as plain!" She turned back to Jeanne with a polite smile. "You were saying, Mrs. Bettencourt?"

"I'd like for you to choose two of the best apples, please, Mrs. Overton. And I'd like a half-pound bag of black tea," Jeanne said with amusement. The Overtons, like most of her guests at the Gayoso, treated her with respect, in spite of her lowly status. Jeanne knew it was because of her upbringing, which had been unorthodox, but her mother had been a gentlewoman and had taught her well. J. B. Cunningham had been right about one thing, at least. She really wasn't like a chambermaid.

Mrs. Overton obligingly put all of Jeanne's purchases, along with her newspapers and pillow slips and soaps, into a roomy canvas bag. "I'll return it tomorrow," Jeanne promised.

"Yes, I know," she said, beaming. "And a very Merry Christmas to you and your little one, Mrs. Bettencourt!"

"Merry Christmas to you and yours, ma'am," Jeanne said. As she neared the door she saw a boy with his face pressed close up to the glass, staring wistfully at the fresh vegetable display. Jeanne felt a deep pang, as she always did when she saw Roberty. But she smiled as he held the door open for her. "Hello, Roberty. I was hoping I'd see you tonight."

His thin, dirty face brightened. "You was? How come was that?"

"It so happens that my stock of matches is very low. I desperately need some kindling, and also I was hoping that you might do me a very great favor," Jeanne said, slowing her step to match his. He was a boy of about ten, she thought, small and thin and hungry-looking. There were dozens, maybe even hundreds, of boys like him in Memphis.

"I got matches, Mrs. Bettencourt," he said eagerly. "And I kept back a good bundle of wood for you, in case. I hid it 'round the corner when I saw you going into Anderton's." He trotted down one of the dank little alleys and came back with an armload of sticks and small branches. "I'll do you a favor, ma'am. Anything, you just ask."

"Well, you know the little Christmas tree you found for me," she said, "we've decorated it some, but I think I'd very much like to have some pine cones to use for decorations. Do you think you could find any?"

"Oh, yes, ma'am! There's a big stand of pines over on Mud Island, and every morning they drop loads of cones. I'll be there first thing of the morning, afore the other wood monkeys get there, and get you the prettiest ones." The boys who scavenged the scarce wood around the city had come to be called wood monkeys. They practically knew where every tree in Memphis was located, and no branch or pine cone hit the ground in winter and stayed there for long. Each day the wood monkeys ranged up and down the waterfront, picking up every splinter lost from the endless line of carts hauling wood to the hungry riverboats.

"I got a surprise for you, too, Mrs. Bettencourt," he said proudly. "I got you some pretty good little sticks of rich pine."

"How wonderful!" Jeanne said. "One can never seem to buy rich pine. And as it happens, today I have a little extra money, and I'd love to have every splinter of rich pine you have. You—you didn't steal it, did you?"

"No, ma'am," he said stoutly. "I don't steal."

"No, I'm sorry, Roberty, I know you don't steal," Jeanne said apologetically. "Are you making it all right? That's a pretty hefty bundle you have there."

"I don't know what hefty is, but it ain't too heavy." Gamely he struggled to match his stride with Jeanne's as they hurried north of town, to the district known as "The Pinch." Originally it had been called the Pinchgut District, because of the gaunt and pinched faces of the poor people, mostly Irish, who had settled there. It was the poorest section of the town.

But Jeanne felt that she and Marvel had a fairly good house, considering that they were indeed very poor. It was a small clapboard shotgun house that was only about ten years old. Shotgun houses were called that because of the open middle hallway from front to rear; you could shoot a shotgun through them. To keep out the homeless drunks and thieves and other, worse criminals, Jeanne and her neighbors, the O'Dwyers, had put up stout bolted doors at each end of the house. The O'Dwyers lived in the room on the right side and Jeanne and Marvel on the left. The one thing that Jeanne treasured most about the single room was that it had a fireplace. That was why she had decided on renting the house instead of living in a more convenient boardinghouse.

Finally they reached her home, and Jeanne dreaded the next few minutes. She felt terribly guilty about Roberty. She didn't know if he had any family, any parents. She didn't even know if he had a home or if he was one of the true orphans who camped out in the summer and slept in a crowded church shelter on the coldest winter nights. But what could she do? Just because he had adopted her, that didn't mean that she could adopt him.

Jeanne opened the door and they went into the dark hallway. From the O'Dwyers, loud voices sounded, arguing about someone's tobacco, and one of the children was crying. The strong smell of onions pervaded the hall. Roberty slipped past her, laid his bundle of wood down at her door, then pulled some sticks out of his pocket. "Here's the rich pine, Mrs. Bettencourt. How many matches do you need?"

"How many do you have?"

"'Bout a dozen left, I think," he said, groping in the dark hallway.

"Good, I'll take whatever you have. Now, I want you to take this, Roberty, for the wood and the rich pine and the matches. And for Merry Christmas," she said, handing him two quarters.

His dulled eyes grew round. "Gosh! Thanks, Mrs. Bettencourt! Merry Christmas to you too, and, and I'll see you tomorrow with the pine cones!" He turned and ran out the door, pulling it securely shut behind him. He always hurried away like that, as if he sensed Jeanne's turmoil over asking him into her home. With regret, Jeanne opened the door to her room and hurried to bring in the wood and put all of her things away.

But somehow Marvel must have heard them, perhaps when the door slammed, for the O'Dwyers' door opened and she came running out. "Mama, you're home! Why didn't you come get me?" she cried, throwing her arms around Jeanne's legs.

"Because I have a birthday surprise here for someone and I was trying to hide it," Jeanne said, swooping down to lift her up and kiss her. "You're going to have to go stand in the corner and hide your eyes."

"That's silly, I haven't been naughty," Marvel scoffed. "I've been very good today."

Jeanne let her slide down to the floor, and Marvel's eyes grew big and round as she saw the bulging canvas bag on the worktable. "Gunness! Are those all your things, Mama?"

"They are mine and yours," Jeanne said, smiling. Marvel always said *gunness*, not *goodness*. "Now, if you'll let me get my breath, and get that fire going good, I'll show you our treasures, and tell you about my exciting adventures today."

"I'll help you," Marvel said happily. "With the fire, not your breath."

Jeanne took off her cape and muffler and then carefully removed her mobcap. It looked clean, but of course her apron got dirty in the course of a day's work. She threw it into a bucket of water with boracic acid in it, for she had found that just soaking it overnight would remove the stains without having to scrub. Smoothing her hair, she put on a black wool shawl and went out in the hallway to fetch a good-sized log for the fire. She and the O'Dwyers split the cost of a cord of wood, which ran about ten dollars.

Marvel stood at the fireplace with the poker, vigorously stirring a good-sized bed of coals and carefully placing small branches on it. The coal-glow lit her intent face. Though she had inherited Jeanne's large dark eyes, she was rather a plain child, with a thin face and mousy sandy-colored hair. Small for her age, her hands were more like a four-year-old's than a six-year-old's. Her legs and arms were skinny, and her neck seemed too small for her head. This was not evidence of malnutrition, because Jeanne was vigilant about feeding her well. Rather, it was because she was frail and sickly. Marvel had been born two months prematurely, and she had never gained normal strength and health.

But she was a pleasing child, because she was bright and alert and interested in everything, even things that most children her age would find a dead bore. Jeanne was alternately grateful and frustrated with her cleverness. She was gratified when Marvel had started learning to read at five years old, and she had been frustrated when Marvel had insisted she explain why the O'Dwyers had six children and Jeanne only had one. Life with Marvel was like that.

Jeanne came in to put the log on the fire. "Did Mr. O'Dwyer give us the coal starter?"

"Yes, ma'am, Angus got home early today and stoked their fire up real good, and Mr. O'Dwyer brought a shovelful of live coals over here just a little while ago," she said.

"Did you remember to thank him?"

"Yes, ma'am. I told you I was very good today."

"Pardon me, I forgot," Jeanne said gravely. "Now I'm going to put this soup on, and while it's heating up we'll take a look at my bag over there." She set up the iron tripod and suspended a cast-iron pot over the hottest part of the fire. All last night she had simmered oxtails, onions, and carrots over the slow fire. Now she added a cupful of cooked rice for a good, thick stew.

"Let's go ahead and put our bed down, shall we?" Jeanne said. They had an iron bedstead with rusty springs, but in winter they always put the mattress down in front of the fire and sat wrapped up in wool blankets. Most nights they read some, and then they talked while Jeanne sewed. Tonight they got the canvas bag and set it down between them.

"First, though, before we see these wonderful things, I want us to say a thank-you prayer," Jeanne said. "Today I had some generous guests that gave me tips. We have to thank Mr. Borden, Mr. Masters, Mr. Cunningham, and Mr. Davis."

Marvel nodded and bowed her head. "Dear Lord Jesus, thank you for Mr. Borden and Mr. Masters and Mr. Cunningham and Mr. Davis. Thank you for the money they gave Mama. Thank you for all the stuff in the bag. Amen."

Jeanne began taking things out of the bag. "Surprise! Kale! Isn't that wonderful?"

"Mama, that bag's got more things in it," Marvel said reproachfully. "You're just joshin' me."

"I'm sorry, I think you'll like this better. Here is milk and a ham hock, which I suppose are almost as amazing as kale. But look at this—and this—" Jeanne pulled out the muslin bag of tea, and the apples.

Marvel's mouth made a small *o*. "Those apples! They're so, so red and shiny and fat! And, Mama is that—" She snatched the bag from Jeanne's hand and lifted it to her nose and sniffed. "It is! It's tea! You got us some tea!"

"Mr. Borden got us some tea," Jeanne corrected her. "And these newspapers. Just look, Marvel, this one has pictures."

"Oh, Mama, could we please, please, have a cup of tea? And we have milk and sugar! Couldn't we make tea, and then read the newspapers while we're having tea?" she pleaded.

"Hmm, I suppose we might, though I'll have to take the stew off the fire," Jeanne said thoughtfully.

"But just this once, to celebrate Mr. Borden and Mr.— and the other gentlemen—may we have tea and bread and cheese and apples for supper?" Marvel said slyly.

"Ah, to celebrate," Jeanne said. "As a matter of fact, that is just about what Mr. Borden told me he'd like me to do with the money he gave me. Yes, tonight we may have tea instead of supper."

"Oh, thank you, thank you!" Marvel said. "I just love tea, and I know it's so 'spensive we can't hardly ever buy it."

"We *can* hardly ever buy it," Jeanne corrected her.

"We *can* hardly ever buy it," Marvel echoed. "Mr. Borden must be nice. You like him, don't you, Mama?"

"Hm? Oh. It's not a question of whether I like him or not, Marvel," Jeanne explained. "In a way, I work for him. He is a generous man, and I am grateful to him."

Marvel frowned. "I thought you liked him, because when you talk about him you sound okay. But when you talk about the others you sound funny, like you don't like them."

"What? No, no, Marvel, it's not that I dislike them. It's just not—the situation—it's one of those things about adults that you can't understand yet," Jeanne struggled to explain.

"Maybe. But I know you don't like men very much, Mama. 'Cept for Mr. O'Dwyer, I guess, and maybe Pastor Beecham. I just don't understand why."

Jeanne blinked several times. She didn't actively dislike all men, of course. But she didn't trust them. She treated them with courtesy, but with cool, distant courtesy. She found it troublesome that Marvel had noticed anything peculiar. In Jeanne's mind, she was equally polite to everyone. How could Marvel have recognized any difference in her attitude toward men? Perhaps it was simply that Marvel was overly sensitive because she had no father.

Jeanne reached over and hugged Marvel. "It is hard for you to understand things about grown-up men and women, little girl. Just don't worry. Because I love you so much, so very much, and I promise I'll protect you and keep you safe."

Marvel buried her face in Jeanne's shoulder. "I know you'll take care of me, Mama. I've always known. I love you, too."

CHAPTER TWO

Venite adoremus
Venite adoremus
Venite adoremus
Dominum!

The thunder of Clint Hardin's tenor voice rolled out through the nave of Calvary Episcopal Church in the last refrain of "Adeste Fideles." After a moment of silence, which generally did happen when Clint finished a hymn at full strength, Choirmaster Altus Lilley, a small nervous man, said, "Wonderful, choristers, wonderful!"

"Someone was flat," Eve Poynter Maxfield said with delicate distaste.

Dr. Augustus Hightower looked down his long generous nose at her and sniffed. "I don't see how you can hear a flat when Mr. Hardin is singing."

"Sorry," Clint said without a sign of remorse.

"Not at all, not at all," Choirmaster Lilley said hastily. "Perhaps there was a flat, Mrs. Maxfield, but then again,

Mr. Hightower, sometimes the acoustics keep us from detecting the very minor flaws, if there should be any. Er—should we try it again?"

"I think not. It is getting late, and Mr. Hardin and I really must practice our pieces," Mrs. Maxfield said. "I believe everyone else can go home."

"Yes, of course, of course," Mr. Lilley agreed. "Splendid rehearsal, everyone. Thank you."

The Calvary Choristers all began to gather their hats, topcoats, gloves, and mufflers. There were fourteen of them: six male singers, four female singers, three male violinists, and twelve-year-old prodigy Constance Raleigh, who played the flute flawlessly. She looked very sleepy and bored as she broke down her flute to place it in the velvet case. The adults were discussing the upcoming Christmas Eve program, the violinists were carefully packing up their instruments.

Clint Hardin walked up to the violinists and asked his friend Vincent Norville, "Hey, Vinnie, meet me at Mütter Krause's about ten? You too, Duffy, Mütter Krause's *Wiener schnitzel* is good for you, make you grow up big and tall."

"Aw, can it, Clint," Duffy Byrne grunted. He was a scrappy Irishman, short on height and short on temper. "I could take you, you know, with that glass jaw you got."

"Probably," Clint agreed with a grin. "You coming, though?"

"Not me," Duffy said. "Shannon's waiting for me at home. Besides, the only person that scares me more than Shannon is Mütter Krause."

"I'm in, Clint," Vinnie said heartily. "I'm not promising to wait for you, though." He was a wiry, tough man with dark curly hair and brown-black eyes. Now he glanced sidelong at Eve Maxfield and said wryly to Clint, "After all, you can't be sure Her Ladyship is going to be all finished up with you by ten."

"I'll be there, I'm as hungry as a bear right now," Clint said. "But you know we must take care to please the ladies." He went back to where Eve Maxfield stood alone.

Vinnie rolled his eyes at Duffy. "He pleases the ladies, all right. I just wish it wasn't *all* of the ladies."

Clint and Eve stood together at the side of the transept, talking quietly. He was bent over solicitously to listen to her, for he was six feet two inches tall and she was only five feet four inches. They made an unlikely pair. Clint Hardin was beefy, with broad shoulders and bulky arms and legs and a workingman's rough hands. His hair was long, growing over the collar of his shirt, a glossy blue-black, straight and thick. One lock perpetually fell over his forehead. He had dark, smoky blue eyes set in a craggy, lantern-jawed face.

Eve Poynter Maxfield was his polar opposite. She was small and slight and dainty. Her hair was a deep auburn, and she wore it in the prevailing fashion, parted down the middle with a chignon in the back and springy ringlets over each shoulder. She had a magnolia complexion, big round brown eyes, a small nose, and short pouty lips. Her dress was exquisite, a winter promenade dress of red-and-green plaid taffeta of such quality that the very whispers it made when she moved sounded rich.

Mrs. Henry Raleigh, wife of Mr. Henry Raleigh of Raleigh Ironworks and mother of the bored Constance, came stalking over to Clint and Eve. Mrs. Raleigh was a fine-looking woman, with dark hair and eyes and aristocratic features and an imperious manner. She was not quite thirty and clung to her youth with fierce determination, constantly setting herself against the young widow Eve Maxfield, an acknowledged beauty.

"Mr. Hardin, Mrs. Maxfield, I really must protest. It was not my husband that was flat," she said frigidly. Mr. Raleigh, short, rotund, with great fluffy sideburns, was one of the two baritones, and though he did have a powerful voice, unfortunately he was sometimes flat.

"I never said it was Mr. Raleigh that was flat, Letitia," Eve retorted. "In fact, I never even said it was one of the gentlemen." Mrs. Raleigh was an indifferent alto.

"Surely you're not accusing me now!" Letitia said stiffly.

With a bored look Eve said, "Why don't we ask Mr. Hardin? After all, he does stand in the center of the group, and his pitch is perfect. I'm sure he could tell who it was."

"Nah," Clint said carelessly. "I sing so blasted loud even I can't hear."

"Liar," Eve said with amusement.

"Am not," Clint said. They exchanged intimate little smiles.

Letitia Raleigh narrowed her eyes. "You know, Eve, you really should be careful about showing undue familiarity with men. You're damaging your reputation, people are talking."

"I know, and I also know exactly who is doing all the talking," Eve said.

"Yeah?" Clint said with interest. "I've always wondered who does all the talking."

"Really, such impertinence!" Letitia snapped, whirling about and hurrying away.

"You're impertinent," Eve told Clint. "Letitia said so. And she is the one who does all the talking."

"At least I've been promoted. Last week she called me a boor."

The choristers were finally filing out, and Clint and Eve waved and said their good-nights. Eve turned to him and said, "Finally, we're alone. All alone."

"Yeah, how'd that happen?" he said, grinning.

"I made sure of it," she said. "So, shall we warm up?"

"We've been singing for two hours already."

"I wasn't talking about my voice," Eve said softly. "I was talking about my hands." She removed her gloves, then put her hands on his chest and moved close to him, looking up at him alluringly.

He backed up just a tiny step so she wouldn't be pressing against him, but he did place his hands over hers. "It is cold in here, Mrs. Maxfield. With your permission—?" He lifted her hands and breathed on them, then gently rubbed them. "Better?"

"Yes, much better, Clint. And I've told you, call me Eve when there's no one around."

"That would be very impertinent of me. I'm like that, you know. People talk."

With an exasperated sigh, Eve pulled her hands free and went to sit on the stool by the grand pedal harp that loomed up behind them. Lightly stroking the strings in a humming whisper, she said, "You always make jokes, Clint. I really wish you would be serious, and speak to me as if you are sincere."

"Sincere about what?" he asked, perplexed. For eight months now, since Eve had practically single-handedly formed the Calvary Choristers, she had been flirting with him, paying marked attention to him, deferring to him in many matters that really were the province of the choir-master. Tonight was the first time she had arranged for them to practice alone, though for many nights now she had drawn close to him to say a warm and intimate good-night. Tonight she had touched him, but he had expected that, for that was the way women like Eve played the game. He knew about ladies like Eve; they liked to dance close to fire, to tease, to tantalize. But they never, ever got burned.

When a respectable gentlewoman like Eve flirted with him, Clint always figured that the last thing they wanted was for him to be either serious or sincere.

Now she looked up at him with a trace of frustration. "You could be so much more than you are. You are intelligent and you are gifted. You have a gentlemanly deportment, when you trouble to display it. But your appearance and your jocular manner don't help you."

"I can't help the way I look and talk, Eve," he rasped.

"Oh, I wasn't talking about your looks at all," she said with heavy insinuation. "Your looks are just fine. Better than fine, in fact. No, I was talking about your mode of dress, always in rough laborer's clothing. If you would wear well-tailored suits, with correct accessories, of course, you could mix in any circles you chose. And neither am I talking about your speech, which is really quite articulate. What I mean is the way that you comport yourself. You should learn to behave more like a gentleman and less like a mechanic."

"That's *machinist*. And I happen to believe that I can be both a machinist and a gentleman. I don't understand what you're getting at, anyway. What good could it possibly do me to dress up like a high-hat muffin? Then I'd just be a machinist in a three-piece suit."

She shook her head. "No, you wouldn't. Again, you could be so much more than you are right now, Clint."

"How's that? Put on some weight?"

She gave him a disdainful look, and he said, "Sorry, sorry, being serious and sincere now. I don't understand what that means, Eve."

"You see, I've been thinking about you a lot," she said in a warm, intimate tone. "I believe that I could help you tremendously. You could be on the stage, Clint. With some training you could be the star of any opera you chose, you could command solo performances. And the first step of

28

working toward that goal is for you to become my voice tutor."

He grinned devilishly. "Well, yeah! And you could be my nanny!"

"You see? You cannot be serious for even one full minute!"

"Because that whole folderol you've got in your pretty head there is funny. Oh, yes, I can just see your father, Judge Eugene Poynter, welcoming me into your drawing room for your la-di-da musicales! And a voice tutor? Just because I can sing doesn't mean I know the first thing about tutoring."

"But you could, you know," she said mildly. "You understand everything about the physical part of it, and your pitch is so perfect you can't tolerate the most minuscule flat or sharp. I've seen you making faces at Henry Raleigh."

"I don't make faces—never mind that. It's ludicrous, Eve. I can see where you're going with this. You dress me up like a pet monkey and parade me around and I simper and fawn to get sponsors, and I spend all day having the vapors because I'm a tortured artist, and I just hate to take filthy lucre to support my gift, but I'm driven, because I'm an artist, and I'm tortured."

"Something like that," she said, smiling. "It would work, too. I know because I'm certain that if I could present you to my father in respectable clothing, and if you would regulate your conduct, he would pay you to be my voice tutor. And when he hears you singing serious music, he would gladly agree to sponsor you. That's what people like us do."

Clint nodded. "People like you may. But people like me don't. So, are we going to practice or not?"

"Yes, we are. But first I would like to ask you two things."

"At your service, ma'am," Clint said instantly. He truly was a gentleman.

"The first is, would you kindly walk me home tonight? I felt bad for Sowerby, so I sent him home."

"You, walking? And on a night like tonight? I'll bet the temperature is somewhere around freezing about now."

"It's only four blocks." She smiled up at him seductively. "And I already know that you can keep me very, very warm."

"That I can do," he agreed. "And the other favor?"

"Just think about what I've told you, Clint. That's all, just tell me that you'll at least consider it."

"All right, Eve, I will at least consider it."

"Good. Now, are you ready?" She placed her fingers on the harp strings and began.

MÜTTER KRAUSE'S KITCHEN WAS a respectable restaurant during the day, when women and their children, or even a lady alone, might dine on the scrumptious German food without a worry that they would be accosted or troubled in any way. There were two things that Gudrun Krause despised: mundane food and troublesome men. So her food was always freshly bought and freshly cooked, and her male patrons were always on their best behavior. Wild river rats, slick gamblers, fighting drunks, smooth pickpockets, and professional thieves found that they were not welcome at Mütter Krause's, not even after six o'clock, when the laborers and craftsmen and dockmen got off work and the restaurant transformed into a tavern/eatery.

Clint came in the front door and saw Vince Norville sitting at the long polished cherrywood bar. Unlike a saloon, Mütter Krause's had tall stools lined along the bar, for men didn't just stand and drink, they sat down and ate, almost always. Gudrun Krause didn't care if the men didn't order food. As long as they behaved, they were welcome to stay and drink as long as they liked. But the delicious smells of spicy sausage, piquant sauerkraut, and tangy hot potato salad generally overcame a man at some point during the night. Right now, at ten o'clock, Clint's stomach rumbled as he settled on a barstool next to Vince.

"Got your beer here," Vince said. "Next one's on you."

"You got it," Clint said, drinking the dark, warm beer appreciatively. "But I've got to have some food, quick. Mmm, what do you think that smell is?"

"I dunno," Vince sighed. "But I'm sure Gretchen will be glad to tell you."

Gretchen Krause was a plump, bosomy, hearty young woman with golden curls and sparkling blue eyes. She threw her arms around Clint, enveloping him in a smothering hug, and smacked him loudly on the cheek. "Clinton! Where have you been? It's been so long, I've missed you!"

Clint returned with a hug that was much more brotherly than Gretchen really wanted. "Hi, Gretchen. I was here just last Wednesday, don't you remember?"

She blinked. "No."

"Oh. Well, I missed you, too, Gretchen."

She beamed again. "You need to eat, you're getting skinny, Clinton." She always pronounced his name Clin-TON, and she always told him he was getting skinny.

"Yeah, I am really hungry. What's cooking that smells so good? I want that."

"That's *gulasch*, with *spätzle*," she told him brightly.

He hesitated, and he heard Vince beside him quietly chortling. "I want that," Clint repeated kindly.

"It's so good, *spätzle* and *gulasch*," she told him happily as she started toward the hinged leaf opening of the bar.

"Yeah, I'll have some of that too," Clint said.

She stopped and looked back at him, her brow furrowed. Slowly her face lit up, and she shook her finger at him. "Ahh! You're joking again, Clinton! What a tease you are!" She flipped up the leaf and went through a brightly lit door into the kitchen. From there they heard Gretchen talking loudly in German, presumably to her *mütter*. They didn't understand anything she said except *"gulasch"* and *"spätzle"* and "Clin-TON." Then they heard both mother and daughter laughing. Mütter Krause rarely came out into the bar at night, preferring to stay in the kitchen and cook and let Gretchen and her two sisters handle the patrons. It was said that if Mütter Krause came out of the kitchen at night with her iron soup spoon, every man in the place had better take to his heels.

Vince was shaking his head. "Gretchen really is a pretty girl, but she's got *Wiener schnitzel* for brains."

"She's sharp enough to handle about a hundred rowdy men," Clint argued, turning around to lean back against the bar and look around the room. "And she's got the best teeth, doesn't she? So nice when ladies have really good, straight, white teeth."

"I've never seen anything like you, Clint. You'd find something nice to say about the cheapest whore in the Pinch."

Clint shrugged. "Whoever she is, I'm sure she didn't decide that's what she wanted to be when she grew up. As far as I'm concerned, any woman's a real lady, given the chance."

"Is that what it is about you?" Vince said curiously. "Is that why all the women fall in love with you? Because you think they're all real genteel ladies?"

"Aren't they?" Clint said. "And besides, they don't all fall in love with me. That's dumb, Vinnie. I just treat them with respect and they appreciate it, that's all. You should try it sometime."

Indignantly, Vince said, "I treat ladies with respect! My mama would pinch my head clean off if I didn't!"

"You slapped Suzette on the behind the other night," Clint argued. "That's not exactly what I was talking about."

Vince rubbed his jaw, remembering. "She clipped me a good one, too. I won't make that mistake again, that's for sure. She could spar with you, Flint."

"Do not call me that stupid name," Clint warned, "or *you'll* be sparring with me."

Vince held up his hands in surrender. "Okay, okay, no need to get such a sore head. But speaking of flint, there's the man you have to thank for the nickname, over there. Did you see him?"

Clint craned his neck around to check the far back table. A four-man poker game was going on. All four of the men were well-dressed, if just a little flashy. One man wore a big, square diamond pinky ring that flashed whenever his hand moved, one had on a wide-brimmed low-crowned black hat with a hatband made of silver coins, one had on a loud purple-and-blue striped satin waistcoat. One of them, however, was discreetly dressed in black with a silvery-gray waistcoat and a plain white-cuffed shirt with gold cufflinks. Alertly, as if he sensed Clint's scrutiny, he looked up from his cards and scanned the room. Spotting Clint, he gave him a curt nod.

Clint turned back to Vince. "Buck Buckner himself, and dressed like a New York dandy. Those other fellows pilots, too?"

"Yeah, not as famous as Buck, but high water/high rollers like him," Vince said, sipping his beer. "It's funny how different so many of the new pilots are from the old breed, the rip-roaring snortin' old river rats. They're almost respectable. Guess making boatloads of money gives you respectability." Vince was twenty-two, the same age as Clint. He had been a roustabout on the Mississippi River wharf in Memphis since he was twelve. He knew every

riverboat, every pilot, every captain, and most of the fire-
men and deckhands.

They looked around for awhile, soaking up the genial
atmosphere. A continual low babble of conversation
sounded, punctuated by laughter and an occasional call
out to an acquaintance. It was a big square room, with
several long rectangular tables and two dozen round four-
seaters. The floor was hardwood, and Mrs. Krause and
Gretchen mopped it with vinegar every single morning.
The walls were plain oak boards, but they were cleaned
every other day and whitewashed once a month. Mütter
Krause's was the only saloon in Memphis with numerous
windows, and they were always sparkling and bright. The
long bar was plainly built, with no ornamentation, but it
was cleaned and then polished to a high gloss every morning with lemon oil. Even now Clint caught the tang of
lemon on the air.

The barroom was thick with tobacco smoke and the
earthy smell of beer. Clint didn't mind either. In saloons
men missed the spittoons far too often, and he found
that habit much more offensive. Mrs. Krause frowned
darkly upon missing the spittoons, and tobacco- and
snuff-chewing men found themselves buying cigarettes
or cigars from Gretchen to avoid her wrath. Also, Mrs.
Krause served liquor but had no tolerance for stumble-
drunks and certainly not mean drunks. Of course a man
could stumble around and pick a fight after having too
much beer, but somehow in Mütter Krause's a man found
he could sip a beer and have a couple of leisurely shots of
whiskey and enjoy the night just as much. Clint certainly
felt that way.

Though there were no cheap prostitutes or saloon girls
here, there were women. Men brought their wives; there
were some old women, probably charwomen; and there

were younger women that might be of questionable virtue but they were quiet and well-behaved. Gudrun Krause was no respecter of persons, but she was a respecter of the peace.

Clint heard a plate scrape the bar behind him, and a fresh waft of the delicious-smelling *gulasch* assailed his nostrils. But before he could turn around, Gretchen hurried around the bar and threw her arm across his shoulders. "Mütter says this is her best *gulasch*, for you. And she asks, will you come sing tomorrow night? She says she'll make her very special *Rheinischer sauerbraten* just for you. Please, please, Clinton?"

He hooked his arms around her waist, which delighted her. "Tell her I'll try. I've got rehearsal, you know, and tomorrow is the twenty-third, the last rehearsal. It might run kind of late."

"You'll be running really late," Vince put in, elbowing Clint, "attending Her Ladyship."

"Who is Her Ladyship?" Gretchen demanded, frowning.

"Don't pay any attention to him, he doesn't know what he's talking about," Clint assured her. "Happens to him a lot. It's kind of sad, really. I'll try to get here by nine, Gretchen. Maybe just a couple of songs."

She clapped her hands and kissed him with relish on the cheek again. "I love, love to listen to you sing, Clinton! I'll be at Court Square on Christmas Eve, too, Mütter says I may! I am throwing you lots of kisses!" Then she proceeded to kiss him twice on the cheek and once on the mouth before dancing away.

"'I am throwing you lots of kisses, Clin-ton,'" Vince mimicked in a falsetto voice. "'Course, I am throwing them a very short way, since my mouth is smack-up on yours!"

"Shut up," Clint said casually. "She's a really sweet girl. You ready for another beer? I am."

"Let me go tell Elza," Vince said hastily, jumping to his feet. "I'm getting tired of watching women slobber all over you."

"Hey, ask Elza to come over here for a minute, I need to ask her something," Clint called after him.

"Shut up," Vince said without turning around.

Grinning, Clint turned to his food with a will. He discovered that *gulasch* was very lean tender cuts of beef and thinly sliced potatoes simmering in a creamy mushroom sauce, and that *spätzle* was soft egg noodles drowned in butter and seasoned with parsley. Mütter Krause listed the menu on a big slateboard with the prices, but she only wrote the German names. Clint and Vince could only remember *Wiener schnitzel* because that was their favorite. If they didn't order that they had no idea what they were getting until it arrived. It didn't matter, though, because everything was piping hot and fresh and delicious. Clint loved spicy, piquant German food.

After a while Vince came back with two pewter tankards of beer, talking to not Elza but Buck Buckner. The riverboat pilot held a cigar and gestured as he talked. They reached Clint, who stuck out his hand. "Hello, Buck. Good to see you. Have a seat, if you don't mind watching me eat."

Buckner was the pilot of the *Lady Vandivere*, the largest and possibly the most elegant steamboat on the river. A four-decker, she had thirty luxurious staterooms, a ballroom, a dining room, and four salons. Buckner was thirty now, but he had piloted the *Lady Vandivere* since she was built seven years ago, when he was at the unheard-of age of twenty-three. Buckner, like many other pilots, had come to understand that if they were going to be rowdy, shouting, cursing, coarse brutes they would never pilot a passenger steamboat that, of course, was designed for the Quality.

These young men had set about to gentrify themselves, and they generally did a good job of it. Buck certainly looked like a gentleman, with carefully coiffed dark hair, clear features, dark eyes, and discreetly tailored suits. His air was one of competence and confidence. Only when he was gambling, which was his passion, did his predatory nature come through in the sharpness of his eyes and the hard set of his mouth. He looked like that now.

"I don't mind watching you eat, Hardin. I'm glad to see it. Going to need your strength, you know," he said, watching Clint's every bite. "How's the workout coming?"

Clint replied, "I haven't had much time to work out. I've been kinda busy."

Buckner frowned. "Singing your sweet little heart out, I guess. I don't think Mike the Hammer's going to be beat by you singing him to death."

"You know, I think Mike the Hammer should be named Mike the Hammer Head," Clint said. "That fellow has the hardest head I ever saw on a man. I know I landed three solid right crosses and he didn't even blink."

"He was too busy beating you to a pulp to blink," Vince rasped.

"Yeah, I remember," Clint said mournfully, wiping his mouth carefully and pushing his empty plate away. "It hurt, a lot."

Impatiently Buckner said, "Hardin, you fast-talked me into sponsoring you for this fight. I'd appreciate it if you'd let me know if Mike's going to knock you flat again. I'll know how to place my bets to recover my financing."

"No, no, don't worry. This time I've got a plan," Clint said grandly. "This time he goes down."

"Uh-huh," Buckner said darkly. "So what's the plan?"

"I'm going to keep him from hitting me in the ribs and gut until I can't breathe, and meanwhile I'm going to beat his head until he falls down," Clint said evenly. Though he was unaware of it, his jaw had tightened and his eyes had darkened to charcoal-blue, and he looked dangerous.

Buckner and Vince stared at him. Buckner said, "That's your plan. That's the whole plan?"

"That's it," Clint said shortly.

Now Vince and Buckner looked at each other. Vince said, "Don't look at me. I don't know anything about the plan. I didn't even know we had a plan."

Buckner considered Clint again. "He's smaller than you, but he's faster. A lot faster. That's how he got to you last time, he darted into your space and pummeled you until you were weak."

Clint nodded. "He did that, for eleven rounds. But that wasn't the reason he beat me. He beat me because I couldn't knock him out first, because like I said, his jaw is like an anvil."

"And you've figured out a way to keep him from tiring you out, and getting in a quick knockout," Buckner said thoughtfully. "How?"

A brief look of discomfort shadowed Clint's face, but when he spoke his voice was hard. "Just trust me, Buck. I'm going to beat him. Bet on me."

"All right, I will," Buckner said quietly, "but if you lose, you're going to owe me a lot of money."

Clint said nothing more, so Buckner went on, now in a light tone, "Good night, gentlemen. Clint the Flint Fist, get to bed early, you need your beauty sleep. Vinnie, keep him on the straight and narrow until Boxing Day, yeah?" With a few nods to acquaintances, he left.

Vince resumed his seat next to Clint and said glumly, "I feel so much better now that I know you got the plan. The one where you win and Mike the Hammer loses."

"Simple, yet elegant. Don't you think?" Clint drawled.

Vince studied him for a moment, and then a slow grin came over his face. "You're watching the clock. What's up? You have an appointment?" A somber Viennese regulator wall clock of walnut and ebony hung behind the bar, and Clint had been glancing at it off and on for the last hour.

"Something like that," he answered carelessly. "Hey, by my reckoning I now owe you two beers. You ready?"

"No thanks and don't change the subject. You've got a lady-in-waiting, don't you?" he punned. "C'mon, it's old Vinnie here. I'm your best friend, you can tell me. Is it Her Ladyship?"

"Vinnie, Mrs. Maxfield is a widow, living in her parents' home. Don't be a complete imbecile."

"Okay, okay, so it's not Mrs. Maxfield. Who is it then?"

"I didn't say it was a lady, I didn't even say it was a person," Clint rasped.

"So, what, got a train to catch at midnight?" Vince rolled his eyes. "I don't get it, Clint. I never have. Not about your women, I've seen enough of that all these years to see why they fall all over themselves over you. But you never talk about them, you never tell me one blessed thing. We talk about everything else under the sun, from religion to politics to music to when my little brother's eyeteeth came in, but you never tell me about your lady friends."

Clint sighed. "No, Vinnie, I know. You just don't see it, do you?" He looked directly into his friend's face and said in a low tone, "Gentlemen never tell, Vinnie. If you get one thing, get that. *Gentlemen never tell.*"

AT MIDNIGHT, AS CLINT went into a narrow dark alley just off Main Street, it started to snow. He paused for a moment to watch with pleasure. Of course there was no streetlight in this little nameless alley, but at the top of the stairwell just above him was a window that glowed a welcoming deep amber. The big powdery snowflakes seemed touched with gold against the lantern light. Humming *The Holly and the Ivy*, he went up the stairs and knocked on the door. A slender, fair woman with her shoulders bare and her hair flowing down to her waist opened it.

"Madame Chasseur, I know the hour is late," Clint said in a low voice, "but I find I am suddenly in need of some cosmetics and perfume. Something to take the chill of this snowfall away, perhaps?"

"Hmm, I see," she said thoughtfully. "As it happens, I not only have perfumes and cosmetics, but just today I received some soothing oil of sandalwood. It would, I think, be very good for a warming massage."

"Giving one? Or getting one?" Clint asked with very great interest.

"Both," she said, and pulled him inside.

The window's lantern-glow lit the snow all night.

CHAPTER THREE

Jeanne lit the last small white candle, the one on the very top of the Christmas tree. Then she and Marvel stood back to look. Jeanne glanced down at her daughter's joyous face, and thought tiredly that it had all been worth it, both the money and the work. Marvel had never looked so happy, or so well.

Marvel took Jeanne's hand and she automatically noted that her daughter's tiny hand was freezing cold. "Why don't we have a nice hot cup of tea?" Jeanne suggested, hurrying to put the copper water pot on the fire.

"That would be nice," Marvel said dreamily. She couldn't take her eyes from the tree. "I think this is the most beautiful Christmas tree ever."

It was a humble little tree, the top of a scrub pine that Roberty had managed to salvage for Jeanne from a wood-cutter's haul. The branches were spare but symmetrical, so it was a pretty cone shape. Jeanne had put it into a small bucket of water on their only table, a rough much-scarred oak worktable that had two bricks under one broken leg. For the last four nights she had brought home something to decorate the tree: first popped corn and cranberries to string together to make garlands, then squares of red and white felt to make stars. As promised, Roberty had brought a dozen little pinecones, and Jeanne and Marvel had fun making "snow" from laundry soap and starch and putting dollops on the top of the pine cones and the tree's branches. Finally, on this night of December 23, Jeanne had brought home the candles. With that final touch, the tree did look pretty.

They settled down on the mattress and bundled up, for it was very cold in their room despite the roaring fire. They had their cups of tea, and each of them had a sugar cookie that Jeanne had splurged and bought them. Afterwards Jeanne got her sewing kit and began darning her winter stockings, for with her work she was continually wearing out the toes and heels. Marvel said, "I can't wait for the Christmas Regale tomorrow. It sounds like it's going to be so much fun. Maybe everyone in town will be there!"

"I hope not," Jeanne said. "That would be a great crush, and I would probably lose you and have to wait for St. Nicholas to bring you home."

Marvel grinned. "Would he bring me down the chimney, do you think?"

"Of course he would. You don't think that St. Nick is just going to come up and knock on the door, do you?"

"No, he wouldn't do that. But you won't lose me, Mama, I know, even if everyone in Memphis is there." Suddenly, like a startled kitten, she yawned hugely. "I'm not sleepy!" she said quickly.

"Uh-huh," Jeanne said with disbelief, setting aside her sewing. "I think I'd better read the next part of our

Christmas book, and then to sleep with you, little girl. We have a very busy day planned tomorrow."

Jeanne had put together all of the verses about the birth of Christ, including the angel's visitation to Mary and then to Joseph, Mary's visit to Elizabeth and the *Magnificat*, the journey to Bethlehem, the story of the shepherds, and the story of the wise men, and had written them all in order in a small book. For a week she read passages every night, to end on Christmas Eve. As she finished the reading, ending with Joseph finding only a stable to shelter them, Marvel was already fast asleep. Jeanne hurried to blow out the candles on the Christmas tree, then bundled up again on the mattress and picked up her sewing. She sewed for a long time, for their clothes were old and worn and needed continual mending and patching. Her back ached, and her eyes watered, because she sewed only by the firelight. Candles and lanterns were luxury items.

She looked back up at the tree and a small smile played on her lips. Marvel had truly been entranced by the little tree. Jeanne had had so many misgivings about spending money on frivolous things like decorations for a Christmas tree. It was difficult for her, because every penny she made had to go for food, for fabrics for clothing, for shoes, for rent, for wood, for supplies like soap and needles and thread, and often for ointments and medications for Marvel when she got catarrh or a cough or skin irritations.

Two things, in particular, bothered Jeanne terribly about their poverty. One was that she couldn't afford to buy books or even papers and pen and ink. When Marvel turned five, Jeanne had bought *McGuffey's Primer*, and within three months Marvel knew it by heart. Then Jeanne had bought the McGuffey's first-year schoolbook. Along with a slate and some chalk, those two books had taken every little bit of her savings, for she desperately tried to put money aside every week, even if was only a penny or two. More than anything Jeanne wanted to buy a little cottage, their very own place. She knew that it would have to be a shack in the Pinch, but even that, if it belonged to them, would make Jeanne immeasurably happy.

For the thousandth time, she reflected that in their circumstances that would be the highest goal they could possibly attain; but when? Every time she managed to put even a few dollars aside it seemed that some new expense dogged her, either an emergency such as Marvel's illnesses, or a simple have-to, as when either she or Marvel wore out their shoes. Jeanne's leather half-boots were much-patched right now. She doubted that she would make it through the winter without having to buy a new pair.

Even as these melancholy thoughts went through her mind, she looked up to rest her eyes for a moment, and saw that it had begun to snow. Quietly she got up and, pulling her shawl closer, went to stand in front of the small four-paned window on the front wall. It faced the back of another shotgun shanty right in front of them, but now the dismal view had become enchanted, for each single puffy flake of snow drifted down on the lightest air and settled into picturesque little drifts at the corners of the panes. Jeanne watched for a long time. Then she bowed her head and whispered, "I know, Lord Jesus, that You're reminding me. There is beauty even here, and there is always hope. Thank You for the snow."

JEANNE OPENED ONE EYE reluctantly. She could hardly see, because thick curls had fallen out of her nightcap and covered her face. But dimly she made out her daughter, in her nightdress, doing a wild pantomime dance. Marvel's skinny arms were high above her head, her face was exultant, and she was hopping and leaping in circles. Not a single sound did she make.

Jeanne sat up and pushed away the curtain of curls from her eyes. "Good morning, little girl," she said with a yawn.

Marvel stopped dancing and ran to the mattress. "Mama! Mama, it snowed, it snowed! It's so pretty, come look!" Again she leaped up and began her dance, talking jerkily. "I tried—to be—quiet—so you could—sleep—"

"You didn't wake me up," Jeanne assured her. "Thank you, Marvel, you're a good girl." For the first time in four years, Jeanne was off work on both Christmas Eve and Christmas Day. She treasured the days she could sleep later than her usual rising time of five o'clock in the morning.

"Thank you. Come see, come see!" Marvel trilled.

"You are dancing in your bare feet," Jeanne said sternly. "And you are dancing without your warm robe. You may dance, Marvel, but only if you put on warm clothes."

"Yes, ma'am," she said, and danced to fetch her stockings and flannel robe. Jeanne, still yawning, got up and stirred the almost-dead coals and began the tedious process of building up a good fire.

They had planned their entire day. After breakfast they were going to both have hot sponge baths and wash their hair. It took hours for Jeanne's hair to dry, but not Marvel's, and Jeanne had promised to roll it up into little rags so that it would be curly for their outing that evening. The afternoon was taken up with preparing everything for Christmas dinner: roasting a small hen, boiling the giblets for gravy, baking cornbread and chopping up celery and onions for dressing, and chopping walnuts and raisins and dried apples for a mince pie. Jeanne had spent most of her tip money on the costly food.

When they finished it was time to get dressed for going to the Christmas Regale. Marvel didn't have a new dress, but Jeanne had washed and ironed her best blue wool, and the ruffles on her cotton pinafore were starched and crisp. She had brand-new cotton stockings that she wore under her wool stockings. Jeanne took down Marvel's hair and pulled the top away from her face, and it fell in soft little ringlets to her shoulders.

Jeanne wore one of her gray skirts and a plain white blouse, and all three of her petticoats, two cotton and one wool. Her hair, now dry, was gleaming darkly, and the curls were rich and springy. She pulled it up to the crown and secured it with four precious hairpins.

"Is it time to go?" Marvel asked, hopping from one foot to the other.

Jeanne smiled. "Just about. Here, it's time to put on your new things." For her birthday Jeanne had made Marvel a new mantle, for her old cape was threadbare and too short. The new one had a hood with a gold tassel, and a little capelet about the shoulders. It tied at the neck with a gold ribbon. Jeanne had also spent a lot of money to buy fine cashmere yarn instead of wool, a bright Christmas red color, and had knit Marvel a long head wrap and mittens. Marvel's skin was very delicate, and wool gave her a rash. Because Marvel always worried that Jeanne never got Christmas presents, Jeanne had also bought cheap wool yarn of the same color and had made herself a muffler like Marvel's. After they were completely dressed, they joined hands and looked each other up and down. "We look beautiful," Jeanne said complacently.

"You do, Mama," Marvel breathed. "But I'm not as pretty as you."

"Yes you are, darling," Jeanne insisted. "You're much prettier than I was when I was your age. And your new red muffler makes your eyes bright and your cheeks look rosy. Now, before we go, I have a little surprise for you."

"Really? A Christmas Eve surprise? What is it?"

Jeanne took down an old wooden box from the mantle and opened it. "There are going to be lots of nice things at the Regale to buy. Here is a dollar. You're going to have to see everything, and then decide what you'll spend your money on."

"A whole dollar?" Marvel breathed. "And I get to spend it all myself?"

"That's right," Jeanne said. "You can buy anything that you want. I'll help you with the arithmetic so you'll know what everything costs, and how much of your dollar it will take, and how much you'll have left. If you reach inside your mantle you'll find a little buttoned pocket on the right-hand side. You should put your dollar there. Now, are you ready?"

"Oh, yes, yes! Can we run?"

Jeanne laughed. "It's twelve blocks, and I think after a block or two we might end up sitting on the street curb, out of breath. But maybe we can skip a little."

They skipped down the narrow alley that opened onto Main Street, and Marvel agreed that perhaps they might walk the rest of the way.

"Everything looks so pretty!" Marvel exclaimed. "I love snow!"

Jeanne did too. It rarely snowed in Memphis, and when it did it was hardly ever enough to stick. But it had snowed all night, laying down a glittering snow-layer on the city that was about nine inches deep. The day had been bright, with a gleaming lemon-drop sun in a powder-blue sky. It was very cold, but there was no wind, for which Jeanne was grateful. When Marvel was in a cold draft she was prone to get ear infections.

As they made their way down busy Main Street, the sun drifted down in the west, and a twinkling silver twilight set in. Lamps were lit in the shop windows, cheery people hurried in and out of the stores, buggies and people on horseback thronged the streets. Marvel was positively goggle-eyed, and Jeanne had to hold her hand tightly, for she kept wanting to dart here and there to see wonders in the store displays.

"The shops will still be open when we come home tonight," Jeanne told her. "You can look at everything then, if you want to."

By six o'clock they reached Court Square, and a soft, quiet darkness had fallen. But Court Square was lit up like a child's most wondrous dreams. Hundreds of lanterns hung from the naked tree branches, paths had been swept through the snow, and as they entered the park they heard laughing and singing from everywhere. Lots of people were streaming in, and for a moment Jeanne was worried. The population of Memphis right now was about eight thousand, and if even half that many came to the four-block-square park it would be so crowded that they wouldn't be able to move, much less see anything. But then she saw that many volunteer sheriff's deputies, dressed in regular clothing but with stars on their chests, were handling the crowd. They stopped and turned away groups of drunken men, they kicked out the rowdy young boys that were not accompanied by an adult, they turned away all the prostitutes. As Jeanne and Marvel made their way into the square, Jeanne could see that the crowd was made up of respectable people, families and couples and some like her, unaccompanied women who were either widows or had husbands at work, with children.

"Oh my gunness!" Marvel exclaimed. "Mama, do you see that?"

"Yes, I do," she answered as they drew nearer to the center of the park. There, a twenty-foot-high Christmas tree had been put up, and it was trimmed with silver and gold tinsel and gold stars. At the top was a great silver star with a candle before it. The other candles on the tree were enclosed in glass boxes with silver and gold trim. A low railing surrounded the tree, and two deputies kept a sharp eye on it, for the decorations were very valuable, but Jeanne and Marvel pressed close. People surrounded it, and *oohs* and *aahs* were heard. Marvel was silent, her face upturned. Jeanne looked down at her, with the candlelight and lantern glow giving her normally pale complexion a soft golden glow, and thought that Marvel did look beautiful just then.

Beyond them the sounds of singing and tantalizing aromas beckoned, and they walked on. Strolling carolers sang, usually finely-dressed couples with songbooks. Groups of people stopped and sang along with them. Jeanne let Marvel lead her, and she went to a group of young couples that were singing "Hark the Herald Angels Sing." Beaming, Marvel sang along in her high piping voice, and Jeanne joined in, her voice a soft, true soprano. From every path the music of Christmas carols drifted, near and far. In the distance Jeanne could hear the cheery jingle of small bells, and wondered where they were coming from.

Marvel pulled on her hand, leading her to a side path where another group of singers was starting "It Came Upon a Midnight Clear." Jeanne bent down to tell Marvel, "The bandstand and the performers will be up there, and I would imagine there'll be lots of other things to see, too. Would you like to walk up that way?"

"Okay," she said, and skipped along in the direction Jeanne had pointed. On Jeanne's walk home from work the previous day she had gone one block out of her way to pass

Court Square, and she had seen them building a bandstand and putting up tables for vendors in the northwest corner, directly across from the County Courthouse. Now as they neared that corner they began to see the vendors surrounding the bandstand in a wide circle, and Marvel stopped in her tracks. Everywhere they looked was like a Christmas fairyland; each vendor's table had a white tablecloth and was decorated with evergreen branches and holly branches with bright red berries. Golden lanterns shone everywhere, lighting the scene with a festive glow. On the bandstand the St. Paul's Boys Choir, the young scrubbed-face boys dressed in ivory white robes, angelically sang carols and hymns.

But it was the vendors that were so enticing. Jeanne was delighted to see that there were no loud hawkers here, no butchers with naked geese and turkeys strung up, no monotonously chanting hucksters. Every table was laden with Christmas goods, and each of them looked like part of a glorious Christmas feast. The fruitseller had piles of oranges, lemons, limes, grapefruits, pears, and red and green apples. The confectioner's table had six great silver cornucopias holding sugarplums, butterscotch drops, coconut caramels, peppermint sticks, candied almonds, and chocolate bonbons. From the baker's table came a delicious scent on the sharp air of gingerbread men and sugar cookies. Next to that was the punch table, with spiced cider, eggnog, wassail, hot buttered rum, and cocoa, all warmed in great silver bowls over candles.

Marvel tried so hard to look in all directions at once that she became dismayed. Jeanne said, "I think that if we start over there, and work our way around past the bandstand and back here, we'll see everything."

"Ooh, and then I can decide what to spend my dollar on," Marvel said with relief.

They began walking around to each table, with Marvel staring with her great smudges of dark eyes at every single thing. The vendors, Jeanne noticed, were not the usual tradesmen, for they were dressed in fine clothing and were very well-spoken. Jeanne decided that they must be members of the City Council and their families. Each one of them smiled at the children and said, "Merry Christmas," to everyone passing by.

As they neared the corner of Court Street and Main Street, where the bandstand was, Jeanne finally saw where the jingling bells were coming from. They were sleigh bells. One of the council members had a great golden sleigh, and the City Council had hired men that morning to pile snow all along the four streets bordering the park. A cheerful man with red cheeks drove the sleigh, and the horse had small silver bells on his harness and bridle. Jeanne had never seen a sleigh, or heard sleigh bells before, and she was enchanted. Marvel was looking up at her, puzzled, and Jeanne picked her up. She was so small that Jeanne could easily hold her. "Is that really a sleigh?" she asked in wonder.

"It certainly is."

"How much do you think it would cost to ride in it?" Marvel asked. Several people were waiting at the corner for a ride around the four blocks of the square. Even as they watched, the driver cracked the whip just over the horse's back, and the sleigh began to glide along, bells merrily jingling.

"Would you like to go see how much?" Jeanne asked, and Marvel nodded. They made their way past the vendors and when they came to the little knot of people they saw a handlettered sign: *Sleigh Ride 25¢*. Jeanne explained a "quarter" to Marvel, and she nodded thoughtfully.

They went back and continued walking slowly along, looking at all of the Christmas wares. It took them more than half an hour to work their way around to the spot where they had begun.

"I don't suppose you saw anything you liked," Jeanne teased.

"Oh, Mama! You know I saw lots and lots of things I like," Marvel said. "It's so hard to know what to buy! I want some of *everything!*"

"Then it's a good thing you can't afford it, because you'd probably be a very sick little girl."

"I know," Marvel said with adult practicality. "I'll never forget that time, with the chocolate." She fell silent, her eyes roving over the tables. "And so if you get something to drink, you have to stand there and drink it, don't you? Because you have to return the cups. Maybe we could have some hot cider, and maybe one sweet and a gingerbread man, just before we go home?"

"That would be nice. And, Marvel, I want to tell you, you aren't to spend your money buying anything for me. I have money, too, so I'll buy my own cider and sweets."

Marvel brightened. "And the sleigh ride?"

"I'll pay my own twenty-five cents, and you will pay yours, and you'll still have seventy-five cents left."

"Oh, let's do that. All right, Mama?"

"I would love to!" Jeanne said happily.

They went back to the corner and had to wait for two couples ahead of them. Finally it was their turn and Jeanne and Marvel climbed up into the sleigh, which had a royal purple velvet-padded seat. The driver turned around and said, "And a very Happy Christmas to you two lovely ladies. Are you ready? Let's go, then!" He turned, snapped his whip, made a clicking noise, and said, "Whup, go along there, Solomon!" The sounds of creaking leather, sweet bells, and snow swishing along the runners of the sleigh filled Jeanne and Marvel with delight. The driver started humming "Deck the Halls" and they joined in, singing softly.

It was over far too soon, but Jeanne and Marvel agreed that it had been well worth the money. "I believe the performances are going to start in just a few minutes," Jeanne told Marvel. "Did you want anything to eat or drink before then?"

"No, but there is something I want," she said slyly. "If I buy one, will you buy one?"

"What?"

"Come on, I'll show you." Marvel pulled her by the hand to a small table that had bunches of holly piled on it. A sweet-faced young woman attended the table, which was fairly busy. Many gentlemen were buying sprigs of holly to put in their buttonholes or in their hatbands, and the ladies were pinning them to their corsages or trimming their bonnets with them. Marvel walked up to the table, pointed, and said, "May I have that, Mama?"

She was pointing to a small wreath made of green ivy with sprigs of holly trimming it. With surprise, Jeanne now saw that the young woman was wearing a like wreath on her head, trimmed with red ribbons. She looked around and saw many children wearing the wreaths, and with dismay she thought that no adults were wearing them. But then, here and there, she saw smiling young women who had removed their bonnets and were crowned with the colorful garlands.

"Yes, of course you may have one, if you like," she said hesitantly to Marvel.

"But will you have one, Mama?" she asked. "Please? Oh, you'd look so pretty!"

"But . . . I . . . ." Jeanne's voice faded away as she saw her daughter's imploring face. Jeanne could hardly think of herself wearing such a thing. It was whimsical, and showy, and she was neither of those things. She dressed dully, kept her hair severely pulled up, her eyes modestly downcast. She might have a type of prettiness, but in her mind Jeanne saw herself as a simple, plain woman. But Marvel looked so hopeful. "All right," she said reluctantly. "I suppose we'll look very festive." She pushed back her hood and unwound the crimson muffler from around her head, and Marvel did the same.

The young lady rose to place the wreaths on their heads. "I think you will both look very lovely," she said. "You, madam, have glorious hair. Here, I'll be very careful, so the holly won't stick you . . ."

Jeanne thought anxiously, *Now there is Marvel with a bare head, and it's so awfully cold . . . the tip of her nose is as red as her muffler, and soon her ears will be, too . . .* But then Jeanne chided herself, *Just stop worrying so much, and let go and have fun! This is for Marvel, and if she catches a chill, well, I'll just deal with it as I always have!* She went down on one knee and shifted Marvel's holly wreath a bit, then puffed up her curls and tied her muffler close around her neck. "You look like a mischievous little Christmas elf," she said.

Happily, Marvel said, "And you look like a Christmas queen with a holly crown."

Just then there was a clamor from the bandstand, for the boy's choir was leaving, laughing and shouting as they clattered down the steps of the stage. Then two stout men came up the steps, carrying what looked like a large wooden box. They set it down in the exact center of the stage and pulled open the two-sided front of the box to reveal a clever puppet theater.

"This is the puppet show, darling, of "A Visit from St. Nicholas." Do you want to get in close?"

"Oh, yes, ma'am!" she said excitedly. Now Jeanne took her hand and pulled her along, threading through the crowds until they were right up against the stage. There were long benches in front of the stage for dignitaries and important personages, but now the adults let the children line up around the stage in front of them. Jeanne got Marvel situated and then slipped back several steps so she wouldn't be standing in front of the children. A top-hatted man mounted the stage and in a warm, pleasant voice began, "'Twas the night before Christmas, and all through the house . . ."

CLINT BREATHED ON HIS wool-gloved hands and stamped to send some blood into his frozen feet. He was waiting on the courthouse steps for Eve Maxfield.

Finally he saw her carriage, and smartly the driver pulled up to the steps. Clint went and opened the door to hand Eve down. In a delicate cloud of flowery scent she alighted, and for a few moments Clint was bemused. She wore deep holly-green velvet and a velvet cape trimmed with that most royal of furs, ermine, a silvery-white with the signature black spots, which was the end of the white ermine's tail and the only color on them. Her hands were buried in a large ermine muff, and instead of a bonnet with the deep brim hiding the face, she wore a hat with a close-fitting leather crown and a wide band of ermine that framed her face. She looked magnificent. "Wow," he said gutturally. "Wow."

She smiled placidly. "Thank you. Please hurry, Clint. It is absolutely frigid out here." She led the way into the courthouse, followed by Clint and Eve's maid, a stolid, rather dour black girl named Beattie. Eve went past the grand staircase to a hallway behind, and walked into an office with an elaborate brass nameplate by the side of the door that read: *Judge Eugene Poynter, Esquire*.

Clint followed her in and looked around the room curiously. He had never been in a judge's office. It was large, and on every wall were books from floor to ceiling. An enormous expanse of a mahogany desk was in front of a double window that looked out onto Court Street. Along one wall was a five-foot-high fireplace, and a great fire roared and snapped. Just to one side of the fireplace was Eve's harp.

"Oh, no, no!" she said angrily. "Look where those idiots put my harp! Right by the fire! Hurry, Clint, come and move it right now."

Obediently, he snatched off the purple velvet cover, lifted it, and gently placed it away from the fire in front of the judge's desk. Her dark eyes stormy, Eve took off her gloves and practically threw them and her muff to her maid. Then she strummed the strings of the harp and groaned, and Clint winced. "It sounds like a cheap Irish fiddle," Eve fumed.

"Yeah, it's definitely sour," Clint agreed. "But you've got time to tune it, Eve. They haven't even started the puppet show yet."

Eve retorted, "I have time to tune it! Whatever makes you think I tune my own harp? Mr. Lilley does it for me. We'll have to find him."

"You know he's working with the boy's choir and the Choristers," Clint said. "Besides, how hard can it be? I've seen you tune a string or two when they went flat during rehearsal."

"Tuning one slightly flat string is very different from tuning the entire harp! I can't do it!"

Clint moved to take her hands. "You *can* do it, Eve. C'mon, I'll help you."

She stared up at him. His eyes were intent on her face, and a slight smile played on his lips. "Yes, I can do this," she said softly. Turning, she ordered, "Beattie, wait outside." The maid silently disappeared, closing the door behind her. "I certainly don't want anyone seeing me fumbling around doing this," she grumbled.

"Except me," Clint said cheerfully. "You won't fumble around."

Eve moved around to the back of the harp, where the tuning pins were. She had told Clint that once Mr. Lilley had been standing in front of the harp, reaching over to the tuning pins, and he had tuned one wire much too sharply. It had snapped and whipped out, leaving a thin red streak on his jaw. After that he had always stood behind to tune, and Eve had no intention of standing in front and having a wire mark her face or put her eye out. She touched the pin for middle C and plucked it.

"No, no, it's—*aaaahhhhh*," he sang a long note, and Eve tuned to it.

She went up an octave, found the correct peg, and plucked the string, turning the pin slightly to raise the tone. Frowning, she plucked the string again and again.

"You're plucking the wrong string, Eve," Clint said with a hint of impatience. "That's the D string."

Petulantly, Eve said, "I can't help it, it's all backwards. And I can't possibly reach over to pluck from the front, where it makes sense."

"Then just—oh, here, let me," Clint said, and went around to the back of the harp. He put his fingers on the correct tuning pin, then reached and plucked the correct string. Eve had not moved; he stood behind her, reaching around her to finger the harp strings. He seemed to have forgotten she was there. She stayed very still as he tuned, expertly and quickly. After a while she stole a look at his face; it was drawn up in fierce concentration, his eyes a dark midnight blue. With very small slow movements she moved back until she was against him, and she could feel his breath on her cheek.

"I didn't know you could tune a harp," she said softly.

"Neither did I. 'Course, you're not making it very easy on me. Kinda hard to concentrate. That perfume you're wearing is hypnotic." Still, he efficiently plucked strings, played chords, tried octaves.

"I wish I could hypnotize you, Clint," she said. "Then I could make you do whatever I wanted."

"Mmm-hmm," he said absently.

She decided to wait until he had finished, and it didn't take him long. He brushed the strings, and the familiar web of notes filled the air in the room. "Now try it," he said with satisfaction.

She turned and put her arms around his neck. "In a minute," she whispered. Then she pulled his head down and kissed him passionately. Clint responded with heat, for he was a full-blooded man and she was voluptuous. His hands went around her waist and he pulled her close to him. She moved to whisper, "My parents are going to a friend's plantation next week for a New Year's celebration. Will you come visit me, Clint?"

"Never say no to a lady," he said, and kissed her again.

They were still kissing when the door opened and Choirmaster Lilley popped in. "Ah—er—ah—" he said, blushing a fiery red.

Neither Eve nor Clint blushed. They merely let go of each other and turned to the poor little man. "Yes, we're ready, Choirmaster," Clint said with a devilish glint in his eye. "As you can see, we're already warmed up."

Without a word, Mr. Lilley whirled and almost ran out the door.

Eve said, "You're wicked."

Clint said, "Madam, you would know."

CHAPTER FOUR

The Christmas puppet show was wonderful, and when it was over the children shouted, "More! More! Again, again!" but the puppeteers took their bow, men came to remove the theater, and the narrator made his bow and left the stage. The children rejoined their parents, and the City Council members, judges, dignitaries, notables, and wealthy planters and their families all filed into the front of the stage to take their seats on the benches that had been brought out from the courtroom.

Marvel came running back to Jeanne, her eyes shining. "What's next, Mama?"

"The Calvary Choristers are going to sing for us, and it's my understanding that they are very good, as good as a professional opera troupe," Jeanne said, taking her hand. "Would you like to go get close to the stage, over on the side there by the stairs?" Of course no one could stand at the front of the stage and block the view of the important persons seated on the benches.

Ruefully, Marvel looked at the wide empty front expanse of the bandstand. "Angus says that we call them 'swells.' He wouldn't tell me what they call us."

"Angus O'Dwyer is ten years old and he doesn't know everything," Jeanne said dryly. Taking Marvel's hand she said, "Come with me. I'll get us close to the stage and hold you up so you can see."

The bandstand floor was four feet high, which was about ten inches over Marvel's head. Jeanne wormed her way through the gathering crowd until she had a spot right at the corner, with only three people in front of her. She hoisted Marvel up to rest on her hip, just as she had done when she was a toddler.

The Choristers were coming onto the stage, beautifully dressed women in wide hoop skirts and frilly bonnets, and men in fancy double-breasted topcoats with brass buttons and beaver top hats. Behind them came three violinists, and Jeanne was a little surprised to see that they were dressed in workingmen's rough clothing. Last was a little doll-like girl with golden curls, dressed in maroon velvet and carrying a flute. She took a seat on one of the four chairs for the instrumentalists and her feet didn't touch the ground. The violinists strummed a few strings, the little girl made a couple of experimental notes. Then the choirmaster in a white surplice came to stand in front of the group.

He held up his slender baton for long moments, and then at his signal the choir started singing "It Came Upon a Midnight Clear." After a few bars Jeanne and Marvel exchanged satisfied looks. The Calvary Choristers were indeed good musicians, the men's voices deep and sure, the women's clear and clean. Even the three violinists, who looked as if they would be more at home fiddling a romp in a saloon, played well. The sweet notes of the flute were perfect.

When they were on the next-to-last stanza of the song, Marvel and then Jeanne were momentarily distracted by a small stir at the steps. They couldn't see exactly, but people moved away from the steps, murmuring slightly. Then the hymn ended, and a man walked up the steps carrying a great purple-clad triangular-looking thing, bearing it easily aloft as if it were a standard. Behind him came a proud-looking lady sumptuously dressed in velvet and furs, and her maid followed behind, her head down. The crowd murmured in low tones, and Jeanne heard someone say, "It's a harp."

The man set the harp down and began to untie the gold satin ties that held the fabric to the harp's shape. Jeanne studied him curiously. He was a muscular man, with dark flashing eyes and rugged features. He wore a shabby but clean brown wool jacket, canvas duck trousers, and sturdy brogans. Instead of a hat he wore a dark flat cap. At first glance, from his dark features, he seemed a looming, brooding man, but he wore a cheerful bright red muffler with a big sprig of holly tucked into it, and when he looked up at the lady he smiled, and looked warm and pleasant. She stood watching behind, like a distant queen, her hands tucked into her opulent white fur muff.

The man stood and pulled the velvet casing off, and it was a grand concert harp, the pillar almost six feet tall and covered with gold leaf. The pillar was topped with an elaborate golden crown. He knelt to check the pedals, and for the briefest moment he glanced around the crowd. When he saw Marvel, his eyes crinkled a little at the corners, and he winked at her. Marvel's eyes widened and then she giggled. Now the man looked straight into Jeanne's eyes. She met his gaze squarely, but then grew a little uncomfortable and felt herself blushing. But she didn't turn away from him. For some odd reason, she felt drawn to him. But he gave her a quick nod, then looked down at his task.

"He winked at me, did you see?" Marvel whispered to her, for the crowd was waiting and watching quietly, with only low murmured words.

"I did see. I'm sure it's because he thinks you're the prettiest girl here," Jeanne whispered back.

"Do you think he's married to that beautiful lady?"

Jeanne almost laughed aloud. "No, darling, they aren't married. I think he's probably just carrying her harp."

"But—" Marvel started to say, but just then the man stood and retrieved a small padded stool from someone at the foot of the steps that was holding it up. He placed it behind the harp's pillar, then turned to the grand lady. Slowly she took her hands out of her muff, handed it to her maid, took off her gloves and handed them, then raised her arms to pull the ermine cape back off her shoulders. Taking the man's hand, she delicately took a seat on the stool and pulled the harp to rest on her shoulder.

The man turned, walked to the center of the stage where he stood alone, took off his cap and held it with both hands in front of him, then turned and nodded to the lady. Soft haunting harp music wafted delicately on the still air, and the man began to sing.

> *Ave Maria! Gratia plena*
> *Maria Gratia plena . . .*

At the first sound of his voice, Jeanne, and many others she was sure, took a sharp indrawn breath. She felt Marvel gasp. His voice was resounding, rich, and powerful. It rolled over them, and they forgot the cold. He sang into a profoundly reverent silence.

Jeanne didn't understand the ancient Latin words, but it made no difference. Whoever or whatever this man was, his voice was a gift from God. The sweet strands of the harp were his angels' accompaniment. The tenor notes soared, then became fathomless depths, and then the last "Ave Maria" was held so long and with such unwavering strength that now Jeanne almost forgot to breathe. A few last whispers from the harp, and the song was done.

Heavy silence reigned in Court Square for long moments, and the man bowed his head. Then the applause began, and men's hoarse shouts of "Bravo! Bravo!"

Marvel turned and in the cacophony Jeanne could not hear her but saw her mouth, "Gunness!"

Jeanne nodded. "Gunness, indeed!"

"Mama, what is that?" Marvel asked with wonder.

Jeanne looked at the vendor's table, where she had seen big round balls of Christmas puddings wrapped up in muslin. But now that the entertainment was over and everyone was making their final purchases, the smiling matron attending the table had unwrapped a pudding. She placed a sprig of holly on the top, poured brandy all around it, and then lit it. Now the sumptuous thick ball glowed with a ghostly blue light. "That's a Christmas pudding, darling one. It takes several days to make, and you eat it at the end of Christmas dinner."

Marvel started to say something, but her eyes focused up beyond Jeanne's shoulder and her eyebrows raised. Jeanne turned, and to her surprise, she saw George Masters bowing low. She had forgotten that he'd said he would see her at the Regale. In fact, she had dismissed it as mere politeness.

"Mr. Masters, good evening," she said.

"Good evening, ma'am," he said. "I am so happy that I finally found you, Je—ma'am."

Jeanne smiled a little at his discomfort. It was an odd situation; at work all of the maids were called by their given names, but in polite company it was considered boorish for a gentleman to call a lady by her first name. "I am happy to see you too, Mr. Masters," she said warmly. "May I introduce to you my daughter, Miss Marvel Bettencourt. Marvel, this is Mr. George Masters."

Marvel made a neat little curtsey and peered up at him. "Mr. Masters? We prayed for you the other night. Well, we didn't really pray *for* you but we prayed *about* you because you gave my mama some money. That was you, wasn't it?"

Master's firm features were ludicrously twisted with confusion after this speech, and he stuttered, "Um—ah—yes, Miss Marvel, I suppose it might have been me. Uh—Miss—that is, it is Mrs. Bettencourt, I'm sure—isn't it? Of course it is! It's just that I saw you, and I thought that she was your sister."

Far from being discomposed at all this, Jeanne was amused. "No, she is my daughter, Mr. Masters. I am widowed."

"Angus says that men always think Mama's my sister," Marvel told Masters disdainfully.

"Angus?" he blurted out.

"Angus O'Dwyer, ten years old, man of the world," Jeanne told him.

Masters stared blankly at Marvel, then asked Jeanne, "And how old is she?"

"She takes after me, I suppose," Jeanne answered lightly. "She looks younger than she really is, at heart."

"I'm six years old now," she told Masters proudly. "I'm going to school in March. Mr. Masters, have you ever eaten a Christmas pudding that's been on fire?"

"Have I—well, yes. That is, not an entire pudding, but a portion, yes, I have." He glanced up at the table, where several people had now gathered and were purchasing their puddings. "They're really very good, Miss Marvel."

Marvel transferred her steady gaze to Jeanne, who said encouragingly, "You may buy one if you wish, Marvel."

Marvel skipped over to the table, and they heard her reedy high voice ask, "May I see that one, please?"

Masters smiled at Jeanne. "She's an intriguing lady, like her mother."

"Thank you, sir," Jeanne said, nervously raising her hand to touch the holly and ivy garland. She felt very self-conscious wearing it.

He studied her gravely. "And may I compliment you on your holly and ivy, Mrs. Bettencourt. It suits you particularly well. I've never seen your hair before, it's lovely." He held out his arm. "Would you allow me to walk you around the displays? They have some fine wares here."

Jeanne lightly rested her hand in his arm and they walked slowly toward the table where Marvel was still considering all the puddings. "You may, because for the third time tonight we are going to each and every table to peruse each and every item on it. I gave Marvel some money, you see, and told her she was responsible for choosing how to spend it. She's a most careful shopper."

"I see," he said gravely. "Then I suppose it wouldn't be quite the thing for me to offer to buy you ladies some Christmas gifts."

Jeanne replied sharply, "No, sir, that would not be quite the thing, for many reasons."

Instead of being taken aback, George Masters looked pleased. "Thought not," he said under his breath. Marvel ran to them then, holding the wrapped pudding in both hands. "This is the fattest one," she said. "I looked at all of them. Now—" she looked uncertainly toward the fruit vendor, and seemed confused what to do with her bulky burden.

Masters made a small bow and said, "Miss Marvel, may I carry your pudding for you?"

"You wouldn't mind?" she asked.

"Not at all, it would be my honor." She handed it to him, and he continued walking with Jeanne, following Marvel. It should have been funny, Jeanne thought, but he was a man of dignity, tall, with a proud posture, and somehow he didn't look silly cradling the muslin ball.

He looked down at her, saw her perusal, and smiled a little. "I don't feel a bit awkward. I've seen men carrying bigger and more ludicrous packages, following their ladies. And at the rate Miss Marvel is going, I think I may be carrying other things before the night is ended. Would that be all right with you, Mrs. Bettencourt? May I escort you and Miss Marvel this evening?"

"Why—yes, I suppose so, Mr. Masters," Jeanne said, a little perplexed. She had thought that he would say a kind word or two to her and Marvel and then return to his friends.

He continued quietly, "For a long time now I've been hoping that we might meet on a social basis. It would never have done for me to have asked to see you while you were working. But tonight is different."

"But it's not," Jeanne said abruptly. "We are far from meeting on a social basis, Mr. Masters. At least, on an *equal* social basis. And there is nothing different about tonight. I am still a chambermaid, and you are still—"

Curiously, he asked her, "Yes? I'm a what?"

"A—a swell," she finished defiantly.

He stared at her, and she stared back at him, and then suddenly Jeanne giggled and George Masters chuckled. "I'm so sorry, Mr. Masters," Jeanne finally said. "I'm afraid that came out all wrong. I'm the one who sounded like the worst snob, only in reverse."

"You're right," he agreed lightly, "but I forgive you."

They followed Marvel around, talking about the foods and decorations and the Choristers' performance, until Marvel had made all of her purchases. George Masters ended up carrying a Christmas pudding, two oranges, a gingerbread man, and a handful of butterscotch drops.

"Mrs. Bettencourt, please allow me to buy you ladies a hot drink," he pleaded. "I'm cold, and I know you must be, and I should very much like to shift all of Miss Marvel's purchases so that I'm carrying them more carefully."

Jeanne said evenly, "I believe it's time for us to go home, Mr. Masters. You've been very kind, and I will take Marvel's purchases now."

"But I hoped you would allow me to escort you home, Mrs. Bettencourt. It's the least you can do to oblige me, you know, after calling me a swell," he said insistently.

Marvel was listening carefully to the conversation, her curious gaze fixing on Masters and her mother as they spoke. Now she announced, "We live in the Pinch, Mr. Masters. It's a long way."

"Marvel, I must remind you about speaking out of turn," Jeanne said more sharply than she intended. Marvel's face fell and Jeanne added gently, "It's all right, darling, it's just that there's no need for Mr. Masters to walk us all the way home. He is here with a group of friends, and I'm sure he has other plans for the evening."

"I'm sorry," Marvel said, both to her mother and to Masters.

After a cautious glance at Jeanne, he said gallantly, "Miss Marvel, I think you'll learn very soon that pretty ladies need never apologize to gentlemen. Mrs. Bettencourt, my plans for the evening are to return to my lonely room at the Gayoso House Hotel. You would really be granting me a favor if you'd stay a little longer and raise a glass of wassail with me. Then, when you're ready, I'd be happy to take you home in a carriage that a friend has placed at my disposal."

Jeanne was very reluctant, for to her the situation was absurd. Their shanty wasn't even on a street, it was bordered only by alleys. For her and Marvel to be driving up in a fine carriage, with a fine gentleman, and they in their shabby gray woolens, seemed a silly satire.

But then she saw Marvel's upturned face, her pleading expression and hope-filled eyes, and she relented. "Thank you, Mr. Masters, that would be very kind of you."

He smiled. "On the contrary, Mrs. Bettencourt, it would be my pleasure."

They went to the punch table, where Jeanne and Marvel decided on hot spiced cider, while Masters had a cup of steaming wassail. He knew the couple attending the table, and said, "Look here, Darnley, Miss Marvel has several valuable purchases here and I'm having a hard time carrying them properly. Would you have a bag or something back there we could use?"

After much discussion, it was decided that Marvel's treasures could be made into a parcel with a big square of brown paper, and they went to sit on the benches and arrange everything properly. Then Marvel decided that the gingerbread man might get crushed, and she wanted to carry it. But Master's gallantry was such that he went and snagged a piece of muslin from the Christmas pudding lady, wrapped it up, and stuck it in his pocket. They all sat down on the now-empty benches to finish their drinks.

"You're a very resourceful man, Mr. Masters," Jeanne said lightly.

"Nothing is too much trouble to make beautiful ladies happy," he said. "Now, I see that you've finished your cider. Would you like more, or perhaps something else? The

Courtier is staying open until midnight. It would give me very great pleasure if you would join me for a late supper."

Jeanne looked at him incredulously. The Courtier was a lavish, very expensive restaurant on Court Square. Did he really think that she and Marvel would dare go into that restaurant, dressed as they were? It was all very well for him. He was wearing the usual outfit for wealthy men, a fine worsted topcoat, black frock coat and satin vest, and a top hat. She and Marvel looked like his scullery maids. What was he thinking?

Then she saw Marvel yawn hugely and blink heavily as she stared down into her silver cup of cider. "I appreciate your offer, Mr. Masters, but as you can see my daughter is practically asleep already. It's very late, it's time we went home."

He looked disappointed, but he merely bowed slightly and said, "Then please wait right here, Mrs. Bettencourt. I'll go get the carriage, and I'll be back very shortly."

She watched him walk toward Court Street, with his confident slow stride and straight back and shoulders. What was all this about? In other men she had met at the Gayoso, she would have been very suspicious, thinking that they were just trying to seduce her. But she had never gotten that uncomfortable feeling from George Masters. The only thing she had ever observed in passing about him was that he seemed a little too kind and solicitous to what was, after all, merely a servant. Perhaps that was it; he was just a kind man who was charitable at Christmastime.

Beside her, Marvel finally surrendered and fell against Jeanne's shoulder, sound asleep. Jeanne took the empty cup out of her limp hand and put her arms around her. In minutes George Masters returned, smiling a little as he saw them. "The carriage is just over there. May I carry her?"

"No, no, thank you," Jeanne said hastily. "I'm accustomed to it." She stood up and pulled Marvel up with her, as lightly as if she were a rag doll. Marvel never woke up.

A barouche box was waiting for them, with a driver in a gray top hat and many-caped driving coat. Masters helped Jeanne get Marvel inside and get Jeanne seated, then asked, "How do I direct the driver?"

"Tell him to go up to the intersection of Main Street and Overton," Jeanne said. "That will be fine."

Masters instructed the driver, then climbed in to sit across from Jeanne and Marvel. When the coach started, Marvel stirred, then woke up. "Mama, you were going to let me sleep? When we're riding in a carriage?"

"I don't know what I was thinking," Jeanne said. "But now you're awake. And apparently," she added with a knowing look at Masters, "Mr. Masters has told the driver to go slowly, so that you can see everything." They were going as slowly as the horse could possibly walk. Masters looked slightly bemused.

Though it was after ten o'clock, most of the shops on Main Street were still open and doing a merry business. The strolling carolers had moved from Court Square to the business section, the snow was still glistening and pretty, the night was cold but clear, the air sharp and bracing. Marvel turned to sit on her knees so she could see out the window better.

George Masters seemed to be struggling to find words. His eyes kept going to Marvel, then back to Jeanne. "Um, Mrs. Bettencourt, I can't tell you how very much I've enjoyed your company this evening. And Miss Marvel's, of course."

"And we have enjoyed yours, Mr. Masters," Jeanne said politely.

"No, I mean I have truly enjoyed our time together," he said insistently. "And I would like—that is, I hope—if you would be so kind—I mean—"

Marvel suddenly sat up stiffly and said, "Mama, look! There's the Singing Man! Right there, walking with those other men! Hello, hello!" she called loudly.

"Marvel, please," Jeanne said, flustered. "Don't shout. Ladies never call out to men. Especially men they don't know."

"But he winked at me," Marvel said in a small voice. "He would know me again if he saw me, I know." She came up to a kneeling position, put her mittened hands against the windows, and stared out. She thought she saw the tall dark man look at her and smile.

"No, he wouldn't. And don't wave." Jeanne said to Masters, "I apologize, sir. Marvel was very taken with the tenor soloist with the Calvary Choristers."

"He's good enough for the stage," Masters agreed. "His rendition of 'Ave Maria' and 'O Holy Night,' with only the harpist's accompaniment, was very powerful. It sort of overshadowed the rest of the performance, I thought."

"I thought the same," Jeanne exclaimed. "The Choristers, as a choir, are the best I've ever heard, but the man was outstanding. And the lady harpist was very proficient, and a fine soprano herself."

"And so beautiful," Marvel sighed. "She looked like a queen."

With amusement Masters said, "I'll have to tell her that you said that, Miss Marvel. She'll be pleased."

Marvel turned to him. "You know her, that lady?"

"I am acquainted with her, yes. Her name is Mrs. Eve Poynter Maxfield. Her father is a judge here in Memphis." He faltered a little as he saw the stiff expression on Jeanne's face. "My family has known the Poynter family for many years."

And here it is, the name dropping, Jeanne was thinking. She turned to look neutrally out the window. An awkward silence prevailed.

But Marvel didn't know it was an awkward silence, and she told Masters, "My mama and I said that when the Singing Man sang "Ave Maria," it made us both forget how cold it is." She said it all together, "avaymaria."

"It is cold," Masters said with emphasis, his eyes on Jeanne's profile. "May I ask you ladies what part of the Regale you enjoyed the most?"

Marvel readily answered, "The puppet show. And the Singing Man. And the huge Christmas tree. And the oranges. And the sleigh ride, I almost forgot! But this is just as nice, in the carriage." She turned back to stare out the window again.

"Mrs. Bettencourt?" Masters said quietly. "I hope you, too, are finding the carriage ride as nice as the sleigh ride."

Jeanne answered, "I admit it is very pleasant, riding home in such a fine carriage. I'm sure Marvel and I will always remember it."

"But you don't have to remember it," Masters blurted out. "No, that's not what I meant. What I mean is, it doesn't have to be the only time. We can do it again. We can ride in carriages a lot."

"I suppose you can," Jeanne said quietly. "But Marvel and I don't have many carriages at our disposal."

He looked extremely frustrated, and started to reply, but just then the carriage came to a stop. Jeanne looked out the window and saw the tawdry little shacks of the Pinch. "Here we are, darling," she said brightly to Marvel.

George Masters opened the door, kicked down the steps, and handed Jeanne and Marvel down, looking around with his eyes narrowed. "Is that your house, Mrs. Bettencourt?" he asked warily, nodding to a weather-beaten clapboard cottage directly on the corner of Main and Overton.

"No, we live a little farther on," Jeanne said vaguely. She took Marvel's hand and held out her right hand to Masters. "Thank you very much for such a wonderful evening, Mr. Masters. It was so kind of you."

Quickly he took her hand, bent over it, then clasped it in both of his own. "I assure you, Mrs. Bettencourt, the pleasure was all mine, and a great pleasure it has been. But please, you must allow me to walk you to your door."

Jeanne gently pulled her hand free. "No, that's not at all necessary. Would you hand me Marvel's parcel please?"

"And my gingerbread man, please, from your pocket," Marvel added.

But George Masters ignored her and frowned at Jeanne. "Ma'am, I'm afraid I must insist. I am not at all comfortable with leaving you on the street like this, in this place."

Jeanne said evenly, "Mr. Masters, I walk to work every day from this street, and I walk home every night to this neighborhood. This is my home. I appreciate your consideration, but surely you must see that it's misplaced."

"No, I don't see that at all," he said quietly. "But I don't wish to upset you, ma'am, of all things. Here is your package, and Miss Marvel, here is your gingerbread man. I hope that you both will have a very merry and happy Christmas. Thank you so much for allowing me to share in your Christmas Eve."

Marvel curtseyed and said formally, "Thank you, Mr. Masters, for taking such good care of me and my mama. You're a really nice man."

Now Jeanne was feeling perfectly horrible, so she mustered the warmest smile she could and said, "Mr. Masters, you have truly made our Christmas Eve a wonderful time, and I thank you. Merry Christmas to you and yours, and good night."

She and Marvel turned and walked in silence. Jeanne was very aware that he stood watching them until they went down the block and disappeared into the alley toward their house. Marvel sighed deeply and said, "See, Mama, I told you. You just don't like men."

And again Jeanne wondered if she was right.

THEY AWOKE TO THE sound of church bells, for all churches had services or mass on Christmas Day. Immediately Marvel ran to the tree, for there were two packages for her, wrapped in plain brown paper and decorated with small felt white and red stars. "Mama, may I open them now?"

"Mmph, just a minute," Jeanne said sleepily. "My eyes aren't even open yet."

"Okay," she said, then went to stand on tiptoe to look out the window. A cheerful golden sun in a periwinkle-blue sky shone down on the snow blanket, making it glitter as if it were strewn with diamonds. It was still bitterly cold, but there was no wind. It was peaceful.

"Why don't you go ahead and light the candles on the tree while I make us some tea?" Jeanne said, tending the fire. "And then you can open your gifts."

"But Mama, we have to wear our holly crowns!" she said excitedly.

"All right, we will," Jeanne said. She had put them in a bucket of water to keep them from wilting, and she went to take them out and dry them on a rag.

Marvel stood on an upturned bucket to light the candles with long thin pine sticks. Then they put on their garlands, got their tea, and settled onto their mattress. Jeanne said, "Open this one first."

It was not one but two long-sleeved chemises that Jeanne had made for Marvel from the Gayoso pillow slips. "Oh, thank you, Mama. They are so soft! May I wear one to church?"

"Well, if you wear a dress over it," Jeanne said. "Go ahead, darling, open the other."

It was a real, store-bought, German-made lady china doll. She had a glazed porcelain head with molded hair painted black, wooden limbs padded with kid, little porcelain hands, and painted blue eyes and a small red cupid mouth. Her full-skirted white dress was made of embroidered eyelet trimmed with delicate lace. For long moments Marvel was speechless, her dark eyes as round as buttons.

"Oh my gunness!" she breathed. "She's beautiful! Thank you, thank you, Mama!"

"You're very welcome, Marvel," Jeanne said happily. "She is very pretty, isn't she? Just like you. What are you going to name her?" Jeanne had made Marvel a rag doll, and because Marvel fancied the name of the owner of Gayoso House, Robertson Topp, she had named her doll Mrs. Topp. She had always been very insistent that Jeanne call the doll by her name.

Now Marvel frowned with concentration. "I think," she said slowly, "I'll name her Avaymaria."

"Avaymaria?" Jeanne repeated with amusement. "That's a nice name for a grand lady."

Marvel touched the doll's head, smoothed her hair, felt of the dress. "Mama, did you know the words to that song?"

"No, darling, it was in Latin. I do know that it's actually two words: Ave Maria, and that means Hail, Mary."

"Mary, Jesus' mother?"

"That's right."

Marvel nodded, her eyes still on the doll. "Why did you say that the Singing Man couldn't be married to the Harp Lady?"

Jeanne explained, "I could tell by their clothes that the lady was rich and the man was poor. Rich people don't marry poor people."

"Ever?"

Jeanne hesitated. She always tried to tell Marvel the exact truth, as much as she could comprehend. "I suppose that it does happen sometimes, but not very often. Rich people just usually don't want to marry someone that is poor, because they think that the poor person just wants to marry them for their money."

Marvel digested this for a few moments, then asked, "Is Mr. Masters rich?"

"I think so. Yes, I know he is."

Now Marvel looked up to meet Jeanne's eyes squarely. "So you don't like him because we're poor and he's rich?"

Flustered, Jeanne said, "No, that's not why—I mean, I guess I didn't explain it properly. I think—that is, Mr. Masters thinks—oh, never mind, Marvel. This is something about adults that you're not old enough to understand yet. And besides, we were talking about rich people and poor people getting married, and that has nothing to do with me and Mr. Masters. In fact, you need to just forget about Mr. Masters, and the Singing Man, too, because you probably won't see either of them again."

Marvel looked downcast. "Yes, Mama."

Jeanne thought, *What's wrong with me? Making my own child unhappy on Christmas morning? But it's not my fault, if she questions these things I have to tell her the truth!*

She reached over and put one finger under Marvel's chin to lift her head. "My darling girl, we're happy, aren't we? You're not sad about Mr. Masters, are you?"

Marvel gave her a sunny smile. "No, Mama. If you're happy, then I am too."

Jeanne nodded. "I am happy, Marvel. The Lord has blessed us so much this Christmas. We have a home, and good food, and nice presents!"

"Like snow, and a Christmas pudding, and Avaymaria," Marvel agreed, hugging the doll. "Thank you, Mama, and thank you, Baby Jesus."

"Yes," Jeanne said quietly, "thank you, Lord Jesus."

CHAPTER FIVE

Jeanne went back to work the day after Christmas, a sparkling and warm day that immediately melted the heavenly snow. Grimly, she realized that her boots were so muddy that Mrs. Wiedemann would never allow her to come into the hotel, and Jeanne would have to sit down outside, take them off, and clean them thoroughly. She picked up her pace so she wouldn't be late. When she stepped off the Main Street boardwalk to cross Union Avenue, she felt the cold muck of the street slide greasily up into her left shoe. The patch on the sole had worn through. Three dollars for new boots. Jeanne could have cried. But she didn't; she squared her shoulders, cleaned her boots, and reported to Mrs. Wiedemann at the service door.

"Only thirteen rooms in the whole hotel," Mrs. Wiedemann told her, "so today only you and Agatha work." She handed Jeanne her list of rooms to clean.

Jeanne collected her supplies and went up to the third floor. She was surprised to see that George Masters was still in residence. Christmas was a time for families to be together, and even the most hard-nosed businessmen gave up work travel to go home for the holidays. Then Jeanne realized that Masters had said something about being alone on Christmas Eve. *I didn't even think about that, or ask him about it . . . How unkind of me . . .* She determined that she would be warm and cordial to him, and she would find a way to ask him about his family and his plans for the remainder of the holidays, and to let him know she wished him well. Jeanne was fairly sure that wasn't exactly the impression she had given him on Christmas Eve.

She knocked on his door and called out, but no welcoming answer came. She was strangely crestfallen, and went into the empty room feeling disappointed. But staunchly she told herself, *Jeanne, you are a plain fool. What did you expect?* Vigorously she began her cleaning, determining not to entertain one more moment's consideration of George Masters.

Only one guest was resident in Jeanne's list of rooms, and he gave her a belated Christmas one-dollar tip, which cheered her up. One-third of a pair of new leather half-boots. On her last room the guest had already checked out, so she left the door open. When she was almost finished she was surprised to look up and see Mrs. Wiedemann come into the room with a gentleman.

"Jeanne? This gentleman needs to speak with you," she said curtly, and left.

Jeanne stood still, her window-cleaning rag in hand, and studied him. He was a man of average height and build, nattily dressed in a gray suit. He had an unassuming air and countenance, with a neat, trim graying mustache and beard and sensitive long fingers grasping a top hat. But his eyes were dark and his gaze intense as he regarded Jeanne. "Good day, Mrs. Bettencourt," he said, nodding his head. "My name is Nathaniel Deshler. I apologize for the unorthodox manner of making your acquaintance, but under the circumstances it was all I could do."

"Oh? And what circumstances are those?" Jeanne cautiously asked.

"I am an attorney, and one of my clients has a legal matter that concerns you, Mrs. Bettencourt."

Jeanne blanched. "What? Am I in some sort of trouble?"

"No, no," he said, shaking his head and coming closer to her. "Not at all, ma'am. I am so sorry, this is a rather complicated situation, and I'm handling it badly. Please, could we sit down for just a moment?" He motioned toward the tea table and chairs.

"Yes, I suppose," Jeanne said reluctantly.

When they were seated Deshler said, "Mrs. Bettencourt, I will tell you plainly all that I can. My client is deceased, and I believe you are a distant relative of his. If this is true, then you are a beneficiary of his will. Understanding that, I need to ask you if you have any connection to a family named Hardin."

"That was my mother's maiden name," she said slowly. "But I'm not aware of any other connection to the Hardin family, living or dead."

He nodded. "It is a distant connection, to be sure, but I feel certain you are a legatee—a beneficiary of a legacy. Do you, by chance, have any documentation showing your mother's Hardin connection?"

"Yes, I have a Certificate of Live Birth that shows my mother's maiden name," Jeanne answered. "But what exactly are you talking about, Mr. Deshler? Who is this deceased person, and what, exactly, is the legacy?"

Regretfully, he answered, "I apologize, Mrs. Bettencourt, but that is another complication. There is another legatee with rights to the property, and I am in the very odd position of having to notify you both that you are beneficiaries, but until I can speak to you together I'm not free to discuss specifics. The other beneficiary has agreed to bring me his documentation and meet with us tomorrow at ten o'clock, at my office. Would it be possible for you to come, and bring your birth certificate?"

Jeanne said with frustration, "Mr. Deshler, that places a hardship on me. I can't just ask to take off work, it's definitely frowned upon, and I need this job."

He smiled, a tidy, close expression. "I'm afraid I have already taken a liberty concerning you, Mrs. Bettencourt. You see, my firm represents Gayoso House, and I'm acquainted with the owner, Mr. Topp, and the managing executives of the hotel. Before I came to speak with you I spoke to your general manager, Mr. Spivey, and explained that you might need to take the day off tomorrow to meet with me on a matter of importance. He was very understanding and said you may take whatever time you need to attend to it. So, here is my card. May I count on seeing you tomorrow at ten?"

"Thank you, Mr. Deshler," Jeanne said gratefully. "I will be there."

BUCK BUCKNER STUCK OUT his hand. Clint took it, and winced when Buckner shook it firmly. "I can't believe it, but you did it, Hardin. I can't believe *how* you did it, either. Where'll you be for us to settle up?" He was shouting to be heard over the blaring din in the warehouse.

Clint said something, but Buckner couldn't hear him, both because of the noise and because now Clint had buried his head under a thick, wet, dirty towel. He was rubbing his head, hard, and wide bloodstains appeared under his six busted knuckles.

"What?" Buckner yelled.

Beside Clint, Vince Norville stood on tiptoe to holler into Buckner's ear, "We'll be at Cozen's Tonsorial Parlor!"

"He's going to get a haircut?" Buck said blankly.

"Naw, a bath," Vince said.

"He's not going to celebrate his win? Clint the Flint Fist downed Mike the Hammer in four rounds?"

"To him a bath is a celebration," Vince said with disgust. "Our buddy Duffy will join you for the tallying-up, Buck." He pointed to the short scowling Duffy Byrne who waited behind Clint, holding his water bottle.

Buckner grinned a shark's smile. "You think I'm going to cheat you, Hardin?"

Clint had surfaced from under the towel. "'Course not, Buck. I mean I don't, and Vinnie doesn't, but I don't know about Duffy. You take exception to him helping you out with counting the money, you'll have to take it up with him."

"I see," Buck said, nodding knowingly. "Knife man, huh?"

"That's right," Vince said expansively. "And I'm the Gun Man, and Clint's the Flint Fist Man. Hey—"

Clint was making his way through the loud, raucous, shouting, shoving, rowdy bunch of men that surrounded him. "Ya did it, Flint! Made me my Satiddy night whiskey money! Busted him up good, Flint! When's the next fight? Hey, Flint, Mike looks like he done got *hit* wid a Hammer!" they catcalled, and other, coarser things.

Clint grinned crookedly at all of them, raising his bloody fists up high, until he made it out the door. His hair was wet, his bare chest ran with perspiration, his hands were covered in blood, his face had blood and sweat on it. The cold air bit him all over, and he gulped in a great icy breath, but it refreshed him. Behind him Vince pushed through several men that were following Clint, cursing, and when he reached him he threw Clint's wool topcoat over his shoulders. "So. You're just going to walk around, naked and barefooted, in the snow. Real smart, Flint-brain."

"You know, it stinks in there, Vinnie, and I'm thinking that a lot of that stench is coming from me. Need some fresh air." He took his heavy brogans out of Vince's hands, threw them down, and stepped into them. "Cozen's is only a couple of blocks. C'mon, it's freezing out here, whatsa matter with you?"

In half an hour Clint was sitting in an enormous tub made of barrel staves. His long legs were fully stretched out, the steaming water came up to his neck, and he lay motionless, his head back, his eyes closed, a dead cigar clenched between his teeth. "Aw, man, what I wouldn't give to have a bath like this every day," he murmured.

Sitting on a whiskey barrel, and sipping some of that very whiskey from a tin cup, Vince regarded him with a critical eye. "Guess you can afford it now, Clint the Flint. You made a big bunch of dollars tonight, buddy."

"Did, didn't I?" Clint said with satisfaction.

"Yeah. By the way, I liked your plan. Good plan, that. It was cold, but yeah, good plan."

Clint opened his eyes—that is, he opened one eye, for the other was swollen shut. He reached up to tenderly feel it, and his rapidly swelling mouth. "Aw, man, how'd that happen? Anyway, what do you mean, cold? I fought fair, straight jabs, no gouging."

"I know. It's just that you were kinda deliberate about it, like you were dissecting a dead frog or something. I've never seen you fight like that," Vince said soberly.

Clint's plan had been simple. He allowed Mike to get close to him, which meant that Clint had to take a lot of gut and kidney punches. But this time, instead of hitting his opponent with professional right crosses and left upper-cuts, Clint hit him again and again in the eyes. He had simply outlasted Mike. Clint took a beating in the belly and sides, but Mike's eyes had swollen up until he couldn't see. In the last round he had doggedly groped his way "up to scratch," the long dug-up streak in the dirt that the fighters had to step up to before beginning to fight, but Mike couldn't see anything at all by that time and couldn't block any punch. Clint had slowly and deliberately hit him twice in the solar plexus to knock the breath out of him, and then had hit him solidly in the chest to knock him down. Mike couldn't recover his breath to get up within the allotted thirty seconds, and Clint had won.

Now he told Vince quietly, "No, and I don't ever want to fight like that again. It wasn't any fun at all. It might have been fair, but it was no sport."

Vince nodded with understanding. "Yeah, I get it, Clint. Now you don't have to fight Mike again, anyway. He's the only one that ever beat you. So, who's next?"

Clint answered lazily, "Vinnie, my friend, there's a possibility that I might be a man of means, and won't have to fight any more. A lawyer fellow came to see me today. It seems like I've got an inheritance coming."

"Huh? From who? What is it? Money? A lot of money?"

"I don't know, don't know, don't know. I won't find out until ten o'clock tomorrow. But tonight," he said, sitting up and contemplating his dead cigar, "I got money to spend. Think I'll take a light, if you please, and see if old Cozens has another fancy shot glass like that one you have there. And you have yourself a cigar and another drink on me."

"I'll do that," Vince said, striking a match to light Clint's cigar. "You know, Her Ladyship's not going to be happy that her favorite's face is all beat up. You might better hit one of those ladies' shops that sell cosmetics, see if you can get prettied up before Madam Maxfield sees you."

Clint smiled. "Good idea, Vinnie. I'll think about that."

EVEN THOUGH JEANNE WAS horribly nervous, she grew amused at herself as she entered the offices of Deshler, Wayne & Beebe as the last stroke of ten sounded on the church bell. *I'm not late, Mrs. Wiedemann,* she thought crazily. The imposing structure was a large two-story building with a pillared front porch and a stalwart-looking front door of oak, respectably blackened with age. Inside was a large foyer leading to a grand marble staircase. Directly on one side was a mirrored hat stand, and Jeanne threw off her hood and unwound her new crimson headwrap, noting that her cheeks were colored a high rose, and not just from the cold. A young somber man with spectacles came out of a doorway on her left and said, "Mrs. Bettencourt?"

"Yes, I have an appointment with Mr. Deshler," she said.

"Of course. Please come this way." He led her into a room that looked like a parlor, with a sofa and spidery side chairs and a generous tea table, and a desk at the back of the room, and beckoned her to a door with frosted glass on the far wall. Opening it, he said, "Mrs. Bettencourt, Mr. Deshler." He held the door open for Jeanne, and she went into a large room with books lining the walls, heavy red velvet draperies framing the windows, and masculine leather armchairs grouped around a sizzling fire.

Deshler rose from behind his desk and came around to hold a chair for Jeanne. "Good morning, Mrs. Bettencourt.

Please, sit down. You're right on time." He returned to his seat.

They exchanged pleasantries for a few moments, about the weather and the state of the streets. Then Jeanne said, "I brought my birth certificate, Mr. Deshler. Would you like to see it now?"

"Yes, I would." She took it out of the pocket of her mantle and handed it to him. He gave it a cursory glance and handed it back to her. "Thank you, Mrs. Bettencourt, this is all the proof I need to substantiate your claim. I found you from the census records, you see, by tracing your mother, so I was already certain that I had the right person. Or rather, persons, for that's the way I traced the other claimant, too."

"I believe you said he is coming here this morning?" Jeanne said politely.

"Yes, he is. It seems he is late, which I don't find too surprising under the circumstances."

"More circumstances," Jeanne said lightly. "I don't suppose I may know these, either."

"Er—" Deshler began, but just then the door opened and Mr. Beebe's sonorous voice announced, "Mr. Hardin, Mr. Deshler."

Jeanne was sitting with her back to the door, and she couldn't restrain herself from turning around to look at her co-beneficiary. She looked—she stared—her mouth opened and she blurted out, "You? The Singing Man?"

He loomed over her, for he was very tall and broad-shouldered, and stared down at her with perplexity, and then astonishment. "You? I saw you! And your little sister! You had on the holly crowns!"

Deshler, who had remained seated, frowned deeply. "Are you two already acquainted? Are you in some sort of theatrical production, maybe?"

They both ignored him. Jeanne said indignantly, "She's not my little sister, she's my daughter."

"Huh?" he said, his one-eyed gaze raking her up and down. "Your daughter? How'd that happen?"

"What?" Jeanne said blankly.

Mr. Deshler rose. "Pardon me for interrupting, but perhaps formal introductions are in order. Mr. Hardin, I have the honor of making known to you Mrs. Jeanne Bettencourt, who is a distant relation of my client's and, therefore, of yours. Mrs. Bettencourt, may I present to you Mr. Clinton Hardin, of the Memphis Hardins. Please, Mr. Hardin, won't you be seated?"

Clint sat down in a chair next to Jeanne's, grimacing a little as he did so.

Jeanne watched him with a mixture of exasperation and consternation. "What happened to your face?"

"My—oh. Uh, accident. Had an accident on Boxing Day," he managed to reply, glancing with amusement at Nate Deshler, who was in on the joke. He had backed Clint.

"You had an accident while boxing up the gifts for your servants?" Jeanne said sarcastically.

Clint said with surprise, "How'd you know what Boxing Day really is?"

"How did I know? Apparently you're the one who thought it was some sort of fistic competition, as in *boxing*," Jeanne replied smartly.

"Well, yeah, but I really did know what it was," Clint said lamely.

"Perhaps we might begin again?" Mr. Deshler said, giving Clint a dire glance.

"Sorry, Mr. Deshler," Clint said quickly, and turned to Jeanne. "I beg your pardon, Mrs. Bettencourt, I've been very rude, I know. It's a great pleasure to make your acquaintance, ma'am."

"I am very pleased to meet you, Mr. Hardin," she said, still a little stiffly. They both turned to Deshler.

He steepled his fingers and said, "First I'd like to explain the connection between the two of you, and my client, Mr. Ira Hardin. I first met him on November 7 of this year, at which time he gave me instructions concerning his last wishes. He died the next day, I'm sorry to say. He wished to leave his property to, and I'm quoting him, 'any Memphis Hardins' I could find. It has taken me almost two months, but through the census records I traced the two of you, who are the only remaining Memphis Hardins."

"I understand Mr. Hardin's claim, for that's obvious," Jeanne said. "But you know that I'm not truly a Hardin, Mr. Deshler."

Deshler said, "It's an odd point of law, but I am obliged to interpret it thus: when Mr. Ira Hardin instructed me the way he did, it meant any blood relation of any Hardin that lived in Memphis. You do have Hardin blood, Mrs. Bettencourt, and so you are entitled, as Mr. Clint Hardin is entitled.

"But let me make it clear to you, my one conversation with Mr. Hardin was not of long duration, for he was extremely ill, and I had no time to press him for the finer points of law as I drew up his last will and testament. I've interpreted his dying wishes as best I could, and I believe that he meant for anyone of Memphis Hardin blood to share equally in his legacy. That, of course, could possibly be open to another interpretation, if either of you feel the need to contest the terms that I have defined."

Jeanne and Clint exchanged furtive sidelong glances, and then both shook their heads.

"I'm sure your interpretation of the will is knowledgeable and expert, Mr. Deshler," Jeanne said. "Whatever you say is just fine with me."

"You've got a reputation as a fair man, sir," Clint said easily. "So I'm happy with whatever it is. By the way, I brought my mother's marriage certificate." He pulled a piece of parchment out of his pocket and handed it to Deshler.

As he had done with Jeanne's birth certificate, he scanned it quickly, then handed it back. "That's fine, Mr. Hardin, thank you. Very well. Now I can tell you everything, because I know you must be monstrously curious, and I'm sorry I had to make you wait."

Jeanne sat up a little straighter and Clint leaned forward, his hands clasped between his knees. Deshler said flatly, "You have both inherited a riverboat. A Mississippi steamboat named the *Helena Rose*."

Jeanne stared at him; Clint stared at him. Deshler was enjoying himself immensely. This was a most unusual will, a most unusual legacy, and two very unusual legatees. He sat back, steepled his fingers again, and waited.

The heavy silence stretched on and on. Finally Jeanne said in a low voice, "A riverboat? I own a riverboat?"

"Half of one," Deshler replied. "Mr. Clint Hardin owns the other half."

Jeanne turned to Clint again. He was staring into space. Finally he turned and grinned at her. "Hello, partner."

Jeanne said, "I'm not your partner. Oh. Oh, I *am* your partner. How very odd."

"Ain't it?" Clint said flippantly, then turned to Deshler. "So, what kind of steamboat is the *Helena Rose*? Pretty name, by the way. Where is she? How big is she? Is she worth much?"

"I have seen the *Helena Rose*, because that's where I was summoned when Mr. Hardin decided to consult me for his last will and testament. He wanted to die on the boat, you see. She's here, right down on the docks. Anyway, I'm afraid I'm no expert on steamboats. What I observed was that she seemed trim and river-ready, as they say. She is not a big boat at all and she is outfitted for cargo only, not passengers. However, I understand that Mr. Hardin was making a tidy profit with her. He did leave a sum of monies. After I settled his outstanding debts, and of course paid my fee, there was just a little more than five hundred dollars in cash remaining, so each of you will receive two hundred and fifty two dollars and some cents."

"What?" Jeanne breathed.

"Wow," Clint said.

"Yes, Mr. Hardin had the cash on the boat, not in a bank. So I have it here, in his lockbox. You may have it now, if you wish."

"No!" they said in unison, then looked at each other in surprise. Quickly Jeanne said, "No, I would really like to go see the *Helena Rose*, and I don't want to be carrying around such a great sum of money, that would be foolish."

"My thoughts exactly, Mrs. Bettencourt," Clint agreed. "You know, I've got a whole bunch of questions about this Mr. Ira Hardin, but I'd kinda like to take some time, think it all over. I do want to see the *Rose*, though."

"Perfectly understandable. In fact, I would advise you both to see the boat first of all, and then consider all of your options. We can meet again to formalize everything, and by then I'm sure you'll have any questions or concerns firm in your minds."

Clint said eagerly, "That sounds right to me," and Jeanne nodded agreement.

Deshler said cautiously, "Now I must tell you that Mr. Hardin specified one stipulation to his inheritors. He had a dog, and apparently Mr. Hardin was very attached to him. He told me that anyone who inherits his boat has to take care of his dog."

Clint looked relieved. "Is that all? Sure, I like dogs."

Jeanne asked, "A dog? What is the dog's name?"

"Hmm? Oh," Deshler said with some confusion, shuffled some papers on his desk, and then pointed. "Here. The dog's name is Leo. He was with Mr. Hardin when I met him, and he's a big, sort of spotty dog," he added informatively. "So I'm assuming that you both agree to Mr. Hardin's stipulation? Good. Now, I will need a couple of days to formalize the title documents and file them appropriately. We can do all the paperwork on your next visit."

"Good, thanks, Mr. Deshler," Clint said gratefully. "So, Mrs. Bettencourt? May I have the honor of escorting you to see our new steamboat?"

"Our new . . . ? Oh, yes," Jeanne said, still feeling slightly dazed. "I mean, of course I want to go see the *Helena Rose.*" She stood up abruptly, and so of course Clint and Mr. Deshler jumped up out of their seats. "Thank you, Mr. Deshler, for everything. I'll see you . . . when should I see you again?"

"Perhaps both of you might come back at the same time on Thursday," he said.

"Ten o'clock, Thursday," Jeanne said, as if talking to herself.

She turned and rushed out the door, and Deshler and Clint exchanged quick helpless glances and then practically ran after her. Deshler hurriedly told Clint, "The *Rose* is at the north end of the waterfront. Mr. Hardin specified that one of his crewmen, a Mr. Ezra Givens, stay on the boat. He'll be able to tell you much more than I've been able to, I'm sure."

"Thanks," Clint said, trailing Jeanne out the front door. She was walking fast, wrapping her muffler around her head and pulling up her hood. He caught up to her and she glanced up at him with a distracted look.

"Hi there. Remember me? Your partner?" He offered her his arm.

She came to a dead stop. "I—this is all too much right now, Mr. Hardin. You'll have to excuse me."

"What does that mean? You're going to the docks, I'm going to the docks. We're going to the same place on the docks. Doesn't it seem like maybe we should go together?"

"No. I mean—yes. I suppose so. But I—I don't know you, you're a complete stranger to me, and I'm not comfortable walking arm-in-arm with a man I don't know," she said darkly.

"But you do know me, ma'am," he said lightly. "I'm your partner. I'm the Singing Man."

"That's silly!"

"You said it, not me. Anyway, what can we do? You want me to follow behind you like a lackey or something?"

"Would you?" Jeanne snapped, her dark eyes hard and brilliant.

He stared down at her for a brief moment, then grinned slowly, for his mouth was still swollen and sore. "Well, yeah. If that's what you want, ma'am."

Jeanne started to fling out a reply, then dropped her head and pressed her fingers to her temples. "I'm sorry, Mr. Hardin. It's just that all of this has been such a shock."

"It's okay, I understand. So does this mean that you'll take my arm, and we'll walk, not run, to the docks, and talk like grown-ups?"

Jeanne's hackles rose again, but she took his arm and said, "Yes, I suppose we must."

They proceeded along for several steps, and Jeanne didn't say a word, so Clint asked politely, "So I assume you're widowed, Mrs. Bettencourt."

"Yes."

"And the pretty little girl, at the Regale. You both had holly and ivy crowns, and I thought you—never mind about that. So she's your daughter?"

"Yes."

"And what is her name?"

"Marvel."

"And how old is Marvel?"

"Six."

"And I'm curious, ma'am, since you don't seem old enough to have a daughter that age. Would you mind telling me how old you are?"

"Yes, I would mind."

Clint sighed, then stopped and turned toward her, placing his hand over hers. "Ma'am, please. I know it's kind of hard to take all of this in, but right now I think it's important for us to get to know each other. After all, in the position we're in, we're going to have to work together, to make some important decisions, together. Isn't that right?"

"I know," Jeanne sighed. "It's just that it's such a bizarre, such an uncomfortable situation, to be forced into a personal relationship like this," Jeanne said.

"Then think of it as strictly a business relationship. That's what it really is, anyway."

Slowly she nodded. "Yes . . . yes. I can do that."

They resumed walking, and Jeanne went on, "My daughter's name is Marvel, and she just turned six years old. I am twenty-five, and widowed, and my parents are both dead. And your family, Mr. Hardin?"

"My mother's dead, and I don't know about my father. I never knew him," he said coldly. "No brothers or sisters, but I guess you knew that, considering we're the last two of the Memphis Hardins," he added in his normal lazy drawl.

"Actually I suppose my daughter is one," Jeanne said. "She would be . . . one-eighth Hardin."

He shot her a quick cautious glance, and Jeanne's eyes widened. "You think—no. No, no. I didn't mean that. I would never try to—to get more, to get a portion for Marvel."

Clint shrugged with apparent carelessness, but his gaze was intent. "Why not? From what Mr. Deshler said, the percentage of Hardin blood doesn't make any difference. It could be argued that she has as much right to the *Rose* as I do. Or as you do, for that matter."

Jeanne shook her head. "No. She already has my share, for everything I have belongs to her. Therefore, she has received the very same thing that I have, and your portion should not be infringed upon at all."

"Wow, you'd make a great lawyer," he said admiringly. "And I'm not just saying that because what you said is all the better for me."

Jeanne made a quick impatient movement with her hand. "It would just be dishonorable and greedy to try to do you out of your share. Not to mention ill-bred."

"That is one thing that you are not, ma'am," Clint said gravely. "So. You're a widow and you're well-bred, we've established that. What else are you?"

"Hmm? Oh. I'm a chambermaid, at the Gayoso."

"You are? But you don't look like a chambermaid!"

"So I hear," Jeanne said dryly, "but so far no one has told me exactly what a chambermaid is supposed to look like, and why, in particular, I don't look that way. No, never mind all that, please, I don't want to discuss the average chambermaid's countenance. Let's talk about the *Helena Rose*. Do you know anything about steamboats, Mr. Hardin?"

"Not a blessed thing," he said cheerfully. "Do you?"

"Actually, I do. You see, I was brought up on a steamboat. My parents and I lived on my father's steamboat, the *Pearl*. He owned it, and he was the pilot and captain. In fact, I learned a lot about piloting a steamboat myself," she said matter-of-factly. "Not on the Mississippi, but on the Arkansas River. Do you know it?"

"Do I know it," he repeated slowly. "Do I know . . . the Arkansas River? And you grew up on a steamboat? And you've even piloted a steamboat?"

"Yes, Mr. Hardin. That's what I said. We are speaking English here, are we not?" she said tartly.

But he only grinned, a wide unconstrained expression, forgetting the pain of his mouth. "Do you know what I call that, Mrs. Bettencourt?"

"I don't know what you would call it," she said, "but I call it a miracle of God."

He rapid-fired questions to her all the way down to the docks. She answered some and didn't know others, but she was surprised at his quickness, at the sharp and incisive nature of his questioning. They reached Jefferson Avenue, which was past the high bluffs and was the first of four avenues that led down the gentle slope to the river. Traffic in town, and on the river, was light, since many people still celebrated the days between Christmas and New Year's day as holidays. Still, there were eleven steamers along the riverfront, their gangways down and roustabouts loading and unloading cargo and a few passengers coming and going. Clint clasped Jeanne's arm a little tighter as they went past the carts and drays and shouting roustabouts. "Mr. Deshler said she's moored up at the north end," he said, and Jeanne nodded.

On the other side of the wharf sat a group of several men, chewing tobacco and spitting and talking. Every one of them was black from head to toe, their red eyes staring out fiendishly. Clint and Jeanne were passing them when one of them yelled, "Clint! Hey, Clint! Hold up!"

They stopped and looked, and when the man got close to them Clint said, "Vinnie! You look awful!"

He grinned, and his teeth shone very white against his ebony face. "Just finished loading up a big ol' girl with coal. What are you doing here?"

He stared curiously at Jeanne, but she was paying him no mind at all. She was looking down the wharf, her eyes narrowed. Clint began, "Vince, may I introduce—"

At that moment Jeanne yanked her arm away from Clint and stalked down the pier.

"Where's she going?" Vince asked blankly.

"I dunno," Clint said. "She does that."

They watched as Jeanne went two steamers down, where a big, high-sided wood cart was being unloaded onto a shabby steamer pulled alongside. "That's Old Man Mock's wood dray," Vince told Clint. "He'll pinch a penny 'til it screams. He tried, once, to scamp some roustabouts out of paying them what he owed them, said they took too long and time was money and it wasn't coming out of his pocket. 'Course, word got around so none of us will load for him now. He hires the wood monkeys, and he picks the ones that are really hungry and pays 'em two cents. Think she knows him?"

"Doesn't look like it," Clint observed. Jeanne had walked up to a short, fat man in a filthy yellow waistcoat who was rapping the three wood boys on the back with a stout stick as they staggered by with two and sometimes three logs. Jeanne's hands were on her hips, and her face was a picture of outrage. Even as they watched, the fat man raised the stick and waved it threateningly. Clint said, "Uh-oh," and he ran toward them, followed by Vince, whose day had just improved mightily.

Before they reached the two, Jeanne reached up with the quickness of a snake and snatched the stick out of the man's hand. "How would you like it if I beat *you* with this stick?" she said wrathfully.

Old Man Mock's face turned a livid purple. "Jest who do you think you are, little girl! You give me my stick back!"

Jeanne contemptuously threw it over his head into the river. Mock took a step towards her, his hand upraised, his expression vicious.

"You don't want to do that," Clint said, suddenly appearing and grabbing Mock's upraised arm.

"OW! Leggo of me, you beat-up sorry—OW!" he howled.

"You don't want to say that either," Clint said calmly, his grip tightening on Mock's fat arm.

"Awright! Awright! Leggo!" Clint released him and he stumbled backwards a step, rubbing his forearm. "You got a grip like a gator! And she—" he pointed a filthy forefinger accusingly at Jeanne and shook it—"she took my stick! And throwed it in the river!"

"Yeah, I noticed," Clint said, and turned to Jeanne who looked as if she'd like to pick up Mock and throw him in the river. Behind him, Vince watched with a wide delighted grin stuck on his face. The three wood boys had stopped loading to watch, and a couple of other roustabouts had come close to observe. "Mrs. Bettencourt, I think—yeah, there she goes," he finished under his breath.

Jeanne walked over to one of the wood boys and said, "Roberty, why would you let that awful man beat you like that?"

He stared up at her helplessly and wordlessly. She sighed and put her arm around his shoulders. "Just drop that wood right now. You're coming with me."

Slowly he let the two heavy logs drop and she kept her arm around his shoulders and walked back up to the pier. She looked over at Clint, Vince, and Old Man Mock, who were all watching her with a kind of dread fascination.

"Well? Are you coming, Mr. Hardin?" She and Roberty turned and began walking.

Clint and Vince looked at each other and then followed them. Old Man Mock shouted after them, "All you crazy people jist stay away from me!"

Over his shoulder Vince yelled, "Better watch yourself, Old Man! She might come back, you know!" Mock looked alarmed.

They caught up to Jeanne and Roberty and stayed a few steps behind them. "Hey, Clint? Think you might let me know what you've got yourself into here?" Vince asked.

"It's a long story," Clint said, frowning. "It's been a long morning. Long and short of it, I'm half owner of a riverboat, and she owns the other half. We're going to see her now."

"Which boat?" Vince asked eagerly.

"Name of *Helena Rose*. You know it?"

"Sure! That's Bull Hardin's boat. She's been docked down there since he died. Uh—you said you own it now?"

"Half of it."

"And that lady up there owns the other half?"

"Yep."

Vince digested this. "Okay. Uh—who's the boy? The wood monkey?"

"Don't have any idea. You can go ask her if you want."

"No, thanks," Vince said vehemently. After a moment he said thoughtfully, "So, you own Bull Hardin's *Rose* now. It never occurred to me that you were kin, even with the same last name."

"I never met him, never heard of him. I guess he's a real distant cousin."

"Is she a Hardin too?"

"No, her name is Bettencourt."

"Oh. What's her first name?"

"I forgot," Clint rasped. "And trying to get her to talk is like trying to pull a stripped bolt."

"You're joshing," Vince said disbelievingly. "You mean there's a live woman on this earth that you can't charm into telling all of her secrets?"

"She's not exactly my kind of woman," Clint muttered. "Anyway, tell me about this boat. What do you know about her?"

Vince pointed. "See for yourself. There she is."

She floated light, with only the gentlest of movements on the long lazy river swells. Painted white, her smoke-stacks and paddle wheel were a bright true red. The main cargo deck was open at the front, with the boiler room and engine room enclosed behind. The Texas deck was completely enclosed, with a railed walkway around, with windows all along the sides and front. On top perched the pilothouse, white with red trim. Painted on both sides and on the back above the paddle wheel in crimson fine script: *Helena Rose.*

Jeanne and Roberty stood still, studying her, and Clint walked up to stand beside Jeanne. "So what do we think?" When she answered him, he was surprised at the warmth and pleasure in her voice.

"She's trim and neat. The paint needs touching up a lit-tle, but the windows are all intact and they're even clean. She looks very well cared for, from the outside at least."

On the cargo deck a dog lolled up into their view and regarded them curiously. "Hello, Leo," Jeanne called. He began to wag, as it were; his whole rear end moved and his skinny tail went around in a lopsided figure eight. His long red tongue flopped out, and it looked like he was grinning. "Silly dog," she said, smiling.

"So do we wade out there?" Clint asked. The boat was about twelve feet away from the shore.

Vince appeared beside him. "Maybe, maybe not. Hey, Ezra! Ahoy the *Rose*! Ezra!"

A man came out of the deep shadows behind Leo. He was in his late forties, with stooped but broad shoulders and long thick arms. He wore a black stocking cap pulled down over his ears. Lifting one hand, he shaded his eyes and looked them over. "Who is all you people?" he asked in an aggrieved tone.

Vince stepped forward. "It's me, Vinnie, Ezra. These are the new owners of the boat. Except the boy. I don't know who he is."

"And I don't know any black fellers named Vinnie," Ezra retorted.

"I'm not a black feller," Vince argued. "I'm just—oh, forget it, Ezra! This gentleman and this lady are the new owners of the *Rose*. Lower a gangway so we don't have to swim."

"Can't you see I'm the only man on this here boat? You think me and Leo can lower away?"

"Why did you—" Vince bawled, then turned to Clint. "Why did he pull off and raise the gangplank anyway?"

"How should I know? So what do we do?"

"I'll wade out there, it's probably not but a foot or so deep anyway," Vince said, plopping down on the muddy riverside to pull off his shoes.

Clint threw himself down beside him. "Somehow I figured as soon as I heard I owned a boat I'd end up getting wet."

"Oh, dear," Jeanne said. "I don't suppose I could help?"

"No!" Clint and Vince said in unison.

Within a few minutes they had waded out and together had manhandled the huge capstan to lower one of the landing stages. Ezra and Leo watched with interest. Jeanne lightly came up the walkway, followed by Roberty with a bemused expression on his face.

Ezra watched Clint and Vince as they wrung out the bottoms of their trousers and replaced their socks and brogans. "Bet thass cold," he opined.

"It's freezing," Vince grumbled. "And I hadn't gotten wet in two days. At least my feet are still white."

Clint rose and stuck out his hand to Ezra. "Mr. Givens, my name is Clint Hardin. Mr. Deshler, the attorney, told us you'd be here, and I want to thank you for watching out for the *Rose*. This is Mrs. Bettencourt. She and I are co-owners of the boat now."

He nodded slowly. "Mr. Deshler, he did tell me that a man and a lady were the new owners. Pleased to meet you, sir, ma'am."

"I'm pleased to meet you, Mr. Givens," Jeanne said. "Mr. Hardin, I'm going to go look at the cabins and the pilothouse first. Roberty, wait here with Mr. Givens, and this is Leo." She gave the dog a cursory pat on his broad head and went toward the outside stairs that led to the Texas deck.

Though he hadn't been invited, Clint doggedly followed her up the stairs to the Texas deck. The door was in the middle of the deck, and they went into a narrow hallway. Just on their right was the galley, with a sliding door that was standing open. Jeanne went into the small room and exclaimed with delight, "A range! A real, honest-to-goodness range! And, oh my goodness, is that an icebox? And pots, and pans, and utensils!" She opened a couple of the high narrow cabinets. "Seasonings, spices, condiments!"

Clint thought the galley was very small and cramped, but he had to admit it was laid out efficiently. On each wall was mounted an eighteen-inch-wide polished oak board that served as a working counterspace. Above the counters were cabinets, tall and narrow, except where the cast-iron stove's pipe went out the wall, and where the single window was. There were six stools neatly stored under the counters, along with some barrels and sacks.

Across the hall another sliding door opened into a plain room with two sets of bunks on either side of the window. One weatherbeaten old chest sat at the foot of one of the bunks, which were all neatly made. "Crew quarters," Jeanne said. She went all the way down the hall, where there were two doors just at the end, and opened the door on the left-hand side. "This would be the captain's cabin, I expect."

It was a long room, with six four-paned windows along the side and two on the back wall. Underneath the windows on the back was a plain desk with nothing on it. About midway down the room two armchairs were pushed against the wall, and a round cherry tea table stood upended between them. At the far end of the room stood a full-sized bed, the bedstead of plain oak with a high headboard and footboard. The mattress was covered with a single sheet. Along the wall next to the hallway stood an enormous armoire, dark and glossy, with curlicue trim and shiny brass knobs and handles.

"Not bad," Clint said, looking around. "It's a lot better than my room."

Jeanne gave him an odd look. "I suppose we should see if that's another cabin across the hall."

They went to it, and it was a cabin, a mirror image of the other, but this one was completely unfurnished. "Wonder what the deal is with this?" Clint murmured.

Jeanne planted herself in front of him and blurted out, "So I suppose you're thinking of living here, on the *Rose*."

"The thought's occurred to me, sure, just like it has to you. But it seems to me that that's kind of long odds. I mean, isn't it the usual thing for a steamboat to have people like, oh, I don't know, a pilot and a captain living in these quarters?"

"Yes, of course. It's just that I hadn't thought about you—living here." She spoke almost as if she were talking to herself.

He waited to see if she would say more, but she remained silent, so he said, "How about we go take a look at the pilot-house? I've never seen one."

Silently she led him to the stairs at the end of the hallway that led up to the hurricane deck. They went into the pilothouse and instantly Jeanne went to the wheel, put her hands on the pins, and stared out the wide front window with a faraway look in her eyes.

Clint noted the seven-foot-diameter wheel, countersunk into the floor three feet so the top of the wheel was four feet high. On the right-hand side was a long tube with a trumpeted end, the speaking tube to communicate with the engine room. On both sides of the door at the back of the wheelhouse were low benches, padded with sturdy canvas bolsters.

He saw the strings running up the sides and across the ceiling, and the different pulls for each bell and whistle. Curiously he stared at a yellow piece of paper glued to the ceiling. It read: *Ira Kenneth Hardin, Certified Pilot. 1852 Licensed as per the Steamboat Act of May 30, 1852. Certified by Albert K. Edmonds, Inspector, Federal Maritime Service.* Clint wanted to ask Jeanne about it, but she was in such a deep reverie that he didn't like to intrude.

Finally she turned to him and said quietly, "Would you like to go see the boiler room and the engine room now?"

"Yes, ma'am." They made their way back down to the main deck. Ezra was in deep conversation with Vince, as he had apparently now recognized that Vince was not a strange black man. Roberty sat on the floor, smiling, scratching Leo's stomach. The dog lolled on his back with his tongue stuck out of one side of his mouth and one long hind leg rhythmically beating. He was, as Deshler had said, a spotted dog, his undercoat a dirty grayish-white with ugly liver-colored irregular markings.

"Ezra was telling me that a bunch of toughs tried to board two nights ago," Vince told Clint. "That's why he had the landing stages pulled up, a couple of deckhands from the *Sultana* helped him the next morning."

"How did you keep them from boarding that night?" Clint asked.

"Shotgun," Ezra said succinctly. "Double barrel."

"You shot them?" Jeanne exclaimed.

"No, ma'am, no call to up and shoot a man when he's done turned tail and running off," Ezra explained.

"Smart men," Clint said. "Mr. Givens, would you come with me now and take a look at the boiler room and engine room?"

"Be glad to, and you call me Ezra," he said. "Don't hardly know how to answer to 'Mr.' Now, I'm an old fireman, and I been on the *Rose* for going on seven year now, since she was built. I know the firebox like I know my own hand. But I can't tell you one sensible thing about that engine, Mr. Hardin."

"That's okay, and call me Clint," he said, stooping to look all around the two barrel-shaped boilers, pulling open the firebox, grabbing the pipes coming out of the boilers. "I know this," he muttered, and went back behind to the engine room. Jeanne followed him.

Still talking to himself, Clint climbed over some pipes to peer out to the paddle wheel housing, threw himself down on the floor to look under the machinery and fingered several valve connections and fittings. "This is easy!" he said, hopping to his feet, beaming.

"What do you mean?" Jeannie demanded.

"This engine. Nothing to it. Boilers make steam, steam pushes the piston, which moves the drive shaft, which moves the Pitman Arm yoke, which moves the Pitman Arm, which moves the paddle wheel crank, and then hey! Paddle wheel turns and off you go. Simple."

"That didn't sound so simple to me," Jeanne said suspiciously. "Are you saying that after looking at this—this stuff for five minutes, you could engineer a paddle wheeler?"

"I don't know about the boilers. Seems to me like that's kind of a matter of experience, to know how to fire them up, keep them just right for the boat."

"I've heard that's true. But what makes you think you know about this engine? There are many experienced pilots and captains who don't know the first thing about a steamboat's engine."

Clint said evenly, "Ma'am, I am a master machinist, and I've made these same valves, these pipes, these rods, these fittings, even these nuts and bolts, a hundred times. When you make the parts, you have to know what they do, and I know how a steam engine works."

"Oh," Jeanne said. "I beg your pardon. I didn't know."

"So now you do. And you see what this means, don't you?" he asked, his dark eyes alight.

Jeanne raised her hands. "Wait. I know what you're thinking. But I need time, I've got to think, this is just overwhelming."

"I know," he said quietly. He came to stand before her and looked down to search her face. "But I would like to tell you something. I don't know you, Mrs. Bettencourt, but

I do know some things about you. You're very smart, and you're determined. You're honest, and hardworking, and you want something better for yourself and your daughter. And I personally think that you can do anything you set your mind to. Including piloting a riverboat."

CHAPTER SIX

 "Is something wrong, Mama?" Marvel asked.

"No, no, little girl," Jeanne replied. "I'm just thinking. How are Mrs. Topp and Avaymaria this evening?"

"Mrs. Topp is going to be Avaymaria's maid, and she was wondering when Avaymaria's mantle and muffler might be finished," Marvel hinted.

Jeanne had told Marvel that she would make the doll a gray mantle just like Marvel's, and knit her a red muffler from the yarn left over from Jeanne's new wool scarf. She and Marvel had sat down on their mattress after supper, Marvel playing with her dolls and Jeanne sewing the doll clothes. But Jeanne couldn't concentrate on her sewing, or anything else for that matter. Her mind wildly darted from one thought to another idea to another question, as she thought about the *Helena Rose* and Clint Hardin. She had been staring distractedly into space, her hands loose on top of the sewing in her lap.

"Please let Mrs. Topp know that Avaymaria's mantle will be finished tomorrow night, and on Wednesday night I may be able to finish her scarf," Jeanne said.

Marvel seemed satisfied and went back to the doll's tea, which consisted of a butterscotch drop each and sips from Marvel's cup of cocoa and whispered conversations between the dolls. Jeanne resumed staring into space.

She hadn't told Marvel anything about inheriting the *Helena Rose*, because Jeanne simply didn't know what to say. Until she made a decision herself, it was impractical to tell Marvel everything. Jeanne was having a hard time trying to absorb everything herself, and she was baffled about what to do with her inheritance.

Two hundred and fifty dollars, in cash, she brooded. That little cottage up on Sycamore is only three hundred.

Her landlord, Mr. Garrison, owned several shacks in The Pinch. He was a hard man, for if a tenant didn't have their rent he gave them exactly one week to come up with the whole amount or he called in the deputies to evict. In the four years that Jeanne had been his tenant she had never once been late with the rent, and consequently he was kinder to her. Two months ago he had told her about the cottage and offered to let her rent it or buy it. She could do neither, for the rent was three times what she was paying now and at the time her savings amounted to eighteen dollars and fifty cents. But she had gone to look at the cottage longingly, for it wasn't a shotgun type, it was a clapboard house with a kitchen, a parlor, a bedroom, and even a small attic loft. The white paint was dismal, but it was solidly built, for it didn't sag as so many houses in the Pinch did, and the roof didn't leak.

Jeanne picked up her needle, but after two stitches she was again lost in thought. *Now that I've seen the Rose, I know we could sell her. I have no idea how much she would bring, but surely five hundred, six hundred?*

These same thoughts had been circling in her mind like a whirlwind. Ruefully, she realized that each time she thought about selling the *Helena Rose*, one part of her brain suddenly started objecting strenuously. All this day she had been thinking about her childhood on the river, her parents, about those far-off heady, happy days before Max Bettencourt had sauntered into her life. She'd had a good life on the river. She knew that Marvel could, too.

But how could that be? How could she make that happen for Marvel, and for herself?

Could she, Jeanne Langer Bettencourt, really be a steamboat pilot?

Dear Lord, what am I thinking? What should I do? What can I do? Jeanne prayed and prayed, but it seemed that she couldn't hear the Lord speaking to her. *Probably because I'm talking so much and so loudly He can't get a word in edgewise,* she thought ruefully.

It was two-thirty in the morning before she finally fell into an uneasy sleep full of dreams of the river.

JEANNE WAS STILL IN a turmoil when she awoke, and the persistent brain-whirl continued as she worked. She barely thought about George Masters, even though he was still in the hotel. Again he was not in his room when she cleaned it. As before, she only had a few rooms, for the Gayoso was still mostly empty, and by noon she was off work.

She went outside and stopped, gasping from the cold. The day was gray and sullen-looking, though it wasn't cold enough to snow. A turbid wind blew, with wild sharp crosswinds that made her cape and skirts flap around her ankles.

Jeanne threw back her hood to wrap her muffler around her nose and mouth, adjusted her hood far up to shelter her face, and pulled her arms inside her cape and clutched it close. Her head down, she started walking.

She was still behind the hotel, walking along past the tradesmen and delivery carts lined up at the service entrances, when she heard, "Mrs. Bettencourt?"

She looked up and George Masters stood there, bowing. "Hello, Mr. Masters. Whatever are you doing here?"

"I wanted to talk to you."

"Why?" Jeanne asked blankly.

"Because I felt that somehow on Christmas Eve I didn't let you know how much I would like to see you and spend time with you. So I determined that I would try again."

"But here? Now?" Jeanne asked, shivering a little.

"I know, I apologize, but I couldn't think of any other way. I didn't want to, uh, accost you in my room. So I bribed a porter to come to the restaurant and tell me when you were leaving. Shameful, isn't it?" He managed a smile.

"Yes—no—I don't know," she said. "Mr. Masters, I'm afraid you've found me at a rather difficult time right now. And I'm in a bit of a hurry."

"Is something wrong? With you, or your daughter?" he asked instantly.

"No, no. In fact, I've had some really good news," Jeanne assured him. "It's just that I have some very important decisions to make in the next few days, so I'm distracted, and to tell the truth I can hardly banter with you right now."

"Then don't banter," he said with a hint of frustration. "I'm a very good listener, so you can talk to me. Won't you please come out with me tonight? Or right now, if you would prefer, we could go have a light luncheon at the Cotton Coffeehouse. But I'd much rather have a leisurely dinner at the Courtier. I promise I won't keep you out late."

Jeanne frowned. "I don't—right now, I'm—it's very confusing, you see—"

"No, I don't see. It's not confusing at all to me," he said forcefully. "My carriage will be waiting at Main and Overton, at six o'clock, Mrs. Bettencourt. I hope you will be there. Now, may I take you home, if that's where you're going?"

"No, I have an appointment down at the docks," Jeanne said, "and no, I'll walk. And I'm not at all sure about meeting you tonight, Mr. Masters."

"Six o'clock, Main and Overton," he repeated firmly. "Good afternoon, Mrs. Bettencourt."

With a yank on the brim of his hat, he turned and went around the corner to the front of the hotel. Jeanne continued walking, and found that she was amused. She wouldn't go, of course. But then again, why not? Seeing him and having that brief conversation had been the only time in two days that she wasn't worried to distraction about the *Helena Rose*. Of course he would look like a fool, tooling around with her in a fine carriage, but what was that to her? He was a grown man, that was his lookout. She decided she would ask for the most expensive item on the Courtier Restaurant's menu.

With that she went back to gnawing on her problems as she fought her way down to the docks. She was surprised when she looked up and was standing in front of the boat. In spite of the cruel wind, she had been so deep in thought the entire walk that she had barely seen or noticed anything. There was no one in sight on either deck, so she called out *"Helena Rose!* Coming aboard!" She started down the gangplank, and the door to the boiler room opened and Roberty came out.

"Hi!" Roberty said, beaming. Jeanne was taken aback, for she had never seen a truly happy smile on his face. His face and hands were clean, his cheeks had a little color, and his normally unkempt tow-colored hair was neatly combed. "Me and Ezra and Vinnie are back here in the boiler room, I mean the firebox, 'cause Clint said we could go ahead and steam 'er up since it's so cold. And he said to tell you when you got here that he's upstairs, I mean up on the Texas deck."

"You sound like a riverman already. I assume you made it all right with Mr. Givens last night?" Jeanne had been exhausted when she left for home last night, and she had just wearily told Roberty to stay on the boat.

Roberty nodded. "Ol' Ezra don't talk nice, but he really is nice. He makes good macaroni. I slept with Leo. I mean, he slept in my bunk with me." He looked up at her anxiously. "Is that okay?"

"If it's okay with you and Leo, then it's okay with me."

They went into the boiler room, where Ezra and Vince were playing checkers on an upturned crate, and they came to their feet when Jeanne came in. One of the boilers was throwing off waves of heat, and the small cluttered room was almost hot. Leo lay stretched on the floor underneath the boilers, and he opened one eye and his tail thumped twice when Jeanne greeted them.

"Please, sit down, Mr. Givens, Mr. Norville. I just wanted to say hello, and to ask you, Mr. Givens, if it inconvenienced you in any way to have Roberty on the boat last night."

"That young 'un wouldn't trouble a dozing cat," he declared. "He's quiet, he don't ask a hunnerd tomfool questions, he looks after hisself, made up his bunk real nice this morning. Had a nice leetle fire already going in the cookstove when I got up at dawn. He can eat a pile of macaroni, though."

"We had macaroni for supper last night *and* breakfast this morning," Roberty told her. "I love macaroni."

"It's a good thing," Jeanne said lightly, though she was thinking, *What is there to eat here? Does Mr. Givens have any money? And if he does, whyever did I just dump Roberty on him and expect him to take care of him?*

"I'm glad you made it all right," she said to Ezra. "We'll all talk later, about the food and things."

She went up to the Texas deck and found Clint Hardin sitting at the desk in the captain's cabin. Several long narrow books were piled on the desk, open, and there was a messy pile of papers. When she came in, Clint jumped to his feet. "Good afternoon, Mrs. Bettencourt. Look at your cheeks, they're all red. No, what I meant to say was that they have a blush like a rose."

"Hmm. And I see that your eye has turned a nice azure blue, and your mouth is a pleasing hue of violet," she said pleasantly. She was removing her scarf and mantle as she spoke, and he reached out to take them, and she saw his knuckles. All four on the right hand, and the two middle on the left, were swollen and gaped open in weeping sores. "Good heavens! I thought you said you were a machinist. I was under the silly impression that machinists were required to use their hands and must be able to see."

He took her things to hang up in the armoire. "Yeah, it helps a lot. That's why I didn't work today. Because of the eye, not the knuckles, I can manage with those." He came back to the desk and held out the straight chair. "Sit down, Mrs. Bettencourt, I've just got to show you all this stuff that Ira Hardin left."

She sat down and picked up one of the books. "Captain's logs, yes, I do want to look at those."

"You really do!" he said excitedly. "You know how you told me you knew the Arkansas River? Well, Bull Hardin ran the Arkansas for almost five years. It's all here, all about the freight he had, the stops, the river, the stuff about snags and sandbars and course changes."

Jeanne nodded. "Yes, that would be what's in the captain's logs, of course."

"So, there it all is! Of course, he was on the Arkansas years ago—see, this first logbook is 1848—but the five years following are all documented thoroughly. Last two years aren't nearly as thorough; Ezra told me that after his wife died, Bull kinda went to pieces. Anyway, I'll bet that we could still contact some of these shippers—"

"Stop," Jeanne said quietly, holding up her hand, and he abruptly fell silent. She rose and paced down the room and back, "Mr. Hardin, you are moving much too quickly, and I must tell you that you really have no idea of what you're talking about. Running a riverboat is an extremely complicated endeavor. Making a profit is even harder. Of course I thought a lot about this, but I have to think about it more, much more. And so should you, before making any decision."

He studied her. "I don't see it that way. You're talking about deciding whether to live on this boat and work her, or sell her off. To me that's a simple decision. I don't want to sell the *Rose*."

"But you know nothing about the river! And though I don't know anything about boilers or engines, I can see that this boat is in good shape, and would probably sell at a good price!" Jeanne argued.

"So you *do* want to sell her? Now who's making a snap decision?"

"I don't want to sell her! I mean, I'm just thinking about it!"

"Why? I don't want to be rude or anything, but I've told you I have no intention of selling," Clint said calmly. "She might bring a nice price sold outright, but she's not going to be profitable enough that you could sell a fifty-percent interest in her."

Jeanne propped her hands on her hips and her eyes flashed like ice on ebony. "This is not fair! You're forcing my hand, you're leaving me with no option!"

"Sorry," he said blithely. "Guess that's a problem with an even 50-50 split."

"Problem? You're the problem!" Jeanne said rudely. "So you're just going to take off in my boat. And this of course, would be *after* you've hired a pilot who, by the way, makes at least a hundred dollars a month, and other crewmen, and other expenses . . . and off you merrily go. When you get back, you have no profit to split with me, if you haven't actually *lost* money. Apparently somehow my fifty percent isn't quite the same as your fifty percent."

"Look, ma'am, you were excited yesterday, I could see it. You started thinking right away about exactly what I'm talking about. *You* pilot the boat, I can engineer it, and together we can figure out how to keep her loaded and running. Why don't we forget this nonsense of selling and concentrate on all that?"

"Because you have no idea what *all that* is," Jeanne said tightly. "You may know about the engine, I understand that. But you have no idea of what it takes to pilot a steamboat. You have to know the river, better than you know your own face in the mirror. You have to know every foot of it, four ways: up, down, day, night. You have to know every snag, every submerged tree, every shallow, and what's around every bend. It's hard, taxing, stressful work."

As she spoke his expression changed from vexation to comprehension. "You're scared. That's it, isn't it? You're afraid that you can't do it."

"I am not!" Jeanne fired back at him. "It's just that I'm an adult, with responsibilities, not a—a—singing machinist!

And while we're talking about this, just where were you thinking you'd live while you're swaggering up and down the river?"

"Where I'll live? Of course I want to live on the *Helena Rose*. Don't you?"

"Yes, I do, I love this cabin. And you?" she snapped.

He shrugged. "Sure, if you like this one you can have it, and all the furniture, too, if you want. The cabin across the hall is the same size, and I'll figure out furniture."

"So, la-di-da, you think you and I are going to live together," Jeanne said furiously. "I knew it!"

He retorted angrily, "You knew what? Pardon me, Mrs. Bettencourt, but what has got into that hot head of yours that you think I'm trying to seduce you? What have I said? Or done? Have I even looked at you funny?"

"Well, no, but—"

"No," he growled, "I have not. I'm half owner of this boat, and the engineer, and I deserve a cabin, and it has nothing to do with you."

"But it doesn't look right!" Jeanne countered heatedly.

"Unless you're planning on having a female crew, that's just part of the deal," he said bluntly.

Jeanne looked startled. "Oh . . . yes, I see what you mean. That is—I wasn't thinking—about that."

"Maybe not, but you are talking about living on the *Rose*, and that means you're thinking about piloting," Clint said with a hint of triumph. "So, can we talk about business now?"

"What? No. I need time to think," Jeanne said absently as she frowned ferociously and bit her lip.

"I thought we already covered all that. *Now* what do we have to think about?"

"I don't know, I don't know! Now I'm worse than when I got here, and it's all your fault!" Jeanne cried.

"My fault?" Clint blustered. "How'd that happen?"

"You don't mind staying overnight with the O'Dwyers, do you?" Jeanne asked.

"'Course not, Mama," Marvel answered happily. "Aideen and Noleen both got dolls for Christmas. Their dolls and Mrs. Topp and Avaymaria are having a weekend party in the country. They're going to dance, and sing, and eat cake and have tea."

Angus O'Dwyer was rarely home, for he was a crewman on a riverboat. Mrs. O'Dwyer was a good sitter for Marvel. She had six children, from ten years old to the year-old-twins. Her two daughters were six and four, and good company for Marvel. Jeanne paid the O'Dwyers ten cents a week to take care of Marvel, and often she gave them little gifts of food. Today she had bought a whole coconut sponge cake and a half pound of tea to give them. Jeanne had offered to pay Mrs. O'Dwyer extra for Marvel to stay the night, for the O'Dwyers usually went to bed at dark and Jeanne was meeting George Masters at six o'clock, which was after sunset in the winter. But Mrs. O'Dwyer had soundly refused the money, saying that she really should be paying Marvel, because she helped so much with the twins.

"Mama, I'm glad you're going with Mr. Masters," Marvel said. "I think he's nice. And you look so pretty!"

"Thank you, little one," Jeanne said. "Maybe sometime we can both go out in the carriage with Mr. Masters again."

"Okay. Um—Mama? Do you think I could go on over to the O'Dwyers now? Mrs. Topp and Avaymaria don't want to miss cake and tea."

"Of course." Jeanne bent to kiss her, and Marvel hurried out with her dolls.

Jeanne went back to look in the mirror, a dark clouded square hung on the wall. Her dark eyes sparkled, and her cheeks were not a chapped red, as Clint Hardin had blurted out that morning, but were flushed a delicate peach. Jeanne didn't own a bonnet, which bothered her in the extreme, for all ladies wore bonnets in public. But she had a bright green grosgrain ribbon she entwined in her curls and tied in a small jaunty bow just above her left ear. Her hair looked particularly well, she thought, with curls piled high at the crown and long ringlets cascading down to her shoulders.

She sighed when she looked down at her clothes. Jeanne didn't own a dress; she only had white blouses and four skirts: two gray, one dark blue, and one black. One of her blouses had a tiny bit of lace around the collar, and she had decided on that one, with a green tie made of the same ribbon in her hair, and the black skirt with three petticoats. She reflected that she was decidedly unfashionable, for her clothes still looked like a maid's Sunday clothes—which they were—and she had no fashionable Basque jacket or pelisse or bonnet or hoop skirt.

St. Peter's church bells began to ring the six o'clock hour, and Jeanne hurried to throw on her mantle and scarf. Then she thought wryly, *Why am I always hurrying to the sound of bells? And he's probably not there, anyway. He's probably come to his senses and is somewhere with his friends, congratulating himself on his narrow escape from mingling with the commoners . . .*

But he was there, standing outside the carriage, watching up the street. As soon as she appeared, he hurried to her. "I didn't think you'd come," he said happily. "I'm very glad you did."

"I am, too," she replied, "somewhat to my surprise."

He tucked her arm securely in his, then pulled her close to shelter her as they hurried to the carriage. The cold wind was still strong, and when it blew from the river it carried little stinging shards of ice. He opened the door to the carriage and helped her inside, then hurriedly climbed in. "Here, this will help, I think. What a bitter night!" He reached over to lay a beautiful fur lap robe over her. To Jeanne it was a curiously personal thing to do, though Masters showed no hint of such as he securely tucked the fur around her. He tapped the ceiling twice with his walking stick, then leaned back in his seat across from her and asked anxiously, "Are you frozen solid?"

"No, thank you, I'm quite warm now. Do you think we may be the only two fools out and about in this horrible weather?" she asked, her eyes alight.

"Oh, no, there'll be lots of other fools at the Courtier, I'm sure," he answered, matching her tone. "It's a very popular restaurant. Have you ever been there, Mrs. Bettencourt?"

"No, I haven't. I've heard it's very grand."

"I suppose it is," he said carelessly, "but what I like about it is the excellent food and the quality of service. Every waiter treats you as if he were your own private butler."

"Really? What a treat for me. I've never seen a real live butler," Jeanne said dryly.

He studied her for long moments. "Mrs. Bettencourt, with your permission, I'd like to speak plainly to you."

"You have my permission."

"I would very much like for us to get past this class distinction," he said quietly.

"But that's ridiculous," Jeanne said instantly. "You're rich—apparently—and I am not. Those are just facts, and it would be silly for me to ignore them."

"And so that is how you define me, and how you define yourself. I am rich. You are poor. That's all there is to either of us."

"I didn't say that," Jeanne objected. "It's just that it's an obstacle."

"Only to you," he shot back. "Not to me. And I have to tell you, Jeanne, that I'm disappointed that you only see me as a sort of mindless puppet, going around spending money. I certainly don't see you as a 'poor' woman. You're intelligent and witty, you're intriguing, you have all the graces of a highborn lady. You are, in fact, a lady that I wish to know better. Couldn't you give me the same consideration?"

Jeanne thought for a few moments, then said, "As a matter of fact, I can, and I will. From now on I will treat you as a gentleman that I wish to know better."

"Good," he said with relief. "So let's start over again, shall we?"

"I'll start over again, there's no need for you to do so, you've been doing just fine. I have been wondering about you, and not just how much money you have," Jeanne said with a smile. "You've been residing in the hotel the entire holidays. Do you have any family?"

"I have an uncle who lives in Charleston, South Carolina," he said, "and some cousins. My mother died eight years ago, and my father died just this past June."

"That's not a long time to get over such a loss. Has the holiday season been difficult for you?"

"In some ways. But as I'm making a new friend that I find is excellent company, and also is lovely to look at, the holiday season is getting better all the time," he said, his blue eyes alight. "If I may be so bold."

"You may. I'm glad I can provide you some diversion."

"A lot of diversion," he said solidly. "Very welcome diversion, Jeanne. May I please call you 'Jeanne'?"

"Now that is bold," Jeanne teased, "and you may. Now tell me about your home. I assume you do have one besides the Gayoso House Hotel?"

George told her about his plantation, Morecambe, that was ten miles north of Memphis, until they reached the Courtier, a two-story stucco building with every window alight and a wide glassed double-door entry. In the foyer a heavy-lidded, disdainful-looking man standing at a podium came forward to greet them. "Mr. Masters, welcome. And madame," he said with a slight nod, looking Jeanne up and down with a jaundiced eye.

"Good evening, Martel," George said pleasantly. "I assume you have the table I requested?"

"Certainly, Mr. Masters. Please follow me."

The main floor of the restaurant had eight large round tables. Five of them were occupied by families with children, two of them had groups of well-dressed gentlemen engaged in earnest conversation. On each side was an enormous fireplace, six feet high and eight feet wide, with great roaring fires crackling hungrily. Along the side walls and back wall, one floor up, was a gallery. Martel led them up a curved marble staircase to the gallery, and indicated one of the walled alcoves with a small table and two chairs. The table was set up against the balustrade overlooking the main dining room. All of the tables were lit with long white taper candles, and along the velvet-upholstered walls were lanterns with golden yellow shades. The entire room glowed with soft light.

Martel took George's hat, coat, and gloves and Jeanne's cape and muffler. "Your steward will be here shortly, Mr. Masters," he said with a low bow and disappeared.

Jeanne looked around with appreciation. "This is lovely. It looks like the great hall of a castle, and we're in the minstrel gallery."

"I think that's what Kinley had in mind when he built it," George said. "But as I said, it's not the trappings I come for, it's the food. Tell me, what would you like? They have all kinds of roast joints, oysters, salmon, lobster, any kind of soup you can think of, and the vegetables are all fresh. They bring them in from Mexico."

"Really?" Jeanne said with delight. "Oh, how I miss fresh vegetables in the winter! I don't care for winter fare, cabbages and turnips, and I hate to admit it but I can't abide brussels sprouts."

"Then you certainly shall not have brussels sprouts. What about meat?"

"I like beef best of all. Any kind of beef."

"Then may I recommend we have beef Wellington? It's my particular favorite. Of course, many ladies say that it's too rich and heavy for them," he added deferentially.

"I don't know what beef Wellington is," Jeanne said, "but since it has the word 'beef' in it, I'm sure I'll like it."

"It's a very lean roasted joint, covered with *pâté de foie gras* and mushroom duxelles and then baked in a puff pastry," he said with animation. "Courtier's is the best I've ever had."

Their starter was a buttery oyster soup, then deviled eggs with a pickled pepper-and-celery relish. The beef Wellington arrived, along with sliced brown carrots, green peas, sautéed onions, and fresh rolls with sweet cream butter. Jeanne took her first bite of beef Wellington and her eyes grew round. "Oh, oh, this is the most delicious morsel I've ever put in my mouth," she said. "I'm afraid now I'll be spoiled, I won't want just plain roasted beef any more."

"Then we'll have beef Wellington all the time," George said. "That would be fine with me. So, Jeanne, I've been very curious about what you said yesterday, that you've had some good news, and you have some important decisions to make. If you feel you can talk about it, I'd be interested to hear."

"You know, ordinarily I wouldn't discuss my personal life with a comparative stranger, but I've been feeling very reckless the past few days," Jeanne said, her dark eyes dancing. "I just don't want to bore you."

"I don't think that's possible, Jeanne," he said gallantly. "Tell me all."

She told him about Deshler, and about Ira Hardin and inheriting the *Helena Rose*. "But one complication is that I'm a one-half partner with the most infuriating man," she said, her color high. "I'm beginning to see that a business partnership can be difficult."

He frowned. "You aren't speaking of an actual working relationship, are you? Surely you're going to sell the *Helena Rose*, so you're just worried about dealing with splitting the proceeds with this man, correct?"

"It's more complicated than that. You see, I lived on a riverboat with my parents until I was seventeen. My father owned the boat, and was the pilot and captain. It was wonderful," she said, starry-eyed. "My mother was my tutor, and my father taught me about the river. In fact, he taught me to pilot."

George's eyebrows shot up. "You can pilot a riverboat?"

"Yes, I can. It's odd, because the *Helena Rose* is so much like our boat, the *Pearl*; they're about the same size, with the same tonnage. Even the pilothouse and captain's cabins are similar. I think piloting the *Rose* would be much like the *Pearl*."

"Surely you can't be thinking of becoming a riverboat pilot!" George exclaimed.

"But I am," Jeanne said spiritedly. "That's the important decision I was talking about."

He sat back in his chair, his face a study in surprise. "I don't understand. It's unheard of, Jeanne, a woman piloting a riverboat. You would be subject to all kinds of abuse from rivermen, not to mention the scandal."

"I don't care about any of that! I'm a chambermaid, George, it's not like I'm a daughter of the Founding Fathers. And as far as abuse from rivermen, I know very well how to handle them. My mother taught me to read and speak and behave with dignity, but my father taught me the river. I can do this, George, and I can do it well."

Now Jeanne was herself surprised, because she realized that in the afternoon she had been arguing with Clint Hardin about selling the boat, and now she was arguing with George Masters about piloting the boat. But even as she reflected, she suddenly knew that she wanted her and Marvel to live on the *Helena Rose*, she wanted to get her pilot's license, she wanted to find out how to get freight, she wanted to know everything about making a living with a boat that she owned. "I'm going to do it," she told George with a bright smile. "Just now, I've realized that this is a blessing from the Lord, and I'd be crazy to sell the *Rose*."

"Well then," he said, sitting up again and spearing a chunk of beef Wellington, "I think you should do it. If anyone can do it, you can. I've seen that already. And what's more, Jeanne, I'll help you."

"Would you?" she said with delight. "Can you?"

"I might be a stuffy old thing," he said ruefully, "but I've got a few tricks up my sleeve. I predict that within two weeks Captain Jeanne Bettencourt will rule the river!"

CHAPTER SEVEN

"Marvel, this is Mr. Clint Hardin that I've told you about," Jeanne said.

Marvel made her little curtsey-bob; Clint instantly went down on one knee so that he would be eye-level with her. "Marvel, I'm pleased to meet you," he said. "Welcome to the *Helena Rose*. I hear you're going to be our captain?"

Marvel giggled. "I'm not the captain, my mama is. Do you remember me? I remember you, you're the Singing Man. You winked at me."

"I sure do. You and your mama were at the Christmas Regale, and I saw you. You had holly and ivy garlands, and I thought you looked like beautiful fairy spirits of Christmas," he said. "I winked because you have to let the fairies know you see them when they magically appear."

"We're not fairies, we're real," Marvel said gravely.

"Ah, I know that now, but I didn't on Christmas Eve," he said. "So just to be safe I had to wink."

Marvel nodded knowingly, then held up her doll. "This is my doll I got for Christmas. I named her Avaymaria."

"Did you? That's a very pretty name."

"I named her after your song," Marvel said earnestly. "I think that song was the best song I ever heard. Would you please sing it to me?"

"Not now, little one," Jeanne said hastily as Clint rose, grinning. "You haven't met the rest of the crew yet. This is Mr. Ezra Givens, our fireman, and Roberty, our deckhand."

Marvel and Ezra Givens exchanged hellos, but Marvel immediately went to Roberty's side. "Mama said you've been bringing us wood this winter. That's good because it's cold. How do you know how to be a deckhand?"

"Ezra's teaching me," he said shyly. "It was nice of your ma to give me a job."

"She is nice," Marvel said. "Where's Leo? Mama's told me all about Leo."

"We can go wake him up, if your mama says it's all right." Roberty looked up at Jeanne. "He's asleep in the boiler room."

"Marvel, do you want to see Leo before you see our cabin?" Jeanne asked doubtfully.

"Yes, ma'am, I'm so excited we have a dog! Where did you say he is?" she asked Roberty.

"He's in the boiler room, but on the river we call it the firebox," he explained, now with a slightly superior air.

With amusement Jeanne said, "Well, Roberty, since you probably know more than I do about the boat, why don't you show Marvel around? Mr. Hardin and I have a lot of business to discuss. Ezra, you'll keep an eye out, won't you?"

"Sure thing, ma'am. She's a purty leetle mite, no bigger'n a butterfly," Ezra said. "I'll watch out for her." They all went into the boiler room, and Marvel squealed as soon as she saw Leo, threw herself across him, and kissed him right on the mouth.

"I didn't see her kiss that dog on the mouth, did I?" Jeanne said darkly as they went up the stairs to what was now Jeanne's cabin. "That does it, I'm going to wash her mouth out with carbolic soap."

"Aw, a little dog slobber never hurt anyone," Clint said. "I think you're joshing anyway. You are, aren't you?"

"Of course, I would never do that to Marvel." They went into the cabin and sat down at the desk, for Jeanne had mentioned that it would be nice for them both to be able to sit there, instead of her craning her neck up to look at him all the time. The next time she'd come to the boat, a second plain straight chair had appeared. Jeanne had forgotten to ask Clint about it, or to thank him.

"I was beginning to wonder if I still had a partner," he said. "It's been a week since I saw you at Deshler's." They had met the previous Thursday at Deshler's office to sign all the papers, go through all the legal documents, and get their cash. Jeanne had told Clint then that she had indeed decided to pilot the *Rose*, and she would let him know when she and Marvel would be moving in.

"I have literally been so busy I couldn't get time to come down here," she admitted. "I had to keep working for three days. I gave them two weeks' notice, but I have a friend that arranged for me to be able to leave without any recriminations. Marvel even had to remind me that it was New Year's Eve. Happy New Year, by the way. What about you? Have you been working? Are you moved in yet?"

"We had a job that had to be finished before I could leave. I've been working for Mr. Warner for ten years, so I couldn't just ride off into the sunset. We finished up that job a couple of days ago, and I moved in yesterday afternoon. Want to come see my cabin? I've got new furniture."

"No, thank you," Jeanne said frostily. "The only thing I'm adding to our cabin is a dining room table and four chairs. They're supposed to be delivered tomorrow morning, and Marvel and I will be moving in tomorrow afternoon."

"You want me and Ezra and Vinnie to come move you?" Clint offered. "I know where we can rent a cart."

"That's not necessary, all we're bringing are our trunks, and I have a friend with a carriage. He's going to bring us."

"Okay," Clint said tentatively. "Then what are we going to do? Live happily ever after?"

"Are you ever serious about anything at all?" Jeanne said sharply. "I've been working on getting the *Helena Rose* on the river, and I have accomplished a lot. When my friend brings us to the *Rose* tomorrow, I want you to meet with us, and we'll discuss it all then."

"What friend? Discuss what?" Clint demanded.

"Our plans for the *Helena Rose*."

"What *our*? I'm your partner, remember? Don't you think you might let me in on *our* plans?"

"Oh. Yes, I see what you're saying," Jeanne said thoughtfully. "But to tell the truth, I'd feel much better if we discuss everything with Mr. Masters. It'll just be tomorrow afternoon, Mr. Hardin. I'm sure you can wait until then."

CLINT DIDN'T HAVE MUCH of a choice, so he waited until the next afternoon and watched with a jaundiced eye as Jeanne, Marvel, and their trunks drove up in an elegant barouche box with glassed windows. Marvel's shining face was at one of the windows, and suddenly Clint recalled seeing her in that same carriage, after the Regale, on Main Street. Mr. Masters must be a good friend indeed, if they had spent Christmas Eve with him. Clint wondered about him and

Jeanne, for it was unusual, he knew, for a chambermaid/ female riverboat pilot to have such a well-to-do "friend." Eve Poynter Maxfield's face rose up in front of his eyes, but then he told himself that he had never ridden in Eve's carriage, certainly not in public. He had been visiting her this past week, while her parents were in the country, but he always came in the tradesman's back entrance to the house.

Marvel ran up the gangplank, with Jeanne and Masters following more decorously behind. Jeanne had on new clothes, Clint noted, a maroon skirt with a matching short cape. She was wearing a new bonnet that he thought was hideous.

"Mr. Hardin, I have the pleasure of introducing you to Mr. George Masters," Jeanne said when they reached him. "Mr. Masters, this is my partner, and the engineer of the *Helena Rose*, Mr. Clinton Hardin."

Clint stuck out his hand, and Masters shook it firmly. He was dressed in a dark blue frock coat, black trousers with a sharply-pressed seam, spit-shined half boots, and a black silk top hat. Clint was wearing his work clothes, as always, a blue flannel shirt over a cotton undershirt, canvas duck trousers, and his old brogans. He had been working in the engine room, and had oil smudges on the knees of his breeches, and that bothered him. At least his hands were clean. And George Masters' hands were as soft as a woman's, he noted smugly.

"Masters," he said.

"Mr. Hardin, a pleasure to meet you," George said pleasantly.

"Mr. Clint, Mr. Masters remembers you," Marvel said excitedly. "We talked about you riding home in the carriage after the Regale. He said you sing really good."

"Really well," Jeanne corrected her.

"Thanks," Clint said shortly to Masters.

Jeanne gave him a cautious glance, then said brightly, "Marvel, why don't we go find Roberty? I'm sure wherever Roberty is, Leo will be with him."

"Okay, Mama. But 'member, I live here now, so you don't have to tell me where to go all the time," Marvel reminded her. "I already know where everything is." She ran into the boiler room and they heard her call, "Roberty! I'm home!"

Jeanne smiled, then asked Clint, "Was the table delivered today?"

"Yes, ma'am, and the four chairs. We put them in your cabin. If you don't like how we fixed it, we'll move it around."

Jeanne, George, and Clint went up to the cabin, and Jeanne surveyed the room with satisfaction. The desk was still underneath the windows along the back wall, the dining table was in the center of the room, and the two armchairs and tea table were down by the bed, across from the armoire. Jeanne had bought a wool carpet with an embroidered rose motif that covered the end of the room where the chairs and armoire were. The room looked homey and comfortable, and it was delightfully warm. Clint had been keeping one boiler fired up, and it heated the entire boat. "That's perfect, thank you, Mr. Hardin," Jeanne said with satisfaction. "Now, one reason I wanted this table is for a worktable, since my desk is small. Please, gentlemen, sit down." She took off her bonnet and cape, then took Master's hat and gloves. "George? We forgot about the trunks. All of our papers are in there."

"Yes, of course," he said, hastily rising again. "I'll go get the driver to bring them up."

"Don't worry about it, George," Clint said airily. "I'll take care of the manual labor."

He sauntered out, and George resumed his seat. Jeanne joined him and said, "I told you he's impossible."

"Maybe. But I have to say that we've put him in an awkward position, Jeanne. Can't blame a man for having a little resentment in this situation."

"What situation?" Jeanne demanded. "After all, you've done nothing but help."

"I've helped *you*," he countered. "To him, I've just come aboard his boat without a by-your-leave."

"So let's say you came on board my half of the boat at my by-your-leave, and I now extend you an open invitation to board any time you want."

"Yes, I'm sure that will make Mr. Hardin feel much better," George said with a chuckle.

Clint and Ezra came in then, carrying Jeanne's and Marvel's trunks. Jeanne said, "Just put them over here, please." They put them down by the armoire, and Ezra made a quick bow and scooted out. Jeanne opened her trunk and took out a logbook, a sheaf of papers, and several rolled maps and dumped them all on the table. "You see, Mr. Hardin, I know the Arkansas River, but I don't know the Mississippi. And that was the problem. The big problem."

"Why is that?" Clint asked. "You learned the Arkansas, you can learn the Mississippi, right?"

"I could, in a couple of years, if I was a cub on a boat with a good pilot," Jeanne answered.

"Ah. That is a problem," Clint said.

"And another problem is that I don't have a pilot's license," Jeanne went on. "The Steamboat Act that was passed in 1852 requires all boats to have a licensed pilot. So pilots started taking cubs, and when they felt that the cub was expert enough, usually after a two-year period, as I said, they would certify to the marine inspector that the apprentice was a qualified pilot, and he would get his license."

Clint frowned. "Is there any good news in this anywhere?"

Jeanne smiled warmly at George Masters. "Thanks to Mr. Masters, it's all good news. He knows a pilot that is going to take me on a short cruise to Helena, then down to Napoleon Trading Post, and then back here, and then certify me to the marine inspector, who is a friend of his. Also, this pilot has kindly consented to coach me on this trip, because with the freight runs Mr. Masters has worked out for us, between here and Napoleon is going to be the only stretch of the Mississippi River I'll have to learn."

Clint leaned forward and clasped his fists on the table. His knuckles had healed up, but they still had red lumpy scar tissue. "Okay, first, what is Napoleon Trading Post?"

"That's a settlement right where the Arkansas comes into the Mississippi," George explained. He unrolled a map, then pointed. "You see? It's nothing but a collection of log huts, but it's been settled since de Soto's time. There are even some Choctaw Indians left there."

Clint ran his finger down the wide green swath of the Mississippi River, then pointed. "Are you telling me that this is the Arkansas River, right here?"

"It is. It's really better than it looks."

"It looks like a skinny wriggling worm," Clint rasped. "And you can pilot that?"

Jeanne looked uncomfortable. "It is difficult from Napoleon to Pine Bluff," she admitted. "But I've done it many times. It's just a matter of knowing the river, and concentrating while you're navigating it. The Arkansas is much smaller than the Mississippi, much narrower, it flows faster, and in many places it's much deeper. But there aren't nearly as many steamboats on the Arkansas River, mainly because only the smaller ones can navigate it. And that has proved to be a big advantage for us."

Clint studied the map for a few moments, then murmured, "I see. Pine Bluff, Little Rock, Fort Smith, those are all sizable towns. If there are only a few steamboats servicing them I would imagine freight would be fairly easy to come by."

"Last year only thirteen boats went to Little Rock," Masters said. "I guarantee you the *Rose* will have freight."

"I'm not going to Fort Smith," Jeanne said curtly. "But Mr. Masters has figured out how we can have profitable runs to Little Rock and back. Mr. Masters is friends with the Memphis postmaster, and he was able to get us a contract to carry the mail, Memphis to Helena to Pine Bluff to Little Rock, and of course it's a turnaround each trip. That means we pick up both coming and going."

"Yeah, I've heard of that," Clint said dryly. "How much does it pay?"

"Only ten dollars per stop/per trip," Jeanne said, "so it's eighty dollars round trip."

"Not bad for a few sacks of mail," Clint said thoughtfully. "We'll have room to haul plenty of other cargo, if we can get it."

"We can," Jeanne said. "Mr. Masters says that Little Rock and Pine Bluff are crying for any finished goods, any textiles, any processed foods like tinned vegetables and fruit, and any coal deliveries in the winter are snatched right up."

"And for return freight, Little Rock has the best crushed stone mines in the United States," Masters said. "Their problem has always been transport. You can pick up all the crushed stone you can hold any time of the year. With that, and lumber out of Pine Bluff, the *Rose* should be able to stay loaded all the time."

Clint said with interest, "You know, crushed stone and lumber are heavy loads, and we're not a big boat. But we can carry a lot for our size. The *Rose* draws six inches empty and only ten inches loaded. That'll work on the Arkansas River, right?"

"Oh, yes," Jeanne assured him. "As I said, it's narrower, but deeper."

"Sounds like you've got it all worked out. Thank you, Mr. Masters. I appreciate your help," Clint said sincerely. "But I just have one question. Where are you going to find this angelic pilot that's going to babysit us for a couple of days? And how much is he going to cost us?"

"There is an excellent pilot that I've already spoken to, and he's very happy to assist Mrs. Bettencourt. He won't charge you anything at all. His name is Francis Buckner."

Incredulously, Clint said, "Buck Buckner's name is *Francis*? And you say he's going to do us a favor, out of the goodness of his heart? I find that hard to believe."

Masters gave him a dry smile. "Believe it, Mr. Hardin. He works for me, you see. I'm half owner of the *Lady Vandivere*."

BY THE TIME THEY finished their meeting, Clint had thawed enough towards George Masters to offer to take him on a tour of the boiler room and engine room. Masters had accepted the offer with a good will, though Jeanne was sure she saw a flash of panic on his face before he did. *He'll probably die of embarrassment if he gets a smudge on his fine frock coat*, she thought whimsically. *I doubt he's ever seen a steam boiler in his life.*

Jeanne took out her list, which was long and complicated, and decided to do the hardest thing first: the galley. She had to take stock of what they had, make a list of what they needed, and then go shopping for it all. Sighing, she went down the hall. The door was open, and Ezra Givens stood at the counter grinding a loaf of sugar through a sieve.

Roberty and Marvel sat close together on two stools, peeling potatoes. Leo's long gangly body lay against the wall underneath the far counter, his head resting on a sack of coffee beans. He looked up and saw her, gave her his usual two-thump with his tail, and wearily laid back down. "Does that dog ever move except to change sleeping places?" she asked.

"He pretty much finds out warm cubbyholes to lie up in winter," Ezra said thoughtfully. "Come spring and summer he gets right frisky."

"Leo, frisky? This I must see. Marvel, your hands are red and they're going to get chapped," Jeanne warned.

"But I'm learning how to peel potatoes, you wouldn't ever let me do it," she objected. "I'm being really careful, I promise. Can't I please, Mama?"

"My child is begging me to let her peel potatoes," Jeanne said to Ezra. "You don't think I've spoiled her, do you?"

"No, ma'am," he answered sturdily. "Seems to me like she's been brung up just fine."

"Thank you, Ezra. Now, maybe you can help me. We're going to go on a four-day run day after tomorrow, and I know that we need to stock the galley. I don't have any idea how much food to buy, or what kind of food to buy, and if we need any pots or pans or utensils. So I need to make a shopping list, and I suppose I'll spend all day tomorrow cooking," she finished half to herself.

"Well, yes ma'am, I can help you with all that 'cause it's already did," Ezra said. "Clint's done bought food, I mean, and all the fixins we need like salt and sugar and seasonings. I sorta got to cooking for Bull and the crew, and so there it is. No need for you to be cooking, Miz Bettencourt, unless you just have a hankering to."

"No, I don't have a hankering to," Jeanne said with vast relief. "But how can you work the boat and be the cook at the same time?"

"Can't, 'less you take on another crewman," Ezra said succinctly.

Jeanne nodded. "Yes, I agree, it takes at least three deck-hands, doesn't it? I'll talk to Mr. Hardin about it. Marvel, are you sure you're not tired? The cabin's all fixed, you could take a nap."

"Do I have to?" she complained. "I'd rather peel potatoes."

"Then I'll leave you to it," Jeanne said with amusement. "If any of you see Mr. Hardin, would you ask him to come up to the cabin, please?"

She went back up to her papers and was poring over a map when Clint knocked once and came in. "Masters doesn't know a boiler from a reach rod," he said with satisfaction. "He's a nice toff, though."

"He's not a toff," Jeanne argued.

"He is. He can't help it. Anyway, I'm grateful to him for everything he's done. It's come in handy, you being friends with the man that owns the *Lady Vandivere*. And the mail. And all of the crushed stone and lumber in Arkansas."

"Silly. No one owns the mail," Jeanne replied. "I've been down to the galley and talked to Ezra. Thank you so much for taking care of the food and supplies. You know, we really should start keeping records of the expenses we incur for the boat."

"Yeah, I'm keeping up with my end. We'll need to get a system going," Clint said. "But not now. I wanted to talk to you about hiring my buddy Vince Norville. He's been a roustabout for years. I know that doesn't mean he knows about crewing a boat, but he sure knows more than I did when I first walked onto the *Rose*."

Jeanne nodded. "If you think he'll be good help, then by all means hire him. And that reminds me, I haven't thanked you for letting me take on Roberty. I just couldn't think of what else to do with him."

"Way I see it, it's not a question of you doing anything with him. He's young and yeah, he's kinda small, but that boy works. If he doesn't have something to do he comes and begs for chores. Feed him some good solid food, fatten him up, give him a warm place to sleep, he'll do fine."

"That's a great relief to me. I've been worrying about him for a long time. Thank you."

"No, no thanks needed," Clint said dismissively. "So, Mrs. Bettencourt, are you ready?"

"Mr. Hardin, I am ready!"

SATURDAY DAWNED, A COLD and crisp day with a cheerful sun. George Masters walked up the gangplank, taking measured steps, rhythmically tapped out with his gold eagle's-head walking stick. Behind him Buck Buckner ambled along, looking over the *Helena Rose* with a disdainful expression. Jeanne and Clint met them, and after desultory introductions Jeanne took Masters's arm and led him to her cabin, while Clint and Buck went up to the pilothouse.

"Never thought you'd be working for me, Buck," Clint needled him.

"And don't think it now," he retorted. "I wouldn't do this for anyone but my owner."

"Masters says you're doing it because you're such a charitable man. That's when I was sure it must be someone else, not Buck Buckner. Oh, I forgot! It was *Francis* Buckner we were talking about!"

"If you mention that name again I'm going to beat you senseless," Buckner said casually.

"Uh—you might have a little problem there, Buck. Remember me? Clint the Flint Fist?"

"So I'll pay someone else to beat you senseless. And just so you won't worry about me, my man, there's no charity about it. Masters is paying me top dollar for this little scheme," Buckner said, opening the door of the wheelhouse and looking around. "So this is it, huh?"

"This is it. What do you think?"

Buck turned to him and crossed his arms. "I think this little hopped-up flatboat isn't going to make you a wooden nickel, Hardin. Don't you have any good sense? Running a riverboat with a bloomin' petticoat for a pilot?"

"She wouldn't like you to call her a bloomin' petticoat," Clint warned him. "I wouldn't do it if I were you. She's tougher than she looks."

Buckner shrugged. "I'll call her Royal Exalted Highness if it makes her happy. But she'll never be able to cut it, you know that. It's a man's world, and no pilot on this river or any other is going to put up with a female pilot."

"You are," Clint said idly.

Buck's smooth brow lowered, but before he could say anything Jeanne and George Masters came into the pilot-house. "Everything in order, Mr. Buckner?" George asked.

"It would seem so, sir. She's a fine, neat little boat," Buckner said politely. Behind Jeanne, Clint rolled his eyes at him.

"Good, good," George murmured.

Jeanne stepped up to the wheel and Buckner turned, solicitously leaning over her as she told him, "Just so we're very clear, Mr. Buckner, I'd like to go over the points and markers before we go. It's been a long time since I've been down the river."

"I'm sure you'll do fine, Mrs. Bettencourt," he said courteously. "Would you like to go over the charts?"

Clint left them then, and George Masters settled down on the bench, his top hat tipped back a little, his legs crossed, and his manicured hands resting on his cane.

"That's correct, Mrs. Bettencourt, President's Island, Council Bluff, Cottonwood Grove, Island Number 60," Buck was saying, pointing to her waterway chart. "Helena's just past there. It's about seventy-five miles to Helena—that's five hours—and from there eighty to the mouth of the Arkansas, another five hours. Do I understand that you want to stay in Napoleon Trading Post overnight? Because I don't think they have a hotel or anything there."

"No, I'm afraid we've had a misunderstanding," Jeanne said quickly. "I have no intention of steaming the *Rose* at fifteen miles an hour. We're not racing, Mr. Buckner. And the way we have our freight worked out, there's no need; we're on a four-day run to Little Rock, and that means overnight in Helena, Napoleon, and Pine Bluff. That suits me just fine, because I have no intention of staying at the wheel for more than eight hours at a time."

Buckner shrugged. "Whatever you say, Mrs. Bettencourt."

"That's very kind of you, Mr. Buckner," Jeanne said gratefully. "Naturally, we'll pay for your hotel in Helena. At Napoleon, I'm afraid you'll have to bunk in the crew quarters."

Seeing the expression on Buckner's face, George said quickly, "I apologize that I didn't make it quite clear to you, Mr. Buckner. I'm sure we can work out any *adjustments* needed."

Buckner's face cleared. "That's fine, Mr. Masters. Mrs. Bettencourt, we'll just go with your schedule, ma'am. Your boat, your call."

Jeanne turned to Masters. "I can't thank you enough, George. I can't tell you how much this means to me and to Marvel."

He rose and bowed deeply, doffing his hat. "Ma'am, it has been a particular pleasure working with you, and I'm glad to do anything to make you happy. Mr. Buckner, I know you'll take very good care of Mrs. Bettencourt?"

"Of course, sir."

George nodded and replaced his hat. "I'll say good-bye then, Jeanne. I'll see you when you get back, I'll be waiting."

After he left, Buckner turned to Jeanne. "Your pilot-house, your call, ma'am."

The *Helena Rose* backed away from the Memphis shore, shivered a little as she filled, then she slipped into the lazy brown waters of the Mississippi River. As they started downriver, Jeanne breathed, "At last!"

CHAPTER EIGHT

Buck Buckner proved to be a good river tutor for Jeanne; he was professional, though a bit cool. He stood by the wheel, arms crossed, saying very little except for pointing out the landmarks and snags and currents. Jeanne was surprised at how much she remembered of the Mississippi between Memphis and the Arkansas River mouth. She was also surprised at how extremely weary she was after piloting for eight hours. But she told herself that that would get better.

After their four-day trip, Jeanne was feeling like an old hand when she pulled the *Helena Rose* up to the familiar docks at Memphis. Buckner turned to her and smiled, a tight controlled expression. "You did very well, ma'am. Good luck to you and the *Rose*. You're going to need it." It was the only smile, and the only hint of his attitude he had given her the entire trip.

Jeanne went down to the main deck. Marvel immediately clasped her legs, and the others crowded around her.

"You did real good, Captain Jeanne," Clint said, extending his hand, and Jeanne readily shook it.

Ezra, Roberty, and Vince all congratulated her, calling her 'Captain Jeanne', and Jeanne decided to let the rather impertinent nickname stand. "You're a good crew," she told them. "I appreciate you all very much."

They all talked excitedly until Clint looked over Jeanne's shoulder and said, "The toff is here, Cap'n."

"He's not a toff," Jeanne said with gritted teeth, then went to meet George Masters at the gangplank. "I did it, George!" she exclaimed. "I can't believe it!"

He tucked her hand into his arm and said warmly, "I can believe it. I passed Mr. Buckner back there, and he tells me you're a good, solid pilot." They slowly walked to the railing on the main deck and stood talking quietly.

Clint and Vince exchanged meaningful glances, while Ezra said, "You Roberty and you Miss Marvel, I'm thinking I might roast up that big fat ham for celebratin' tonight. I could use some help." He led them to the stairs, their young voices piping excitedly about some promised fried apples.

Vince said to Clint, "Looks like the captain's going to be occupied for awhile. Want to go check in at the Bell and Whistle?"

"Sure," Clint agreed, watching Jeanne and Masters thoughtfully. "But don't start a fight this time, Vinnie. My knuckles have just now healed up."

"I keep telling you to carry a gun. All you have to do is wave it around a little, puts a stop to all the nonsense."

"Then why do I keep getting dragged into saloon brawls with you all the time?"

"Aw, admit it, it's fun. You brawl all the time, Clint the Flint Fist."

"Yeah, but that's because people give me money for it."

Jeanne and George, still arm-in-arm, joined Clint and Vince. Jeanne said, "We're going to pick up our first load Tuesday, Mr. Hardin. It's all set. May I ask if you'll be on the boat tomorrow?"

"I was planning on it," Clint answered. "Why, did you need something?"

Jeanne glanced up at George hesitantly, but he merely smiled at her. Finally with some difficulty Jeanne said, "Mr. Masters has invited me to visit his home tomorrow. But someone needs to be here, just in case there's any business that needs to be done with the shippers or suppliers. And then there's Marvel . . . I suppose I need to take her to the O'Dwyers."

"Why? The *Rose* is her home, and she's got the whole crew wrapped around her little pinky finger," Clint said. "She'll be fine here. And yes, I'll be glad to take care of anything that comes up, Captain Jeanne."

As JEANNE WALKED DOWN the gangplank to meet George, she saw that he had traveled in a new carriage. It was bigger than the one he had borrowed, with brass lanterns and door latches, and the body painted midnight blue. The driver was a dignified-looking black man with his coachman's cloak and tall gray top hat. It was hitched to a couple of dappled horses that pranced and snorted, their breath making little steam bursts in the cold air. George helped her into the carriage and then got in and as always tucked a fur around her lap.

"This is a new carriage," Jeanne said. "Did you buy it?"

"No, Dr. Hightower just got tired of loaning me his barouche. I sent word to the plantation and instructed my driver to bring my own carriage into town yesterday. Do you like it?"

"Oh, yes, it's as big as a parlor," Jeanne said. "And the seats are so much more comfortable."

"They are, aren't they? I think Hightower skimped a little on his padding. So, Jeanne, now we have time. Tell me all about your trip."

They talked all the way about Jeanne's experience piloting again, about Buck Buckner, about the *Helena Rose* and her upcoming first freight run. After about two hours George glanced out the window and said, "Well, there's my home. How do you like it?"

Jeanne was ready for something better than ordinary but was taken aback at the sight of Morecambe, the Masters family plantation. A long sweeping drive lined with massive oaks and broad enough for three carriages led up a gentle slope to the mansion crowning it.

Morecambe House was a two-story building with white Corinthian columns across the front and along both sides. A balcony, set off by an ornate iron grill painted black ran all the way around the second floor. Tall wide windows could be seen on both floors of the house, with pale blue shutters breaking the luminous white of the stucco. The steeply pitched roof ran up to a center point broken by three gables on each side. High-rising chimneys capped with curving covers of brick added further beauty to the building. They pulled up in front of the house, and a black servant wearing a butler's tie and tails came out to open the carriage door, bowing deeply as Jeanne alighted.

George and Jeanne mounted the steps and the pair of enormous oak doors opened as if by magic. As they passed into the foyer Jeanne saw two black maids curtseying by the open doors. Jeanne's attention was immediately drawn to a broad, graceful stairway leading up to the second floor.

The entrance hall and the staircase were of marble with a twilight gray swirl, and the elaborate wrought-iron stair railing looked like black lace.

A dignified-looking lady in her fifties came up to them and George said, "This is Mrs. Rawlings, my housekeeper." The lady nodded and took their hats and coats. George asked Jeanne, "Would you like to see the house?"

"Yes, very much."

George led Jeanne around the first floor of the house and the tour included a somber, well-stocked library, with glassed cases and busts of Roman emperors displayed. "I haven't spent much time in here," George admitted.

"I think I would have a hard time ever leaving this room," Jeanne said. There must have been four or five hundred books.

"You're a big reader, are you? A bluestocking," he teased. "You've surprised me again, Jeanne. How about we take a look at my favorite room?"

She followed him across the hall, and he opened the double doors. "The dining room," he said with a boyish grin. "You might know it would be my favorite."

It was at least twenty by twenty-two feet in size and floored from wall to wall with Aubusson carpet. The walls were wallpapered in gold with a bright green fleur-de-lis pattern. At the far end, overlooking the front grounds, were twelve-foot-high glassed French doors. On each side was a fireplace, the marble mantles holding pairs of silver George III six-light candelabras on a spreading circular base. Candle chandeliers of silver and crystal hung over the dining table, which was of mahogany and seated twelve. Lining the walls were Elizabethan carved chairs that looked like small thrones. "What an elegant room," Jeanne breathed.

"It's not really my favorite," George admitted. "It's far too formal. We have a smaller family dining room that I like to use unless I have a number of guests. In fact, that's where I told Mrs. Rawlings to serve dinner tonight. I hope that's all right with you."

"Oh, but I was so looking forward to being stranded about a mile and a half from you at the end of that monstrous table," Jeanne said.

"Sorry, I had something a little closer in mind. Over here, across the hall, is the ballroom." The empty room, with gleaming oak flooring, had a graceful arched entryway. George continued, "This comes in handy for big parties. In the summer we sometimes have as many as fifty or sixty of our neighbors come for two or three days. We have picnics and barbecues, hunting and archery, horse races, things like that, and dancing at night."

"It's very beautiful! I never saw a house with its own ballroom. You didn't build this house, did you, George?"

"No, my great-grandfather did. We've added onto it, though. In fact, it was my father that added the ballroom. He did love dancing."

"You must miss him very much."

"I do," George said quietly. "He was a good man, and a good father."

He then led her upstairs, where there were nine bedrooms, all roomy and grandly furnished. Jeanne's mind whirled. Even the smallest bedroom was much bigger than her room at the Pinch. But she was careful to say nothing like that; ever since she had come to understand that it was she, not George, who was so mindful of the difference in their stations, she had determined not to be so class-conscious. She admired all the rooms, and George led her back downstairs. "I'd like to take you on a tour of the plantation. I have an open landau that I thought you might like. It's sort of like a sleigh, only without the snow. But it is cold today, so we can put the top up if you wish."

"No, I'd love the open landau," Jeanne said. "It's a still day, with no wind, and the sun is warm. I think we'd be perfectly comfortable."

"I was hoping you'd say that," he said with pleasure. "In fact, I ordered Marcus, my coachman, to go ahead and bring the landau around."

They put on their outerwear again and went outside. A long black carriage drawn by two white horses and the mum coachman waited for them. It seated four, and instead of George sitting five feet across from her he settled in beside her. "May I?" he asked.

"Of course. How many horses do you have?" Jeanne asked curiously as they went around the graveled drive that circled the house.

"Eighteen carriage and saddle horses, and twelve farm horses."

"You have thirty horses," Jeanne couldn't help but say. "And how many carriages?"

"Four: the barouche, the landau, a stanhope, and a gig."

"That is a lot of carriages for one man," Jeanne observed.

"I don't plan on being one man forever," he said lightly.

Jeanne cocked her head and asked, "You've never been married, have you? May I ask why?"

He frowned slightly. "I was engaged, once. I was twenty, and I asked a young lady to marry me. But as soon as we became engaged, she changed. I don't like to speak ill of a lady; all I'll say is that as the year of our engagement went on, I came to realize that I had asked her to marry me because it just seemed the thing to do, to settle down and have a family. I didn't love her. I tried to make the best of it, you know, but after a while she knew of my feelings, or lack of them, and she released me. It was a very good thing for both of us. She's happily married now, with two children."

"But what about you? There's been no one since then?"

"No one I wanted to marry," he said delicately. "Because I've never been in love. Enough about me. What about you, Jeanne? You've never said anything about your husband."

Jeanne turned from him and looked straight ahead. "I know. He was a soldier, and he died."

"I see," George said, though he didn't. In a lighter tone he went on, "Here we are in one of our pecan orchards. It was an excellent harvest this year. As you can see, the trees are still making."

Jeanne roused out of her brown study to look around. "Oh, they are. The ground is still covered with them! May we pick some?"

"What? You mean, you pick them up yourself?" George said, startled.

"Yes, George. And it wouldn't hurt you to pick a few either," Jeanne said mischievously. "Mm—Marcus? Isn't that your name, sir?" she called to the driver. "Would you stop here, please?"

The coachman pulled to a stop and turned to look at Masters with stunned surprise. "It's all right, Marcus," he said, alighting and handing out Jeanne. "I am ordered to pick pecans."

"Yes, sir," the coachman said blankly.

Jeanne bent down and picked up eight plump nuts without having to take a step. George took two of them and cracked them easily between his palms. Holding them out he said, "Try them."

Jeanne popped the fat morsel into her mouth and said, "Oh, they're good. I always loved pecans."

"We've got barrels of them at the house," he said. "I'll send you home with all you want."

She looked up at him and asserted, "You're not going to pick any up, are you, George?"

"It's a problem, you know. Where am I going to put the things? Not in the pocket of my frock coat, it'll ruin the lines. And not in my hat either, this is my best beaver," he grumbled.

Jeanne laughed. "Oh, very well. I didn't mean to subject you to such demeaning manual labor. Come on, I promise to behave myself from now on."

Much to George's relief they climbed back into the landau and drove on. "We're coming to the north cotton fields. They look dead now, but in August the fields look like they're blanketed with snow. We had the best harvest this last fall that we've ever had."

"George, if you don't let the *Helena Rose* carry your cotton next fall, I'm going to be very angry," Jeanne warned him.

He laid his arm along the back of the seat and smiled at her. "Madame, you may have all of my cotton, all of my pecans, you can even have the kitchen garden crop if you want it. Because the last thing in the world that I want is for you to ever be angry with me."

THE FAMILY DINING ROOM was indeed smaller and more intimate, and pleased Jeanne much more than the cold grand dining room. A round table covered with a white damask tablecloth was set in front of the fireplace, where a small hot fire warmed the entire room. Twelve white candles in a silver candelabra lit the table with a gentle glow.

They were seated close together, and George took her hand and asked, "May I say grace?"

"Please do."

He prayed a simple prayer of thanksgiving, and a Negro maid brought in the first course, a creamy cauliflower and leek soup. After that was baked salmon, pink and delicate and falling away from the fork, then a remove of curried sausages with raisin and fig relish, which Jeanne had never had and found delicious. Finally the entrée, a spicy, lean, tender steak au poivre with cognac sauce. "Steak au poivre," Jeanne said reverently. "I've only had it once before in my life, and it was nothing at all to compare to this. I thought that I couldn't eat any more, but I'm going to finish this if it takes me all night long."

"Jeanne, we have ices, dessert, and nuts and cheese for the other courses," George objected. "I had the cook make a chocolate buttercream torte for dessert that I know you'll love."

Though she was chewing a little, Jeanne said firmly, "I'd rather have this steak than a torte. I told you I love beef."

"So you did," he agreed. "Never in my life did I expect to meet a woman that likes beef better than cake. You're an original, Jeanne, and you're delightful."

They talked through the entire meal, sometimes interrupting each other, and with much laughter. The conversation ranged from cotton to books to music to fabrics, as Jeanne told George how Marvel couldn't wear wool. They spoke of favorite nature scenes, of streams and hills and sunsets and forests. George told her about the exciting sprawling city of New York, and she told him of places and people she'd seen on the river.

"I think it was the most beautiful sunset I've ever seen," Jeanne said dreamily. "There at Widow Eames' landing. It was just me and my father and mother, sitting outside on the main deck. The sun was crimson, and the sky was purple and royal blue and the river was dark and mysterious and quiet. We didn't say anything for an hour, as we watched." She sighed deeply. "It was the last sunset I ever saw with my mother and father."

He leaned close to her, then slowly reached up and touched her hair. He took a thick shiny curl between his two fingers and savored the feel of it. "Your hair is lovely, Jeanne, and a man could get lost in your eyes."

George Masters had known many women, but he had never seen one exactly like her. He considered her, noting that she was shapely and her eyes mirrored some sort of wisdom he was not accustomed to seeing in women. She was looking at him silently, and a woman's silence, George knew, could mean many things. He was not sure what it meant in her, for she was mysterious to him. He felt a slow run of excitement as if he were on the edge of a discovery.

She had courage, simplicity, and a tremendous capacity for emotion, he knew. She wasn't smiling at that moment but the thought of a smile hovered around her mouth. Her nearness suddenly sent off shocks within him and carefully and slowly he reached out and brought her forward and kissed her. She didn't resist; she yielded to him. He felt some sort of wild sweetness that was here, something that he had not found in any other woman. He had felt desire before, but this was a deeper feeling, a need in him that had never been satisfied. He thought that this, that she, might take the last loneliness and incompleteness from him. Finally, after years of searching, George Masters knew love.

CHAPTER NINE

A soft knock, and then silence. Jeanne sat up in bed, startled, and looked around with wild eyes. She was in the cabin, her cabin, the captain's cabin on the *Helena Rose*. She still hadn't gotten accustomed to her new home. Cold gray light came in the eastern windows, and Jeanne knew it was dawn on the day of the first run of the *Helena Rose*.

Beside her Marvel stirred, then peeped over the three quilts covering the bed. "That's Roberty. He's funny, he just knocks and runs away."

"He's just shy," Jeanne said, climbing out of bed and going to the door. Outside, as usual, was a copper kettle full of steaming water and a breakfast tray holding biscuits, a wedge of cheese, link sausages, boiled eggs, and a tin coffeepot with the delicious aroma of fresh coffee rising from it. Jeanne was pleasantly surprised to see the *Memphis Appeal* from the last two days rolled up neatly on the side of the tray. "Someone's brought us the newspaper," she said.

Marvel sat up and rubbed her eyes. "Mr. Clint bought them for us. I told him how much we liked reading newspapers, and when he went to the Post Office yesterday he bought those."

"That was nice of him. How did everything go yesterday, Marvel? Did you have a good day?"

"Oh, yes. I did my daily reader and spelling, and then we had dinner and it was so good, it was ham sammiches. Me and Roberty made our own, and—"

"Roberty and I."

"Roberty and I made our own and we had pickles. Then I was down in the boiler room, I mean the firebox, playing with Mrs. Topp and Avaymaria, and Ezra watched me to make sure I didn't get into no nonsense. Then some men were yelling outside and Mr. Clint and Mr. Vince went outside and yelled back at them. Then a man came and talked an awful lot about coal—"

"Just a minute," Jeanne interrupted. "What men were yelling outside?"

"I don't know," Marvel answered. "Mr. Clint said it was nothing a fine lady needed to hear about, and I guess he meant me 'cause I was the only lady there. Can I have a sausage?"

"May I have a sausage, and you can just get yourself up here to the table and eat a proper breakfast," Jeanne said. "I'm sorry, Marvel, but this is a very important day, so I'm going to hurry and get dressed and go talk to Mr. Hardin. When you've finished and you get dressed, you may come down to the main cargo deck for awhile before you start your lessons."

Jeanne had bought new clothes with some of her inherited money. She was a sensible woman, and knew that the frilled, beribboned, ruffled, hoop-skirted dresses that fashionable women wore would never do to pilot a riverboat, so she had bought plain gathered skirts and plain white blouses. Hurriedly she pulled on a dark blue skirt and blouse, tied up her hair in a matching blue ribbon, and grabbed her new blue shawl. When she went outside, the first pale yellow rays of the sun were tentatively creeping out behind the city.

She came into the boiler room, and Ezra looked up from loading one of the furnaces. "G'mornin', Cap'n."

"Good morning, Ezra. Has Mr. Hardin come down yet?"

"Oh, yes'm. He's back in the engine room, with Vince, checking everything over last minute."

Clint came out then, wiping his hands on a rag. "Good morning, Captain Jeanne. First run, first day! The *Rose* is rarin' to go."

"Everything is all right then? You're sure?" Jeanne asked anxiously.

"Yes ma'am, that engine is running so smooth she hums a tune. And yesterday I talked to our coal shipper, the wagons should be here any minute now, and Vinnie's already got the roustabouts lined up to help us load."

"Good. What about the mail?"

"I went to visit the postmaster yesterday, just to make sure we were all set. The mail cart will be here before eight o'clock."

Jeanne nodded. "It seems that you have everything well in hand, Mr. Hardin. I'm going on up to the wheelhouse, call me if you need me." She went up to the pilothouse, pulled out a chart, and sat down on the bench. She studied the chart for a long time, muttering to herself. After a while she leaned back, closed her eyes, and prayed: "Dearest Lord Jesus, help me, please. Help me remember, help me know, help me be strong and sure." With her eyes closed and whispering prayers, visions of the little river, and of her father standing at the wheel, rose in her mind.

WITHIN TWO HOURS THE *Rose* was carrying a full load of coal and three sizable sacks of mail. Clint came into the pilothouse, and Jeanne saw with dismay that he was literally covered in coal dust. In the morning sun she could see little puffs floating in the air from his shirt. His face was black, his hair was sooty, but Jeanne noticed with surprise that his hands were clean. "We're all ready, Captain," he said. "She's steaming, she's loaded, and she's ready to go."

"Did you load coal? I thought you had roustabouts," Jeanne said.

"Yeah, well, I'm a man in a hurry. Got a beautiful lady waiting on me. Uh—I mean the *Rose*, not you. Not that you're not beautiful, but—"

"Never mind, Mr. Hardin," Jeanne said dryly. "I know what you mean. All right, go on below, I'm ready here."

He opened the pilothouse door, then turned and asked, "You are all right, aren't you, Jeanne? You don't need anything? Or want to discuss anything?"

"No, thank you," she said coolly. "I'm fine."

"Okay. If you need anything, just holler. You know," he said, pointing to the speaking tube. Then he left.

In a few minutes the lazy wisps of steam coming from the *Rose*'s 'scape pipes turned into shrieking columns of wet steam, the smoke from the stacks billowed, and then she was on her way.

Eight days later Jeanne jauntily sounded the steam whistle, a loud alto shriek, and rang the Big Bell, the great brass one mounted on the hurricane deck, as they pulled back into Memphis. Jeanne even showed off a bit, pulling hard and fast very close to the docks before sounding the engine room bell for All Stop. The *Helena Rose*, like the trim lady that she was, surged proudly until she was checked, and then she came to a gentle rolling halt.

Within a few moments Jeanne heard shouts from the main deck and the creaks of the great capstan turning as Vince and Ezra lowered the landing stages. She stood, staring ahead without seeing, the triumphant smile fading. Jeanne took a deep shuddering breath, then had to make herself loosen the death grip she had on the pilot's wheel. Her shoulders sagged, her knees trembled, and like an old woman she took the three steps back to the bench and collapsed on it. "Thank you, God," she said wearily. "Thank you, God."

Thirty minutes later George Masters was there, and he admitted to Jeanne that he was paying an errand boy to keep a lookout for when the *Rose* docked, and to run to the Gayoso to alert him. The next night he took her and Marvel to the Courtier Restaurant. Then the *Rose* left for her second run, loaded with textiles and canvas and five hundred windows that gave Jeanne nightmares worrying about breaking them before they unloaded them in Little Rock. They had one more run before bleak January slipped into the first bright days of February. When Jeanne and Clint balanced the books for January, the *Helena Rose* had made a clear profit of three hundred and forty-two dollars.

"One hundred and seventy-one dollars for one month," Jeanne marveled. "At the Gayoso I made fourteen dollars and forty cents a month."

"Told you so," Clint said, grinning crookedly.

"Told me so what?"

"Told you so everything," he replied.

IN JUST THREE TRIPS, life had settled into a regular routine on the *Helena Rose*. Jeanne was in the pilothouse all day, of course. Marvel studied her *McGuffey's Pictoral Primer* and *First Reader* in the mornings. At first she had stayed in the cabin alone, but after a few days she began taking her books and dolls down to the boiler room. Ezra had made her a little seat out of three crackerboxes, and a few days after Ezra had made her makeshift chair, Clint showed up with a lavish embroidered brioche cushion for it. It was wildly out of place in a riverboat's boiler room—as was Marvel herself—but she loved it, and took it to the cabin with her every night for Avaymaria to sit on. Roberty cleaned Marvel's little corner of the firebox, and her chair, twice a day with ammonium chloride. Vinnie rasped, "That two square feet of this boat's clean enough to serve a lord's luncheon on."

Roberty wasn't really much use as a crewman; he was too small. He struggled mightily to bring one single log from the deck to the firebox to feed the hungry boilers, and there were few cargoes with items small enough that he could help load and unload. After seeing him half kill himself trying to drag a fifty-pound sack of coal on board, Clint had told him, "Boy, you're gonna bust a lung trying to haul stuff like that. Now I know you want to work, and you are a good worker. But you don't have to haul wood and cargo. You help out Ezra in the galley, you keep everything so clean it's kinda embarrassing to be on such a prissy riverboat, and you help out Captain Jeanne and Marvel. So from now on you just keep on with what you're already doing and leave the wood to me and Ezra and Vinnie and the cargo to the roustabouts."

As the routine shaped up, Roberty became, in essence, Jeanne's and Marvel's servant, bringing hot water and meals, washing their linens, cleaning the cabin every single day that Jeanne was piloting, and taking her coffee and tea when she was in the pilothouse. He also started studying with Marvel, for when she found out he couldn't read she started bossing him shamelessly about lessons.

For Jeanne, it was a curiously dual life. On board the *Rose* she was the pilot, and she rarely spent much time at all with the crew. Evenings, of course, were spent with Marvel when they were on a run. But always, when they came back to Memphis, George Masters was waiting. Jeanne would spend at least one day with him, for they usually took a two-day layover. She no longer worried about Marvel staying on the boat, for Ezra and Roberty had come to care for her so well that Jeanne thought it was as if Marvel had a brother and a grandfather. Clint and Vince also took good care of Marvel, but they weren't always on the boat at night. Jeanne assumed they went out to saloons every night, which bothered her, but she decided that as long as they weren't drunk and rowdy on the boat, it was really none of her business. Her business was Marvel, and the *Helena Rose*, and George Masters.

Thinking these thoughts as she steered the boat around Island Number 60 and came in sight of Helena, she wondered if she were getting her priorities straight. Naturally her first concern was always Marvel. But what about George Masters? How important was he to her? He seemed to be a big part of her life, and Jeanne knew that he was falling in love with her. But what exactly were her feelings toward him? She was physically attracted to him, she enjoyed his company, he had been a terrific sponsor of the *Helena Rose*, and however offhand George Masters may be about his money, it was definitely a plus for Jeanne. None of those things, however, said one thing about her feelings for him. Jeanne admitted to herself that she just didn't know her own heart. It had been closed off for so long that she thought it may never be tender and open to a man's love again.

HELENA, ARKANSAS, WAS A riverboat town. As more and
more steamboats plied the Ol' Mississippi, it quickly
became an important landing. Conveniently situated
between Memphis and Vicksburg, Tennessee, with a thriv-
ing lumber industry, steamboats made their wood stops
at Helena as the larger cities and the areas around them
quickly got deforested. Helena always had plenty of wood
at a good price, and as George Masters had observed, any
finished goods were easy to sell in the growing town. By
1830 Helena's docks were as busy as Memphis's.

Where the river is, there will always be thieves, gamblers, prostitutes, panderers, and other assorted outlaws.
In 1835 the upright citizens of Helena formed the Helena
Anti-Gambling Society, and soon after that the Helena
Temperance Society, and they elected strict High Sheriffs
that hired no-nonsense deputies, and the town got civi-
lized. By the time Jeanne was driving the *Helena Rose*,
Helena had three newspapers, six private schools, thirteen
churches, four subscription libraries, and twice-monthly
public lectures.

Of course, where the river is, there are also rivermen.
Therefore, there must be saloons, and drinking, and gambling, and prostitutes, and thieves. Such a tide might be
stemmed but not stopped, even in Helena. Clint and Vince
had found three saloons the first time they'd stopped
overnight in the town, on Jeanne's trial run. All three were
grim-looking shacks huddled at the end of the waterfront
in a line with a rundown inn, two tobacco and liquor stores,
a couple of brothels thinly disguised as boardinghouses,
and a sad-looking and scanty grocery. Clint and Vince
went to the first one, farthest down the docks, but Clint
stopped dead in front of the propped-open sagging door

and sniffed. "Is that horse manure? How come a saloon smells like horse manure?" he complained.

"I don't wanna know," Vince said. "C'mon, let's go try the Hairpin Bend Tavern. I like the name," he added hopefully.

They stood in front of the Hairpin Bend Tavern, considering it. "It has a window," Vince said. "It's not even broken or anything."

The door burst open, and a man came staggering out, clutching a half-empty whiskey bottle. He stared at Vince and Clint, said, "Huh? Whadja say?", sunk to his knees, then toppled over like a chopped tree, face-forward, arms sprawled out.

Vince and Clint looked at each other. "Huh-uh," Clint said. They turned and walked two buildings down to a saloon cleverly named Island No. 60, the riverman's landmark for Helena. It had two windows, with neither of them broken, which was a hopeful sign, and as they hesitated at the doorway no one came out and fell down. They went in.

It was like a thousand other saloons in a hundred other river towns, with thick tobacco smoke and liquor reek on the heavy air. On the right was a bar, with men "bellied up," one foot propped on the brass rail below. On the left were tables, all with rough-looking men sitting at them, drinking and talking about the river. Only one table had a poker game going, and the four men seemed sober and subdued. Clint and Vince had stayed and had a couple of beers, but they were accustomed to other, friendlier watering places and soon they went back to the boat. On the next couple of trips they didn't return to Island Number 60.

But the day was cheery, and cool, not cold, and they had docked at about three o'clock, so Clint and Vince decided to give Island Number 60 another try. As they walked down the waterfront to the slums at the far southern end,

Clint said, "I'm going to stop in the tobacconist's and get the papers."

"Why do you buy papers for her?" Vince asked. "She doesn't appreciate it, Clint."

"Yeah, she does. She always thanks me. Well, almost always."

Vince shook his head. "I don't get it. She puts on airs and she treats you like a servant. It's not right."

"I don't think it's really putting on airs. I think she's really had a tough time, and she's had no one to depend on or to help her, and so she just keeps herself to herself. And she treats me fine."

"She sure doesn't treat you like other women do. She's not all gaga over you. Bothers you, doesn't it?"

"Nah, she's crazy about me," Clint said loftily. "She just doesn't know it yet." He ducked into the dank tobacconist's and came back out holding the *Helena Daily World*. He glanced at the folded-up bottom half of the first page and murmured, "Hey, look at this."

Vince craned his neck to see a small headline below the fold: THE STEAMBOAT *HELENA ROSE* RETURNS HOME WITH A LADY PILOT! The article was written by a lady named Mrs. Honoria Putnam, and was fulsome and fruity. The first paragraph read:

> *Many of the esteemed citizens of Helena will remember the* Helena Rose, *the steamer owned by Mr. Ira Hardin, who was married to our favorite daughter, Rose Dulany. After Mrs. Hardin's bitterly tragic death we sorely missed both of our "Roses" terribly. Mr. Ira Hardin recently passed on to a Better Place, and joined his Beloved Rose, but his stout riverboatman's spirit still plies the Grand Old Mississippi in the* Helena Rose, *now*

owned, captained, and PILOTED by Mrs. Jeanne Bettencourt, the first FEMALE PILOT on the Mississippi River!

The article went on to fulminate about Captain Jeanne's DARING and HARDY PIONEER SPIRIT as she conquered the Mississippi River, apparently single-handedly. It went on to list the *Rose's* stops, and the fact that she was entrusted with the mail, and how dedicated Captain Jeanne was in plying the treacherous river, toiling to faithfully deliver the mail near and far.

"This is kinda making me nauseated," Vince joked. "It's like when you eat too much candy."

"Aw, man, Jeanne's gonna be steamed," Clint groaned. "I don't think I'm going to give her this paper."

"Why not?" Vince said cheerfully. "Captain Jeanne's famous now." He placed one hand over his heart and flung out the other arm as he recited sonorously, "As the valiant Captain Jeanne toils, under heavy burdens of care, in the driving snow, alone, without friend or boiler or engine, just she and the *Helena Rose*—"

"Vinnie," Clint said, grinning, "Shut up."

They went down to Island Number 60, which was quiet this early in the afternoon. Six men stood at the bar, tossing back shots of whiskey and spitting into a nearly full spittoon. A dozen men were scattered around the tables. Clint and Vinnie stood at the bar and the bartender, a big bruiser as they always seemed to be in these kinds of saloons, came up to them, polishing a glass. He had black hair parted down the middle and greased with macassar oil, and close-set eyes in a round, red-cheeked face. "G'day to you gentlemen. What'll you have?"

They ordered beers, and Clint spread the paper out on the bar. "You know, it was kinda sad about Ira Hardin. Ezra told me a lot about him. He was a rompin', stompin' pilot until he met this Rose Dulany here in Helena, and they got married. That's when he had the *Helena Rose* built. Seems like she really gentled him down, that's when he started running the Arkansas River. Ezra said he was a snorting bull—that's why they nicknamed him—but with Rose he was as gentle as a spring lamb. After she died a couple of years ago, he went back to his old river rat ways. Ezra said he was only thirty-five when he died. That's kinda sad, isn't it?"

The bartender set down two mugs brimming with beer, and they took appreciative sips. "Good beer," Clint said to the bartender.

"Thank you, sir. I heard you talking about the *Helena Rose*. Did you two know Bull Hardin?" he asked.

"Never knew the man, I'm sorry to say. He was a distant cousin of mine, and he left me half of the *Rose*." Clint pointed to the newspaper and went on, "But it seems like Mrs. Putnam missed my story."

"Mrs. Putnam," the bartender said disdainfully. "You orter be glad she don't have you in her sights, mister. So, you work the *Rose*? I heard she just came in."

"I'm the engineer, and Vince here is a deckhand," Clint said.

"And you two have a lady pilot," the bartender said thoughtfully. "Is that—"

Vince had noticed four men further down the bar who had been listening to the conversation, grinning and punching each other. They were working men, probably roustabouts or deckhands, dressed in coarse dirty clothes, unshaven, with dirty stringy hair topped by greasy floppy hats. Now one of them loudly interrupted the bartender. "Hey, you two boys! Did I hear right? We got two crewmen from the famous *Helena Rose* here?"

Warily, Clint answered, "That's right," then turned back to the bartender.

But the man, who was missing his two upper front teeth and all four lower front teeth, kept on calling down the bar in his nasal voice. "Whew-ee! Ain't you got a mutt's life! Got a female pilot! What's she do there, boy, flash her knickers when she wants more steam?" The four of them snorted loudly with laughter.

Clint stood upright, took four steps down the bar, pulled back his right fist, and planted a bone-crunching right cross on the man's jaw. He flew backwards a couple of feet, and crashed to the ground. The other three were still standing there dumbfounded, staring down at him, when Clint planted another right on another jaw, and he went down. By this time the other two had waked up, and they grabbed Clint's arms, and one of them bit Clint's ear. Vince reached them, and as quick as a snake, did a vicious head-butt to the biting man. A general scuffle ensued.

Clint was sitting on top of one of the men, banging away at his face, when from behind two men grabbed his arms and hauled him to his feet. A couple of feet away from him another deputy grabbed Vince, who had his nearly unconscious man against the wall, belting him in the belly.

The saloon grew very quiet. Standing behind the two deputies holding Clint was a tall man with a bronzed leather face and black eyes, wearing a big silver star pinned to his chest. In a voice like gravel he said, "My name is Hank Burnett, and I'm the sheriff. Now boys, I know you ain't from around here, so you ain't had time to learn the rules. We don't like this kind of thing here in Helena. This is a nice town, with good folks, and they elected me to keep the peace. And that's what I intend to do, and that's why ever one of you fools is under arrest."

"CAPTAIN JEANNE IS GOING to kill us," Vince groaned.

"She probably won't actually kill us," Clint said. "Not literally kill us dead."

"She'll make us wish we were dead."

"Yeah, that sounds about right." Clint stood up and yelled at the cells at the far end. "Hey, you down there. Which one of you people bit my ear? I didn't know you had enough teeth between the four of you!"

Only low mutters sounded from the four cells; the deck-hands from the *One Eyed Jack*, as it turned out they were, had definitely calmed down. All four of them were nursing cuts and scrapes, knots on their heads, black eyes, and busted lips. "Funny," Toothless said in a low voice, "I knew he was a big feller, but he 'peared like a sweet johnny. Calm and speaking low, like."

"Yeah, 'til he turned inter a big mad b'ar," the beat-up man in the next cell said. "Don't nobody tell him I'm the one what bit his ear."

"Niver seen nothin' like it," Toothless said in wonder. "One minnit I'm a-talking, and next minnit I'm flat on my back and I'm watchin' little spangly stars goin' round and round."

Clint dabbed at his ear, which was still bleeding slightly. It was the only injury he had; even his knuckles, by now hardened like anvils, weren't scraped or swollen. Vince had a big red bump on his head from his head-butt, and that was the only injury he had.

At six o'clock a grinning deputy brought them coffee and pork and beans. Clint asked, "Can you tell us what we're in here for, and how long we have to stay?"

"You fellers were disturbin' the peace," he said, hooking his fingers in his belt, which was stretched thin over a large paunch. "Penalty for that is five days in jail."

"Five days! That's kind of severe, isn't it?" Vince said.

"Yup. Sheriff Burnett, he don't hold much with fights. See, you fellers get into a brawl down on the docks, and it disturbs the peace of the good citizens of Helena, and then the Anti-Gambling Society and the Temperance Society disturbs the peace of the sheriff."

"But we weren't gambling! And we only had one beer that we didn't even finish!" Clint protested.

"Well, them is some circumstances, all right. But it don't matter, disturbing the peace carries a five-day jail sentence. I got you some good news, though," he told them with another huge grin. He was enjoying himself enormously. "Your bail is set for five dollars each, and there's been a nice lady here that's paid it. Howsomever, you still have to stay overnight. You'll get out in the morning." He left, going back into the office.

"She was nice?" Vince said blankly.

"Yeah," Clint said thoughtfully. "How'd that happen?"

Clint hardly slept all night, because the mattress on his cot was hard and lumpy, and it smelled atrocious. Finally dawn came and the same grinning deputy came in and unlocked their cells. "Miz Bettencourt done vouched for you and filled out all the papers, so the rest of your sentence is suspended. Might better spruce up a little there, she's a-waiting for you."

There wasn't any "sprucing-up" to be done in the bare cells, so Clint and Vinnie followed the deputy into the sheriff's office. Sheriff Burnett was standing next to Jeanne, his arms crossed, and she looked at them expressionlessly as they came in. The only warning sign was the dark flickers in her eyes.

Sheriff Burnett looked amused, though his voice was heavy. "Now you boys know the rules, right?"

"Yes, sir," Clint and Vince mumbled.

The deputy handed Vince his gun, a Colt six-shooter that he kept stuck in the back of his trousers. Painstakingly, the deputy counted out the six bullets. Sheriff Burnett said, "I 'spect you understand the rule about guns, don't you, sonny?"

"Yes, sir. The rule is: no guns," Vince said obediently.

"That's right," Burnett said with satisfaction and turned to bow slightly to Jeanne. "Miz Langer, I'm right glad that you're back on the river. Your daddy would bust a button, he'd be so proud of you. Now you need anything, anything a-tall, you just let me know, all right?"

"Thank you, Sheriff Burnett. You've always been a good friend to me and my family, and though I'm sorry about the circumstances, I'm glad we met again. I appreciate your help so much," she said, and without a word to Vince and Clint walked out the door.

She walked down to the docks, with them trailing her. She stopped, and they moved up sheepishly to let her get it all out. She said evenly, "I knew what I was doing when I had Marvel, and I knew what I was doing when I adopted Roberty. What I didn't know was that I'd have two other children on the boat."

"But I can explain, Jeanne—" Clint began.

Jeanne stuck one imperious finger in the air. "Not one word." She turned and stalked off.

Clint and Vince followed some distance behind her. "You were right," Clint finally said. "I wish she woulda just gone ahead and killed us."

CHAPTER TEN

The *Helena Rose* steamed on to Napoleon Trading Post, where they stayed the night, and then a long haul to Pine Bluff, then Little Rock.

Jeanne talked to Clint each morning and when they docked for the night. She said nothing about bailing them out of jail, not even when Clint had repaid her the ten dollars for his and Vince's bail. "Thank you," she merely said.

"No, thank *you*, Captain Jeanne," he said lightly. "I owe you."

She just shrugged.

They were on their return trip, back in Pine Bluff for the night. Jeanne was sitting at her desk, doing her logs. Marvel sat in one of the armchairs, playing quietly with her dolls. "Mama, are you mad at Mr. Clint and Mr. Vince?" she asked.

Jeanne put down her pen and turned to her. "No, I'm not mad at them. They didn't say anything to you, did they?"

"About you being mad? 'Cause they got thrown in jail? No. They just talk to me like they always do. But Roberty told me."

"Roberty told you what?"

"Roberty heard Mr. Vince telling Mr. Ezra about how these mean men in the saloon were talking bad about you, and Mr. Clint got mad and hit them. Roberty said it always makes Mr. Clint real mad when somebody says something about your petticoats, like when those men came to the *Rose* and yelled and Mr. Clint and Mr. Vince went out and yelled back at them. But Roberty said that those saloon men must have really said something not-nice for Mr. Clint to hit them, 'cause usually all he does is holler back at them. If Mr. Clint would have just told those saloon men to shut up, maybe he and Mr. Vince wouldn't have gotten thrown in jail."

Jeanne sat there, stunned. She suddenly recalled Marvel telling her about the "men yelling" that day before their first trip. She had been so absorbed in her own piloting problems that she had completely forgotten about it. In fact, she had been in a thick, muffled cocoon since she had started piloting the *Rose*. She rarely went anywhere by herself; she never went into town at their ports, and when she was in Memphis she was with George Masters. She had seen the article in the *Helena Daily World*, but she had dismissed it as silly and of no consequence. Now she realized that the river gossip about her must be widespread and crude.

Jeanne jumped up and started pacing, frowning at the floor, thinking hard and fast. So Clint and Vince had been defending her honor. Angrily she thought, *I can take care of myself, I don't need their help! And it's stupid, anyway! What are they going to do, go into every saloon and whorehouse on the river and pick a fight with anyone who says something ugly about me?*

"Mama?" Marvel asked softly. "Did I upset you?"

Swiftly Jeanne went to kneel by her and give her a hug. "No, no, little one. I'm just thinking, that's all. But I need you to do me a favor, all right? Please go down and ask Ezra to come up here for a few minutes. I need to talk to him, so you stay down with Roberty until Ezra comes back, okay?"

"Sure, Mama," she said, hopping up and skipping out the door.

Jeanne paced until she heard the knock, and called, "Come in, Ezra."

He came in and stood in front of the door, his hands behind his back as if he were about to recite. Jeanne looked at him as if she was seeing him for the first time, and perhaps she was. He was short, with brawny shoulders and arms. His bald pate shone, and the brown fringe beneath was neatly combed down. His face was weathered and ageless. He wasn't at all uneasy, Jeanne saw; he was regarding her with something like compassion warming his dark eyes. She was about to ask him to sit, but then she realized that he wouldn't feel comfortable with that. She sat down in one of her desk chairs, folded her hands in her lap, and said, "Ezra, please tell me what happened in Helena, with Clint and Vince."

Unemotionally he related the events to her in his earthy voice, including colorful metaphors and descriptions but leaving out exactly what the deckhand from the *Red Queen* had said. "Clint and Vinnie took their exceptions to them boys, and there was a ruckus, and they all ended up in jail."

"I see," Jeanne said evenly. "And Marvel has told me something about some men on the docks in Memphis, *yelling men*, she called them. Was that a similar event?"

"Yes ma'am, Cap'n. And it ain't jist been in Memphis, neither. We've had to take some exceptions to some roustabouts here and there on this ol' river since you been driving the *Rose,* ma'am."

"You too?"

"Yes, ma'am. I might jist be an old river rat, but I niver have took to men insultin' ladies. It ain't right, and as long as I'm walkin' and talkin' and breathin' I ain't gonna put up with it."

"That's a fine sentiment, Ezra, and I appreciate you defending my honor," Jeanne said, "but I don't see you getting into fights with idiots in some seedy bar. I hardly think that helps my reputation."

He cocked his head and asked her curiously, "So you're all het up with Clint and Vinnie 'cause you think they ain't helping your reputation?"

"No, I see now that they were—trying to help," Jeanne said hesitantly.

"So you're all het up 'cause they got throwed in jail?"

"No—no. Not exactly. I guess."

"So you're all het up 'cause they was in a saloon?"

"I don't know," she said distractedly. "I'm confused now."

He nodded knowingly. "Miz Bettencourt, I'm a-gonna speak frank to you. See, I'm a Christian now, I done got saved and sanctified ten year ago, at a camp revival meeting. Afore that I wasn't nothing, I didn't have no honor, I didn't have no dignity, I didn't have no good sense, all I had was sin to keep me company, and poor company it were, too. But the good Lord saved me from my sin, and I come to figger out He saved me from everbody else's sin too. I got a hard head, and it tuck me awhile, but finally He got through to me. I had enough in my own lap without tendin' to other folks' problems. He'll deal with them, sure as He dealt with me."

Jeanne said evenly, "You're telling me that I shouldn't be angry with Clint and Vince for being in a saloon."

"Well, are you, ma'am?"

She thought for long moments, then answered quietly, "Yes, I am. And you're exactly right, Ezra, and I'm exactly wrong. I do have plenty enough in my own lap without tending to other folks' problems," she echoed him with a faint smile. "Thank you, Ezra."

"Cap'n," he said, bobbing his head, then he turned and left.

Jeanne stared into space. *Lord, I've been a mean-spirited busybody. It's none of my business what Clint and Vince or anyone else does. I'm so sorry.*

As soon as she told this to the Lord, she thought: *I owe them an apology.*

Somehow, Jeanne thought, she wouldn't have any trouble apologizing to Vince. He was employed by her, and she had made a mistake, and she could easily say to him, "I apologize for my attitude toward you, sir, what you do when you're not on my boat is none of my business. Let's just forget it, shall we?"

But it wasn't that simple with Clint Hardin.

Why not? Jeanne wondered.

She wrestled with herself, trying to pin down the answer. But somehow it was a harder question than it should have been, and finally she gave up. She resolved to be more polite to Clint and Vince from now on, that there really was no need for her to go apologizing all over the boat.

Why not? Jeanne thought.

JEANNE WAS NICE TO Clint and Vince, in fact she was very cordial to them. No one said anything more about their Helena escapade; Marvel didn't ask any more questions, Ezra gave no hint to anyone about his talk with Jeanne, Vince went on roustabouting around as he usually did, and Clint was the same easygoing, charming man he'd always been.

They got back to Memphis and as soon as the *Rose*'s engine shut down, Jeanne hurried down to the main deck. Clint and Vince were lowering one of the landing stages, kneeling down to turn the handle of a big capstan with a ratchet-and-pawl mechanism that slowly let out the stout ropes and lowered the landing stage. It was hard work for two strong men, so Jeanne went inside the boiler room to say hello to Marvel.

Outside four roustabouts gathered on the shore. "Hey, Vinnie!" one of them called. "We heard the Petticoats beat the tar outta the One Eyes down there in Helena!"

Vince hopped up. "Eddie, you call me a Petticoat one more time and you're gonna be eating this lumber instead of unloading it!"

"Aw, keep yer galluses on, I didn't mean nothing by it," Eddie hollered at the top of his lungs. "Them One Eyes is some rough boys. If they got beat by you Petticoats, I sez good-all for ya!"

Clint grunted, "A little help here, Vinnie?"

Vince knelt back down and grabbed the capstan handle. "Petticoats!" he muttered darkly.

Just inside the boiler room, Marvel was standing on a box looking out the window, with Jeanne right behind her. "Those must be some of the yelling men," Marvel observed. "What are they talking about?"

Jeanne's mouth twitched and she answered, "Oh, just river talk. Nothing to worry about."

When the landing stages were down, Jeanne went out on deck to talk to Clint. "We had a very smooth run this time," she said. "Any problems?"

"No, Cap'n Jeanne," he said, eyeing the roustabouts as they filed on board. Each of them nodded politely to Jeanne and murmured, "Ma'am," or "Captain."

"I know it's Thursday," Jeanne continued, "but do you think we could lay over for two nights and load up Saturday? I'd like to take Marvel shopping tomorrow."

"It's early yet," Clint said, for it was only two o'clock. "How about you do me the honor of allowing me to escort you and Marvel to town this afternoon? There's plenty of time for shopping, and there's a new confectioner on Main Street that's got this whole castle made out of chocolate in the window. I think Marvel would love it."

"Thank you, but I need to take Marvel to buy some new clothes, and that takes a while," Jeanne said. "And I am engaged this evening anyway. Maybe some other time."

"Sure, Cap'n, any time."

Jeanne hurried to the stairs and Vince came back to Clint's side. "Face it, buddy. She's only got eyes for the Big Bug."

Clint looked troubled, but then his face cleared and he said easily, "Guess you're right, Vinnie. Hey, you want to take Marvel and Roberty to the new confectioner's shop? You know, the one with the chocolate castle?"

JEANNE BARELY HAD TIME to wash her face and touch up her hair before she saw George Masters strolling down the docks from her window. She went back down to greet him at the gangplank but Clint, holding Marvel's hand, stopped her at the bottom of the stairs. "Hey, Captain, would you mind if Vinnie and I took Marvel and Roberty to that confectioner's I was telling you about?"

Jeanne said with surprise, "You and Vinnie? Going to a confectioner's shop?"

"Well, yeah! I like raspberry ices, even in winter," Clint said.

"Please, Mama?" Marvel pleaded. "I want to see the castle!"

Jeanne's every instinct was to say no, but then she saw George coming up the gangplank with an armload of flowers so she said hurriedly, "I suppose it would be all right. Er—Mr. Hardin, it is just the confectioner's, isn't it?"

His eyes narrowed but his tone was light. "Yes, ma'am. Where else did you think I would take your daughter?"

"Nowhere, I was just checking," Jeanne said hastily. "Thank you, Mr. Hardin, it will be a treat for Marvel and Roberty."

"Hurray!" Marvel said, running back inside the boiler room to tell Roberty.

With an awkward smile Jeanne went to meet George, uncomfortably aware of Clint Hardin's cold blue gaze on her back. "Hello, George," she said with less welcome than she had intended.

"Hello, Jeanne, my dear. These are for you, I suppose you've guessed," he said, handing her the bouquet of pink roses and white lilies.

"Mmm, they smell heavenly! And such flowers, in winter!"

"Yes, the *Lady Vandivere* buys them by the boatload from a hothouse in New Orleans. How are you, Jeanne? How was the run?"

She took his arm and they went to stand on the other side of the deck, for the roustabouts were still unloading the lumber. Jeanne frowned. Finally she answered, "It was fine, a clean there-and-back with no problems at all. What about you? How are you, what have you been doing?"

"I had several meetings the last couple of days. In fact, there are a couple of things that came up that I'd like to discuss with you," he said, his smooth features bland. "We are still on for this evening, aren't we?"

"Of course. I'll be ready."

He took her hand and lifted it to his lips, as he often did now. "And I'll be here."

Jeanne went upstairs to bathe and dress. Marvel came into the cabin and said, "As soon as the yelling men finish unloading, we're going to town. Are you and Mr. Masters going to a restaurant tonight?"

"Yes, it's called Gladstone House. I've never been there before, but Mr. Masters says it's wonderful."

"Those are pretty flowers," Marvel said, sniffing and caressing a pink rose. "That was nice of Mr. Masters, to bring you flowers. You should wear them in your hair, Mama. You would be beautiful."

"No, I have my new bonnets. Now listen, little one. You wear your cape and muffler and mittens, all right? It's still cold enough for you to catch a chill. And don't eat too much chocolate."

"I won't," she said solemnly. "Not after that time, with the chocolate." She dressed Avaymaria in her wool cape and muffler, then got her own things and left the cabin.

Jeanne took her time with bathing and dressing, and at a quarter to five she was standing in front of the mirror, putting on her bonnet. She was wearing her one coordinated outfit, the maroon skirt with the matching short cape and bonnet. She tied the wide ribbon in a perky bow under her chin, then made a face. She actually hated the bonnet, because she thought that the style of completely covering the hair with a big fabric pouf, and then a brim completely encircling the face, so wide that the wearer couldn't see to the right or left without turning the head completely around, looked silly. But it was trimmed with maroon satin flowers with pink pearl centers, and it was fashionable.

Jeanne untied the ribbon and threw the bonnet down on the table, then took a rose and two lilies and put them into her hair. She took off the short cape and got her old gray mantle and settled the hood gently onto her head so as not to crush the flowers.

George arrived with the barouche right on time, and soon his grays were prancing up Jefferson Avenue. They arrived at Gladstone House, which actually was an old house converted to an inn, with six bedroom suites on the second floor and the entire first floor turned into six separate dining rooms. Jeanne and George were seated at a small table in the corner of what would have been a parlor, and the room had only one other table occupied by an elderly couple. A silent black man in a white coat and gloves took their outerwear. George eyed her hair and said, "You look very exotic, Jeanne."

"Thank you, sir," she said, wondering if looking exotic was truly a compliment.

"This is rather an old-fashioned place," George told her as the waiter promptly brought them crystal goblets of mineral water and a clear onion consommé as soon as they were seated. "They don't go in for newfangled things like serving from a menu. At Gladstone's there is a bill of fare for each day, and that's what you get. I've always found that it's good, hearty food, though. I think you'll enjoy it."

"I'm sure I will," Jeanne said rather automatically. "George, I've been so very curious. What happened in your meetings that could possibly concern me?"

George took a sip of the soup before replying. "Perhaps I misspoke. You weren't the topic of the meetings, Jeanne. What I wanted to talk to you about was that article in the Helena newspaper. You did see it, didn't you?"

"Of course. I thought it was trite and ridiculous. It was hardly what I call newsworthy."

"Perhaps not, but it is all the talk," George said gravely. "And just today, the *Arkansas Gazette* had a similar article. Several gentlemen of my acquaintance have mentioned the articles to me."

Jeanne slowly put down her soup spoon and folded her hands in her lap. "And this is a problem for you?"

"For *us*, Jeanne. Wouldn't you agree? I mean, for a lady to have her name bandied about in the newspapers—well, it's just not done." He sipped another spoonful of soup.

"No, in my case it is indeed already done. Do you have any suggestions for undoing it?"

He stated the obvious. "Can't undo it now, I'm afraid. You are upset about it, aren't you, Jeanne?"

"No, George, I'm not. I've just recently learned that having a silly newspaper article written about me is the least of my worries."

He nodded. "Yes, I knew there would be indecorous gossip about you on the river, and I decided to just ignore that. No gentleman would take notice of the things those river rats go on about anyway. But to be so publicly exposed, that's another thing."

"You decided to ignore it," Jeanne repeated. "River rats." Suddenly the contrast between George Masters and her crew—especially Clint Hardin—seemed extremely unfavorable for George just now. Frostily she said, "I'm so sorry that my choice of livelihood has been a cause of offense to you, George."

He looked up quickly. "You're angry with me. Why are you angry with me, Jeanne? What did I say?"

"I'm not angry, George. I just wasn't aware that this would be such a problem for you. And put quite simply, there's no help for it."

"I know, not for the articles that have already been written," he said hastily. "But I just wanted to warn you, you see. Since you've gained such public notoriety, I don't doubt but that other journalists, the ne'er-do-well sensationalist kind, will be seeking you out for interviews. I just thought that I'd tell you—that is, I was going to ask you, respectfully, for the sake of your own reputation, not mine of course, not to give any interviews. That's all I meant, Jeanne. Please don't be angry with me, it would make me very unhappy."

He really was upset, she saw, and she softened a bit. Picking up her spoon again, she said, "I don't want you to be unhappy, George. I'm not angry, and I won't give any newspaper interviews. Let's just forget the whole thing, shall we?"

"Yes, let's do that," he said with relief. "I've already forgotten."

Jeanne wondered, *But will I?*

"CLINT, FOR SHAME ON you," Ezra scolded. "You're worsen the chilluns. They ain't got no better sense than to spoil they supper by eatin' sweets, but you shoulda knowed better."

"Vinnie was there too!" Clint said defensively. "He's the one that bought them the cherries!"

"But all they ate was fruit," Vince argued. "Fruit's good for them."

"Uh-huh," Ezra growled. "Pears and plums and oranges and such drownded in sugar syrup and cherries dipped in a vat full o' chocolate ain't like crunchin' on a good red apple, you ninny."

Marvel said wistfully, "Oh, how I wish I hadn't eaten so much. I love fried hominy so, and I can't eat it."

They were sitting in the galley, all perched on the high stools pulled up to the counters that lined the walls. Leo had managed to worm in between the wall and Marvel's and Roberty's stools, and at suppertime he even sat up and stayed awake. At least Ezra, Vince, and Clint were eating supper. Marvel had taken exactly two bites of the hot, creamy chicken fricassee, and one bite of fried hominy. Roberty was trying to eat the fricassee, for it was one of his favorites, but he, too, was just picking at it. His normally fair complexion looked slightly yellow-green. He had had four candied orange slices, a coconut chew, and three chocolate-covered maraschino cherries.

Looking at Roberty, Clint said guiltily, "Okay, I guess I was supposed to be the responsible grown-up. Roberty, quit trying to look like you're eating, it makes my stomach hurt. Marvel, I'll make you some more fried hominy tomorrow, for tonight you're excused from supper."

"Thank you," she sighed with relief.

"I'll git you some bicarbonate of sody, Roberty," Ezra said. "It'll make you feel better."

"Thanks, Ezra," he said faintly.

The men finished eating and everyone helped wash up. Roberty was feeling better, and Marvel seemed none the worse for their visit to the confectioner's.

Clint said, "Vinnie, why don't we have a little music tonight?"

"Fine with me," he agreed. He left to fetch his violin, and the others all went down to the firebox. It was a small room, crowded with the two boilers, all the pipes, and with wood stacked along the walls. But it was very warm, almost hot, so Clint opened the double doors out onto the main deck. Leo laid down across Ezra's feet, and he scolded him, so he ambled off and collapsed just under the boilers, panting like it was an August noon.

Vince came back down and took a few minutes tuning his fiddle. Roberty asked Clint, "Can you sing that song you were singing this morning? That Mr. Foster song?"

"I sure will, and it's easy, so I expect you and everyone else to help me after you catch on," Clint said. Vince played a few chords, and Clint sang:

> *I come from Alabama*
> *With a banjo on my knee*
> *I'm going to Louisiana,*
> *My true love for to see.*

> *Oh, Susannah,*
> *Oh don't you cry for me*
> *For I come from Alabama*
> *With a banjo on my knee.*

Ezra, Vince, and Clint sang the verses and the children hummed, but after the second verse they sang the chorus with gusto. Then Clint sang "Old Folks at Home," "Cockles and Mussels," and "Yankee Doodle."

"How 'bout this one?" Vince said, grinning, and started playing a lively tune. Clint sang:

> *As I was a-gwine down the road,*
> *With a tired team and a heavy load,*
> *I crack'd my whip and the leader sprung,*
> *I says day-day to the wagon tongue.*

> *Turkey in the straw, turkey in the hay,*
> *Roll 'em up and twist 'em up in a high tuckahaw*
> *And twist 'em up a tune called Turkey in the*
> *Straw!*

Clint sang all five verses, and Marvel and Roberty clapped when he finished. "What's a tuckahaw, Mr. Clint?" Marvel asked.

"That's where they put the turkey after he's rolled up and twisted up," Clint answered with a grin.

Marvel sniffed. "It is not. You just made it up."

"It's a good word, though, isn't it? I like it, *tuckahaw*. I think you should name your next doll Tuckahaw."

Next they sang "De Camptown Races," and when they were finished Clint said, "Miss Marvel, would you do me the honor of dancing with me?"

Marvel said, "But I don't know how to dance!"

"'Camptown Races' is a good polka song. C'mon, I'll teach you." He nodded to Vince, who began to play. Clint scooped up Marvel in his arms. "Heel, toe, away we go!" He danced and Marvel giggled, her eyes starry. Roberty and Ezra clapped and sang, and Vince played the song all the way through twice.

"Gunness!" Marvel said when Clint set her down. "I didn't know dancing was so easy! And so much fun!"

"And so thirsty," Clint said. "How about some cider, Ezra?"

"Be right back wid it," he said, and went upstairs to the galley.

Roberty went over to sit by Vince, who started showing him how to hold a violin and run the bow across the strings. Clint sat down on a cracker box next to Marvel's cushioned chair. "So you like to dance, huh? Then I think that Vinnie should teach you a couple of jigs, and I'll teach you a waltz. Would you like that?"

"Yes, I would so much!" she said. "And I want to learn all the words to 'Turkey in the Straw.'"

"Yes, ma'am," Clint said. "After I get something to drink we'll all learn 'Turkey in the Straw.'"

Marvel asked, "But first would you please sing 'Avaymaria' for me? I just loved that song, when you sang it on Christmas Eve. Please?"

"I wish I could, little one, but I'm afraid it's not possible," he said gravely.

"Why not?"

Clint explained, "See, when you heard me sing on Christmas Eve, I was singing in what's called my *operatic voice*. It's different from when I sing 'Turkey in the Straw.'"

Marvel nodded knowingly. "You've been singing really good tonight, but it's not like Avaymaria. But it's still you singing, why can't you sing your 'pratic voice now?"

"It's hard, it's real hard to sing like that. To be able to sing like that all the time, you have to practice every day. And before you sing a real song, you have to warm up the muscles in your throat and neck and shoulders and chest and even your stomach."

"But you already have big muscles," Marvel said insistently. "And why don't you practice every day?"

Clint grinned. "Because it would be so silly, everyone would laugh at me, and I'd probably laugh at myself. When you practice you do this." He stood up, placed one hand theatrically over his heart, threw out his other hand, and thundered out an operatic: "LA-LA-LAAAAAA!" Leo scrambled up and looked around in alarm.

Marvel laughed, and Clint sat back down. "See? Told you. And I gotta tell you, Marvel, for you I'd sing anything if I could, but 'Ave Maria' is kinda hard anyway."

"It is? Why?" she asked curiously.

"When you sing, you want the sound to come from way deep inside your chest, and kinda roll out of your throat. That's why when you sing opera, you open your mouth really wide. Here, do this." He opened his mouth and sang middle C, "Ahhhh."

Obediently, Marvel opened her pink mouth to a round *o* and sang, "Ahhhh."

"That's good," Clint said. "Now listen: Ah-vay-Ma-REE-uh. Try opening your mouth and singing REEEEEE."

Marvel tried, then said with disgust, "It's coming out my nose."

"Yeah, it does." He reached over and gently pinched Marvel's nostrils shut. "Now try."

Marvel sang: "REEEE. Now it's coming out my ears!"

"Uh-huh. Such are the woes of singing in your operatic voice," Clint said lightly. "That's why I'm too yellow-bellied to try it when I haven't been practicing."

Ezra came in from the outside stairs then, holding a tray of steaming mugs. Jeanne followed him in. "Clint's been singin' us up a storm tonight," Ezra was saying.

"Really?" Jeanne said with interest. She pulled back her hood and took off her cape in the warm room. "And I've missed it!"

"We're going to sing 'Turkey in the Straw' some more, Mama," Marvel said eagerly. "You put the flowers in your hair like I said! Oh, you look beautiful."

Clint, who had risen when Jeanne came in, said softly, "You sure do, Jeanne. Just like the fairy queen and the fairy princess, when I first saw you and Marvel."

Jeanne blushed a little with pleasure. "Why, thank you, Mr. Hardin. That's very kind of you."

"Not really," he said, offering her his crackerbox. "You're going to join us, aren't you?"

"I certainly am. I don't want to miss 'Turkey in the Straw.'"

They all sipped their hot cider and talked about loading up the *Rose* in the morning, and Jeanne's and Marvel's upcoming shopping trip. "Marvel simply must have some new dresses," Jeanne said. "Mr. Masters is going to accompany us and introduce us to the finest dressmaker in Memphis. Isn't that wonderful, Marvel?"

"Yes, Mama. May I have pink?"

"You may. And blue to match your eyes, and green for coming spring."

Clint whispered something to Vince, who nodded. Clint said, "Before we learn 'Turkey in the Straw,' I want to sing a song for Marvel. I can't sing the one you wanted, Marvel, but maybe you'll like this one."

Vince played a slow sweet, haunting strain and Clint began to sing.

> *Black, black, black*
> *Is the color of my true love's hair.*
> *Her lips are like a rose so fair*
> *And the prettiest face and the neatest hands,*
> *I love the grass whereon she stands*
> *She with the wondrous hair.*

Marvel thought the song was for her, and perhaps it was; but as Clint sang he looked only at Jeanne Bettencourt.

CHAPTER ELEVEN

On the river Jeanne counted time differently. Days were not days, they were distances marked off by islands, snags, sandbars, points, chutes. Nights were not dusk to sunrise. The night was the town: Helena, Napoleon, Pine Bluff, Little Rock, Memphis. Weeks did not translate as seven days. Jeanne counted and logged trips, which were eight days. By the middle of March, she was taken aback to see, thumbing through her logs, that she had made only six round trips as pilot of the *Helena Rose*. She had been in the wheelhouse driving so much that it seemed she had been on the river for a long time.

It was the middle of their seventh trip, and the middle of March. They were overnighting at Pine Bluff on their return home. Jeanne sat at her desk with her captain's logbook, a lantern casting a bright aura around her and the rest of the cabin into deep shadow. She looked up at the window. A wild storm shot fat drops of rain that splatted noisily against the glass. Occasionally a garish glare lit her face, a bolt of lightning, and immediately afterwards *basso profundo* growls of thunder.

Jeanne put her head into her hands and closed her eyes. *What if the creeks are flooding?* she worried. As spring had grown nearer, so had her anxiety. She wished devoutly that she could talk to someone about her concerns. Once, she thought, she would have told George Masters her fears that she wouldn't be able to handle the *Rose* on the lower part of the Arkansas River during the spring rains. But since he had talked to her about the article in the newspaper, his attitude seemed to have changed from wholehearted support of her venture to a sort of patient indulgence. She was reluctant to tell him about any setbacks or hardships on the *Helena Rose*. She had the feeling that he was just waiting for an excuse to talk her out of piloting. In spite of her current fears, Jeanne was far from ready to retire from the river. She must have as much of her father in her as she did her mother, she reflected.

The natural person to talk to should be Clint Hardin, her business partner and the engineer. But Jeanne refused to contemplate confiding in him, for she simply didn't trust him. He and Vince always left the boat on their overnight stops, and she knew they must be going to saloons. They were careful, and courteous, she admitted. They must get all their drinking and carousing done before they returned to the *Helena Rose*, because Jeanne had never heard them come back, even though the door to Clint's cabin was directly across from her cabin door.

But there were also the two- or three-day stays in Memphis after they concluded a trip. Clint and Vince left in the evenings, as usual. One morning when Jeanne left her cabin after they had arrived in town the night before, she could smell the essence of sandalwood in the hallway in front of Clint's door. She only knew what sandalwood smelled like because a gentleman at the Gayoso had always brought his own soap, sandalwood soap. To Jeanne the scent represented something costly, glamorous, mysterious, and it was outlandish to think that Clint Hardin would buy it. It had to be something to do with a woman.

Also several times she had caught the barest whiff of a woman's perfume in the hallway. Jeanne wondered if the sandalwood woman and the perfume woman were the same person before she berated herself harshly for wasting her time even thinking about such things.

And then, of course, there had been the infamous Suzette incident. One day as they were in Memphis loading up, a buxom girl of about eighteen with raven hair and dark snapping eyes danced onto the *Helena Rose*. Jeanne was standing up on the hurricane deck, just above the bow, watching the roustabouts load. When Suzette boarded, she could hear Vince and Clint laughing. Later Vince had said something to Clint about going to see Suzette at the Bell and Whistle that night, or she'd have a thing or two to say when they got back.

None of these things were Jeanne's concern; but she felt she had good reasons not to trust Clint Hardin.

As these things ran through her mind, she took a mental step back. *It's not that I don't trust him, I trust him with Marvel and I trust him with money. That is a lot of trust. It's just that I can't confide in him, talk to him about personal things.*

At the moment Jeanne's troubles weren't personal, they were about the *Helena Rose*. It was her own conflicting emotions about Clint Hardin that were in the way. But she was tired and she didn't want to analyze all that. She would see what the morning would bring.

VINCE CAME INTO THE engine room and said, "Ezra's nervous." He had to shout because the engine was always loud and on this stormy morning the rain made a deafening staccato beat against the sides of the *Helena Rose*.

"How can you tell?" Clint shouted back. He was kneeling down on the starboard side, looking underneath the complication of pipes that led into and out of the *Rose*'s pumps.

Vince came to kneel beside him and help him look. "He's standing out on deck, staring at the riverbanks. We got a leak or something?"

"No, but listen how hard the pump's working. I'm thinking we're drawing up more sludge than water."

"How can you hear the pump?" Vince complained. "All I hear is a deafening hurly-burly racket."

"Good ears, I guess." He stood up and crossed to the port side to kneel again, and he said something that Vince couldn't hear, of course.

Sighing, Vince stood up and was about to kneel by him again when not one but three jangling rings of the attention bell from the pilothouse sounded. Then they heard Jeanne scream, "Clint, Clint! Hurry, I need help!"

Clint stood and bounded out of the engine room, took the stairs three at a time, and was in the wheelhouse in ten seconds. It was dark, the windows completely clouded up. Jeanne was standing on a spoke on the left-hand side of the wheel. "Help me! We've got to turn to port!" she cried, jumped, and stamped on the spoke, hard, but the wheel didn't move.

Galvanized, Clint took two pins at the top and pushed left. For eternal moments he struggled, the tendons and veins on his arms bulging. Slowly the wheel gave, and he was able to move four pins left. Jeanne jumped off the wheel and cried, "That's enough! We've got to—"

But Clint had already guessed the situation and he shouted, "Vinnie! Back and fill, back and fill!"

This command effectively put the boat in neutral, and sluggishly she wallowed to a stop. Clint turned the wheel, still with some difficulty, until the kingpin, the one that was wrapped in marlin as an indicator, was straight up. This meant the rudder was exactly straight.

"What's happened?" he asked Jeanne calmly.

Her face was pale and her hands shook. "I was trying to come out of a hairpin right turn. From the east Choctaw Creek is flooding, and it created a strong cross-current and the rudder got stuck in the right turn. I couldn't get her out of it in time."

"Can you hold her steady?" he asked, and Jeanne stepped up to the wheel.

Clint went outside and wiped the rain away from his face. The storm clouds were so low and black that it was more like late evening than eleven o'clock in the morning. Around him all he could see were gaunt trees with naked spiky branches. The water was black. As he began to comprehend what he was seeing, he realized that the *Rose* was in a swamp, surrounded by cypress and tupelo trees. He ran to the side of the boat and looked around, and barely in the torpid light he could see great cypress knees—hull-killers—rising up out of the water. He oriented himself, and realized that the *Rose* had turned sideways to the current that had swept them in.

He ducked back inside the pilothouse. "Is the way back to the river landmarked in any way?" he asked.

Mutely she shook her head. He went to the speaking tube and didn't bother with the attention bell. Shouting in an operatic voice was loud enough. "Vinnie, Ezra up here now." He took a rag out of his pocket and wiped the windows, but like a wraith, the steam slowly stole back into the corners.

Vince and Ezra came in and Clint said, "We're in a cypress swamp, and we can't back out. The *Rose* is turned port side against the current. What we're going to have to do is reverse, fill, forward, fill, reverse, fill, forward, fill, and so on 'til we get her head-on. Then I'll give you a shout to stop."

"Got it, Clint," Vince said.

He and Ezra started to leave, but Ezra turned back and asked, "Cap'n Jeanne, we's in Dead Man's Slough, ain't we?"

"Yes," she answered dully. "Have you ever gotten caught in here before?"

"No, ma'am, but don't you worry, we'll have her outta here in no time," he said reassuringly, and closed the pilot-house door.

Clint said, "Jeanne, you're the pilot, you know this wheel. You want to do this?"

"No, I don't," she answered tensely. She stood by the wheel, her fists clenched at her sides.

He nodded, and slowly the engines geared up again, and the *Rose* began to back up. Clint worked the wheel, and then they filled, and he turned it the other way; this went on as they inched their way around, turning in a tight half-circle. At last the *Helena Rose* was facing due east. Clint leaned over the speaking tube and called, "That's good, boys! Shut 'er down!"

When the engines came to a full stop, Clint ran outside again to see if the Rose was still being pushed farther into the swamp by the flood current. But the dark water looked still except for the raindrops splashing on its gloomy surface, and he could see no telltale ripples against her nose, so he went back inside the pilothouse. Jeanne was sitting on the bench, her hands limp in her lap, staring into space. He sat down beside her.

"I've always heard the river plays the very devil's tricks on you," he said lightly. "This was a humdinger."

"It wasn't the river," Jeanne said numbly. "It was me. I was afraid this was going to happen."

"Jeanne, boats get shoved around every which way by flood currents all the time. It's not your fault."

"It was my fault. I'm too weak to handle the *Rose*. If a grown man had been piloting he could have made the turn."

"Maybe, maybe not. Ezra told me that pilots have a saying. 'It takes one upstream, but sometimes downstream it takes three: two to fight the wheel and one to holler encouragement.'"

"Fine. So we need three grown men to pilot."

"No. We need you," Clint said quietly.

"Don't patronize me, I am not a child!" Jeanne stormed, jumping to her feet to stand before him, her bloodless fists on her hips. "You don't know anything about what I'm going through! You just tra-la-la, trip your way around life, everything comes so easy for you! You sashay onto a riverboat, and oh, sure, this is *simple*! Steam boilers, reaching jerkins, pooling rods, no problem! I've been a master machinist since I was two years old! Oh, what's the matter, poor little Jeanne, can't turn the wheel? Here, I'll do it with my pinky finger, see how *simple* it is? And you just open your mouth, and glorious sounds like an archangel's anthem just come rolling out, but you fiddle-faddle around and sing about stupid *tuckahaws*! And, oh, Vinnie, help me, I just can't decide between my sandalwood woman or my perfume woman or my tavern maid with the black, black, black hair!"

When this tirade had begun, Clint's inclination had been to rise to his feet, because it was so deeply ingrained in him not to remain sitting when a lady stood. But after Jeanne's first few words he realized he'd better keep his seat. Clint had seen ladies having hysterics before, but he'd never seen one quite as wrathful, nor as acidly articulate, as Jeanne. Despite himself he was fascinated. And so he sat, looking up at her, struggling to keep his face expressionless.

She shut her mouth abruptly, pressed her fingers to her temples, and squeezed her eyes shut. "What am I saying? I must be out of my mind." She collapsed back onto the bench.

Clint watched her warily, but she seemed deflated and listless, and remained silent. Finally he said, "I'm sorry about all of that, Jeanne. But right now I guess we'd better figure out what to do. Should we just stay here until the storm stops?"

She looked down. "I don't want to stay in Dead Man's Slough overnight."

He nodded. "Okay. It's only about noon now. We'll see how it goes for the next couple of hours. By two, if it hasn't let up, why don't we try this. We can take soundings, and drive out of here one paddle at a time."

"That's fine," she said dully. "But I'm not driving. You do it. And I don't want to go south when we get back in the river. About ten miles north is a big landing, Widow Eames' Landing. I'm sure Ezra knows it. I want to stay there overnight."

"Then that's what we'll do," Clint said steadily. "You look really tired. Why don't you go rest for awhile?"

She rose and without looking at him or saying a word, she left the pilothouse. He watched her thoughtfully. She didn't try to shield herself from the rain. Her shoulders stooped, she walked slowly to the stairs and didn't look back. When he was sure she'd had enough time to get into her cabin he went down to the boiler room. Vince, Ezra, and Marvel were there. Marvel was sitting in her chair, clutching Avaymaria and Mrs. Topp. She looked scared. Instantly Clint went down on his knee beside her and took her hand. It was very small and cold. He smiled at her. "The river played a dirty trick on your mama, and whooshed us right up into a swamp. But everything's okay, Marvel. Your mother is fine, she just had a tough morning and needs to rest for awhile."

She stared at him with her wide-spaced almond eyes, so like her mother's. Then she nodded slowly. "I understand. Roberty's already making tea, the black Indian that Mama likes. Should I take it to her?"

"Yeah, I think that would be real nice."

Marvel left to go to the galley, and Clint turned to Ezra. "What in blazes is Dead Man's Slough?"

Grimly, Ezra said, "Hit used to be just a bog about a quarter-mile east of the river, called Choctaw Bayou. Indians used to go in there to gather thet moss on the trees, makes good stuffing for pillows and mattresses and such. But the Choctaw Creek acrost flooded and cut a swath over to the bog, so's now it's connected to the river by a narrow ditch of fast-flowin' water, in heavy rain times. Story is that back in the bad days when all the Indians was gittin' shipped out to the west, some of 'em would try to hide in Choctaw Bayou. But rivermen that got caught just like we done did told tales of finding Indians hanging from the trees back up in here, lot's of 'em, all over. That's when they started calling it Dead Man's Slough. And that's when it started to be said that Choctaw Creek tries to push the white man's boats up in it."

"You don't believe that though, do you Ezra?" Vince asked uncertainly.

He shrugged. "Choctaw Creek does push boats inter the bog. That's how we got here."

Clint asked, "But you said you'd never been here before?"

"No, Cap'n Hardin wasn't named 'Bull' for no reason. He was strong as a team of ox. He could fight that rudder right round when it got flat-up a-whomperjawed by the river. I niver did know of him to lose the boat 'cause of that. I reckon that's what's happent; going downstream, and them currents pushed the rudder right bang-up agin the housing."

Hesitantly, Clint said, "Jeanne says it's because she wasn't strong enough to turn the wheel."

"Prob'ly true. They's been other pilots that's been caught up inter Dead Man's Slough, though. Rip-roarin' river men. If that's what she's done got in her head."

"That's what she's done got in her head," Clint said dryly.

"But did these other pilots see any dead Indians?" Vince asked, his brow furrowed.

"Not that I know of," Ezra answered. "But dead men or not, it just ain't a good place to be stuck in."

"I don't think Jeanne's going to be able to get us out of here," Clint said evenly. "Could we take soundings and go real slow?"

"Sure 'nough," Ezra replied. "But who's going to drive the *Rose*?"

"I guess I am," Clint said. "Captain's orders."

THE NIGHT SKY WAS washed clean by the rain, and countless stars glittered. A solemn half moon hung low, too close to the horizon to reflect in the river. The *Helena Rose* was at rest at Widow Eames' Landing, a solid dock made of cypress. Up a long, gentle hill six lantern-lit windows glowed from the Eames house, three windows downstairs and three windows upstairs. Clint thought that it was a lot of lights for one widow, but then he didn't know if she was lucky enough to have family living with her.

He was sitting up on the hurricane deck in the soundless night, just staring up at the sky. It was unusual for him to be so still for so long. But he felt tranquil, not restless, as he watched the old moon and the stars and smelled the rich fragrance of wet earth and felt the tentative warmth of early spring.

Jeanne came onto the deck and crossed over to him. "I'm so sorry," she said quietly.

"Don't be," he said hurriedly. "Here, take my front-row seat. I'll go get me another one." He went into the wheelhouse and came out with another long bolster, the padding from the benches. Jeanne was already seated, her legs crossed beside her, her back against the 'scape pipe. Clint arranged his pillow and sat down. "Hope you don't mind me abusing your bench padding."

"No, I don't. I never sit on the bench anyway. So. How did you make it?"

"Okay. I kind of zigged and zagged along, because I couldn't get the hang of the wheel for awhile. I yanked us this way, then I'd shoot us over that way. Ezra said I was driving like a Sattiday night drunk. Begging your pardon, ma'am."

He couldn't see her face very well, but he sensed her smile. "I didn't feel any zigging or zagging. I think you must have done fine."

"Thanks, Captain."

"You're welcome."

She turned her face upward, and it was lit by starlight and faint moonglow. Her profile was clean, her nose small, her lips youthfully full, her neck long and slender and graceful. "I've seen so many nights here, at this landing. Widow Eames used to have a big eight-sided gazebo painted white right there. She had a large family, you see, and her sons built it. In summer sometimes the Eames and families from all around used to come down here and picnic and swim and dance in the gazebo. That gazebo was probably the most familiar landmark on the Arkansas River."

"What happened to it?" Clint asked curiously.

She sighed deeply, a sad sound. "There was a tornado. It destroyed the gazebo and the dock and—and the *Pearl*, my father's boat. My parents were killed."

Clint drew a sharp indrawn breath. "I'm so sorry, Jeanne. You weren't on the boat?"

"No, I was married, and Marvel was five months old. We were living in Memphis. The tornado was on May 7, 1849, and it caused a lot of damage between Little Rock and Arkansas Post, and eighteen people died. Anyway, I didn't even find out about my parents for a week and a day. I came back here. They're buried up there, in a little cemetery about a mile from here. But there was nothing left of the *Pearl*, nothing at all. It was as if she had simply disappeared."

"You've passed this place on every trip," Clint said quietly. "It must have been hard for you."

"The first trip was very hard. But that all happened six years ago, and it's true that time, and the Lord, can heal all sorrows. One day I wanted to stop and visit their graves, but I'm not quite ready for that yet. Now I try to remember the good things, the summer nights with the *Pearl* all lit up, and a hundred torches on the hill and all around the white gazebo. Two of the Eames boys were very taken with me, and they used to fight to see who was going to ask me to dance first. Of course, we were about eight or nine years old at the time."

Clint was wondering about her husband, and where he was when Marvel was only five months old and she lost her grandparents. But Jeanne's tone had turned light now, and he didn't want to question her about her marriage. It was miraculous that she'd told him about her parents. So he merely said, "You can't blame a fellow for fighting to see who's going to dance with the most beautiful woman at the ball, even if she is only eight years old."

"Hmm. And what about you, Clint? What were you doing when you were eight years old? What about your parents?"

He shrugged. "I never knew my father. By the time I was eight years old, I didn't know my mother any more." He stopped, but Jeanne felt he wanted to continue so she remained silent.

"She told me that he left her before I was born," he finally went on. "She said that he'd decided that she wasn't good enough for him, and so he knew that I wouldn't be good enough for him. He paid for me to go to Calvary Episcopal School, though. And I think, I'm not sure, that when I was young he was paying for our house. But my mother started drinking, and we lost the house, and moved to a cheap boardinghouse. She just literally wrecked herself, she got so bad."

"The drinking?" Jeanne asked quietly.

"It started out with whiskey, but then she got addicted to laudanum. It killed her," he said bluntly. "When I was fourteen. For three years she had been hitting the streets to pay for her little blue bottle. When that was gone, and she didn't have money for more laudanum, she drank rotgut whisky. Finally it was both. She didn't die well," he added bitterly.

"Oh, Clint, I am so sorry," Jeanne said compassionately. "It's when I hear things like this that I realize how very blessed I've been. I should never complain, or feel sad, or scared."

"Everybody's got a story," Clint said in a hard voice that was unheard of coming from him. "Mine's better than some, worse than some. Anyway, I got the *Helena Rose* from a cousin of my father's, so something good came out of it."

"It's funny you should say that. I have the same kind of mixed feelings about Ira Hardin's boat coming to me. You know that my mother was a Hardin, and she was from St. Louis."

"Ah, the infamous *St. Louis* Hardins. Good thing we're the *Memphis* Hardins or we never would have inherited. What's the story with them, anyway?"

"I don't have any idea," Jeanne said, sighing. "My mother never spoke of her family when I was a child. When I got older, she sat me down and had a talk with me, but she was—guarded, I suppose you'd say. She told me that her parents had disapproved of my father. When she married him anyway, she said that over time they had grown so far apart that they really weren't like her family any more. My father and I were her family."

"It sounds like you had a really good family, without the St. Louis Hardins. I'll bet they cut her right off, just like my father cut off me and my mother. I'll bet something like that happened to Bull Hardin, too. To tell the truth, I'm glad we're just fifth cousins twice and a half removed from them."

"You're a fourth cousin of Ira's, and I'm a fifth once removed," Jeanne reminded him. "And I have to be grateful that I'm a Hardin, no matter how distant. As you said, that's why we've got the *Rose*."

"Okay, so I'm grateful. Speaking of the *Rose*, how's the pilot doing?"

Jeanne sighed. "I guess we do have to talk about it."

Clint propped one knee up and rested his arm on it. "I wish it wasn't that we have to, Jeanne. I wish you just wanted to talk to me about it."

"I know, and I am trying. It's hard for me, Clint. I'm just not accustomed to asking anyone for help."

"Yeah, I noticed. But I can help you, Jeanne, I know I can. And I'm not just saying this because you're a woman and you're weak, and I'm a man and I'm tough. It's because I'm your engineer and you're my pilot, and you had a mechanical problem, and it's my responsibility to figure out a way to fix that problem."

"So you think it was just a mechanical problem?"

"Well, yeah. I mean, all that stuff about the angels singing and the tuckahaw and what on earth do you think a reaching jerkin is? No, I can't help you with all that. But I can fix it so the rudder's not so close to the housing and not so tight, and that will make the wheel easier to turn. It may happen again anyway—*because it happens*. It's just the way of the river."

"The way of the river," Jeanne echoed softly. "Yes, the river can be cruel and heartless and dangerous. But he can be dreamy and slow and sweet, too. Maybe you're right, Clint. Maybe it's not just me."

"It's not just you, Jeanne. And please, please listen to me. You're not alone in this. Whatever it is, no matter how bad it is, or how little the problem, give me a chance to help you."

She nodded slowly. "Okay, Clint. I'll give you a chance."

CHAPTER TWELVE

Neither Clint nor Jeanne mentioned their impromptu meeting on the hurricane deck that night to anyone. It had an effect, though; Jeanne and Clint talked more and more about the *Helena Rose*. Jeanne got into the habit of having breakfast with the crew in the galley, instead of just her and Marvel in their cabin. After the day's run, instead of going immediately to do her logs and paperwork, Jeanne came down to the main cargo deck as they were loading or unloading, and she and Clint talked to the shippers and attended to the mail together. As spring melted into summer, Jeanne came to respect him, and she even found that she enjoyed his company. Before she had always felt vague hostility toward him, mixed with disdain.

"Yes, I know I've told you that he's sometimes arrogant, and yes, sometimes he infuriates me," Jeanne explained to George Masters. "He and Vince must live in saloons, I think, when they're not on the *Rose*. And his women! I imagine he has two or three in every port. But still, he's an excellent engineer, and he's proved to be a shrewd businessman. That makes him a good man for a business partner."

"Mmm," George said noncommittally. They were sitting on a bench in Court Square, feeding peanuts to the squirrels. It was a hot day in July, and Jeanne was wearing a brand-new summer dress of light green muslin with a pink rose print. The sleeves were "pagoda" sleeves, the outer sleeve triangle-shaped with white embroidered eyelet undersleeves. For this one dress, Jeanne had bought a hoop skirt, and the eight-ruffled skirt was wide and made her waist look tiny. Her bonnet was trimmed with a dozen satin roses, and she had a dainty parasol of white Battenburg lace. She looked about eighteen years old.

The Court Square squirrels were famous in Memphis, for they were the fattest, boldest, most spoiled animals that ever lived. Now one bright-eyed squirrel that had been hogging the peanuts scampered up to Jeanne, climbed up onto the toe of her boot, and sat up, begging. "You little minx!" she said with delight. Slowly she reached down with a peanut. He took it in his clever paws, stuffed it into his cheek, and then ran off. Jeanne laughed. "He's as bad as Leo! That dog has gotten so that he lays his big slobbery head on my lap every time we're eating. I have to wash my skirts every night, it's as bad as trying to keep my aprons clean at the Gayoso."

"Do you know, I can count on one hand the times I've heard you laugh," George said. "You sound happy. I hope that some of that happiness has to do with me?"

"Of course it does. After all, we never could have done so well with the *Helena Rose* without your help."

"So your happiness is all about the success of the *Rose*. Your success, and Clint Hardin's success. That's not what I was talking about, Jeanne."

Jeanne reached into their bag of peanuts and threw some out to the waiting dozen or so squirrels around their feet. "I know," she said quietly. "I understand what you're asking, George. Yes, you make me happy. Can we leave it at that right now?"

"I'm glad I make you happy," he said slowly, and then turned to search her face. "But I need more, Jeanne. Evaluating this conversation alone, Clint Hardin makes you happy, the squirrel makes you happy, Leo makes you happy, and I make you happy. How am I supposed to feel about that?"

"I didn't say Clint makes me happy," Jeanne said hastily. "It's just that—oh, forget about him. George, please try to understand my position," she said, dropping her voice so that passers-by strolling in the park couldn't hear her. "Do you realize that you are the only man I've ever kissed besides my husband? Our relationship, our warmth and closeness, are all strange territory to me, something brand-new and a little frightening."

"You've never been frightened of anything in your life, Jeanne."

"You are so wrong, and the reason you're wrong is because you don't really know me as well as you think, and I don't really know you either. That's my point. We share a lot of things between us, but there hasn't been enough time for me to be sure of my feelings."

"It's been seven months, and I am very sure of my feelings, dearest," he said, taking her hand and caressing it in both of his. "Can't you give me some encouragement, can't you at least tell me what you're thinking about us? No matter how many times we kiss, and how close we become, I always know that you're holding back. I can sense that you deliberately put distance between us, and it's hard for me."

With some difficulty Jeanne said, "George, I meant it when I said that you make me happy. I enjoy our time together immensely. You're interesting, you're interested in me and you show it, you listen to me and you respect me. And I—I find you a very attractive man, and I'm drawn to you in that way. But more than this I can't say right now."

He lifted her hand, turned it over, and pressed his lips to her palm. "Then it will have to be enough, Jeanne. I can wait."

THE NIGHTS HAD GROWN sultry. Jeanne slept with not even a light sheet covering her, only her cotton nightgown. She tried to stay very still so as not to wake Marvel, who never seemed to get too hot. But after about an hour, Jeanne felt perspiration beading on her forehead, and she got up. She bathed her face in cool water scented with mint, which she found to be cooling and refreshing, but it also had a tendency to make her feel wide-awake. She went to the window, propped her crossed arms on the sill, and rested her chin on her hands. There was a very slight breeze, and it felt good on her tingling face. Again she thought how grateful she was to Clint for replacing all of the windows on the *Rose* with six-by-six windows that opened. It had been an extravagant expense for a steamer, but Clint had known a glazier that gave them a good price, and he and Ezra had installed them. Ezra was an experienced carpenter, and Clint had learned quickly, Jeanne thought ruefully. Naturally.

It was early, so there was still activity on the docks. The music of a waltz drifted on the air, probably from the steamship docked two down from the *Rose*, a big luxury steamship with twenty staterooms and a ballroom, Vince had told her. He seemed to know everything about every boat on the river. Jeanne hummed along with the waltz. In the capricious breeze, occasionally a man's deep voice would carry to her, or a woman's light laughter.

Then she heard two voices quite clearly. Clint and Vince were coming back on board the *Rose*. ". . . trying to tell me you're not staying over with her, Clint? C'mon!"

"I'm trying *not* to tell you anything, Vinnie."

"I know, but you might as well give over, man. Don't you think we all know who that little colored boy is, with his red vest and black trousers, that brings those messages? Her Majesty sure knows how to dress up her slaves, even the errand boys. Little popinjay, carrying around those purple notes that smell like perfume."

"Hey, Vinnie? Did you notice that I happen to be standing here talking to you for some reason I can't understand and not at her house?"

"Yeah. How'd that happen?"

"Shut up, Vinnie."

Their voices faded as they went into the boiler room. Jeanne had been motionless, outrage growing in her. Now she stood up and banged the window down. It sounded loud, but Marvel didn't stir. Jeanne paced. *Staying with* Her Majesty! *And this woman is sending little love missives down here to my boat? How dare she! And I wonder how they explain those perfumed notes and the popinjay to Marvel? I could kill Clint!*

Jeanne raved on for a while, and managed to make herself tired. She lay back down but found that she couldn't make her mind stop going over and over the conversation. It was a long, restless night.

When she awoke in the morning she could tell she had slept late, for the light streaming through the windows was already white and hot. Marvel was already gone to breakfast. Jeanne splashed her face again and again and dressed hurriedly. She went down the hallway to the galley, stepped inside and looked around at Ezra, Vince, and Roberty, then glared at Clint. "Where is Marvel?" she demanded.

"Good morning, Captain," Clint said pleasantly. "Don't worry, she ate a good breakfast. She's out playing with Leo."

"Thank you," Jeanne said stiffly, and hurried out.

Vince stared at Clint, his brown eyes wide with alarm. "What'd you do?"

"Me? Nothing! It must have been you."

"Huh! She didn't bite my head off, buddy. Besides, you're always the one the women are mad at. I've told you and told you, they don't take any notice of me when you're around, and when they're in a huff I'm really, really glad."

Jeanne went out on the main deck, and Marvel wasn't there, and she wasn't on the Texas deck either. Muttering to herself, she went up the stairs.

The hurricane deck, where the pilothouse was perched, was the flat roof of the boat. It was about twenty feet above the water, and it had no railing. Jeanne saw Marvel throw a stick that, ludicrously, had pink ribbons tied to the ends. Leo, his ears flopping crazily, loped over to it, picked it up, shook it, and then bounded back to Marvel. Jeanne said sharply, "Marvel! What are you doing!"

Marvel whipped around and the laughter on her face faded. "I'm playing with Leo, Mama." The dog sat down by her and drooped his head guiltily.

Jeanne walked over to them. "Haven't I told you not to play up here? It's dangerous! You could fall overboard!"

Marvel looked down and fidgeted with the stick in her hand. "I'm sorry, Mama, but no, you didn't tell me that. This is the first time I've played with Leo up here."

"Oh," Jeanne said uncertainly. "I didn't realize . . ." She knelt and lifted Marvel's chin. "I'm sorry, Marvel. But I really don't want you playing up here, all right?"

"All right, I won't. But Leo comes up here, doesn't he?"

Jeanne reached over to pet the dog's wide head. "Yes, he likes to come up here and lay down in the shade of the wheelhouse. I guess it's probably the coolest place on the boat. Leo, you big mooch, you always find the most comfortable spot, winter or summer."

"But won't he fall off?" Marvel asked worriedly.

"No, he doesn't have much sense but he's got more sense than that," Jeanne said affectionately, scratching his ear. "It's little girls that might fall off. Now, listen, Marvel, I need to ask you something. Have you seen a little black boy come to the boat, with a red waistcoat on?"

Marvel looked mystified. "Huh? I don't know what you're talking about, Mama. I don't know any little black boys 'cept those ones that bring fish sometimes."

"So you haven't seen a boy dressed in a red waistcoat and black trousers bring a note or letter to Mr. Clint? Here, on the boat?"

"No, ma'am."

Jeanne sighed and stood back up. "Good. Now, I haven't had my breakfast yet. Why don't you and Leo come down and keep me company?"

They went back down to the galley, and Jeanne managed to make herself agreeable to everyone. Their freight, a load of dry goods and housewares, had been loaded yesterday, so as soon as Jeanne finished breakfast they were on their way.

They reached Helena eight hours later, and Jeanne came down to talk to Clint. "You're sure you know what's being off-loaded here?" she asked cautiously. "All that stuff looks like a big jumble to me."

"No, we got it, Cap'n. I made sure it got loaded in order. Roberty's been a big help with multiple shippers and offloads, you know? Ever since we gave him charge of the mail sacks, he's turned into a little organizing fiend."

"Really? That's nice," Jeanne said shortly, and went upstairs.

Jeanne was much like that the entire trip, though she didn't stay shut up in her cabin. She was just very cool to Clint. It seemed he didn't even notice, which for some reason only made Jeanne more angry. By the time they were coming back from Little Rock, she had almost forgotten the reason she was upset with Clint in the first place.

They were steaming easy along. The river was wide and slow, almost like a big orange-brown pond. The sun was just past noon-high, and the heat of the sunbeams on Jeanne's face made her cheeks burn a little. A fly had gotten trapped in the wheelhouse, and its busy buzz and the huffing of the 'scape pipes and the rhythmic water whishing of the paddle wheel were the only sounds.

Then Jeanne heard a curious beat, like a far-off snare drum, *whit! whit! whit!* for a few seconds, and then it turned into a jangling *clank! clank! CLINK-CLINK-CLANK! CLANK!*

"Shuttin' her down, Cap'n!" Clint shouted in the engine room speaking tube.

Jeanne positioned the kingpin, then went outside. She saw Leo standing at the far end of the deck, right at the edge, looking down. The wheel was still turning, though much more slowly, and the noise became *clank . . . clankety . . . clankety . . .*

"Dumb dog," Jeanne muttered, and stamped down the deck. When she reached him she grabbed the folds of loose skin behind his head and said, "LEO! You're going to—"

The dog started, jumping as if he'd been scalded, and then she felt a weight on her foot as he landed on it. She then jumped and struggled to get her foot out from under his big paw; her skirt and petticoat flapped around the dog's head, she lost her grip on him and stumbled, and down Jeanne went, dog and all. Her shoulder hit the paddle wheel, and then the warm milky water of the river closed over her head.

At first she panicked, struggling wildly because she was trapped, something was pulling her down. But immediately she calmed down and realized that her skirt had gotten tangled in the paddle wheel and it was all bunched up and twisted tight around her. She tried to pull it free, and realized that she didn't have the strength to tear the fabric, so she reached around to undo the single button at the waistband. Like all experienced swimmers, she had instinctively taken a deep breath before she hit the water.

She felt a tug on her sleeve that pulled her arm away, and she saw Leo, trying to pull her up. She wrenched her arm back and reached around herself again. Then there was a splash, and strong arms grabbed her around the waist. She felt a strong yank, and for a moment her skirt held her, but then another bone-crushing yank crushed the breath she had left out of her. Her skirt gave way, and then she was above water. She gasped and coughed, then drew in a deep breath. Clint was holding her up, his hands around her waist.

She pushed his face. "Let go of me, you—you!"

"Huh? But I'm helping you! Here, Jeanne, I'll pull—"

"No! I can swim, you moron! Just let go of me!"

"Okay, okay!" he said, and struck out toward the shore, which was only twelve feet away. To get back on the boat they'd have to swim all eighty feet down to the bow. Jeanne did have trouble, because she was choking a little and her petticoat was tangled between her legs. Still, she reached the muddy riverbank and pulled herself up to collapse beside Clint, who was sitting there calmly, petting a dripping, downcast Leo.

"Oh! You almost yanked me in two!" Jeanne shouted to Clint.

"You were drowning. I pulled you up."

"I wasn't drowning, I was just unfastening my skirt!"

Clint's eyebrows shot up. "You were unfastening your skirt," he repeated slowly. "So sorry, I didn't realize I was supposed to be saving your skirt."

"Mama!" Floating over the water, Marvel's thin voice sounded panicky.

"It's all right, darling, I'm fine!" Jeanne shouted, and waved. Vince, Ezra, Roberty, and Marvel lined the port side railing.

"Did you fall off?" Marvel called anxiously.

Clint, Vince, and Ezra couldn't help it. They all burst into laughter.

Jeanne was furious with them, and spluttered inarticulately. But then the absurdity of the situation hit her, and she started chuckling, and then giggling. Finally she managed to call out, "Yes, I fell off, Marvel. But I'm fine."

Clint's white teeth gleamed. "Thought you were a river—er—lady. Only landsmen fall in."

"Actually Leo pushed me in," Jeanne said, gasping a little. "But then he tried to pull me out, so I guess we're even."

She plucked at her torn blouse sleeve, and then she realized how she looked. Her blouse, now completely transparent, clung to her like a second skin, and she felt cool air on her back; it must be completely torn in two from Leo trying to pull her up. Her skirt was completely gone, except for a few raggedy tatters hanging down from her waist. Her single petticoat was wrapped soggy around her legs. She remembered hitting the paddle wheel, and reached back to feel of her upper shoulder.

Clint frowned and said, "You got a mean red streak back there, Captain. Did you hit the paddles?"

"I just glanced off them, it's not really bad," Jeanne said, working her arm around. It was then that Jeanne really looked at Clint. His hair was slicked back and gleamed ebony in the sun. His eyes were a bright royal blue, and tiny water drops in his long thick eyelashes sparkled. He wasn't wearing a shirt. He had gotten tanned on the boat this summer, and the expanse of his bronzed chest and the thick muscles of his shoulders and arms distracted Jeanne for several moments. Quickly she turned her head. "I must look a perfect fright."

"Nah," Clint said. "You look real nice. A little damp, but you're still pretty."

"Liar," Jeanne said with amusement.

"Am not," he said lazily. Then a curiously unsettled look crossed his rugged face, and he said, "So. You want to swim back, or have Vince and Ezra put down one of the stages? They'd reach."

"No, that's way too much trouble. I'll swim. But not just this minute, I'm still catching my breath. What happened, anyway?"

"You fell in," Clint teased. "Okay, okay, sorry. It's one of the reach rods, or as some captains call it, a reaching jerky."

"That would be a *reaching jerkin*," Jeanne corrected him, her dark eyes dancing. "Can you fix it? No, what am I saying? Of course you can fix it. You can fix everything."

"Not everything. For instance, no way I can fix that sad drownded skirt of yours. But yeah, I can fix the reach rod, it just whanged right out of a connection. What really gets my goat is that I oiled all the connections this morning and I didn't even notice it was loose."

"How'd that happen?" Jeanne said with a mischievous grin.

"My question exactly. You know, I think this is the first time I've ever seen you laugh. Are you happy, Jeanne?"

"What?" she blurted out. They stared at each other.

Vince yelled, "Hey, you people want a gangplank? Or I could bring you over a picnic!"

"That'd be nice," Clint yelled back.

Jeanne laughed.

CHAPTER THIRTEEN

"I've got a great idea," Clint said. "I want to take you all out to eat. We can celebrate Captain Jeanne's Dunk. You ever have German food, *kleines Mädchen?*"

"I don't know," Marvel replied, puzzled. "Mama knows. Do you speak German?"

"No, but I can sing in German," Clint said airily. "I know 'O Tannenbaum' and 'Stille Nacht.'"

"Yeah, but Her Ladyship says you sing German with an Italian accent," Vince joked. Clint gave him a dire warning glance.

They had just finished unloading in Memphis. Ezra had made lemonade, and Clint and Jeanne kept the boat stocked with the luxury of ice in the icebox. Everyone was sitting out on the main cargo deck, watching the furious activity on the docks. Twenty-two steamers were lined up in the waterway, and hundreds of people—roustabouts, crews, passengers, shippers, receivers, errand boys, woodmen—swarmed all over, shouting and shoving. After the *Rose* had been unloaded, they pulled down to the far end of the wharves and docked to get out of the way. Ezra had brought out crates for them to sit on, and Clint had remarked that he was going to go to town and get them some nice deck chairs. Now, after Vince's tell, he glanced cautiously at Jeanne. She pressed her lips together and looked down the docks, but said nothing.

Marvel asked, "Do you sing 'Avaymaria' in German?"

"No, that's actually in Latin," Clint replied. "And Vinnie has a big mouth, so he's going to tell you I sing Latin with a German accent. So, how 'bout it, everyone? I'll hire us a cart and we'll go to Mütter Krause's for dinner tomorrow. You too, Ezra. You gotta get off this boat sometime or you're going to start looking like a boiler."

He grinned. "Just so happens I love Mütter Krause's *Weiner schnitzel*. You betcha I'll go. How're you for sech a thing as *Weiner schnitzel*, Captain Jeanne?"

"I've never had it," she said distantly. "And I'm afraid that I have a previous engagement tomorrow, Clint." She was still looking away.

"I knew it, you always go with Mr. Masters," Marvel said impatiently. "But I can go with them, can't I? I want some weinersnits."

"Yes, you *may* go," Jeanne said. She rose and said, "Speaking of Mr. Masters, I see him coming now. If you all will excuse me, I think I'll go meet him."

He was strolling along dressed in a cream linen suit with a straw top hat. Jeanne had teased him about his "summer" walking stick, made of blonde ironwood with a silver knob with inlaid pearl.

After their greetings Jeanne tucked her arm into his as they walked slowly back to the *Rose*. "I see you brought me a present! How thoughtful, I love *Frank Leslie's Illustrated*

Weekly. It's so good for me to read with Marvel. She can't read nearly well enough for a newspaper yet, of course. But with pictures, she sounds out and learns new words. And Roberty too."

"Then I'll start bringing you one every week," he said gallantly. "It's little enough, since you won't let me buy you any gifts. It's depressing to be limited to flowers and newspapers. So how was the trip, Jeanne?"

"I fell in the river," she said with amusement. "The crew is calling it Captain Jeanne's Dunk."

He stopped walking and turned to grab both her arms. "You fell in! Are you hurt?"

"No, no, I'm just fine. I banged my shoulder against the paddle wheel, and I've got a lurid bruise that's quite dramatic, but it looks worse than it feels. To tell the truth, the whole thing was kind of funny."

"Funny," he repeated darkly as they started walking again. "You banged your shoulder, so you fell close to the paddle wheel. You could have hit your head, or even broken your back, Jeanne. That is *not* funny."

"But I didn't. So it did turn out to be funny, considering—"

"How did you get out?" he demanded. It was the first time he had ever interrupted her. His smooth classic features were dark and troubled.

"I'm an excellent swimmer," Jeanne retorted.

"You swim? And just how are you clothed when you swim?" he snapped.

"My father taught me to swim when I was very young. And after I got older, he found us a swimming hole just out of South Bend that was private, and we all swam there, even my mother. I haven't been swimming since I was sixteen years old, but even if I had it's none of your business what I wear," Jeanne said indignantly.

They had reached the *Rose*'s landing stage, and George turned to her again and took her hands. "All right, let's forget all that for the moment. It's just that I'm worried, Jeanne. So many things can happen to people on riverboats. What you're doing is dangerous; steamboats are dangerous, the river is dangerous, the weather is dangerous, the people are dangerous. You just don't take care of yourself at all, otherwise you would never have fallen off the boat. You don't have any idea of what you're doing, do you?"

Jeanne pulled her hands away from him gently. She was very aware that everyone on the *Rose* was watching them. "So you honestly think that I don't know what I'm doing? How can you say that to me, George?"

"You're deliberately misunderstanding me. I was talking about you being more aware of the dangers on the river. That's all."

"Fine. I'll be more careful."

"Do you promise? Promise me, Jeanne. I worry, because I care about you so deeply," he finished in a low heartfelt voice.

Mollified, she nodded. "I know you do, George. I care for you too. Let's just not talk any more about me falling in. I can see that you'll never see that it really was funny. Anyway, I wanted to ask you, were you still thinking that we'd go somewhere tomorrow? Because unless you have special plans, I thought I'd go out with the crew and Marvel tomorrow for dinner."

He frowned. "But we always go out while you're in Memphis. As I've told you, it's very difficult for me, and I hope for you too, just seeing each other on your layovers. Of course I want to spend the day with you tomorrow. Go out with the crew? Surely you're joking! Where are you going to go with a riverboat crew, a saloon? You shouldn't even be seen in public with them!"

Jeanne drew herself upright and her eyes flashed. "I said, with the crew and Marvel. You are being insufferably rude and snobbish!"

"You did? I'm so sorry, Jeanne," he said instantly. "To tell you the blunt truth, when I realized you were saying you didn't want to see me tomorrow, I got terribly jealous. That's why I said what I did. Please forgive me, I didn't mean a word of it."

"Jealous? Oh, George, that's ridiculous!"

"I can't help it, I want you all to myself," he said with a half smile. "So now I'm rude, snobbish, and selfish."

"You're none of those things," Jeanne said quietly. "I know that very well."

"Then you will spend the day with me tomorrow?" he asked. "Please, Jeanne. The days I have with you are important to me above all things."

"All right," she said, tucking her arm back into his as they went up the gangplank. "But only because you brought me the *Illustrated Weekly*."

Though Jeanne smiled at him, she still had misgivings. She really did want to go with the crew tomorrow. The reason she had been rather cool toward Clint was not because of Vince's mention of "Her Ladyship"; Jeanne had resigned herself to Clint's women. It was because she was thinking of how entangled she was with George Masters now. When they were in Memphis she saw very little of Marvel. Now she realized that George Masters hardly ever wanted Marvel to be with them. She supposed it might be understandable. He was a single man with no children and he was, she knew, in love with her. It was only natural that he wanted to be alone with her. He did ask for Marvel to come with them occasionally, and several times he had asked if he could buy Marvel some gift, which Jeanne always refused, but still it was generous of him.

Still, it troubled her that he showed very little interest in her daughter.

Clint Hardin spent a lot of time with Marvel, and with Roberty. In fact, Clint asked Marvel to do things with him, such as helping her with her arithmetic and making up math games. He and Ezra were making a dollhouse for Mrs. Topp and Avaymaria, at Clint's suggestion. At night when he and Vince were on the boat, Clint sang what Marvel wanted to sing, and he often danced with her. Clint actually seemed to like Marvel, and deliberately sought out her company, and not because she was Jeanne's daughter. And like George Masters, Clint Hardin, too, was single, with no children of his own.

With an effort, Jeanne brought her attention back to George as he said, "Anyway, it does happen that I have plans for us tomorrow. I've found a charming eatery, and during the dinner hour it's perfectly respectable for ladies. It's German food, and if you like German food it's absolutely delicious."

"Is it Mütter Krause's?" Jeanne asked dully.

"Why, yes. Do you know it?"

"No. But I don't really want to go there, George. Not tomorrow, anyway."

THE FIRST OF AUGUST, far from being the height of the dry season as usual, had heavy rains. The storms weren't theatrical, just heavy steady downpours of warm rain. Both the Mississippi River and the Arkansas River turned into fast-flowing sepia-colored mud.

When Clint had first seen the map, he had said that the lower part of the Arkansas River looked like a squiggly green worm. That was actually pretty accurate. From

Niccottoo to the mouth of the Arkansas where it flowed into the Mississippi, the kingpin was never straight up. Pilots had to carefully tend the wheel, making constant turns: some sharp, some meandering. Countless streams flowed into the lower Arkansas: some wide and fast, like Choctaw Creek, some so insignificant that they were unnamed, but all of them had to be carefully evaluated by the pilot in a rainy season. As a precaution, Jeanne had told Clint to stand by just in case she needed him to help her with the wheel again. She had realized that she wasn't the only pilot on the river that sometimes was defeated by heavy rains and the currents they created.

There were no less than four oxbows in this stretch. Oxbows were formed when a slow-moving river meandered off the main course to make a circle. If the narrow entrance of the circle closed off, and if the water was deep enough, the formation became an oxbow lake. On the lower Arkansas the water hadn't eroded the interiors of the circle enough to form lakes, so they were four circles of water just off the river, with sand in the middle. It was Noble's Oxbow that gave the *Helena Rose* trouble.

Jeanne rounded a bend she had named Lean-to Corner, because just on the left-hand side of the shore, in the middle of deep thick woods, was a tiny clearing with a three-sided lean-to shack. It was deserted, and obviously old, because the wood was bleached out by many years of sun to an oyster white. She glanced over to look at it, and noticed that it was covered with honeysuckle vines, for it had thousands of tiny yellow blooms, making the lean-to look like a bower. The clearing was carpeted with black-eyed Susans. She was thinking that she'd never noticed flowers there before, and thought everything might be blooming because of the rains they'd had for a week, when abruptly she heard a raspy crunching sound and the *Helena Rose* jarred to a stop.

The paddle wheel kept working, making a horrible grunting noise. She rang the attention bell and started to yell into the speaking tube, but Clint's voice sounded in the tube from the engine room. "I'm shutting her down, Jeanne!" Immediately the wheel slowed, then stopped. Jeanne ran downstairs.

She headed for the side door that led directly into the engine room, but Clint was already outside at the stern, and she joined him. The paddle wheel was only submerged into the water about four inches. "It's a sandbar," Jeanne groaned. "I knew it." She pointed to starboard. "That's Noble's Oxbow, it's got a very shallow entrance."

Clint nodded and began to walk along the rail, staring over the side. "Yeah, you can see the sand depositing right now. The middle of the boat's not even in water." Ezra and Vince came out, and they walked all around the boat. She was stuck, slightly nose-up, completely out of the water until about two-thirds down the boat's length. There, a crosscurrent ran from west to east, or port to starboard on the *Rose*. Clint jumped over the side and went to stand behind the paddle wheel. "Yeah, there's a little drop-off back here, and the current's pushing more sand to starboard. It might deepen enough right under the wheel in an hour or two that we might be able to back off."

"I hope so," Jeanne said miserably. "Once my father got stuck on a sandbar, and we were there for six days. This is all my fault, I should have seen it."

Ezra shook his head vigorously. "It ain't your fault, Cap'n Jeanne. I ain't never heard of Noble's Oxbow getting sand-barred up."

Clint climbed back on board and said to her, "When are you going to get it into your pretty head that everything this ol' river does isn't your fault? Might as well say the rain's your fault."

"But I was looking to port, at the flowers," Jeanne argued. "I might have seen the sandbar if I'd been looking over here."

"So it's the flowers' fault, Cap'n. Okay, Ezra, Vinnie, let's get some shovels and see if we can heave her off."

The three men, along with Roberty, worked for two hours, digging under the paddle wheel. At high noon Jeanne went to the stern and leaned over. "Take a break, gentlemen. Marvel and I fixed you some dinner."

Clint looked up at her and grinned. "You cooked?"

"Yes, I've been slaving over a hot cutting board for an hour, slicing ham and roast beef," Jeanne answered sarcastically. "Come on up to the bow, we've set up a picnic on the deck."

Jeanne had made a dozen curried eggs, tomato-mushroom catsup, chow-chow, boiled jacket potatoes, corn fritters, fried hominy, and macaroni with cheese and bacon. Ezra had made fresh bread that morning, and Jeanne sliced some of it up for sandwiches. When they came back on board, Roberty and the men stared at the four crates pushed together and covered with a white sheet that held all the food. "Macaroni," Roberty breathed. "My favorite."

"My favorite is everything on that table," Clint said. "Thanks, Captain. Hey, maybe we should fire you as the pilot and make you the cook."

"Just try it," Jeanne said.

Everyone fixed their plates and got seated, and Leo laid his chin on Jeanne's lap as usual, staring up at her longingly. Resignedly, she gave him a small chunk of ham and asked, "So what's the verdict?"

Clint shook his head. "We're not going to be able to dig her out. About an hour ago the current shifted and started piling more sand up under the paddle wheel, so now it's buried about four inches in sand, faster than we could shovel it out. But Ezra thinks that may be a good thing."

Ezra said, "If it don't rain no more, the mud'll settle. Ol' Arkinsaw River's done righted hisself, runnin' north to south, so oncet cleans up agin she'll have water under her, you mark me."

They all looked up at the sky. It was a hot deep blue, with an enormous glaring sun. In the east were banks of storm clouds, a long low line of charcoal gray on the horizon. "Think it's moving west?" Vince asked Ezra.

"Dunno. If'n it does, it'll be Cap'n Jeanne's fault for sure," he said slyly.

It was the first time Ezra had ever teased Jeanne, and after she got over her surprise she laughed along with the others. "Another disaster to put in my log," she sighed theatrically. "*The flowers caused us to get stuck on the sandbank that just popped up out of the river because it knew I was coming, and then my own personal storm stirred up the mud so much we were here for days.*'"

"Aw, I was just joshin' you, Cap'n," Ezra said. "I think them there storm clouds are the leavin's of the storm we had this mornin', passin' west to east. Looks like hit's gwine to be a clear rest of the day and evenin'.'"

"I gotta tell you, Captain, I don't think there's any use in us trying to shovel out right now," Clint said. "The current has picked up, but it's like Ezra said, it's pretty much like a sandslide right now, piling up under us."

Jeanne said, "Okay. We might as well take the rest of the day off, don't you think?"

"So we can do whatever we want?" Marvel asked brightly.

"No, you may not learn to swim," Jeanne said sternly, eyeing Clint. "This is not the time and certainly not the place. But you can wade around or play with Leo on the sandbar—*as long as someone is watching you.*"

Clint said, "Now you know I'll be with her all the time, Cap'n. Can't you come out and play too?"

"No, I've been putting off our July accounts, and I need to go ahead and finish them."

"We made a bunch of money, I bet," Clint said happily.

"I'd rather like to narrow it down to more than just *a bunch*," Jeanne said dryly.

Ezra started gathering up plates and the platters of food, but Jeanne said, "No, I'll do the clearing up, Ezra. You cook and clean up every day. It's your day off. Go do something fun."

He grinned, his leathery face crinkling into smile and eye creases. "I did have a mind ter look for some minners in them shallows, Cap'n. Catchin' some fat crappie or bass would make fer a fine supper."

Jeanne cleared up all the food and dishes, cleaned the galley, and checked the pot of water she had put on the stove. It was exactly right; warmer than tepid but not hot. Happily she hauled the five-gallon copper pot to her cabin and threw fresh mint leaves in it. Stripping down, she took the longest, most leisurely sponge bath she'd ever had, and then soaked her feet in the pot. She put on a loose chemise and her lightest pair of bloomers. With a cool wet cloth on her forehead, she fell sound asleep.

After about an hour, she awoke, feeling refreshed and delightfully clean. It wouldn't last long, she knew, because it was suffocatingly hot and when any breeze came in through the windows it was lukewarm and fickle. Sighing, she dressed and sat down at the pile of papers under her clerk's ledger on the desk. Even though it was hot, it was a gorgeous afternoon. The sunbeams were a translucent gold, and Jeanne could see airy dust motes dancing in them. A rich wet mud smell, not dirty but earthy, pervaded the still boat. A fat honeybee came flying in, making erratic up-and-down circles as it investigated Jeanne and her desk, and it finally wandered out the opposite window. Birds were singing, dozens of them, it sounded like. Jeanne didn't hear anyone on the boat. They must be on the far bank fishing, she thought. She decided to join them as soon as she finished.

The accounts were more complicated than she had realized, and she worked for a couple of hours and still wasn't finished. She heard a commotion on the main deck as the others came back on board. She rose, stretched and put her hands to her aching back, and went downstairs. On the stairs she heard Clint say, "I think Marvel's crappie is the biggest one."

"That's 'cause Ezra let me use the fattest minner," Marvel said.

Jeanne came around the corner and stopped in amazement. Clint was holding up a stringer filled with fish, and they were all gathered around him. They turned to Jeanne and Clint said, "Jeanne, Marvel's the best fisher . . . What's wrong?"

"What's wrong!" Jeanne cried. "Look at all of you! Marvel, what have you done to yourself?"

They were covered with mud. All of them, even Ezra, had apparently slathered thick red-brown mud all over their exposed skin: their faces, necks, arms, and hands. Marvel's hair was pulled straight up on top of her head and tied into a messy knot with some fishing string. The only exposed skin was her eyelids. "Did you actually stick mud in your *ears*!" Jeanne demanded in outrage.

"Not in my ears," Marvel explained. "But around the outside. It's 'cause of the mosquitoes, Mama. We were all getting ate up."

"Eaten up," Jeanne said automatically.

"Calm down, Jeanne," Clint said easily. "It's the best mosquito repellent, the Indians used it all the time. It washes off, okay? No harm done."

Jeanne relaxed. "Except for you scaring me half to death. I thought a bunch of mud-goblins had boarded my boat. I've never seen human beings so dirty."

"It's itchy, too, when it dries," Marvel said. "But it's better than mosquito bites. I caught the biggest fish, Mama! See? That one!"

"You did? Good for you, Marvel. Now how about we rinse you off and then go get a proper bath?" Jeanne said firmly.

Jeanne fetched rags, and Clint got a big tub full of fairly sediment-free water. They rinsed off their river mud and Jeanne hustled Marvel upstairs to bathe and change clothes. Ezra, Vince, and Roberty started cleaning the fish. Clint said, "I'm swimming over there, to that lean-to. Be back in a few minutes."

He didn't have to swim, the deepest part across the river came only to his waist. He cut several long honeysuckle vines, their sweet scent filling his nose. Then he picked an armload of black-eyed Susans, the bright yellow flowers with their velvety brown centers, some of them as big as his hand. Back on the boat he put the flowers into a bucket of water. Then he went to sit down by Vince, Ezra, and Roberty. They were sitting on the deck at the stern, their legs hanging over, cleaning and filleting the fish. "I'd help y'all," Clint said airily, "but I got something important to do here."

"Playing with flowers? I'm worried about you, Clint," Vince said. "If I didn't know you were Clint the Flint Fist, I might think you were a sissypants."

"You're Clint the Flint Fist? The fighter?" Roberty asked eagerly, leaning over to stare at Clint.

"I hate that name," Clint sighed, "but yeah, that's what they called me. It's been awhile, though."

"You could fight anytime we're in Memphis," Vince argued. "And you could beat any one of them that's challenged you, too."

"Maybe. But it's more trouble than it's worth. They hit you, you know, Vinnie. It hurts."

"That didn't used to bother you before, and it's not what's bothering you now. It's because your ladies don't like you getting that pretty face bashed in, isn't it?"

"He ain't pretty," Roberty said indignantly.

"No, I ain't," Clint said, grinning. "No lady's ever accused me of that."

Jeanne and Marvel joined them. Clint looked up at Marvel, then scrambled to his feet. "Oh, no, baby girl, what's all this?"

Marvel was covered with mosquito bites. She had them all over her hands, on her neck, and on her face there was hardly a place to put a finger. The big red bumps covered her nose, her cheeks, even the tips of her ears. Her right eye was almost closed because she had a bite on her eyelid, and the sensitive skin had swollen up. Except for that one, every bite had a splotch of white paste on it. She looked like she'd been thoroughly splattered with white paint. "Guess they got me before we put the mud on," she said miserably.

Jeanne said, "That's baking soda paste, it's the only thing I've ever heard of that stops the itching. I never believed I'd say something like this, but from now on please cover Marvel with mud *before* she goes into the woods."

"You mean you aren't mad?" Clint asked in astonishment.

"I was at first. But what am I going to do? Tell her she can't go outside? Who am I going to be mad at? I gave her permission to go."

"Yeah, but stuff like that's never stopped you from being mad at me," Clint said ruefully.

"Oh, don't worry, before too long I'll probably get mad at you," Jeannie joked. "It's been a couple of days. So, how are the fish coming?"

"All done," Ezra said with satisfaction. "Tonight we're gonna have the biggest, best mess of fried fish you never saw."

That night Marvel pleaded with Jeanne to let her wash off the baking soda paste. "It stings when it's wet and it itches when it dries," she complained.

"I know, little girl, but I'm afraid you'll scratch in your sleep. I don't want you to get any open sores, they might get septic. Look, you're rubbing your eye right now. I'll put a cool cloth over your eyes and you try to go to sleep, okay?"

As soon as dawn's first tentative gray light appeared, the crew was back out at the stern of the boat, shoveling sand. Their voices awakened Jeanne, who got up and dressed hurriedly. She went out on the rear deck and called down to them. "How is it?"

Clint looked up. "It's looking good, Jeanne. Paddle wheel's in about ten inches of water. It might be enough to draw."

"Why don't we give it a try? It won't hurt the engine or paddle wheel, will it, if we're still stuck?"

"No, not if we don't rev her up and keep her straining. C'mon, boys, let's go load her up and get some steam."

Jeanne went back to look down at Marvel. She had had an uneasy night, Jeanne knew. She had tossed around, and once or twice Jeanne awoke to see her scratching her face in her sleep. The baking soda paste had dried out completely, so she had little dustings still clinging to her. Jeanne was sure she was lying in grit. She woke her up to bathe her and begin again the painstaking process of covering each bite in the paste.

Within an hour the boilers were hot and the engine was humming. Jeanne went up to the wheelhouse and gave the engine room the go-ahead bell. She felt the boat come alive and shift a little. Then they opened the steam valves to give the *Rose* a full head, and the paddle wheel slowly started turning. Jeanne had a death grip on the wheel, and she turned around to look behind them. The paddle wheel flapped emptily, then they slowed as they picked up water. The *Rose* began to slide backwards. Jeanne held the wheel perfectly steady. The boat was sluggishly moving, then it picked up speed, and then Jeanne felt the welcome buoyancy as she settled into deep water. "Thank you, Lord!" she said exultantly, and rang the forward bell twice.

The *Helena Rose* started steaming down the river as nonchalantly as if she hadn't been high and dry for twenty-four hours. Down in the engine room, at last Clint relaxed as he stood by the gear indicator. "I've been helping her go by holding my stomach muscles tight," he joked to Vince. "Think I can let go now?"

"Yeah, I'll keep mine all knotted up," Vince answered. "Just in case."

Clint went into the boiler room and knelt by Marvel's chair. She still had big red splotches, with white splotches in the middle of them, on her face and neck and hands. "How are you feeling, little girl?" he asked gently.

"Better than last night. But Roberty said I look like someone stuck a bunch of cherries with blobs of cream on my face," she said mournfully.

"I didn't mean it bad," Roberty said regretfully. "I like cherries with blobs of cream."

"But not stuck on your face," Marvel retorted.

"Never mind, I think you're still beautiful," Clint said, rising. "I've got something that's going to make you even prettier, too." He went out to the main deck and came in with the vines of honeysuckle he had woven. "Here, I made this for you. I didn't want to give it to you last night because I could tell you didn't feel good." He set the garland on her head. It was skillfully woven, with six strands of honeysuckle full of blooms, and two long tendrils that hung over her shoulder. "Now, you look like my fairy princess again."

"Ooh, it's beautiful! Thank you, Mr. Clint. I wish my face wasn't all splotched up. I don't feel like a princess."

"Don't you worry about that, Marvel. When we get to Memphis I'm going to get you something for those bites, and I know a secret potion to keep mosquitoes away," Clint said, kneeling by her again. "It smells good to people but not to mosquitoes. And it sure looks a lot better than mud. I really am sorry you got all those bites, Marvel. I'm not going to let that happen to you again."

"Really?" Marvel asked, her eyes shining. "You'd do that for me?"

"That, and a whole lot more, little girl," he said quietly. "But let's not tell your mother, all right? She's very strict about not letting people buy things for you, but since this is my fault I'm the one that needs to fix it. Okay?"

"Well, I don't think it was your fault that a hunnerd mosquitoes bit me," Marvel said. "But okay, I won't tell Mama unless she asks me. Then I won't lie."

"I know, baby. I'll tell her when it's all done. Now, I've got about a hundred flowers out here. How about we go fix some of them to put in your cabin? And Roberty, when you take up Captain Jeanne's tea, we'll send some up with you. It'll make that boring old wheelhouse look nice."

In two more days they arrived back in Memphis with no more incidents. They had shipped a load of crushed stone out of Little Rock, and as usual the receivers were there to snatch it up as soon as they docked. Clint told Vince, "I've got to go into town real quick. Can you make sure all this gets offloaded? By the time they're finished I figure Jeanne will be down, but just in case, you collect half from Mr. Carruthers, it's his company that's the receiver. He owes us two hundred dollars. You can take a bank draft, he's good for it."

"Got it," Vince said, and Clint sprinted off the boat.

Jeanne was in her cabin, washing up, changing clothes, and fixing her hair. She smiled as she looked at the big bucket of flowers by the door. It was odd how cheerful flowers made a room look, she thought.

Marvel came in. "Hello, Mama. They're unloading the rocks, and it makes a lot of dust and makes me sneeze."

"I know, darling. You don't need to be down there in the way, anyway." Marvel's mosquito bites were much better, though some of them were still angry red bumps. She sat her dolls in one of the armchairs and went back outside to bring in a pail of water that held the remnants of the honeysuckle vines. "I'm going to make Mrs. Topp and Avaymaria some garlands to wear, and then Avaymaria can be the fairy queen and Mrs. Topp can be the fairy princess."

"That's nice, dear," Jeanne said absently. She thought that George Masters would probably be very worried since they were a day late. They had planned on having a picnic at Court Square today. It was too late now, but she thought he might want to go out for supper, so she changed into her good pink muslin with the crinoline. It took a long time to get her hair presentable since she hadn't been dressing it on this trip. She tried to hurry, for she was sure George would arrive at any moment. Finally she had tamed it into a neat bun at the back of her head, with long ringlets over her shoulders. She looked out the window at the docks, and didn't see him, so she went down to the main deck. Vince was supervising the roustabouts as they unloaded. "Where's Clint?" she asked him.

"He went into town. It was urgent," Vince added hastily when he saw the look on Jeanne's face. "He told me about Mr. Carruthers, and the payment, Captain Jeanne. That's all right, isn't it?"

"Of course, Vince. I guess I'm just surprised he took off so quickly. Um—Mr. Masters hasn't been here, has he?"

"I haven't seen him, ma'am. You want me to ask one of these fellows about him? Us roustabouts, we know everybody and all of their business, too," Vince said lightly.

"No, of course not. I'm sure he'll be here," Jeanne answered.

She went back up to her cabin and played with Marvel and her dolls. Apparently there was trouble in the household, for Mrs. Topp wanted to be the queen and Avaymaria the princess. "Mrs. Topp is older, so she says she should be queen," Marvel said thoughtfully. "I guess that's true." They had started re-weaving their crowns when a knock sounded on the door and Vince called, "Captain Jeanne? Excuse me, but I need to speak to you."

Jeanne went to the door and motioned Vince to come in, but he shook his head. "No, thank you, ma'am. We're not through unloading but I got a piece of news I thought you'd better know quick. One of the roustabouts told me there's yellow fever in town. He's not sure, but he said the last he'd heard there were about six hundred cases, and one of the fellows says there's a bunch of new graves at Elmwood Cemetery. The City Council and the Board of Health knows about it, but they don't want to quarantine the docks because it's bad for business."

Jeanne went pale. "Are any of the roustabouts sick? Or have they been around anyone that has it?"

"My friend I was talking to, he says not. These men that work for us, they're my old buddies I used to work with when I was a roustabout. We can trust them."

"All right," Jeanne said tightly. "Don't let anyone on the boat that you don't know and trust, Vince. None of you leaves this boat, do you understand? Do you know where Clint went?"

"No, ma'am. No, really, Captain Jeanne, I don't know. If you want I could go to our—uh—regular places and look for him."

"No, Vince, I really mean it, no one leaves the boat. And send Roberty up here. He and Marvel need to stay in my cabin until we can get out of here."

"Yes, ma'am. And Captain? An errand boy from the Gayoso brought you a letter." He handed her an envelope made of thick cream parchment.

"Thank you," she said slowly. She closed the door and sat down at her desk to open the letter. It was from George.

> *Dearest Jeanne,*
>
> *I apologize for my absence. I deeply regret that we won't be picnicking when you come in.*
>
> *I'm sure you've found out by now that there is a yellow fever epidemic in Memphis. Fortunately, Dr. Augustus Hightower is an old friend of mine, and he's on the Board of Health. He was kind enough to alert me of the first few cases. I've returned to Morecambe, and I plan on staying until the danger is past. I wish I could have brought you and Marvel with me. I advise you to leave the city as soon as possible.*
>
> *I'll miss you very much, dearest, and I hope to see you soon. God bless you and keep you, and as always I remain,*
>
> *Your obedient servant,*
> *George Masters*

CHAPTER FOURTEEN

Madame Chasseur was an acknowledged beauty in Memphis. She was slender and fair, with translucent blue eyes and a pleasing, low soft voice with a charming French accent. Her clients, who were all of the upper-class ladies in Memphis, knew that she was a widow and still grieved for her husband. He had died ten years ago in a duel, defending his wife's honor against a brute that had insulted her. Madame Chasseur had fled New Orleans to hide from this blackguard, and had made a new life for herself in Memphis with the establishment of Madame Chasseur's Cosmetics and Perfumery. Her reputation in Memphis had grown quickly as a gentlewoman of pure ideals, for she never entertained any man's attentions, always maintaining that her love for her husband, even after death, was so strong that she could never think of marrying again.

It was true that Madame Marie Chasseur, whose real name was Mary Chase, never thought of marriage, either in the past or now. In New Orleans she had not been the type of woman that men married, although they enjoyed her company—and her charms—very much. And now that she had left that behind and was a respectable woman, she had no intention of allowing any man to interfere with this life she had created for herself. It was extremely lucrative, for women were pure fools when it came to spending money to beautify themselves.

Mary could buy a jar of rose oil, mix it with a little jasmine water, re-bottle it with her name on an ornate label as "Madame Chasseur's Essential Complexion Restorative" and charge ten times what the ingredients cost her with the promise that it would keep wrinkles from appearing at the corners of the eye. It took another, different expensive preparation to keep wrinkles from appearing at the corners of the mouth. It wasn't that Mary thought her cosmetics were fakes, she just knew that women paid too much for them. She truly believed in her remedies and restoratives, and used them all herself.

That was why she was extracting essential oil from frankincense and myrrh resins now. The perfume from the oil would keep away the yellow fever miasmas. When she heard of the outbreak, she immediately started advising her ladies to wear veils with the frankincense and myrrh oils dabbed on them if they must go outside their homes. Mary herself used a steam distillator to extract the essence, and she knew that the fragrant steam in the shop would keep the pestilential vapors away.

The bell on the front door jangled, and Mary went through the curtain from the back room to attend her customer. She stopped with shock when she saw that it was Clint Hardin.

He grinned at her and said, *"Bonjour, Madame Chasseur. Comment allez-vous, cherie?"*

"What are you doing?" she hissed. "We agreed that you would never come here!"

"Relax, Mary, I'm here because I need a cosmetic or a perfumery," he joked, looking around the shop. It was a small, intimate place. On one side of the room were shelves from floor to ceiling with jars, bottles, tins, and boxes neatly arranged. A long glass-enclosed case containing more jewel-colored bottles and ivory boxes was along the back wall, with four silver mirrors on top. On the other side a sofa, a settee, and two Queen Anne chairs surrounded a small fireplace. Madame Chasseur often served China tea to her clients there as she consulted personally with them. There was no one else in the shop. Clint added, "Looks like you'd welcome a paying customer." He leaned up against the glass counter.

From behind it she leaned close to him and spoke in a half-whisper as if they could be overheard. "The only time men come in here is when their wives drag them in. What do you want, Clint?"

"I just know you've got something that smells real sweet, and that will keep mosquitoes from biting you."

"Yes, I do, and ladies love it," she bit off. "You're telling me that you came to buy some fragrance for another woman?"

"No, not another woman, a little girl. We got stuck on a sandbar out in the wilderness, and she got eaten alive. I figured you'd know something to do about that."

She went to the shelves and picked out a small amethyst-colored bottle. "This is lavender and rosemary essence. It repels all insects. It smells so good that many women use it for perfume, too. See?" She uncapped the bottle and held it under Clint's nose.

He shook his head. "I can't smell anything but whatever that is you've got cooking back there. It smells like an

Araby brothel in here. I'll have to take your word for it that that stuff smells good."

Mary asked evenly, "So, this is for the little girl on your boat? The lady captain's daughter?"

"Yeah, it seems like she gets the short stick all the time. We haul coal, she sneezes and coughs. We haul crushed stone, she sneezes and coughs. If there were ten thousand mosquitoes where we were, they'd ignore everybody else to try to get to her. Is that the biggest bottle you've got?"

She pulled it back and replaced the cork. "Do you know I haven't seen you in more than a month? And now you come in here, and all you can think about is some kid that's gotten a mosquito bite?"

"Has it been over a month?" Clint said with surprise. "I kind of lose track, out on the river. Aw, c'mon, Mary Mary Quite Contrary, you know you don't really care one way or the other. When I'm here, I'm here, and when I'm not I doubt you hardly notice."

"That's not true," she said stiffly. "I do notice. I notice a lot of things. Like all of the talk about you and Eve Maxfield. She's one of my customers, you know."

"So is every other woman in Memphis. Anyway, you're not going to try to tell me that Eve has been talking to you about me," Clint said dismissively. "She wouldn't do that, she's got a lot more to lose."

"No, she doesn't. Because she tops the social ladder, and since she's a widow, she can do anything she wants, and she'll never suffer any consequences. The only thing that happens to her is that people gossip about her. That's how I know about you and her. Letitia Raleigh and Mrs. Dr. Hightower were in the other day, and that's all they talked about. How everyone knows that you're her *amour.* Her current one, anyway," she added maliciously.

Clint stared at her in disbelief. "I can't help what people say, Mary. Where's all this coming from? We never talk about other people when we're together. I sure wouldn't question you about your personal business."

"Because you don't care!" Mary burst out.

"And since when do you care? I don't think you do, even now. I think that your pride's just hurt because you've got it in your head that you're in some bizarre competition with Eve Maxfield. And that's just nonsense."

"Why? You are her lover, aren't you?"

Clint said darkly, "You shouldn't even ask that question. It's none of your business. I would never discuss you with anyone on this earth, and I'm not going to talk about Eve Maxfield, either. Now are you going to sell me this stuff or not?"

She deflated and answered dully, "All right. It's five dollars."

Clint knew that was outrageous, but he merely said, "I'll take two bottles, please." He handed her a ten-dollar bill and stuck the bottles in his pocket. "Hope business picks up, Madame. Funny, Main Street seems almost deserted, so it's not just you. I'll see you, Mary."

He turned to leave and she came from around the counter to pluck at his sleeve. "You just came in, didn't you? So you're going to be here tonight. Why don't you come to me, just after dark?"

Gently he pulled away from her. "Not tonight, Madame Chasseur, but thank you."

As he left, she knew that she wouldn't see him again. Again rage seethed in her, rage at Clint, at Eve Maxfield, at her own inability to keep him, even at the little mosquito-bitten girl he cared about so much. She was glad she hadn't told him that there was a yellow fever plague. Maybe he would catch it and die.

But deep down Mary Chase knew that losing him because he died wouldn't make her feel any better than losing him because he didn't love her . . . as she loved him.

JEANNE SAW CLINT WALKING up the gangplank, smiling, and she ran to him. "Where have you been?" she demanded.

"I had a little errand to run. For Marvel," he explained. "Why, what's the matter?"

"You don't know? There's a yellow fever epidemic. You didn't see any sick people?"

"No, I didn't know, and I didn't see anyone that was sick. I hardly saw anyone at all on the streets and I guess now I know why," he said thoughtfully.

"We have to get out of here," Jeanne said, grabbing his arm and hauling him into the boiler room. The roustabouts were still unloading the sacks of rocks, filing back and forth on the gangplanks. "They should have quarantined the docks, but they didn't. There's been no official notice at all. Vince says that word on the docks is that hundreds are sick, and some have already died."

Clint nodded. "Okay, Jeanne, but it's Sunday. We can't pick up the mail or get loaded today. You do realize that, don't you?"

Jeanne wrung her hands. "No, I didn't realize that. Are you saying that we'll have to stay here tonight?"

Clint put his hands on her shoulders. "I'm not saying that at all. It's just that I had yellow fever when I was a kid, and they tell me that once you've had it you're immune. I can stay and explain to the postmaster and to Mr. Baxley that the *Helena Rose* left because of the fever. So you can leave right now if you need to."

Jeanne paced up and down for a few moments. "I don't know. I hate to do that, we have commitments. Especially the mail. Who knows how long it would be before they get their mail in Pine Bluff and Little Rock?"

Vince came in the boiler room and said, "Sorry to interrupt, but I wanted to ask you, Captain Jeanne. My men said they'd come back to load us up when the stoves show up. That way we won't have to let anyone that might be exposed onto the boat."

Clint said, "I saw you've got Duffy and Eddie and the others loading. You talked to them?"

"Yeah, Duffy told me about the yellow fever. None of the guys or their families have it. There have been a couple of roustabouts that have caught it, but Duffy says they don't work with them."

Jeanne looked pleadingly at Clint. "What do you think?"

"I know the postmaster goes to Calvary Episcopal Church, and I can go find him there and tell him we need that mail now. And Kaufman's warehouse is always open, I can go tell their manager that we want to load up today instead of in the morning," Clint answered matter-of-factly. "I know it's a risk, Jeanne, but that Kaufman contract was hard to get and we need their business. If only two fellows on the docks have gotten sick, then it must not be too bad down here."

"All right," Jeanne decided. "Let's get it done as fast as we can, because we're leaving as soon as we're loaded. And, Clint, while you're in town stop at Anderton's and get them to send us two barrels of vinegar. I'm scrubbing this boat inside-out and top to bottom as soon as it gets here."

The vinegar arrived before the mail or the Kaufman stoves, so Jeanne, Ezra, and Vince scrubbed the floor, walls, ceiling, wheel, the windows, and all the fixtures in the pilothouse. Jeanne sent Marvel and Roberty up there as soon as they'd finished. Roberty protested, "I can help, Captain Jeanne! I feel fine."

"No, Roberty, not this time," she said sternly. "You and Leo keep Marvel company while we clean our cabin, okay? Once we get underway it'll be all right for you two to roam around again."

They scrubbed Jeanne's cabin, and by that time Clint had come back with the mail, and the carts of stoves were lining up on the docks. Jeanne, Clint, and Vince kept scrubbing everywhere while Ezra supervised the roustabouts. It was almost nine o'clock before the *Rose* was loaded and ready to go.

Jeanne hadn't been piloting at night for the simple reason that she didn't know the river by night. It was a completely different world from daytime navigation. And she was utterly exhausted. But she was determined to get out of Memphis, so she told Marvel and Roberty that they could go down to the main deck and she took the wheel. The *Helena Rose* backed away from the plague city and slipped off into the night.

After about an hour she heard a soft knock on the door, and without turning she called, "Come on in, Roberty."

"Sorry, it's not Roberty, it's me," Clint said. "I had to beat him up so he'd let me bring your tea." He set a tray down on the bench and came to her side, holding a steaming mug with the spicy aroma of black tea wafting from it. Jeanne stared straight ahead, her jaw clenched, and held out her hand. He slipped the mug into it. "Ezra took Marvel up to bed a little while ago. He said she barely said 'good night' before she went to sleep."

Jeanne nodded. "That's good. She needs her rest more than other children. She has a frail constitution, you know."

"I remember, you told me she was born early. But she's better than she was, don't you think, Jeanne? Since you've been on the *Rose* she's gained some weight, she's not so pale, her cheeks have a pretty pink color, her eyes are bright. It's the same with Roberty. He doesn't even resemble that half-starved dirty little street urchin you brought on board."

"It's true. Living on the *Helena Rose* is good." She sounded strained, and even in the darkness of the cabin Clint could see the tension in her shoulders and her hands.

"I brought you a sandwich and some fruit, Jeanne. Why don't you take a break? You look and sound done in."

"I can't. I've never done this before, at night."

"So I'll stop the boat. You can rest. But if the next coupla miles are like this I don't see why I can't just stand there and hold onto the kingpin. Looks to me like we're going straight and steady."

She hesitated, then said, "No, it is straight on, dead middle of the river, until we get to Island Number 60. And I don't mean the one in Helena, either," she said with feeble humor. "To tell you the truth, I would like to sit down for a few minutes."

"Then sit, and eat. If anything happens you can jump right up and rescue me."

Jeanne almost had to pry her hands loose from the wheel, it was so ingrained in her never to let go of it. But she gritted her teeth, closed her eyes, and told herself, *Just let go!* and she did. Wearily she sat down and looked at the tray. It held a fat sandwich and a big green pear. She picked up the pear with delight and sniffed it. "I'll bet this pear smells really good," she told Clint ruefully, "except I can't smell anything but vinegar."

"Yeah, I'd bet there's not a live vermin crawling on this boat anywhere. I'm surprised your scrubbing didn't eradicate Leo."

"Bet it killed his fleas, if he had any." Jeanne took a bite of the crunchy, juicy pear and chewed with enjoyment. At least she could taste it.

Clint said diffidently, "Jeanne, can I ask you something?"

"Mmm, yes. You can ask," she said heavily.

"Yeah, I get it, you don't have to answer if you don't want to. But it's a pretty innocent question. I've just always wondered how Marvel got her name. She told me her grandfather named her, but that's all."

Quietly Jeanne said, "It was in wintertime, and I slipped and fell on some icy stairs. She came almost two months early, and I—we had a hard time. When my father first saw her he picked her up, held her high up over his head, and said, 'Thank You, Lord Jesus! She's a marvel, a real marvel!'"

"So she is," Clint said. "She's smart, but it's not just intelligence. She's clever, and she has a sort of intuition that's way beyond her age. She's a special little girl."

"Yes, she is. I have to admit that I'm surprised she's turned out as well as she has. Because she hasn't had a father, you see." She took another bite of the pear and Clint waited in silence, amazed that Jeanne had mentioned her husband. After awhile Jeanne went on, "My husband left us when Marvel was only five months old."

"But—I thought you said that your parents died around then?" Clint asked.

"Yes. My husband disappeared on May 12, 1849. My parents were already dead on that day, though I didn't know it. I found out about my mother and father three days later. But I never saw or heard from my husband again."

"I'm so sorry, Jeanne," Clint said gutturally. "So sorry for you and for Marvel."

"It's all right now," she said, and Clint could hear the small smile in her voice. "Now we have the *Helena Rose*. And we have friends that are almost like family. It's almost as if Marvel has a father now, too."

Clint knew she was talking about George Masters, and he said nothing more.

But she wasn't.

They reached Helena at dawn, and Jeanne and Clint went ashore to check with the harbormaster as soon as they docked. There was no yellow fever in Helena, none reported on any ships that had come through there. Jeanne fell into bed and slept until noon. She felt fine, so they went on to Napoleon Trading Post, at the mouth of the Arkansas River. Clint checked with the general store, for there was no harbormaster at the tiny settlement. "No yellow fever, not even word of it here," he reported back to the *Helena Rose*.

With relief Jeanne said, "Then we're overnighting right here. I know it's only four o'clock, but I'm going to bed. I think this will be the first time I can sleep soundly since the night before we docked in Memphis."

They set out up the Arkansas at dawn the next day, and Jeanne felt completely relieved, rested, and strong again. She was glad, for this was the most difficult part of their trips. After four hours they reached Noble's Oxbow, and she gave it a wide berth, though it looked as though the entrance to the sand island was well under water again. Just after they passed it Clint came into the pilothouse without knocking.

"Jeanne," he said gravely, "you're going to want to stop."

"What? Why?"

He laid one of his hands on top of hers on the wheel. "I'm so sorry," he said quietly. "Marvel is sick."

CHAPTER FIFTEEN

Jeanne bolted out of the pilothouse and flew downstairs to the cabin. Marvel was kneeling by the bed, vomiting into a pail, with Ezra holding her head. When Jeanne knelt down to hold Marvel, Ezra slipped out. When Marvel finished, she was gasping weakly, and Jeanne picked her up and laid her in bed. She wet a cloth in the washbasin and sponged her face. "I'm sorry I'm sick, Mama," Marvel said.

"Hmm, so you're doing this on purpose? Then stop it right now," Jeanne said gently.

"Okay, I'll try." She closed her eyes.

"Tell me how you feel, and where it hurts."

"I started feeling like I had a fever awhile ago, Mama. Then my tummy started rolling around and around and then I felt really sick and Ezra carried me up here. Then I had to throw up."

Marvel's forehead was hot, and Jeanne knew she had a fever. She asked, "So you felt like you had a fever before you got nauseated?"

"I don't know, really. I just know I all of a sudden started feeling bad."

"It's all right, darling. I'm going to get your clothes off and sponge you down and get you in a nightdress. But right now I'm going to go get some fresh water, okay? I'll be right back."

"May I please have Mrs. Topp and Avaymaria?"

"Of course." Jeanne put the dolls in bed with her, grabbed the water pitcher, and went out into the hall. Ezra was standing there, waiting. "I need some fresh cool water, Ezra." Instantly he hurried down the hall to the galley and in a moment reappeared with the pitcher filled with cool water from the icebox. "Thank you. If you look in the cupboard you'll find a tin with dried chamomile. Will you make some tea?"

"Yes, ma'am. Does Marvel have a fever?"

"Yes, but I really think she got sick because of the vinegar," Jeanne answered with artificial brightness. "She's got a tender tummy, and I didn't think about the strong odor all over the boat. A lot of times when she gets nauseated she gets a slight fever."

"Yes, ma'am," he said gravely. "Cap'n Jeanne, I'm a-guessin' that Clint's driving. You want we should dock somewheres?"

Jeanne frowned. "We were just passing Noble's Oxbow when he came to get me. Dead Man's Slough is coming up, and he's driven from there to Widow Eames' Landing. Go talk to him, Ezra. See if he feels like he can get us there."

Jeanne went back into the cabin and undressed Marvel. As she was bathing her, Marvel started shivering. "I'm freezing, Mama."

Her skin was burning, her cheeks were a lurid crimson. Jeanne said soothingly, "I know, little girl. Let me just finish, and I'll put on your soft nightdress with the pink roses and you'll feel a lot better."

As soon as Jeanne ran out of the wheelhouse, Clint took the wheel and searched the river ahead with narrowed eyes. He had no idea, really, of where they were. The lower Arkansas all looked alike to him, a narrow trench heavily wooded on both shores. Rarely could one see more than a hundred feet ahead because the river curved this way and that, with hardly any straight stretches. Grimly, he put the *Rose* in the exact middle of the river and steered. At least he had gotten fairly familiar with the wheel, and could steer smoothly instead of jerking it back and forth, as when he'd driven them out of Dead Man's Slough. Just thinking of the name of that place made his throat tighten.

He thought about just pulling the *Helena Rose* into the next cove, no matter how small, and docking her. But that wasn't at all practical. Marvel needed a doctor. Aside from that, the river was narrow, and he didn't have the expertise to know where to dock the boat so that it would leave room for another boat to pass them. They rarely met other boats, for not many of them ran freight on the Arkansas River, but it did happen. And that gave Clint a start, because he realized he didn't know the protocol for passing by a boat if they should meet one. Was it port to starboard, or starboard to port? He searched his memory, but he had no recollection of Jeanne ever mentioning it to him. He was just about to yell down to Vince in the engine room to see if he knew when Ezra came into the wheelhouse.

"How ya doin', Clint?"

"Well, I don't know where we are, I don't know where we're going, and if we meet another boat I'm just going to lay on the steam whistle to let 'em know there's an idiot at the wheel," he said grimly. "How's Marvel?"

"She's purty sick. Cap'n Jeanne, she thinks mebbe Marvel got a sick belly from breathin' in all the vinegar fumes."

Hope surged high in Clint's breast. "Is that what you think, Ezra?"

Quietly he answered, "Leetle girl's got a high fever, Clint."

As quickly as it rose in him, the hope went away. He nodded helplessly. Ezra went on, "Now as to where we's at, I'm a-thinking we're 'bout ten mile south of Dead Man's Slough. Far as I know there ain't any tricks nor snags 'tween here and there, and you've done piloted from there to the Widder Eames' Landing. That's where Cap'n wants to go. You think you kin do it?"

"I can do it. I *will* do it," Clint said vehemently. "I want you to go back down to the firebox, Ezra. You load this old girl up as hot as she'll bear. We're not dawdling along at ten miles an hour, we need to get Marvel to a doctor quick. Hopefully there'll be one around the Landing, but if there isn't then we're going to have to go on to Pine Bluff. So you stay down there and help Vinnie, Ezra. He'll be okay with the engine, but only you know about the boilers."

"I do know that, and I'm a-tellin' you that if'n you kin keep from crashin' inter something we'll be at the Widder's landing in a coupla hours," he said sturdily. "And by the by, if'n you meet another boat, you jist git outer their way. They'll be doin' the same thing. Y'all will figger it out. So you reckon we orter let Roberty go up and sit outside the cabin if'n they need something?"

"No," Clint said bleakly. "Keep him down in the engine room. He doesn't need to be exposed. Jeanne will understand that." *Maybe not now, if she's telling herself that Marvel's nauseated because of the vinegar. But when we find out for sure that it's . . .* He couldn't finish that thought.

Two hours and nineteen minutes later Clint rounded a familiar bend and saw Widow Eames' Landing ahead. He furiously rang the backing bell two gongs, which when the boat was in motion meant "dead slow." He immediately felt the engines powering down and the paddle wheel slowing. They neared the dock at a reckless pace, but Clint didn't care. He rang the stopping bell once and the *Rose* came to a dead stop only a foot or two from the dock's pilings. Vince and Ezra jumped onto the dock to tie her off. Clint rang the Big Bell furiously, the low gong sounding startling and dire in the quiet afternoon. Then he stamped on the steam whistle pedal three times. These were signals for "Emergency."

He wanted to run down to Jeanne's cabin, but he hesitated. He didn't know whether to bother her and Marvel or not, and he didn't want to intrude on Jeanne if she didn't want him. He waited in the hallway to see if Jeanne would come out, but she didn't, so he ran on down to the main deck.

Vince and Ezra stepped back aboard the boat; the dock was only about ten inches higher than the main deck. "I know that someone still lives up in that house," Clint told them. "When we stopped here before I saw lights."

Ezra said, "Bull niver stopped here, but lotsa times in summer we'd see folks down here, picnicking. Big family, I reckon. Saw lotsa chilluns."

"Anybody seen Jeanne?" Clint asked.

Roberty and Leo were standing behind Clint, and now Roberty said reproachfully, "I wanted to take Cap'n Jeanne her tea, it's time. And I was gonna make some for Marvel, too. But Ezra wouldn't let me."

Ezra reached down and mussed the boy's sandy hair. "We need to see what Cap'n Jeanne wants us to do, boy, afore we go bustin' up in there with Marvel sick and all."

Roberty said, "That's not why you don't want me up there, is it? It's 'cause you think Marvel's got the fever and you don't want me to catch it."

Ezra sighed and said to Vince and Clint, "Niver try to lie to a innocent. Hit jest don't work."

"There's a man coming down the hill," Roberty said, pointing.

He was of average height but of stocky build, dressed in brown canvas work trousers with suspenders and a pull-over work shirt. He wore a wide-brimmed slouch hat, and when he reached the dock he took it off, wiped the sweat from his forehead, and asked, "Hello, the boat. You folks having some kind of trouble?"

Clint stepped forward. "We've got a little girl here that got sick on our way from Napoleon. I stopped here, hoping you might have a doctor that could come take a look at her."

He nodded and came onto the boat. "My name is Jacob Eames, and I'm a doctor. You say it's a little girl?"

"Yes, she's six years old. Her mother is the captain and pilot. I'm Clint Hardin, this is Ezra, this is Vince, and this is Roberty."

They all shook hands and Eames absently patted Leo's head. "Okay, Roberty, tell you what. If you'll just run up to that big house on the hill, you'll find my mother and family. Tell them that I need my medical bag. You want to take me to the little girl, Mr. Hardin?"

"Just a minute, Dr. Eames," Clint said cautiously. "We were in Memphis three days ago, and they've got yellow fever." He swallowed hard and continued, "When we found out, we scrubbed the boat down with vinegar, and Marvel's mother thinks that smelling it made her sick. She's a frail little thing, you see. But still, it's a possibility—I mean, we think—"

Dr. Eames nodded wisely. "I see. Take me to the little girl, and then I'll go get what I need."

He followed Clint up to the Texas deck and Clint knocked softly on the door. "Jeanne? We've got a doctor here."

Jeanne wrenched open the door and stood there, staring starkly at Jacob Eames. She was pale and her face and posture was a picture of tension. "Jacob? Jacob Eames?" she muttered.

His brown eyes grew warm with recognition. "Jeanne . . . Jeanne Langer. So you're the lady pilot, and this is the *Helena Rose*. We read about you in the paper, but we didn't know it was you." He stepped forward and hugged her tightly.

She clung to him, then wrenched free. "It's my daughter, Marvel. She's sick. You're—you're a doctor?"

"For five years now, so I didn't just hang up my shingle," he answered reassuringly. Jeanne led him into the room and closed the door behind them, leaving Clint standing in the hall.

Eames walked over to the bed, sat down, and took Marvel's hand. "Hello, Marvel. My name is Dr. Eames. I hear you're not feeling too well."

"Hello, Dr. Eames, it's a pleasure to meet you," she said, managing a small smile. "No, I don't feel good. I keep throwing up." Her thin face was whiter than snow, except for the bright red of her cheeks. The limp hand Eames held was hot and dry. As she spoke, Marvel shuddered with a chill.

"Throwing up is no fun at all, is it?" he asked, laying his hand on her forehead. He gently pulled up one eyelid, then the other.

"No. This is even worse than that time with the chocolate," Marvel said miserably. She shivered so hard her teeth chattered.

Eames took both of her hands and cradled them in his. "Well, I might have some medicine that will help your stomach feel better. The thing is, my medicine and all my doctor stuff is up at my house, because when I heard the bell and the whistle I didn't know it was someone that was sick, and I came running down here without it. So I'm just going to go get you some medicine and I'll be right back, okay?"

"Okay," she said weakly. "Gunness, I wish it could have been me that got to ring the Big Bell and the steam whistle. Mama wouldn't ever let me do it."

"When you get better I'll let you ring the bell and the steam whistle all you want," Jeanne said tightly. She followed Eames out into the hall, where Clint was still waiting. "So what is it?" Jeanne demanded.

Eames answered slowly, "Jeanne, I really need to examine her more closely, and ask her some questions. Please, just wait. I'll go get my things and I'll be back in minutes." He hurried to the stairs.

Jeanne looked at Clint as if she didn't recognize him. "He—I know him. Knew him."

"I know, I remember. He's about your age, I figure he's the lucky one that got to dance with you," he said softly. "How's Marvel doing?"

"She is horribly sick. She keeps throwing up, and her fever is sky-high. Go tell them," she said as if the words were wrenched out of her. Then she went back into the cabin and closed the door.

Marvel was throwing up again, slumped over the bed-side. Jeanne went to her and held her head. She finished and she was so weak that Jeanne had to lift her back on the bed to lie down. Jeanne pulled up an armchair and sat, holding Marvel's hand as she shivered and clung to her dolls.

Eames returned and Jeanne stood behind him as he examined Marvel. "Light a lantern and bring it over here, please, Jeanne." The room was still lit with strong afternoon sunlight, but the bed in the alcove was deeply shaded.

As Jeanne got the lantern, the doctor took Marvel's pulse, staring at a pocket watch. Jeanne brought the lantern and he took out an instrument with a big round polished silver face and a tiny magnifying glass in the middle. "Hold that above her head so that the glow falls directly on her face." Again he pulled up Marvel's eyelid and almost touched her face as he bent close to look through the tiny aperture at her eyes. "Open your mouth wide, please, Marvel," he instructed. With blunt forceps he depressed her tongue, motioning Jeanne to hold the lantern so the light streamed down Marvel's throat. "Okay," he said quietly. "Now, Marvel, would you please sit up for me? And Jeanne, if you'd pull up her gown." He took out his stethoscope and held the chestpiece between his palms to warm it. Then he listened for long moments to different places on Marvel's chest, and then her back. "Here, let's get your nightgown back on, and cover you back up." He plumped up Marvel's pillow, tucked the quilt around her, and took her hands between his again. "I need to talk to you, Marvel. Do you feel like you can answer a few questions?"

"Yes, sir."

"When did you start feeling sick?"

"This morning, after breakfast but before dinner."

"So you ate breakfast this morning? Did you eat a good breakfast?"

"Yes, Ezra made fried hominy, my favorite, and fried eggs and I had some toast with maple syrup poured all over it. I ate a lot, 'cause I didn't feel bad then." She winced. "Now it doesn't sound too good, 'cause I threw it all up."

"Yes, that's what happens when you throw up, it makes you not want to eat that same food for awhile," Eames said sympathetically. "But don't worry, there'll come a day when fried hominy will sound good to you again. Now, when you started feeling bad, exactly how did it happen? Did you feel sick to your stomach first, or did you have the fever first?"

"I can't hardly remember. I was just sitting on my cushion down in the firebox, and then I got dizzy. Ezra had to carry me."

"I know it's hard when you get sick all of a sudden. Try and think what you were doing when you got sick. Maybe that'll help you remember how it happened," Eames said encouragingly.

Marvel shivered a little, though the chills were lessening in intensity. "Roberty and I were doing our arithmetic. I was trying to work eight plus three, and I was trying not to count on my fingers 'cause Mama says that's not the right way to learn. And then, and then, my head started hurting. It hurt really bad. I forgot that."

"It's okay, you're doing very well," Eames said. "You're a smart little girl, I see. So your head started hurting, and then what happened?"

"I closed my eyes and laid my head down on the table, on my arms. Roberty asked me what was wrong and I said my head hurt. He said he'd get me some water, and he left and brought me some iced water and I drank some and laid my head back down. Then after a little while I started feeling that kind of raw, prickly feeling all over my skin. Not the good prickly, it was that kind when even soft clothes feel itchy. And I drank some more water and I thought it was real cold but then I knew that my lips were hot, and then I knew I had a fever. And then I got sick to my stomach, and Roberty told Ezra, and Ezra carried me up here, and I threw up." She seemed exhausted. She turned her head and closed her eyes.

"Very good, Marvel, thank you. That helps me know how to take care of you," Eames said soothingly. "You rest now, try to go to sleep if you can. I'm going to talk to your mother."

Marvel nodded slightly without opening her eyes. Eames led Jeanne out into the hallway and said in a low voice, "Is there somewhere we can talk?"

"Down here, in the galley," she said and they went down the hall. Clint, Vince, Ezra, Roberty, and Leo were all there. The men jumped to their feet when Jeanne came in, and they stood in a tight circle around her and the doctor. She didn't greet them, she just turned to Eames and said, "Well?"

"You already know that she has a fever, Jeanne," he said gently. "My examination doesn't tell me definitively whether it's yellow fever or not, because she's not jaundiced. But Mr. Hardin said that there was yellow fever in Memphis when you were there three days ago, and so it makes sense to diagnose that. This would be the early stages and, therefore, she wouldn't necessarily be jaundiced yet."

"I don't understand," Jeanne said harshly. "I thought jaundice was something babies got. Marvel was jaundiced when she was born, but it went away."

"Jaundice is caused by bile in the blood, because the liver isn't functioning correctly," Eames explained. "That's the primary symptom of yellow fever; in fact, that's where it gets the name, because of the yellowing of first the whites of the eyes, and then the skin. You're right, Jeanne, many times babies can be jaundiced but usually mother's milk corrects the problem."

"All right, assuming it is yellow fever and it is in the early stage, what's going to happen to her?"

"She's going to have nausea, chills, fever, headaches, and body aches for three or four days. Mr. Hardin tells me that Marvel doesn't have a strong constitution. Would you say that she is frail? Very frail?"

"I—I don't know," Jeanne said in confusion. "She's better, stronger than she used to be. What—what do you mean? What does that mean?"

"I'm trying to figure out what prescriptive might work best for her," he replied. "A blue mass pill is hard on the digestive tract, so I'm afraid it would just nauseate her more, if she's susceptible to stomach upset. Calomel is easier on the stomach but harder in the mouth, if you get what I mean. It tastes terrible. And quinine is bad on both."

"But these medicines, they'll cure her, if she can keep them down? They cure yellow fever?" Jeanne asked eagerly.

Eames hesitated and glanced at Clint, whose mouth had tightened and eyes narrowed as Eames had been talking about the drugs. "I'll be brutally honest with you, Jeanne. Those drugs are always prescribed for yellow fever. But there are no statistics that have been compiled as to their success. I've had patients with yellow fever before, but not enough of them to really know whether the medications do any good or not."

"I want them," Jeanne muttered. "I want all of them."

Eames nodded. "I brought all three of them, but I must caution you. The reason I was trying to determine about Marvel's general constitution is because these drugs are very difficult for a person to keep down. The more Marvel vomits, the weaker she gets. The weaker she is, the harder it's going to be for her to fight this off."

"What are you saying!" Jeanne almost screeched. "Do I give her the medicine or not?"

Calmly he replied, "Please understand, I'm only trying to explain everything as clearly as I can. I recommend that we try the blue mass pills first. If she can keep them down, then we'll try adding the calomel. I don't know about the quinine, it really is harsh. I just really need to keep assessing her to know the exact course of medications to give her. And I'm going to do that, Jeanne. I'll stay here until we know for sure."

"Thank you," she said tightly. Then she turned to Clint, her color high, her lips bloodless. "This is all your fault. You brought this plague on the boat. No one else even went into town, but no, you had to run off, probably to see some woman! If Marvel d— if she—" She choked, a dry sobbing sound, and ran out of the galley.

Dr. Eames said quietly to Clint, "People do this, you know. Especially mothers with sick children. They get angry, and want to blame someone, and say hurtful things that they don't really mean."

Every bit of color had drained from Clint's face when Jeanne turned on him. He looked as sick as Marvel did, and his voice was dull and lifeless. "She did mean it, though. And you know what? She was right. She was exactly right."

CLINT WENT OUT AND sat on the dock, leaning against one of the tall pilings. He bent one knee and threw his arm across it, and the other long leg was hanging down over the water. He was perfectly motionless except for that leg kicking, his face chiseled into grim lines, his eyes a murky slate blue as he focused on nothing. He had no idea how long he had been sitting there, except when Vince sat down beside him he suddenly realized that night had fallen.

Vince put his hand on his shoulder and said, "Clint, you can't take to heart what Captain Jeanne said. She's so scared she doesn't know what she's saying or doing."

"I told you, she was exactly right. Her attitude doesn't matter," Clint said woodenly.

"No, she wasn't exactly right. I know you. I know you didn't just pop off the boat and go see one of your women. And Jeanne herself sent you back into town, remember? I don't know what you were doing when you left the first time, but I know it wasn't the way Jeanne made it sound."

"None of that matters now, does it? Anyway, Vinnie, I'd really like to be alone just now. Get it?"

Vince rose slowly. "Yeah, I get it, and I'll go with it, for now. But I'm worried about you and I'm going to be watching out for you, brother."

"You don't have to worry about me unless that little girl dies," Clint muttered. "And if she does I won't need or want you to watch out for me."

Defeated, Vince left.

Clint thought, *So what will I do if Marvel dies?*

Already he felt so guilty and miserable, it was difficult for him to envision what he would do if she died. It was difficult for him to think, period. His mind was filled with darkness, with rag-tag bleak thoughts, with bits and pieces of Marvel's face, pale in death, with Jeanne's fury-filled visage. He swallowed hard and realized he was thirsty, but he hadn't the will to get up even to get a drink of water.

Awhile later—perhaps much later, Clint thought with confusion—Dr. Eames came out to sit down by him. "It's almost two o'clock in the morning, Mr. Hardin. You've been sitting here for six hours. My prescriptive for you is that you eat something and go to bed."

"I don't need your help," Clint lashed out at him. "How's Marvel?"

Eames sighed. "She is a very sick little girl. She's not holding down the meds, or anything else for that matter. The next two or three days are going to be hard for her, and her mother."

"And there's nothing at all I can do," Clint said bitterly. "There's not one single thing I can do to make up for it, or to help."

"As for helping Marvel, really none of us can do anything except pray. Are you a praying man, Mr. Hardin?"

"I am not."

"That's too bad," Eames said mildly. "The Lord Jesus is the only comfort we have in bad times. I'll pray for you, Mr. Hardin, that you'll find Him, because I know He will give you rest and peace."

"Yeah, thanks," Clint said dryly.

"You're welcome. I also want to talk to you about yellow fever."

"I've had it. I know about it. What is there to talk about?"

Eames shifted a little to a more comfortable position and stared out over the river as it whispered softly by in the still night. In a cool lecturing voice he answered, "I doubt you do know all about yellow fever, Mr. Hardin, because even doctors don't know much about it. We really don't know how the disease is transmitted. Some think it's in the air, some think it's in the water, some think you have to touch an infected person. Now, suppose it is carried on the air. Why do some people in a household get the fever when others don't? Same thing with the water. If people drink from the same well or source of water, why don't they all get yellow fever? And by touch: Why does it so often happen that people caring for yellow fever patients don't contract the disease themselves?"

For the first time Clint turned to look at Eames' face. It was a plain, honest face, and he had kind eyes. "You're trying to tell me that maybe I didn't cause Marvel to get the fever."

"I doubt very seriously that you did," he said sturdily. "I got Ezra and Vince to tell me everyone's movements after you returned to the boat. Apparently you didn't even see Marvel until after you had disinfected the entire boat, did you?"

Clint frowned. "I—I hadn't thought about it, really. But yeah, Marvel and Roberty stayed in Jeanne's cabin while we finished scrubbing up, and that took until late afternoon. Then Jeanne let her and Roberty come down."

"Again, why would Marvel catch the fever from you, particularly after you had disinfected yourself, along with the entire boat? Yes, Vince told me you doused yourself in vinegar, even washing your hair with it. So why didn't Ezra, or Vince, or Jeanne catch it? They all were with you right after you came back from town."

"I don't know," Clint said wearily. "All I know is that Jeanne thinks I infected Marvel, and that's all that matters."

"No it is not," Eames said vehemently. "You can't bear the guilt for this, Mr. Hardin. However Marvel got yellow fever, and I don't think we'll ever know, you did not *cause* it. You are not to blame."

Clint turned to stare blankly into the darkness again. "Then who is? Never mind, I'm really tired of talking. I appreciate you trying to help me, Dr. Eames, but right now I'd much prefer to be left alone."

"All right. There's just one more thing I wanted to let you know. I am going to have to quarantine the *Helena Rose*. Of course my family and I want you all to feel free to come out here on the dock, fish if you'd like, anything like that. But please don't let anyone go anywhere else, and no one is going to be allowed to come down here while Marvel's sick. Except me, of course. I'm going to go get some more things from my house and then I'm coming back to stay the night."

Clint looked up at him curiously. "Aren't you afraid you'll catch it, Eames?"

"Sometimes," he replied lightly. "But most of the time I trust in the Lord, and I believe that I am in His hands. Just as Marvel is; just as we all are. He is much more comforting than any doctor or any prescriptive, I find. And as I said, Mr. Hardin, I'll pray that you find His comfort, too."

CHAPTER SIXTEEN

Marvel was terribly sick. Jeanne suffered more anguish than Marvel did. She was so angry even the taste in her mouth was sour. She was so bitter that every conscious thought was pure misery. Always when Marvel had gotten ill, Jeanne had had to deliberately keep herself from letting Marvel see her cry. This time she couldn't cry. She was gentle and tender with Marvel, of course, but she felt that inside she had a leaden weight where her heart used to be.

With an effort she made herself be courteous and grateful to Dr. Eames. He stayed all night the first night, and tried various things to help Marvel keep down the medicines. He gave her sips of barley water, he tried rice gruel, he tried ginger tea, but nothing worked. Finally they were only able to give Marvel small chips of ice to hold in her mouth. She was always desperately thirsty, but if she took even tiny sips of water it came right back up.

At last the dawn came. Jeanne had sat in the armchair all night, her eyes wide and gritty, never feeling the least bit sleepy. Dr. Eames dozed in the other armchair by Marvel's bed. Jeanne watched the gray light of dawn turn into the cheerful yellow sunshine of an August day, streaming unconcernedly through the windows. Jeanne hated it, and wished for night again.

Eames stirred and rubbed his eyes. Then he checked Marvel, who was sleeping, though fitfully. She still had a fever, but it had been several hours since she had vomited. "I don't think we need to try to give her anything else today but the ice chips," he said.

Jeanne nodded. "I know. You'd better go home and rest. Thank you for everything."

He stood up and rubbed the back of his neck. "If you don't get some rest you are going to get sick yourself, Jeanne. I mean it. I told you, Marvel will likely be sick for the next two or three days. You cannot go without sleeping, or without eating, for four days. You won't be doing Marvel any good at all."

"How can I eat when the thought of food makes me sick? And how can I possibly make myself go to sleep? I feel like any minute I'm going to jump up and start screaming and not be able to stop!"

He considered her for long moments, then went to his bag and pulled out a small flat bottle. "This is brandy, and don't look at me like that, Jeanne. This is definitely for medicinal purposes. I want you to drink a very small glass of it, what's commonly known as a shot. Then eat. Then take another shot, and lie down and go to sleep. If you won't agree to do that, then I'm going to come back and *make* you do it."

Jeanne felt rebellious, but then realized that there was

no reason to argue with him. "All right, I will," she said dully. "In a little while."

He grimaced, then left without saying anything. He came back with a mattress from one of the crew bunks, a pillow, and clean linens. "Here's your bed. Ezra is fixing you some soup, and I want you to go to the door and answer it when he brings it to you. Apparently this is not a drinking man's boat, because there's no shot glass on board, so here is a coffee mug. Look. I'm pouring out one, two, three. That's a shot." He handed it to her. "It's good brandy, sip it, don't gulp it. If there's any change, have them ring the Big Bell. Otherwise, I'll be back this afternoon."

Jeanne barely noticed when he left, for she was lost in thought. And dark thoughts they were, indeed.

How could You let this happen, God? It's not fair! She's an innocent child! Why not me, or someone, anyone else? You have to heal her, You have to make her well!

Even through the rage she felt, Jeanne knew this wasn't right, but she had forgotten how to pray. *All right, I know I'm saying this all wrong, God, but please, help me. I can't stand it if Marvel dies, I couldn't live! I know that since we've been doing better, with the* Helena Rose *and all, I haven't been as close to You as I used to be. I know I've been ignoring You, and I'm sorry! Just please heal Marvel, and I swear I'll come back to You. I promise I'll do better, I'll be better!*

Jeanne had been a Christian a long time, and she wasn't a fool. She knew this was attempting to bargain with God— no, worse, she knew she was actually trying to bribe Him. The realization of her folly only made her feel worse. Now she was not only angry with Clint Hardin, and with God, but she was angry at herself. She didn't even try to overcome it. She gave up. The room may have been lit with glorious light, but Jeanne saw only the blackness of her own soul.

The next two days were just like the first. It was all a long nightmare to Jeanne, of bathing Marvel, watching her sleep, giving her ice chips, watching with sickening dread every time her fever rose and when she vomited. Dr. Eames came and went. Jeanne flatly refused to see anyone else, except when Ezra brought her food. Then she took it without saying a word. She completely lost track of time. She ate robotically, slept when she couldn't stay awake any longer. And she kept railing at God.

On the fourth morning after Marvel had gotten sick, Jeanne started awake with a jolt. She sat up on her thin mattress, bewildered, and looked around. She had been having an evil dream, but she couldn't remember what it was, but a lingering sense of dread assailed her.

"Hello, Mama."

Jeanne bounded to her feet and went to the bedside. Marvel was looking up at her, and her eyes were clear, not fever-dulled. "Did you say something?" Jeanne asked tremulously.

"I said, 'Hello, Mama,'" she replied in a weak half-whisper.

"Oh, child!" Jeanne half-picked her up and caressed her in her arms. Her body was treacherously limp, and she could feel Marvel's rib bones right through her nightdress, but she wasn't hot. "Oh, baby, do you feel better?"

"Yes, ma'am. I'm awfully thirsty, though."

Jeanne laid her back down on the pillow and said, "I know, sweetheart. For right now you'd better just suck on some ice, okay?"

Jeanne sat on the bed, putting small ice chips in Marvel's mouth. She was so weak she could barely lift her hands. Marvel asked, "I've been really sick, haven't I? How long have I been sick?"

"I'm not sure," Jeanne said with an attempt at lightness. "It seems like a long, long time to me. But I think it's only been three days."

"Where are we?"

"We're at Widow Eames' Landing. Remember where we came after we got stuck in the swamp? Dr. Eames lives here, and he's been taking very good care of you."

"He's nice," Marvel said. "He's got a nice smile."

A single soft knock sounded just then, Dr. Eames' signal, and he came in. He smiled when he saw Marvel, but Jeanne noticed that he didn't seem at all surprised that she was better. "Good morning, ladies. So, I see you're feeling better this morning, Miss Marvel." He sat on the bed and took her hand.

"I do. Can—may I have some water?" she pleaded.

"Sure, but I want you to sip it, not gulp it, okay?"

Jeanne fixed her a tumbler full of water and put some ice chips in it. Marvel sipped obediently, then fell back onto the pillows. "Gunness, I can't even sit up."

"You've been very sick, and that makes you weak," Eames said gravely. "But I tell you what. If you'll try to eat, you'll get stronger. In fact, I have a little surprise for you. My mother sent you some rice flummery. She used to make it all the time for me when I was sick, and it always made me feel so much better."

Marvel's eyes brightened a little. "Rice flummery? I like that name. It sounds fun."

"It does, doesn't it? Now first I'm going to examine you, and then it'll be time for rice flummery." He proceeded to examine her thoroughly. She still was very pale, and her eyes were still slightly jaundiced. But her skin was cool. When he was finished he smiled at her. "No fever, and your tummy's not making angry noises like it was. I think you can have all you want to drink now, of whatever you want to drink."

"More water, please. And may I have some apple cider? With my rice flummery?"

"You certainly may," he answered. "Is there anything else you want right now?"

She looked over at Jeanne. "Mama, would it be all right if Roberty and Leo came to see me? And Ezra and Mr. Vince and Mr. Clint?"

"No," Jeanne said vehemently.

Dr. Eames said soothingly, "Marvel, let me explain something to you. You remember I told you that you have yellow fever? Well, it's contagious. That means that other people who haven't had it before can catch it from you. I know you're better, but we need to wait for two days before we let other people come around. Do you understand?"

"Yes, sir," she sighed, then she brightened. "But Mr. Clint has had it before. I remember you told me, Mama. He could come see me, couldn't he?"

"No, Marvel, I just want you to stay in here and rest today. I'll stay with you, darling, and maybe if you feel better later we can play with your dolls," Jeanne said tightly.

"Okay. But Dr. Eames, can dogs catch yellow fever?" she asked hopefully.

Jeanne blurted out, "No, Marvel, I said—" She realized that she sounded like what she was at the moment—an angry, cold woman. Eames was watching her curiously. Lamely, she went on, "So, Dr. Eames, can dogs catch yellow fever? Even if the patient kisses them on the big grinning slobbering mouth?"

He smiled a little and rose. "No, dogs can't catch it. I'll bet Leo would be glad to see you both. Just don't let him eat your rice flummery, Marvel. That dog is the best beggar I've ever seen. C'mon, Jeanne, come with me and we'll go get Marvel her food and Leo."

Jeanne followed him to the galley, and he pulled out two stools. "Sit down for a minute, Jeanne."

Her eyes narrowed. She had purple shadows under them so deep that they looked bruised. She was as pale as Marvel, and her prominent cheekbones stuck out sharply, her cheeks deeply hollowed beneath them. Her hair was an untidy mess, and she hadn't changed her clothes, and her blouse was soiled. She sat down jerkily. "Something's wrong. I knew it."

"Maybe, maybe not," Eames said calmly. "I do have something to tell you; it is perhaps the most difficult thing about this disease. Marvel is better today, and she may be cured. All yellow fever patients are better after three or four days. On the next day, after what's called the remission stage, some go on to the third stage of the disease."

"And what is that?" Jeanne asked in a choked voice.

Evenly he answered, "It's called the intoxication phase. The patients very suddenly worsen, with fever so high it can cause convulsions and delirium. They may get nauseated and vomit. The jaundice gets worse, so the skin turns yellow."

"And that's when they die," Jeanne said with gritted teeth. "She's better today! She has to be cured! Why would you tell me this, Jacob? What good could it possibly do? Why would you say such horrible things?"

His gentle features were a study in pain. "Jeanne, I struggle with this every single time I have a patient with yellow fever, particularly children. If the patient is an adult, of course I must tell them, even though I feel that they are cured. But with children, if I don't tell their parents I would be criminally wrong. Surely you see that?"

She stared at him with burning eyes.

He went on, "I want you to listen to me carefully, Jeanne. Marvel came through this very well, considering that she is small and thin and delicate. Today she may be completely free from yellow fever. If she isn't, we'll know by morning. And even if she does go into the intoxication phase, she may live through it. Yellow fever is very frightening because large numbers of people contract the disease, all at the same time. But out of all of the people that get it, very few of them die."

"Yes, well, it's also frightening because you may be one of the few that dies," Jeanne said sharply. "You sound as if you have no idea whether Marvel is cured or if she's still sick, and will go into this third stage. Is that true?"

"That's true, Jeanne. I have no idea. Some patients who seem completely recovered during remission go into the intoxication phase. Others who are still jaundiced and nauseated get better, and never go into the third phase."

Jeanne jumped to her feet and stood over him. "We're not talking about some patients, we're talking about my daughter! As far as I can see, you are practically useless! You have medicine, but it may not work. Yes, give her medicine, but no, she's vomiting so don't give her medicine. She may be cured, or she may die. You don't know anything!"

He stood up and placed his hands gently on her shoulders. "I do know some things, Jeanne. I know that Marvel is in the Lord's hands, as we all are. She is calm and free from fear, and has been all through this, and that is a miracle of God. I know that she's better today, and she has joy in her spirit, I can see it. None of us knows what tomorrow will bring. Be joyful with Marvel, Jeanne, for this is the day that the Lord hath made."

Her shoulders sagged, and her head drooped. "I will try," she said in a ragged whisper. "Maybe she is going to be fine. So I'll try. For Marvel."

DR. EAMES WENT DOWN to the boiler room. Roberty and Ezra were playing checkers, with Leo sleeping by their upturned cracker boxes. Through the open double doors to the engine room he heard Vince and Clint's low voices. "I've got some good news for you," he said. Roberty jumped up and went to get Vince and Clint. When they were all together Eames went on, "Marvel is much better today. Right now she's eating my mother's rice flummery, and if that doesn't cure all her ills nothing will."

They all pulled up boxes and sat down, grinning and sighing with relief. Except for Clint, who crossed his arms and looked thoughtful. "How's Jeanne?" he asked.

"She's not doing too well, and I'm afraid I didn't help her much. I guess I need to tell you all, too, it seems like you're like family. But first, Miss Marvel wants Leo to come keep her company for awhile."

Roberty jumped up eagerly, but Eames went on, "Sorry, Roberty, but Marvel still may be contagious, so you can't see her for another day or two. Better let me take him up."

"Maybe I could," Clint said hesitantly, looking at Eames with pleading dark eyes. "I've had yellow fever, and so I couldn't catch it again."

"I'm sorry," Eames said helplessly. "It'll just be better if I take him."

Clint nodded and sank down on a crate, his head between his hands. Eames took Leo upstairs and returned quickly. Then he told them what he'd told Jeanne.

"Yeah, I knew this," Clint said hollowly. "I've seen it. But chances are she's over it, right?"

"I'm praying that she is," he answered. "We all need to keep praying for her. And for Jeanne, too. Jeanne is suffering just as much, and I think even more, than Marvel."

Vince, Roberty, and Clint were all sitting in their camp, a small level piece of ground on the wide slope up to the Eames house. It was situated just a few feet from the starboard side of the *Helena Rose*, and though they hadn't said it aloud, they all knew that through the open windows of Jeanne's cabin they could hear if she called. From the first day they docked, Ezra flatly refused to cook anything in the galley. "That there stove is sitiated right down by Marvel's head, and it's hot enough as 'tis, she don't need no quick hot cookin' fire just on t'other side of the wall. And she don't need no cookin' smells, neither, nor me a-banging around in there."

Ezra had gotten all the pots and skillets and utensils they needed, and they had been cooking over a campfire. They hadn't had to cook much, though, for Dr. Eames' family—and they had learned that there were over thirty Eames, Franklins, and Greenes living on the Eames place—sent them enough food every day to feed them twice over. But now Ezra was in the galley, cooking up about half a dozen things he'd thought of that Marvel might like to eat.

In the last three days Ezra had scoured the boilers and furnaces three times. Vince and Clint had worked in the engine room, oiling and tightening and testing all the parts, some of them several times. Roberty had painted all of the red trim on the boat except for the paddle wheel. Dr. Eames had brought a tall ladder, and he had climbed up twenty feet to paint the smokestacks, though the men had cringed at the sight.

Clint said dully, "I think I'm going to paint Marvel's dollhouse and the furniture."

Vince sighed. "At least we don't have to take the engine apart again. That's really boring, Clint."

"Why don't you let me paint them, Clint?" Roberty pleaded. "I didn't get to make anything for it, and I want to do something for Marvel. I need to."

"Yeah, I know," Clint said. "Okay, you paint, then." Roberty got up and ran to the boat.

"So what do you wanna do, Clint?" Vince asked. "How about we go fishing? Dr. Eames said just around the bend there is a real good little cove with lots of minnows in the shallows and bream and bass and catfish."

"No, you go, Vinnie."

"No, the point is that I'm trying to get you to go. I'm trying to get you to do anything. You've been sitting around like a stump, Clint, just staring into space. You don't talk, you don't listen, it's like you're not even here."

"I'm here," he said listlessly. "I just don't have anything to say, and I don't care what anyone else says either."

Never in his life had Vince gotten angry with Clint, but now he was. "You're acting like a selfish little kid. What's the matter with you? Marvel's better, she may be just fine! And even if she's not, then we need to be strong and acting like *men*! I know you think Jeanne hates you, and maybe she does *right now*. But I know that she really cares for you, you big stupid ninny! No matter what happens, she'll remember that one day. So you just quit sulking and get yourself out of that hole you dug and threw yourself into!"

A humorless half-smile twitched at the corner of Clint's lips. "Okay, okay, Vinnie, don't blow a gasket. You want to go fishing? Let's go fishing. But first I want to tell Ezra where we're going. I want to make sure they can find us if . . . if Marvel needs me."

BY TWO O'CLOCK IN the afternoon Marvel was able to sit up in the armchair, with her legs propped on three pillows that Jeanne put down for her. She had a light quilt over her, for though the day was a typical hot August day, she felt a little cool. Jeanne constantly checked her, and it wasn't because she had fever. Dr. Eames said it was just because she was so weak and her blood was so thin.

Jeanne set an enormous plate of steaming macaroni on the cherry side table by Marvel's chair. Leo immediately sat up and rested his chin on Marvel's lap. "Ezra says if you eat enough macaroni you get fat," she told Marvel with amusement. "So he'll be disappointed day after tomorrow if you're not a chubby little girl."

"I prob'ly will be, if I keep eating like today," Marvel answered. "Ezra's made me so much stuff I think he forgot the whole crew's not eating it." Ezra had made fresh bread, had sliced mild yellow cheese thin and had cut the slices into funny little shapes, had made mashed potatoes, chicken broth, oatmeal, a cherry ice, fresh warm applesauce, and baked pears stuffed with raisins. Marvel was able to eat a few bites at a time, and she had eaten some of everything. Now she took three or four bites of the macaroni and sighed.

"It's all right, darling, I was just teasing you," Jeanne said. "You eat what you can eat, but don't make yourself if you don't want it."

"Okay. Um . . ." she petted Leo's head and looked hopefully at Jeanne.

"You might as well give it to him," Jeanne said resignedly. "He's already sleeping in our bed and sitting in our chairs. I guess when we start eating at the dining table again, he can join us there, too."

Marvel set the bowl down and Leo began to eat. He was a very polite eater, he never wolfed down his food. His long snaky tail began going in the funny lopsided circles that moved his whole rump. Marvel giggled a little. Her voice had grown stronger, though it was still weak. She glanced up at Jeanne, who was watching Leo with a blank expression. "Mama? Is something wrong?" Marvel asked.

"No, no, of course not. I guess I'm just tired."

Marvel nodded. "I know, I don't remember much about while I was so sick, but I remember you were always awake, it seemed like. I know you were worried about me, Mama, but I'm better now."

"Yes, you are, and I'm so thankful, Marvel. I'll be better, I promise. Would you like to play with Mrs. Topp and Avaymaria?"

"Yes, ma'am, but first may I ask you something?"

"Of course."

Marvel cocked her head a little and looked troubled. "You said you're thankful, Mama, but we didn't have a thank-you prayer. We always have thank-you prayers for everything. I've said thank you to Jesus, but not out loud, like we usually do."

Jeanne flew to kneel by her chair. "Oh, Marvel, I'm so sorry. Of course I'm thankful to the Lord. I guess—I guess I've just been so worried about you that I'm not really thinking straight. Let's pray right now."

Marvel bowed her head and closed her eyes and began thanking Jesus for everything she could think of. Jeanne bowed her head, too, and closed her eyes, but when she heard Marvel say, "Thank you that I'm all well now, God," her eyes opened to narrow slits. She had lied. She wasn't thankful to God at all. All day she had tried to believe that Marvel was healed, but she didn't. As soon as Dr. Eames had told her about the course of yellow fever, Jeanne had gotten so fearful that she had gotten nauseated. Throughout the day that fear grew and grew, and crushed any hope she might have had. Now she was so deathly afraid that Marvel was going to get sicker and then die that it had become almost a certainty. All day desperately she tried to act with Marvel as if she was recovering, and she had done fairly well; but she didn't believe it at all.

All she believed was that Marvel would die. And she knew that it was because God was punishing her, Jeanne, for her carelessness and selfishness. Why else would He do this to Marvel? It was the only thing that made any sense.

And by this time Jeanne herself might have been dead, because she just didn't care.

MARVEL GOT TIRED JUST about dark, and Jeanne put her to bed. Leo lay beside her, looking up at Jeanne with his hangdog pleading eyes, and Jeanne allowed him to stay, patting him on the head and grumbling. Marvel said sleepily, "Thank you, Mama. G'night."

"Good night, my darling," Jeanne said, and kissed her on the cheek.

She sat down in the armchair by the bed and watched Marvel as she dropped off into a peaceful sleep. Her expression was very different from when Marvel had been awake. As soon as Marvel had closed her eyes, Jeanne's face, as if someone had slapped her, grew tight and tense, her eyes as empty as bottomless wells. Even Leo seemed to notice, for he looked at Jeanne for a while. Jeanne whispered, almost a hiss, "Go to sleep, Leo." His tail thumped twice, then he laid down, ludicrously on a pillow just by Marvel's head.

Jeanne sat and watched. Marvel slept. Leo slept. Jeanne's whole body was so tense she ached frightfully everywhere.

As the hours wore on, her temples began to throb. Soon she had an agonizing headache. Even the low light from the single lantern on the table by her chair hurt her eyes, so she closed them.

She jerked painfully and tried to look around, but she was in darkness. Leo was whining, a soft low cry that almost sounded like a child. She realized that she had fallen asleep, and the lantern had gone out. Jeanne jumped up and felt her way to her desk, grabbed the lantern, and lit it, then hurried back to the bed. Leo jumped down and was staring at Marvel, keeping up his soft keening. Jeanne thought that Marvel was the same, for she looked as if she were still asleep. But then Jeanne saw the sheen of sweat on her forehead and that her nightdress was soaked.

At that moment Marvel started convulsing.

CHAPTER SEVENTEEN

Marvel's whole body was rigid, and her arms and legs thrashed wildly. Jeanne set the lantern down and grabbed her arms. She tried to hold Marvel still, but all she could do was keep her arms from jerking up and down. Jeanne saw that Marvel's jaws were clenched horribly, and she was afraid she might grind her teeth so hard they would break. With a groan she searched around the room for something to put in her mouth, and cursed herself for not asking Dr. Eames for the precaution. There was nothing. Marvel's convulsions went on and on.

Finally the spasms lessened in intensity, and Jeanne was able to let go of her biting grip on Marvel's arms. She jerked two, three times, then her body seemed to sink into the mattress. She had never opened her eyes, and they remained closed. Her mouth was slightly open, and Jeanne had to bend over her face to see if she was still breathing. Her respiration was fast and shallow. Jeanne could feel the sickening heat coming from her body; even the sheet and light quilt covering her were soaked with sweat. "Marvel?" she whispered.

She didn't stir or open her eyes, and Jeanne knew she was unconscious.

She flew out into the hallway and out the back door. Close by on the shore was the dying campfire, with lumps of sleeping figures around it. But Clint was sitting up, and he was staring right at her. Jeanne started to call out to him but he jumped up and started running. He reached her and started to grab her arms, but dropped his hands with a jerk. "Is she—" he gulped.

"No," Jeanne said in a dead voice. "Not yet. But I need your help."

He followed her into the cabin and Jeanne knelt by the bed. Clint knelt by her. Neither of them said anything. Clint thought that Marvel already looked dead. The skin was stretched across her face, and all childlike roundness was gone. It looked like a small skull. Her hair was in dank strings, and Clint could smell the sour odor of the very ill emanating from her.

"She's convulsing," Jeanne said. "I couldn't find anything to put between her teeth."

Clint reached into his pocket, drew something out, and went to wash it in the washbasin. He dried it off and returned to kneel by Jeanne's side. She saw then that it was three round strips of leather braided tightly together. "Leo's collar," Clint said. "Roberty and I are making it."

Marvel started convulsing. Clint put the leather between her teeth and slid behind her, cradling her upper body and holding her arms. Jeanne kept her legs from striking the bed so hard.

Again, it was a long seizure. When they were finally able to let go of her, they knelt again by the bed. Her breathing became more and more like panting. Jeanne felt of her forehead, and it was so hot that Jeanne thought if she licked her finger and pressed it to Marvel's flesh, it would sizzle, like a hot iron. She wasn't sweating now; she was just burning. She convulsed again, and then after a few minutes the spasms started again. Each seizure was longer than the previous one. Clint and Jeanne stared helplessly at each other. Both of them were as pale as death.

After some time Marvel jerked, and her head yanked around toward them, and they both started to grab her. But then she grew still and her eyes fluttered, and then opened. Her gaze seemed unfocused for long moments, but finally Jeanne could tell that Marvel was looking at her. Jeanne took her hand and said, "Hello, my darling. Just lie still and rest."

Marvel's mouth moved, but no sound came out. Jeanne started to tell her not to try to talk, but then she saw the thing that she dreaded even more than death. She saw fear in her daughter's eyes. "No, no, Marvel," she said in a desperate croak. "Don't be afraid, please don't be afraid. I'm right here, I'm here, everything's going to be all right, my darling one. You're strong, and the Lord is with us, always. Please, please don't be scared."

Jeanne leaned over her, her ear next to Marvel's lips. "Okay, Mama. I'll . . . try."

Jeanne collapsed back and she pressed her lips to Marvel's burning hand.

Slowly Marvel looked at Clint, and he thought that his heart would burst with pain. He managed to smile back at her. "Hi, sweet baby."

He saw that she was trying to say something to him, so he bent over her. "It was . . . like angels singing . . . and Jesus was there . . . when you . . . sang . . ." She seemed unable to go on.

Clint kissed her cheek and lifted his head to look at her. "When I sang 'Ave Maria.'" She nodded. With dread he made himself look into her eyes, and he saw the desperation, and the pleading there. "Then I'll just sing it right now, for you, little one. Just for you."

He rose to his feet and left. Jeanne lifted her head and saw that Marvel's eyes were closed. She still breathed.

As soon as Clint got outside the cabin, he leaned up against the wall and squeezed his eyes shut with anguish. *I can't do this! I would give that little girl anything, anything, even my life, but I can't give her the one thing she asked for!*

Clint had not sung since Christmas. He saw himself standing beneath Marvel's window, opening his mouth, and a sorry pathetic croak coming out. He heard a weak travesty of the majestic prayerful song. He thought it would be so pitiful it was almost evil, like a monstrously cruel trick that the devil would play on a dying little girl.

As if he were unconscious, but still moving, he walked slowly down the hall to the side steps. He felt so weak, and so weary, that he thought it was as if he were an old, old man. He climbed up onto the dock and stood there, looking at the sky, bewildered. The moon was full, and there were countless stars, and the night was beautiful. Barely knowing what he was doing, Clint bowed his head and prayed. *Dear God, help me do this. Please. Help me sing for her. Not for me, but for her.*

He lifted his head, filled his lungs with the sweet night air, and began to sing.

> *Ave Maria, Gratia plena*
> *Maria Gratia plena*
> *Maria Gratia plena*
> *Ave, ave Dominus!*

It was the strongest and best he had ever sung. He felt his spirits rise, and remembered that he had had this same feeling before as he sang well. It uplifted him, made him reverent, made him aware of a higher plane than this vale of tears. But now he prayed as he sang. He thanked God over and over again in his spirit. He forgot everything except music. Now he knew that the song wasn't coming from him. It never had. It was coming from God Himself.

The song was almost four minutes long, but to Clint, as he finished, he thought with amazement that he might have gone on singing for hours. Instead, he dropped to his knees and murmured, "Oh, thank You, God. Thank You, Christ Jesus. Why, why would You give me such a gift? I'm nothing. I'm a sinful, wretched man. How can You forgive me? I don't deserve anything but death!"

I already died for you, because I love you. I made you and fashioned you before the foundation of the earth, and I gave you this gift. I gave it to you because I am your Father, and you are my son.

Clint never knew whether God had spoken to him in an audible voice, or if He had put the words into his mind. It didn't matter. With wonder he prayed, *My Father . . . my Father. Forgive me, Blessed Father. Forgive me for it all. Thank You, thank You, from now until all eternity, thank You. Finally, now I understand . . . and I want to come home.*

WHEN CLINT LEFT, JEANNE thought dully that he simply couldn't face it any more, and she didn't blame him. Marvel hadn't opened her eyes again, and neither had she had convulsions. She was so still and limp and bloodless that Jeanne kept her eyes fixed on her chest to watch it rise and fall in her quick shallow breaths. Jeanne wondered at her own calmness. But it didn't matter, really. If—when Marvel died, Jeanne was just going to lie down and never move again. She hoped that God would kill her. If it was slowly, by starvation or from thirst, then so be it. It was no more than she deserved.

Then the sound of heavenly music came floating into the room.

Ave Maria . . .

Jeanne sat transfixed, motionless. As the song went on, she felt as if she was not merely listening to it, but that she was breathing it in, that it was filling her, slowly but surely, with a kind of soft quietness. Her head stopped pounding, her jaw relaxed, her fingers lost their tension, she even felt herself settle down on her knees, relaxing her body. It was as if the music was warm oil, and it was being poured right over her. She saw Marvel's eyelids flutter, and she opened her eyes for a moment. Slowly they closed again.

Jeanne's mind was restful, tranquil, as Clint sang. She felt the presence of the Lord very strongly, for the first time in a long time. When he finished she laid her head down on the bed and prayed.

Oh, dearest Lord Jesus, my blessed Savior, please forgive me. I've been so angry, I've hardened my heart to stone. I've spit in Your face as surely as those who crucified You did. I'm sorry, so desperately sorry, please forgive me! Instantly Jeanne knew she was forgiven. All of the terrible things she had done, particularly since Marvel had gotten sick, were gone from His sight just as if they had never happened. Jeanne sagged with relief.

Thank You, Blessed Lord. Now strengthen me, comfort me, let Your Holy Spirit fill me with Your boundless love. I know what I must do, and thank You for giving me the strength to do it.

She rose, and was slightly surprised that she didn't ache any more, either her body or her mind. Going to the window, she saw Clint kneeling on the dock, his head bowed, and her eyes filled with tears. It was the first time she had wept, and these weren't tears of sorrow; not yet. These were tears of joy, for Clint. She went down to the deck and called softly, "Clint? Please come back up to Marvel with me."

He looked up, and tears were streaming down his face, too. He wiped them away, and smiled at her. It was a beatific smile, gentle and kind. He rose and looked over at the campfire. Everyone had awakened when he sang, of course.

Jeanne followed his gaze and for the first time realized that Dr. Eames was there, asleep in a bedroll. That afternoon she had told him to leave her and Marvel alone, they didn't need him any more. Now she called out softly, "It's all right, she's still—with us. But you can all come wait in the hall. In fact, please do come, and pray for us."

Clint walked with her to the stairs. "Are you—are you sure you want me, Jeanne?"

"I'm sure. And Marvel asked for you, Clint. I'm so sorry, so very sorry."

"I know," he said sincerely. "Me, too."

They went back into the cabin and knelt by the bed. Both of them were sure of what to do. They laid their hands on top of Marvel's, and with the other they held hands, and then bowed their heads.

Jeanne prayed a simple prayer for Marvel's healing, and thanking God for many things, including Clint, and that he had found the Lord. Then Clint prayed, too. After that they silently prayed, their heads bowed and eyes closed. They felt Marvel stir the tiniest bit, and they both looked up.

She was looking at Jeanne, and she managed a whisper they could both barely hear. "I'm not scared . . . any more, Mama. I'm just . . . so tired." So slowly, as if it was against her will, her eyes closed.

"I know, little girl," Jeanne said soothingly. "I know. Sweetest Marvel, you know that the Lord Jesus is here, right here. Don't worry about me, I'm not afraid any more either. So if you get too tired, my love, you just go on. You'll know if that's what you need to do. The Lord Jesus will tell you if it's time for you to go home with Him."

Marvel gave no sign.

Jeanne and Clint wept again, but silently.

The hours passed, the night waned, they wept and prayed. The lamp flickered and hissed and went out. Finally dawn came, with dim fingers of first light creeping through the windows. Jeanne raised her head; she hadn't been asleep, just resting her head on the bed. Clint was staring at Marvel, and Jeanne's eyes went to her daughter's face, expecting to see her death mask.

Marvel was looking back at her. She smiled.

CHAPTER EIGHTEEN

Clint stood up very slowly, for he was stiff from kneeling by Marvel's bed for so long. He kept his eyes fixed on her face in wonder, and started backing up towards the door. He stumbled against something, and looked down. Leo had been hiding underneath the dining room table all night, and was now standing at the door, big silly dog's grin on his face, tongue lolling, his tail making his crazy figure-eight circles. Clint wrenched open the door and rushed out into the hall and again almost fell, over Vince's outstretched legs. He was sitting against the wall, Roberty's head was on his lap, and he was asleep. Ezra and Dr. Eames were sitting Indian-style, with a Bible opened between them. All of them jumped up when Clint appeared.

"Dr. Eames? Come quick! I think she's all right!" Clint said urgently.

Eames hurried into the room to sit on Marvel's bed. Jeanne stood up to make room for him, her tired face lit up like a happy child's. Eames smoothed Marvel's hair back from her forehead and rested his hand lightly on it. "Hi, Marvel. Feeling better, are you?"

She nodded and moved her mouth, but Eames realized she was too weak to talk. "Shh, don't worry about talking yet. I just want you to suck on some ice chips right now. Later we'll try some water, and maybe even some apple cider. But for now, just let the ice melt in your mouth. And if you feel like you can sleep, you just go right ahead and go to sleep, okay? You don't have to stay awake and entertain us."

He put an ice chip in her mouth and waited. She thirstily licked her lips and he gave her another one. She made a small contented smacking sound, and her eyes fluttered and closed.

He stood up and grinned at Clint and Jeanne. "This little girl is healed! Even her eyes don't show any sign of jaundice! Praise God, it's a miracle!"

Smiling at Clint, Jeanne said, "I think God performed more than one miracle last night. And I must tell you, gentlemen, if Marvel were awake, she would tell us that it's time for a thank-you prayer."

"It's past time," Clint said. "And I want to be first."

The next week was actually very busy for all of them. Marvel recovered slowly, but as the days wore on she regained much of her strength and also gained weight and color in her cheeks. Jeanne was with her every minute, and now she found that she could sew again. While Marvel had been sick Jeanne hadn't been able to do anything at all. She liked sewing, and she was an expert seamstress. By the end of the week she had made Marvel a new dress of pink muslin with a red rose print, and a pinafore.

Marvel said little about being so gravely ill, and finally Jeanne asked her, "Darling, do you remember being so sick?"

She answered cheerfully, "I 'member some things. I 'member when I felt so bad, and I kept throwing up, and all I could have was chips of ice, and then rice flummery."

"But after that," Jeanne pressed her. "After the rice flummery, do you remember anything about that night?"

A dreamy look came into Marvel's eyes, and she wrapped her arms around her dolls and held them close. "I 'member feeling better after the rice flummery, and going to sleep that night. Then I had a dream. I dreamed I was in this nice, pretty place, sitting under a tree. There was a river, but it wasn't the Mississippi River or the Arkansas River, it was real blue and sparkly and it went fast and made a nice sound. And I was hot, and I thought I would get in the river, 'cause it looked like it would be cool. And then Jesus said, "Not now, Little Girl.' He called me *Little Girl* like you and Mr. Clint."

"You—you saw Jesus?" Jeanne asked in a half-whisper.

Marvel shrugged. "No, I just knew He was there somewhere. Then He told me that this was where I needed to rest for a while. So I laid down, and the grass was thick and soft and cool, and I went to sleep. It was funny, going to sleep in a dream, when I knew I was already asleep. But I didn't think about that being funny then. I was just tired, and I went to sleep. When I woke up I saw you and Mr. Clint. And Leo, under the table."

The men, along with men and boys from the Eames families, rebuilt the gazebo. Jacob Eames had told them, "We've had the lumber for the gazebo for two years now, but somehow we just never got around to building it." It was larger and the gingerbread trim was more ornate than before. They painted it a glowing white and Roberty painted the trim *Helena Rose* red. Clint and Ezra made a sign, with the Eames' permission, that read: *Marvel's Rest*. They mounted it over the gazebo doorway opening, which faced the river. After that, over time, instead of the Widow Eames' Landing, the landmark became known as Marvel's Landing.

Just after dinner on Saturday afternoon, six days after Marvel's miraculous healing, she yawned like a newborn kitten. "Gunness! I'm sleepy again. It seems like all I do is sleep and eat."

"That's your job right now, little girl," Jeanne said, smoothing Marvel's hair. They had washed it for the first time this morning, and her fine sandy hair with blonde highlights seemed thicker and healthier than it was before she had gotten sick. "I have to admit that I'm sleepy too. Why don't we take a nap together?"

They laid down and both went right to sleep. When Jeanne woke up, she could tell by the light that she had slept for a couple of hours. She was sleeping almost as much as Marvel was, recovering from her own ordeal. She carefully crawled out of bed, leaving Marvel still sleeping soundly. Jeanne splashed her face with mint water and went to look out the window at the men working on the gazebo.

Her gaze went first to Clint. He was standing talking to Jacob Eames, and his younger brother Isaac, the brother that had unsuccessfully competed for Jeanne's attentions when they were children. Clint pointed up the hill, and the brothers nodded.

For a few moments Jeanne was lost in her womanly admiration of Clint Hardin. He was not classically handsome, for his features were too rugged and his hair, shining almost blue-black in the summer sun, was coarse and couldn't be styled in waves and curls as was the fashion. He was so tall he stood heads above most men, and so muscular as to make them look weak and effeminate. He had gotten more sun this week, and his skin seemed to glow a golden bronze. Jeanne's heart beat a little faster, and she felt a treacherous warmth spreading throughout her body. *He is absolutely gorgeous! And he doesn't even seem to know it!*

With a jolt that shocked her to her very soul, Jeanne suddenly realized that she didn't just admire Clint's looks. She was deeply, helplessly in love with him. She drew in a sharp breath and for a few moments she felt lightheaded. When the dizziness passed she watched him again, with new eyes. *I love him . . . for how long? How'd that happen?* she thought with a half-hysterical giggle. Cautiously she looked back at Marvel, and was relieved that she still slept soundly. Jeanne definitely needed time to think, to absorb this horrible-wonderful love for Clint that she had so abruptly come to know. Realizing it had been something like being hit on the head with a club, and also like it used to be when she swam, taking a deep breath and diving underwater to swim in the perfect silence, surrounded and cradled by cool, clean spring water.

I don't know when, or how . . . over the past months we've become such good friends, and I thought that was all that I wanted from him.

But then Jeanne discovered that somehow during that time she had come to love him. She had slowly been pushing George Masters away, withdrawing more and more from him. Her thoughts had been filled with Clint Hardin, and she had wanted to be with him, not George. Clint was always fun to be with, he wasn't a moody man. He was filled with energy and worked hard. He was witty, he was interesting, and he had an active mind that made him interested in practically any subject that came his way. And he was the most charming man Jeanne had ever met.

Now her heart plummeted as she watched him. That was why she had deliberately fought hard to keep from acknowledging to herself that she was in love with him. Jeanne thought that probably every woman to whom he paid the least attention fell in love with him. He wasn't a predator, Jeanne knew that for certain. She had had a lot of experience with seducers in her four years at the Gayoso, and Clint Hardin was not one of those. He didn't have to be, she was sure. She knew Clint now. She knew that women seduced him, not the other way around.

And here she was, another in a long line of silly women to fall for his manly looks and irresistible charm.

No, be honest! I'm not just infatuated with him, I know him, I know that he's a kind, honest man, and I am in love with him. Even if he didn't look like he does, even if he had no charm, I would still love him. I love the man, not the trappings.

Jeanne must have known how much she loved him and depended on him the night Marvel almost died. She didn't want Dr. Eames or anyone else with her. She wanted Clint, and he was right there for her and Marvel. Even though she had been horribly cruel to him, he had forgiven her and had been a pillar of strength for her. She had instinctively known that he loved her and Marvel.

Jeanne sighed deeply, and would have become depressed from the hurt she felt; but instead she prayed. *Blessed Father God, help me to be strong. I know that Clint loves me and Marvel as if we were his own family. I treasure his friendship, his care for us. Help me never to let him know that I love him as a woman loves a man. I know he doesn't feel that way about me, and I don't want to threaten our relationship in any way. Help me to be strong, and kind, and forgiving, and help me never to feel jealousy when he finds the woman he truly loves. I know that he will always be our faithful friend, and I thank You for him.*

AFTER A JOLLY SUPPER—ACTUALLY, a picnic on the dock—Jeanne sat down at her desk to write a letter. It was, she thought, the most difficult letter she had ever written, and it took her four hours before she was at least satisfied with it. The letter was to George Masters. When she finally finished she was so tired she thought about crawling into bed and passing out.

But then she thought, *I really have been wandering somewhere out of this world for the past two weeks! Just how am I going to mail this letter? And what about the mail we had picked up . . . forever ago, it seems like.* She stood up, slightly panicked, but then she thought of the empty cargo bays. Someone had picked up their load of stoves, obviously, and Jeanne knew that Clint would have sent the mail on. But Jeanne had to get this letter to George, it was the only honorable thing she could do, under the circumstances. She went to find Clint, and Ezra told her he was out on the dock.

The night was milky-warm, the starlight bright. The waning moon was high in the sky, its reflection waving on the slow current. He was sitting at the end of the dock with a bucket beside him. As Jeanne went to him she saw him reach into the bucket and throw something out into the river. It made a soft *plop*.

"Hello, Clint," she said softly.

It startled him, and he jerked around and then smiled. "Hi. Want to join me? I'm stoning the moon reflection. It's funny how it kinda breaks up into pieces when I hit it head on."

Jeanne sat beside him. "You just can't sit still, can you?"

"I'm not so good at that, no. Ezra says I'm worse than Roberty, always fiddle-faddlin' around and gittin' inter somewhat. And then he told me to get out of his galley, someone else would have to teach me how to make rice flummery." Marvel had asked for the cold, creamy pudding over and over again. Ezra had gone up to the Eames house and demanded that Widow Eames teach him how to make it.

Jeanne chuckled. "He's right, you know. You are always inter somewhat. Anyway, apparently I have just today come back into my right mind, and I remembered that we are on a boat and that this boat hauls cargo. What happened with the stoves? And the mail?"

"When we first put up the yellow quarantine flags, the next boat that came by stopped to see if they could help." He looked amused. "It was the *One-Eyed Jack*. Maybe you've seen it."

"I have. And I believe their crew is called the One Eyes. Just like my crew is called the Petticoats. I would apologize for that, but personally I'd rather be called a petticoat than a one-eye."

"Me, too. Anyway, I was kind of surprised that they were so helpful. They took the mail on for us, and when they got to Pine Bluff they telegraphed Mr. Baxley at Kaufman Stoves warehouse. They sent on the *Club King*, one of the *One-Eyed Jack*'s sister boats, to pick up the stoves. In the last two weeks four different boats have come by, and every one of them has stopped to see if they can help. Guess when it comes down to it, there is a brotherhood on the river."

"So someone could take a letter for me?" Jeanne asked anxiously. "I know that the Eames probably have a mail-man that picks up and takes their mail to Pine Bluff, but I'd rather not go through the regular mail. I'd really like for it to be delivered by messenger as soon as possible."

Clint jumped up and started pacing back and forth. Jeanne craned her neck around and said, "Clint, don't walk around behind me like that. It's like having a tiger prowling around behind me."

"Sorry. But I have to stand up. The letter's for Masters, isn't it?"

Jeanne got to her feet and leaned up against a piling to face him. "Well, yes, it is. I have something—something very important to tell him. Since I don't know when I'll be seeing him again, I felt that I needed to write him and tell him this—this—information as soon as possible. What's the matter with you, Clint? I know you don't care for him, but surely you can't be upset that I'm writing him."

Clint stopped pacing, took a deep breath, and came to stand in front of her. "Yes, I'm upset that you're writing him. I'm upset about a lot of things. And I want—I need to know what's in that letter, Jeanne. But before I ask you about Masters, I have to tell you something. I—I have to talk to you. I think."

"Clint, you're not making much sense. I don't mind you knowing what's in the letter. It's personal, but you're my friend and if you really want to know, I'll tell you," Jeanne said with confusion. "And if you need to talk to me, of course you can, anytime, about anything."

He resumed his restless pacing. "I've prayed and prayed about telling you this, because now, for the first time in my whole life, I really want to do the right thing. But I'm so new to all this, to being a Christian and trusting in the Lord, that I haven't been able to understand what He wants me to do. But now, I think I have to tell you the truth, because—because—you're marrying the wrong man, Jeanne."

"What?" she said, astounded.

"I said you're marrying the wrong man," he repeated deliberately. "I know it. Ezra knows it, Vinnie knows it, Roberty knows it, even Marvel knows it. No, no, Jeanne, of all times please don't get mad at me now. We don't talk about it among ourselves, I promise you. It's just—it's just something that the people who really know you, and love you, can see, even though you can't."

"But I can see it, Clint, you half-wit," Jeanne said with some heat. "I've changed my mind, I don't think you need to know what's in this letter, because it's really none of your business. I don't go telling you how to pick and choose your women, do I?"

A spasm of pain crossed his face. "Jeanne, I'm so sorry about all of that. The Lord's forgiven me, and I'm different now. Those women—I mean, from now on my life is going to be different. Can't you forgive me? *Will* you forgive me?"

Immediately Jeanne's anger melted away. "Oh, Clint, of course I forgive you, and now you must forgive me. You weren't wronging me in any way, and I know very well that you've changed since that night that the Lord saved you. I'm sorry. I just—it's hard—I'm just sorry. I'll never, ever treat you like that again." Then hurriedly she added, "I just told George that I wouldn't be able to see him any more. For—for a lot of reasons. Perhaps I was thinking of marrying him, at first. But not now, it will never happen, and I have to let him know that as soon as I possibly can."

Now Clint seemed stunned. "You're not marrying him? How'd that happen? Oh, forget it! Forget about him! I have to tell you something, Jeanne. Right now." He stepped up to stand close to her but he didn't touch her. He looked down at her, and by the glitter of the starlight Jeanne could see the intensity on his face. "I love you, Jeanne. I'm so in love with you that I can hardly breathe when I'm with you. I wanted to tell you, even though I knew—I thought—that you were in love with George Masters. I just wanted you to know how much I treasure you, how I want to be with you, for as long as I can, even though it hurts, because I know you don't feel the same way about me."

She stared up at him, her dark almond eyes gleaming first from shock, and then from joy.

"Clint," she whispered, "I love you." She threw her arms around his neck and pressed the back of his neck, and he bent and she kissed him. Jeanne felt so much joy, so much happiness, her whole body felt delightfully warm. His lips were heated, and his hands pressed urgently against her back. She felt passionate desire, and she knew it was right. His kiss was hungry, demanding, yet gentle. Jeanne didn't want their embrace to end; she felt she could stand there on that dock, kissing him, for hours, days, forever. But finally she did gently draw her hands down to press against his chest.

He lifted his head and held her close. "Thank you, oh, Lord, for giving me the desire of my heart," he murmured.

"My beloved is mine, and I am his," Jeanne whispered. "Thank you, fairest Lord Jesus."

After a while, as if they were of one mind, they sat back down, holding hands.

"I can't believe you love me," Clint said wonderingly. "How? When? When did you know?"

"Just today," she answered mischievously. "I felt like someone had dropped a Kaufman Stove on my head."

"Really? Just today? Then it's no wonder I didn't know it. You've always treated me like a tiresome little boy. And I know, I know, I act the pure fool most of the time. No wonder you didn't mistake me for a man."

She put her hand on his cheek and turned him to face her. "You know very well that's not true. Who did I want, who did I desperately need when I thought Marvel was dying? You. Only you, because you're strong and you're loving and you give of yourself to your friends, to the people you care about. And as far as you acting like a fool, I don't think so at all, I never have. You're clever and you're witty and you're fun to be with. You have a merry heart, and it doeth good like a medicine."

"Yeah? Is that in the Bible?"

"It is. It's in Proverbs, I can't remember the chapter and verse. We can look it up."

"Yeah, I've been studying the Bible with Isaac Eames. Did we tell you that he's a preacher?"

"No, I didn't know that. I've been very distracted lately," she sighed. "I haven't thought about anything but Marvel . . . and you. Do you know, George Masters had not once entered my mind all this time, until today. And then it was only because I was staring at you through my window like a starved she-wolf, comparing him to you. He came up very, very short."

He squeezed her hand. "Jeanne, I have to ask you this. You—you aren't just angry with him, are you? I mean, because he left Memphis, because of the fever?"

"I was angry with him, yes, and it hurt me extremely. At first. Now I'm relieved. You know, he's in love with me, I guess, and today I was thinking that my letter was going to hurt him terribly. But then I realized that if he really, truly loved me as a man should love his wife, or at least the woman he was considering making his wife, he never would have left me and Marvel behind in Memphis. So I think his pride may be hurt, yes, and maybe he will feel some loss. But not much, and not for long."

"Good," Clint said cheerfully. "I don't want to talk about him any more. I want to talk about us. Me and you. Will you marry me?"

Jeanne laughed, a silvery trilling sound that was delightful to hear. "You really don't sit still for a minute, do you? Yes, my love, I will marry you. But not now. Not soon."

"Yes, I know," he said, now soberly. "I've talked to Isaac about everything. He's taught me about what it means to become a Christian. I talked to him about you, about how I love you so much, and I told him that you were going to marry George Masters. He kinda brushed that aside, for some reason. Anyway, he really drilled me about whether the love I had for you was true, and real, and godly. And it is, and I'm sure of that, I've prayed about it for hours and hours. When Isaac finally believed me, he told me that I should tell you. But then he went on to explain that brand-new Christians should spend some time to get to know their Lord before they get all taken up with getting married. I know you need time, Jeanne, and I know I need time. We can have a long engagement, as long as you say. But I had to ask you, I had to make sure. So—so we can be engaged? You'll be mine, really?"

"I already am yours," she said simply. "I am honored that you love me and want me to be your wife, Clint. When it's time for us to marry, the Lord will let us know. Both of us."

THEY STAYED ANOTHER WEEK, until the *One-Eyed Jack* brought them the news that the yellow fever epidemic, which had never been officially announced, had been officially announced to be over. That week was the happiest time of Jeanne's life. She and Clint spent every possible moment together, with Marvel and the crew during the day, and by themselves after Marvel went to bed. They talked about everything under the sun, of their plans and their dreams and how they wanted to spend their lives together.

The only thing they didn't talk about was Jeanne's marriage. "Please, Clint. I promise I'll tell you the whole sad, shabby story when we get back to Memphis. But right now, in this place, in this time, I want to be happy. I don't want to think of him, or talk about him."

"That's fine, my love," he had said quietly. "I understand."

One night they sat out on the dock, this time with Clint throwing rocks into a moonless river. "At least six more," he said airily, as they were discussing Marvel and Roberty, whom they decided to officially, legally adopt. "Three boys and three girls, please."

"Six? Why not eight? An even dozen?" Jeanne said with mock outrage.

"Yeah, I'd like that. I'll really, *really* be glad when we get to start working on it."

"Clint? Shut up."

He took Jeanne and Marvel to visit her parents' graves. The Eames had built a church at the back of one of their cotton fields, and Isaac was the pastor. In the cemetery next to it Mr. Eames was buried, and two Eames children that had been stillborn. Kurt and Constance Langer were buried side by side, with two simple wooden crosses marking their graves. On them Jeanne had directed the Scripture from the Song of Solomon: *I am my beloved's, and my beloved is mine.* Jeanne's mother had loved the Song, and when Jeanne got older she came to understand that it was how her mother felt about her father, and he about her. Jeanne learned that it was the perfect picture of Jesus as Husband to His Bride of Christ.

Weeping softly, Jeanne whispered to Clint, "Now I know. It was a blessing from the Lord for them to die together. Neither of them would have wanted to live without the other."

It was the first of September when the *Helena Rose* docked in Memphis. They had decided to go to Mütter Krause's to eat, and Jeanne was wearing her best dress, the pretty muslin with the flounced skirt and hoop skirt, and her lace parasol. As Jeanne and Clint went to the gang-plank, arm in arm, she said, "It may be my imagination, but it already seems a little cooler, don't you think? I love autumn."

"I love you," he said. "And autumn. Spring's fun. Winter, though, yes, I love—"

Coming up the gangplank was a man that Clint didn't know. He was tall and slender, with sandy blond hair and pale blue eyes and a deeply tanned face. He was dressed in a black frock coat, red waistcoat, natty blue trousers, and a top hat set at a jaunty angle. Clint thought he might be a riverboat gambler, because he was flashy-looking, with a watch chain too large and ostentatious hanging from his vest button, and a flashing red ruby pinky ring.

Jeanne had frozen beside him. Clint glanced at her. Her face had gone utterly pale, her eyes were wide and stark, and her hand on his arm was trembling.

The man sauntered up to them, doffed his hat, and bowed deeply. "Hello, Jeanne. I've been looking for you for a long, long time. You're even more beautiful than I imagined."

"M-Max?" she stuttered in a broken whisper. "Max? How . . . you . . . I thought . . . ?"

"I know, but I'm alive," he said carelessly. Now he turned his cold gaze on Clint. "My name is Max Bettencourt. Whoever you are, I want you to take your hands off my wife."

CHAPTER NINETEEN

The oddest thing happened to Clint. He remembered his fight with Mike the Hammer, the one he had lost, and he remembered how he had felt when Mike's last blow had landed, because that was how he felt when he heard the man say "Max Bettencourt." He felt as if he'd been slammed in the gut with a sledgehammer, and that there was no air to breathe.

His eyes narrowed to glaring iron-blue slits as he stared at Bettencourt, who met his gaze flippantly. Jeanne's arm slowly slipped away, and then he felt a tiny soft hand take his. He looked down, and Marvel was half-hidden behind him, holding his hand. She looked confused and scared.

Bettencourt looked down at her and gave her a slick smile. "Hello, Marvel. You don't remember me, do you? I'm your father. You've grown into a very pretty little girl. You look a lot like me, bet she reminds you of me all the time, huh, Jeanne?"

"No. She has never reminded me of you, Max. She's nothing like you," Jeanne said between gritted teeth. She had recovered from the initial shock of seeing her husband alive, and some of the color returned to her cheeks. "Why are you here, Max? What do you want?"

"Those are stupid questions, Jeanne. I'm your husband."

"I know that," she said helplessly. "But what do you want?"

His eyes went to search the *Helena Rose*. He looked all around, up at the pilothouse, the Texas deck, the main deck, at Vince and Ezra and Roberty and Leo gathered behind Clint, Jeanne, and Marvel in a phalanx. "Nice boat. I hear you've been doing very well for yourself, Captain Jeanne, with this little moneymaker. That cute little outfit you're parading around in, I'll bet that cost a pretty penny." His eyes narrowed and he said deliberately, as if he were speaking to a backward child, "We have to talk, Jeanne. Now let's go on up to your cabin so we can be alone."

"No!" Clint and Jeanne said in unison.

Max's brow lowered. "I'm not talking to you, Hardin. You just keep your mouth shut. This is between me and Jeanne."

"Thought you didn't know who I was," Clint said in a hard voice. "This boat is half mine. I'm not giving you permission to board her, now or ever. In fact, take yourself off my gangplank before I throw you in the river."

"This is half Jeanne's boat," Max retorted. "And that means it's half mine. So I'm standing on *our* half of the gangplank."

"No, that is my gangplank," Clint said, taking a threatening step toward him. "That other one that hasn't been lowered is Jeanne's. Now get off my gangplank."

"Stop it," Jeanne said dully. "Clint, I have to talk to him, of course. And no, Max, you are not coming up to my cabin.

So do you want to stand here and argue all day, or do you want to go somewhere so we can talk?"

"This isn't the end of it, by far, Hardin," Max warned, grabbing Jeanne's hand and tucking it tight beneath his arm. "Don't wait up for her, lover boy." He turned and half-dragged Jeanne down the gangplank onto the wharf.

Clint's vision was rimmed with crimson, and he took a step forward, intending to follow them, and that might have been very bad news for Max Bettencourt. But Vince stepped up in front of him and put his hands on Clint's shoulders. "Man, this is bad, and I know how you must be feeling, like you wanna kill something right now. But what's done is done, brother. We need to take care of the little one." He nodded toward Marvel.

Clint's jaw tightened and he kept watching Max and Jeanne until they disappeared into the crowd on the docks. Then he took a deep breath, settled his face into a less tense expression, and turned to go down on one knee in front of Marvel and take her hands. "Hey, little girl. I know this is hard. But don't you worry, everything's going to be okay."

Marvel was pale. Clint realized with a jolt that her facial features were those of Max Bettencourt's, except for her wide-spaced dark eyes. She had the same long thin nose, the same pointed chin, the same wide thin mouth. Her hair was like his, too. But he understood perfectly what Jeanne had said. Max's face was hard, as hard and bitter as a dark winter night. His blue eyes were cold, with no semblance of any emotion whatsoever. Even though he had sounded angry, he had looked utterly uncaring, as if he were dead. Marvel's sweetness showed in her face, her love, her purity, her innocence. She was nothing at all like her father.

She asked, "So that really was my father? That awful, mean man?"

"I guess so," Clint muttered.

"So you can't marry Mama now?" Tears sprang into her eyes.

Clint picked her up and held her close. She threw her arms around his neck and sobbed on his shoulder. "You know what?" he said softly. "Let's go pray. That always makes you feel better, doesn't it? I know it sure does me."

But this time he wasn't so sure even prayer would help.

"IT IS SO RIDICULOUS for us to sit in a public place to discuss our future," Max said sarcastically. "You're going to have to do better than this, Jeanne."

They had gone to Dooley's Confectionery, the shop that had had the famous chocolate castle in the window. When warm weather came it had disappeared, of course, replaced by watercolor signs advertising the candies and ice cream and the prices. Dooley's had done so well, particularly with the ladies, that he had opened up a little courtyard behind the shop, with wrought-iron tables with big umbrellas to shield the patrons from the hot southern sun. Even now Jeanne felt a pang as she recalled that she had gone with George Masters that day instead of coming here with Clint and Marvel and the crew.

With an effort she made herself pay attention to Max. "Do better than what?" she asked.

"I have no intention of having intimate discussions with my wife in a confectioner's shop. Right now I want to make this clear to you: what you own, I own. Tonight I'm moving onto the boat, into our cabin."

"How dare you," Jeanne said between gritted teeth. "Did you actually think that you could just show up on my doorstep and we'd go back to being husband and wife? After everything you've done?"

He shrugged carelessly. "So what if I did take the money? It was mine. And you've obviously done all right for yourself."

"It was not your money, my father gave it to me! You left me penniless with a five-month-old baby! How Marvel and I managed to live is only by the grace of God. And it's none of your business how I'm doing. You've been dead to me for six years, Max! What do you expect?"

"Hmm, well, I expected that my wife would at least ask me how I've been, what happened to me, why it seemed as if I were dead for six years."

"I knew where you went, or have you forgotten that among all your women you did mention to me that you were going halfway across the world to the Afghan Empire. Under the circumstances, I assumed you had been killed."

"I almost was, many times," he snarled. "And I was captured and taken prisoner, and tortured, Jeanne. You think I was off having a party in the Punjab? You have no idea of the tortures they've devised in that heathen part of the world!"

"Oh, really? Just let me get this straight," Jeanne said calmly. "You went as a mercenary and joined the *Khalsa*, the Sikh Army, didn't you? Because Maharajah Ranjit Singh needed artillerymen, mercenary English and American artillerymen, to train his army."

"Yes? So?"

"So who, exactly, took you prisoner, Max? You were fighting for the Sikhs. Did the British East India Company capture you and torture you? What did they do, mess up your hair?"

He grinned a shark's smile. "You always were sly in some ways, Jeanne. Stupid about men and their needs, but otherwise you're clever. Okay, so let's forget the past six years. It doesn't matter now anyway. What matters is that I am most certainly alive and you are my wife, and I am going to claim what's mine."

"I'll never forget the past six years! In spite of the hardships Marvel and I have gone through, they've been very good years—without you! So I don't want you or need you now!"

"Yeah, I've heard all about that too. Everyone on this river, and the Arkansas River, knows you and Hardin are living together on the boat. How convenient. I can see that you're so besotted with him that you wish I really were dead right now. But I'm not, Jeanne. I'm alive, and I am your husband, in the eyes of the law, and in the eyes of God, like you always preached at me. That's a fact and you're going to have to learn—again—to live with it. And to live with me, because I'm moving in with you tonight."

"If you so much as set foot on that boat, I'll let Clint Hardin deal with you," Jeanne said evenly. "I'm warning you, Max. He will hurt you, and I won't be able to stop him, even if I wanted to."

"Oh, really? But Jeanne, my dear, I thought you were supposed to be a Christian woman. At least, that's how you see yourself, and you put on a good act, so holy and pure, ask the Lord for this, pray for that. So you've prayed to God, and He told you to set your big mutt on me and beat me up?"

"Stop it!" she cried, much too loudly. Two finely dressed ladies sitting nearby stared at her with disapproval. How did Max Bettencourt do this to her? He always made her feel ugly, inside and outside, and ashamed. He was so reprehensible, so cruel and heartless, how was it possible that she was always the one who felt guilty?

He went on, "And what about Marvel? Are you going to deny me the right to see my own daughter? And have your river rats assault me, right in front of her, I presume, if I try?

Where does it say that in your Bible, Jeanne? You should be ashamed of yourself, anyway, the way you're raising her. On a riverboat, with river rats as her only companions. And you living in sin on that boat with Clint Hardin."

"I am not living with Clint Hardin!" Jeanne said, stung. "I've never had a man in my life, except for you!"

"Ah, so there's nothing between you and him?" Max said knowingly.

"I—I didn't say—it's none of your business!"

"But it is my business," he said with a great show of patience. "You are my wife. Marvel is my daughter. You two are my only family." Then he leaned over, grabbed her arm and squeezed hard, and muttered in a spiteful undertone, "And I'm warning you, Jeanne. I have a legal right to anything and everything that you own. That's the law of Tennessee, believe me, I've already checked into it. So you'd better just call off your big mutt, because if he so much as lays a finger on me I'll have him arrested for assault."

"You're hurting me," Jeanne hissed.

"Yeah, I know," he said maliciously. With one last brutal squeeze he let go of her upper arm. "You were a stupid little girl, and now you're a stupid woman. You'd better think about this, Jeanne. You haven't got a chance of running me off. The law is on my side."

Jeanne rubbed her arm and looked down, her cheeks flaming. This situation was so intolerable she felt nauseated. She remembered now, all too well, that in the last months before Max had left she found every second in his company, rare though it was, to be a nightmare of shame and crippling remorse. And she had no one to blame but herself. She had married him. She had *wanted* to marry him.

Finally she looked back up at him defiantly. "You know, Max, you've made a lot of plans that you're going to have trouble carrying out. In the first place, if you try to board my boat, I will tell Clint, and Ezra, and Vince, to remove you forcibly. And as I said, you will get hurt, probably extremely hurt. Any one of those men will be all too happy to go to jail, probably just overnight, for beating you senseless. And in the second place, I will never consent to you claiming a husband's right to my property. If you think that's what you're going to do, you'll have to take me to court. If that's your choice, then fine. But until I get a decision by a judge, you cannot set foot on board the *Helena Rose*. As far as seeing Marvel, I'll have to think about that. Even if I do decide to let you see her, it will never be unless I'm with her, and not on the *Helena Rose*."

"I can get the sheriff to escort me on board!" he blustered.

"Not without a court order, he won't," Jeanne retorted.

"You'd better not do this, Jeanne. I'm warning you, you're going to pay for it if you defy me," he said balefully. "And when that day comes, your payment is going to be a lot more than you bargained for." He jerked to his feet, overturning the small wrought-iron chair, and stalked out of the courtyard. Everyone stared at Jeanne, and she buried her face in her hands.

No matter how unfair it was, she was once again the one who felt shame.

WHEN MAX BETTENCOURT LEFT Dooley's, he felt that he had made a grand exit. He'd left Jeanne sitting there like a cast-off whore, and she'd have to make her own way back to the boat alone. He considered waiting for her somewhere along the way, but decided against it. It was still several hours until dark and he had no intention of taking such a risk in broad daylight.

He stopped at a dank, dark liquor store and bought the cheapest gallon of whiskey they had. A few blocks down was his hotel, a filthy flophouse that rented rooms by the half hour, the hour, or the night. Paying for another night, he went up the rickety stairs, almost choking from the stench of body odor, rotten fish, and urine. In his room he pulled the single chair up by the window and leaned his whole upper body out of it. Uncorking the whiskey, he took four harsh gurgling swallows from it. This hotel, which apparently had no other name than Rooms to Rent, had no such luxuries as glasses or sheets or even pitchers and washbowls. To wash up he had to go to the pump out back, which was right by the privy. It occurred to him that a pitcher and washbowl would cost less than the whiskey, but cursing silently he decided to use one of the empty gallon jugs—there were two of them in the room, the idea that this place had any maids to clean up was farcical—to fetch water for washing. He couldn't afford a pitcher and washbowl. His lip curled in a snarl, thinking that Jeanne had backed him against the wall, telling him that he'd have to take her to court. Lawyers cost money, and Max Bettencourt's money was almost gone.

He cursed Jeanne in his mind, over and over again. Though she had always been a little spitfire, he had always been able to manipulate her, in fact, to bully her. She had grown much less vulnerable; in fact, it had been an extremely unpleasant shock to him that she so strongly and openly defied him. And she had that big bruiser Clint Hardin to defend her. But he wouldn't stay by her side and protect her all the time, Max thought confidently. He had heard on the river that Hardin was quite the ladies' man. To Max that meant that Hardin was like him. Oh, yes, soon enough Hardin would be out chasing whores. No matter what Max said, he knew that Jeanne would never take a lover, she really was way too holier-than-thou religious. Hardin had needs, like any man, and he wouldn't be finding them satisfied by prudish Jeanne Bettencourt. All he had to do was watch for his opportunity.

There was only one thing that Max liked about this room. The hotel was on Front Street, the waterfront that ran right along the river. Sandwiched between a beef warehouse and an icehouse, the only windows were on the front of the hotel. His window looked right over the river, the northern part of the docks, in fact. He got up and got his field glasses and settled back down in his chair. They were sensitive, and it took him a few moments to adjust them, but finally they were in such good focus that he could read the letters on the side of the boat: *Helena Rose*.

JEANNE'S RETURN TO THE *Helena Rose* was slow and torturous. She walked as slowly as she had ever done, feeling barely able to drag one foot in front of the other. Still, she went several blocks out of her way, walking in circles for a couple of hours. She had to think.

But her mind wasn't working properly; her thoughts were incoherent. All she could do was cry out to the Lord. *What am I going to do? Oh, my God, my loving Father God, whatever can I do? I can't stand the thought of him anywhere near Marvel!* An abominable picture of Max Bettencourt picking up Marvel and holding her as she and Clint did, loomed up in her mind. She stopped dead and bent over, clutching her stomach. She actually thought that she was going to vomit.

But the picture faded and she kept on her dogged way. Eventually her mind cleared somewhat, though her thoughts were as painful as if she were being stabbed. *I am his wife, and he is Marvel's father. But I will never, never live with him. And I don't care what the law says or even whether it's right or wrong . . . no, I know it's right. That man shouldn't have any part of Marvel's life. If I have to, Marvel and I will run away. Thank you, God, that I have the money! And he'll never find me again!*

Sudden hot tears stung her eyes, and she stifled a sob. *Oh, Clint, Clint, my lost love! What have I done to us! I thought it was unbearable before, my regret at marrying him, but now, how can we stand this pain, this sorrow? Not together. If I have to run away, it will be from you, too, my beloved . . .*

She had almost reached the *Helena Rose*, so she dashed the tears away from her eyes and scrubbed her face with her handkerchief. They were all sitting outside, on the main deck, in the deck chaises. Marvel was sitting in Clint's lap, resting her head against his shoulder. He was caressing her hair, smoothing it back over and over again.

When they saw her, they all jumped up and met her at the gangplank. She said, "All of you, please, go ahead and sit back down. Ezra, will you bring me a chair? Here, Marvel, my darling, come sit with me."

They all got seated except for Clint, who stood and paced. His tanned face was tense, his jaw hardened, his eyes dark and foreboding.

"I suppose there's no way to explain this except just to say it," Jeanne said quietly. "I met Max Bettencourt when I was sixteen years old, and I fell in love with him. Or at least I thought I did, now I don't think what I felt had anything whatsoever to do with true love. He was older, he was handsome, he was dashing, a captain of artillery in the army, stationed at Fort Smith. My parents were horrified that at sixteen I wanted to get married, and they made me promise to wait at least a year. And so we did, and when I turned seventeen we married. Max's term of enlistment had expired, and so he resigned from the army. We moved to Memphis, and he got a job at the Victory Ironworks, making cannons and ammunition. He was quickly promoted to supervisor of the light arms division, and there he learned how to make handguns and rifles. He was all right, for a while . . . but . . ." She choked back tears. Marvel started crying.

Clint said, "Jeanne, you don't have to explain yourself to us. I don't even think you have to explain it all in detail to Marvel. When she's older she'll need to understand, but please, right now just tell us whatever you feel you need to. If that's anything at all."

Jeanne sighed, a mournful sound. "I don't, I hate talking about him. I'm sorry, Marvel, so sorry for everything. If you all would bear with me, maybe later I can explain it better to all of you. For now, you need to know that Max is going to claim that since he is my husband, he co-owns my half of the *Helena Rose*. I've told him that he's going to have to take me to court to settle this, and I guess he will, because it's true, in this state a husband does legally own everything that his wife owns, and he'll certainly win. Anyway, I told him that for now he's forbidden to come onto the boat. And to that he said that if any of you try to physically stop him, he'll have you arrested for assault."

"Assault? That's way too nice a word for what I'd do to that vermin if he tries to come on board this boat," Clint growled. "Unfortunately, however, I know that he won't give me the chance. I don't know him, but I don't have to, all I need to know is that he deserted you and Marvel. So he's a coward. He wouldn't even have the guts to face down Roberty."

"If I had to fetch the stepladder I would, so I could punch him in the nose," Roberty said stoutly.

"You would really?" Marvel said, sniffing and looking fascinated. "Mama, could we watch?"

Somehow Jeanne managed a ragged smile. "I hate to say it but I wish we could. But I think you're right, Clint. He may come here again, but he won't dare try to come on board. Now, if you all would excuse me, I want to go up to my cabin and wash up. Marvel? Why don't you and Roberty go get us some fresh water for the cabin, okay? I'll be up in a minute."

They all left, except Clint. He stood by the railing, staring out over the river, a dark brooding look on his face. Jeanne came to stand by him but didn't touch him. "He is my husband. Lawfully, and as he so carefully reminded me, in the sight of God."

"That is the biggest travesty I've ever heard of," Clint said heatedly. "Jeanne, that man is a swine. He shouldn't be able to raise his eyes to look at you. I can't—I won't—"

He grabbed her and tried to pull her to him, but she quickly pushed him away. "Clint, you know that this is the end. This is the end of us. I know that God has forgiven me for marrying him, but sin has consequences in this world. I married him. I'm his wife. I'll never live with him, I'll never let him so much as touch me. But it would be wrong, very wrong of me to have a relationship with you now. You see that, don't you?" She fought back the tears, but she couldn't control her grief. It was as if she was dreadfully wounded, and with each word she spoke that wound was agonizingly opened again and again. She bent her head and blindly felt for the railing as she sobbed.

Clint reached for her again, but then he slowly dropped his hands and turned again to look out over the river. "I'll never love anyone but you, Jeanne. I don't know why the Lord allowed this to happen to us. I prayed so much, and searched my heart, and I knew, I *knew* that He meant for us to be together, that we are bound together as surely as Adam and Eve were. And I'm going to hold to that. One day I believe we'll be man and wife, Jeanne. Already I know that I will love and honor you, from this day forward, forever."

CHAPTER TWENTY

"I'm not very hungry," Marvel said. It was breakfast, and Ezra had made her favorite food these days, rice flummery. She had eaten one spoonful and then just fidgeted with the cold pudding.

Jeanne sighed. Instead of joining the crew in the galley, she had asked Roberty to bring them breakfast and coffee. "I know, darling," she said. "Is there anything at all that you can think of you could eat? You were a very sick little girl, and you still haven't gotten all the peaches in your cheeks back."

Marvel puckishly reached up and pinched her cheeks, as women did instead of wearing wicked rouge. "Is that better?" she asked, smiling a little. "Roberty says it's funny that Mr. Clint says we have peachy cheeks instead of rosy cheeks. Hmm . . . do we have any peaches?"

"I don't think so, but if we don't I know Roberty would be glad to go get us some," Jeanne said, rising. "I'll go tell him and I'll be right back." She returned in a few minutes.

Marvel was clearing the dishes, and Jeanne said, "Never mind that right now, Marvel. Come sit with me, I want to talk to you."

They went to their armchairs and Marvel pulled up her knees and wrapped her skinny arms around them. "It's about my father, isn't it," she said in a low voice.

"Yes, it is. I've thought so much about it, and prayed about it, and I know I have to explain some things about him," Jeanne said quietly. "When I met him, he wasn't like—like what you saw yesterday. He wasn't a mean man. He laughed a lot, and he made me laugh. He was very nice to me back then. He told me, so often, how much he loved me.

"I was only sixteen years old. I know it's hard for you, Marvel, because I know that at your age all adults just seem old. But I want you to think of Dorie Eames. You remember her, don't you?" Dorie was one of Widow Eames' many grandchildren, a bright, perky sixteen-year-old girl.

"Yes, I remember her. She was nice. She made a daisy chain for me, and then put yellow roses in my hair and teased me about having yellow roses instead of yellow fever," Marvel said with a child's amusement. "I think I see what you mean, Mama. She's not a little girl like me but she's not like you, either."

"I would say that she's closer to being an innocent child like you. And that's how I was, when I met your father. He was a soldier, and he was tall and handsome and so dashing in his uniform and with his sword. He was eight years older than I was, and he seemed like all anyone would want in a husband. Your grandfather made us wait for a year before we could get married, but Max wanted to marry me as much as I wanted to marry him, so we waited."

Jeanne hesitated, for she knew very well now that the only reason Max had married her was because that was the only way he could seduce her. It was the thrill of the chase, of getting something that he couldn't have. It wasn't long after their wedding that she had seen that marriage vows meant little to him, and that once he had conquered her he cared nothing for her. He had still claimed his husbandly rights as far as the marriage bed, and Jeanne, who believed that she must be a dutiful wife, allowed him to without complaint. At least, she was submissive until she got pregnant, and then she began to refuse him. That was when he had started flaunting all his other women, throwing them in her face. He had never forced her, however. Back then he wasn't a violent man, but Jeanne had seen the brutality in him clearly yesterday. Her arm was bruised where he had grabbed her. Max Bettencourt had changed, and not for the better.

"So you loved each other," Marvel murmured.

"I know now that your father never did love me," Jeanne said firmly. "And this is the main thing that I want you to try to understand, Marvel. I thought that I loved him, and maybe I did. But it was wrong from the beginning. It was a sin for me to marry him, because I never asked the Lord if he was the right man for me. I guess I knew, deep down, that he wasn't, because he wasn't a Christian man, and the Lord teaches us that it's not wise at all, and it doesn't please Him, if a person that has been saved by the Lord Jesus Christ marries a person that doesn't know Him. And so I think that's why I didn't dare ask the Lord to bless our marriage. I just went ahead and married Max anyway."

"You make it sound like it's all your fault, Mama," Marvel said unhappily. "But you're a nice lady, and a good mother, and you love Jesus. It wasn't all your fault."

"No, but it was my sin, and now, it seems, I must bear the consequences of that sin. But listen to me, Marvel. Even though I made such a terrible mistake, and was so wrong, the Lord forgave me. He even made something good, some-thing wonderful, out of the mess I'd made of my life."

"Huh? What, Mama?"

"You. You are the best thing that ever happened to me, Marvel. I thank the Blessed Lord for you every single day. And He is faithful and true, and He'll take care of us, always."

They hugged, and Jeanne said, "Why don't you and Roberty come up here and we'll do your lessons in the cabin today?"

JEANNE TRIED VERY HARD, but she was unable to concen-trate on much of anything. She longed to be with Clint, to let him hold her and comfort her, to feel his strength, to know his love. But she couldn't do that any more, and she had a hard time maintaining a pleasant demeanor for Marvel. All she really wanted to do was crawl in bed, pull the covers over her head, and cry.

She kept going to the windows, watching the docks, expecting Max to show up any moment. Upon reflection, she was fairly certain that Clint was right, that Max wouldn't risk a direct confrontation, a physical confrontation, with Clint. But she thought that he very likely would come to demand to see Marvel. Or she thought that he might very well show up with a deputy sheriff to escort him on board. Jeanne had been bluffing about that yesterday; she really had no idea about the actual legal ramifications of the situ-ation. All she did know for certain was that in Tennessee a man owned his wife as surely as he owned a slave, and all of her property was considered to be equally his.

She nagged and worried herself half to death all day long. Finally, at about four o'clock in the afternoon, she went down to the engine room to talk to Clint. "I can't stand this much longer," she said desperately. "Yesterday I just wished he would go away, and now I wish he would come here so I would know what he's going to do."

"Why are you sitting here waiting for him?" Clint said brusquely. "I don't care what he says, he's got nothing to do with the *Helena Rose*. Not unless a court of law decrees it, and there's no law that says you have to sit here and wait for a summons that may never come."

"But what should I do? I can't just pretended that yesterday never happened."

"I know that, Jeanne, my love," he said softly. "But we can still live our lives, he can't take that away from us. What were we going to do when he popped up in front of us yesterday?"

"We were going to contact the postmaster and our shippers and see what we needed to do to start moving freight again," Jeanne said slowly. That seemed like ages ago.

"So, let's contact the postmaster and our shippers and get some freight and go to work," Clint said steadily.

"But it's late afternoon already."

"Right now that doesn't matter. I know you've seen the docks today. The cotton's coming in. Every business, whether it has to do with cotton or not, is busy. We'll have plenty of time to go see the postmaster, and telegraph all of our shippers. Even if there's some problem with our regulars, we can haul all the cotton we could stuff into this old girl."

"Yes. You're right, of course. But I don't really want to go into town, Clint, not today."

"Don't you worry about a thing, little lady," he drawled. "Vinnie and I can take care of it. You're not worried about staying here by yourself?"

"No, I think you were right yesterday," Jeanne answered. "Max is a coward, and he wouldn't dare chance having to face you. I imagine he's talking to some slick lawyer right now. Anyway, I'll put the stepladder out on deck. That way, if he shows up, Roberty can climb it and punch him in the nose."

MAX BETTENCOURT WAS WATCHING, and he saw Clint and Vince leave the *Helena Rose*. He knew it, he knew that real men wouldn't stay cooped up on a riverboat babysitting a do-gooder nagging woman and a little kid when they were in a port town with plenty of saloons and brothels. He tried to watch where they went, but it was impossible. All four lanes that led down to the riverfront, and the docks themselves, had been crowded all day long with endless lines of carts and wagons bringing cotton to the waiting steamboats. Hundreds of slaves, roustabouts, shippers, clerks, errand boys, and riverboat crews jostled together in huge crowds. There were passengers, too, for there were a couple of the big luxurious passenger riverboats docked in Memphis. Max had particularly noted the grandiose *Lady Vandivere*, and had spent some of his day planning the trip he would take back to New Orleans on it, after he'd gotten Jeanne's money and had sold her boat.

When he'd left New Orleans, he'd been sick of Sin City, mainly because he'd been in the hospital for three days. He had almost died from alcohol poisoning. The doctor attending him had said sarcastically, "Mr. Bettencourt, if you aspire to be a drunkard, you're going to have to start more slowly. Drink a little all day long. Don't worry, before long you can drink gallons of the swill and it won't kill you."

The doctor didn't know that Max had gone almost six long years without a drink. The Sikhs didn't allow alcoholic beverages in their country. When Max first arrived he'd thought that if he had known that, he wouldn't have come, even though the money was good. Soon, however, he had gone native and chewed khat as practically everyone did in the Afghan Empire, men, women, and children alike. It gave one a supremely euphoric feeling, and also imparted a burst of energy. It had the added effect of making men aggressive, and they all chewed huge mouthfuls of the leaves before they went into battle. When Max had fled Afghanistan, he had only brought with him a small amount of khat that was gone after a few days on the ship. He'd had trouble finding any stimulant to replace it, until he had finally settled on laudanum and whiskey. The laudanum gave him a dreamy feeling of well-being, and the whiskey, once he drank enough of it, made him feel strong and tough.

As for women, as in any place where men lived, there were prostitutes. They were dark-skinned, exotic, dressed in exciting filmy veils and scarves and golden bangles. The Sikh culture regarded prostitution as a criminal offense, punishable on the first offense by cutting off the hands; if any woman was convicted of a second offense, her feet were cut off; and although it was unheard of, on a third offense they were beheaded. Consequently, the prostitutes were very exclusive, always beautiful women, skilled and eager to please—and outrageously expensive. But to Max they were the most alluring women in the world, and he loved them only a little more than he loved guns. He had spent all of his money on prostitutes and arms and fine clothing, and he would have been glad to live out his life in Kashmir. But the Sikhs had lost the war, and he had been forced to flee.

The British mercenaries that had been captured by the British Army had been hung as traitors. Max didn't know what they might do with Americans, and he didn't wait to find out. He stained his skin with walnut juice, killed an old man who lived alone, and took his clothing and the ruby ring that he wore. He went to the docks dressed as a Sikh with the *dulband,* a long black scarf wrapped around his head, and the *kirpan,* the short curved ceremonial sword strapped to his waist. He traveled under the name of Arjan Bhuppal, a fig merchant.

It was late afternoon, a blazing day that promised a late sunset. Max told himself that he wanted a couple, or three or four, more whiskeys before he went to the *Helena Rose.* It never quite came up to his conscious mind that he was waiting for the dark. What he was planning to do was night work. So he took a sip of laudanum and kicked back, the jug of whiskey on the floor beside him, and started rolling a cigarette. He had plenty of time.

JEANNE STOOD AT THE window, watching the docks. Even an hour after sunset, they were still a hive of activity. During cotton season, they often loaded steamers all night long. The marine service set up torches all along the warehouses and shipping offices on Front Street, down the avenues to the riverfront, and all along the docks. The roustabouts worked overtime. In September and October they earned more in one day than in five regular days shipping. All along Front Street, the first street of Memphis high on the bluff, every warehouse and office had lanterns in every window. The figures of men and horses and carts going in and out of them looked like little beetles to Jeanne.

She turned to watch Marvel. She sat on the floor in front of her dollhouse. It had taken both Clint and Vince to move the dollhouse from the main cargo deck up to the cabin, because by the time they had finished it, it had turned into an ornate house, four feet wide and six feet tall, with a steeply pitched roof painted red, and a high chimney made of small stones glued together.

The dollhouse had two stories and six rooms. The first floor had a parlor on one side, with two settees and a sofa, four little tables, and a fireplace with tiny sticks of wood stacked in it. Ezra had even sewed cushions for the settees and sofa, made out of one of Clint's old blue flannel shirts. Jeanne sighed at the poignant sight. Even the simplest reminder of him made her think of how much she loved him.

In the dollhouse, across the hall from the parlor, was the dining room with a table and two chairs, and at the back of the room was the kitchen. Ezra had actually made little cabinets with doors that opened, and Clint had made a little step stove, just like the one in the galley, painted black, with a real piece of curved pipe that went into the wall. Upstairs both Mrs. Topp and Avaymaria had their bedrooms and each had their own sitting rooms. Marvel was enchanted with the dollhouse, and could sit and play for hours with her dolls. Now Jeanne heard her whisper, "Mrs. Topp, may I serve you tea in my sitting room this evening?" And in a different tone, "Why, yes, Avaymaria, I'd be delighted."

Jeanne felt herself grow more peaceful and relaxed than she had been all day long, watching Marvel. There had been no sign of Max Bettencourt, and no sheriff. Maybe Max had just left Memphis when he realized that he had much more to deal with than just bullying his wife.

Marvel was saying, "Perhaps, Mrs. Topp, we may ask our butler Ezra to make us a rice flummery. I do love rice flummery so." Jeanne smiled at Marvel's endearing imitations of adult conversation.

The door opened, and as quick as a snake, Max Bettencourt stepped in and locked the door behind him, and pocketed the key. Jeanne never locked her door, so the key was simply left in the keyhole. "Hello, Wife," he said, casually leaning against the door. "Hello, Daughter."

Jeanne and Marvel froze, then Marvel scrambled to her feet, her eyes as wide as silver dollars. Jeanne ran to stand protectively in front of her. "What are you doing here? Get out!"

"No." He walked over to her desk and opened the drawers. "I know you, Jeanne, I know you've got some money around here. You're just like a little mama rat, always stashing money somewhere in your little nest."

He was slurring his words, his face was a flushed, and his gait was unsteady. Jeanne realized he was drunk. She had given her last dollar to Roberty that morning for peaches. At the time she thought that she should go to the bank and get more cash, for she always kept some on hand. But she didn't go into town, and now she bitterly regretted it, for she thought that if she could give Max some money he might go away. "I don't have any money in here, Max," she said defiantly. "You're always telling me how stupid I am, but I'm not stupid enough to keep cash here."

His head wavering a little, he turned to stare at her. "Quit lying to me. I know you got some pocket money, some working money somewhere. Where is it?"

"Clint keeps a little money for things for the boat. Why don't you ask him for some?" Jeanne retorted. "Now get out of here and leave us alone!"

He spit out, "I'm not going anywhere. I warned you, Jeanne, I'm your husband and what's yours is mine. In fact, *you* are mine. You're my wife and before I'm through you're going to remember that." He stalked over to her, reached around, and grabbed Marvel's arm. "C'mon, you little brat. Get out. And don't you go whining to that old man or the little boy, or they're going to get hurt, you get me, kid?" He hauled her to the door, opened it, and shoved her outside. Then slowly, leering at Jeanne, he locked the door again. "So, you gonna get in that bed or you want me to drag you?"

Jeanne started backing up, and he rushed her. She tried to push him away, but he brutally backhanded her, knocking her to the floor. He reached down, grabbed her shoulder, pulled her up, and shoved her hard toward the bed, tearing her blouse almost completely off her. One final push, and she sprawled across the bed. Finally she came to her senses and started screaming, "No! Get off me, take your filthy—"

The door burst open, completely off the hinges. Clint charged in like a maddened bull. Max Bettencourt's eyes bulged, and he reached in his trouser pocket for his .22 derringer. He managed to pull it out and point it, but he was fumbling, and it was too late. Clint reached him and grabbed his arm to wrench it down. They grappled for a few seconds, and then the gun went off.

Bettencourt flinched, then reeled backwards. Clint made a whipping motion, and ended up with the small gun in his hand, a wisp of smoke rising from one of the barrels. With the other hand he reached for Bettencourt's neck, but Max shrieked, "You shot me! You've killed me!" He fell back across the bed, and quickly Clint looked around to see Jeanne standing across the room, holding Marvel in front of her. Vince and Ezra were standing at the door.

Clint bent over Bettencourt. A lurid red stain was spreading on the left side of his white shirt. Clint tore his shirt open. "Quit crying like a baby, you little weasel. You shot your own idiot self in the shoulder. Get up. Get up!"

He grabbed Max by the back of the collar and hauled him to his feet. "I'm going to bleed to death!" Max yelled, and then started alternately cursing and moaning. Clint pulled him out into the hall, with Ezra and Vince following him. Roberty and Leo were out in the hall. Leo pushed in front of Roberty, every hackle raised, his eyes glowing a baleful yellow, snarling and foaming as soon as Max was propelled through the door.

Clint half-pushed, half-carried Bettencourt down the stairs, across the deck, and down the gangplank. He pushed Max down into the filthy Mississippi River mud, and Max writhed like a beaten dog at his feet, howling. Clint looked down; he was still holding the gun, and with a quick movement he turned and threw it out into the river. Then he growled to Max, "If you ever touch her again, I will kill you and throw you in that river, just like I did your little girlie gun. There's no one on this earth that would miss you, Bettencourt. Now get out of my sight!"

Clint bounded up the steps back to Jeanne's cabin. Jeanne was sitting in one of the armchairs, with Marvel on her lap. Jeanne clutched Marvel close, but her eyes were unfocused and filled with horror. Clint knelt by the chair and tried to take Jeanne's hand that was clasped around Marvel's waist. He couldn't pry it loose, and it was cold and trembling. He looked closer at Jeanne and saw an angry red mark across the ride side of her face, and her lip was bleeding. He went down to the galley and saw Ezra there, already chipping ice and placing it in a muslin cloth, thickly folded with many layers. Clint said harshly, "Where's the brandy?"

"Got it right here," he answered, reaching into his trouser pocket and handing Clint the small brown bottle. Clint grabbed a glass, rushed back to Jeanne, and poured three fingers of alcohol. Jeanne was still staring into space, and now Clint could see that her face and lips were beginning to swell. Anger, dark and vicious, rose in him again, but he swatted it away and said, "Jeanne? Jeanne, listen to me. Drink this. Drink it right now."

She started, then stared up at him. Her hand shaking as if she were palsied, she took the glass and sipped, then took a bigger mouthful and shuddered convulsively when she swallowed.

Marvel's face was buried in Jeanne's shoulder, and she was sobbing fitfully. Clint knelt by them again and started stroking her hair. "It's all right, little girl, it's all right. Jeanne, you're going to be okay. He's gone, and I promise you he's never coming back." He went on talking soothingly and quietly to both of them, lightly putting his arms around them, encircling them protectively.

Ezra came back with a bowl full of ice chips and a small yellow bottle. He wet the muslin cloth with it, muttering to Clint, "Witch hazel. Silly skeery name, but hit's good fer bruises." Gently he patted the ice pack to the corner of Jeanne's mouth and then placed it against her cheek and held it there. Jeanne seemed not to notice.

Finally, bit by bit the frightening blank shocked look went away from Jeanne's face, and she relaxed. She reached up to hold the ice pack herself and murmured, "Thank you, Ezra."

Slowly Marvel's sobs stopped, until she was hiccupping. She sat up and looked around the room mournfully, as if to make sure where she was. Clint kissed her on the cheek and whispered, "Angel girl, don't be scared any more. I promise you that from now on I'm going to make sure nothing like this ever happens again. Okay?"

"Okay," she said weakly.

Clint stood up and for the first time paid attention to the room. Roberty knelt next to Leo by the sagging door, his arms around the dog's neck, tears streaming down his face. Vince stood helplessly by Jeanne's chair, swallowing convulsively, his expression a mix of anger and regret. Ezra was preparing another cloth, soaking it in witch hazel.

Clint said, "Vince. Vinnie! Take care of that door. Roberty, I need you to go make some nice hot cocoa for Marvel. Ezra . . ." He pointed. There was a bloodstain on Jeanne's bed, and a trail of blood smears out the door.

Vince, Ezra, and Roberty all hurried out. Clint held out the glass of brandy to Jeanne. "My sweet love, drink the rest of this, please. You—you scared me. This will help, I promise."

"All right," she said, and took the glass.

Clint watched her take a sip, and then she looked up at him and tried to smile. Clint said in a deep voice, "Jeanne, I love you, and I'm so sorry. Marvel, I love you, and I'm so sorry."

Then he turned and went to the bed. He grabbed the far side of the mattress and folded it up double, then walked out the door with mattress, sheets, quilt, pillows, and all. He took it down to the main cargo deck and laid it out at the muddy riverside. Later he would burn it all.

He went back upstairs, went into his room, and got clean sheets, a blanket, both of his pillows, a light cotton blanket, and picked up his mattress. Returning to Jeanne's room, he made up their bed. "This is mine, I hope you two don't mind. Tomorrow I'll go get you all new things."

"It's fine," Jeanne said, her voice stronger. "Thank you."

Ezra was down on the floor, with a bucket next to him that smelled the faint chemical odor of boracic acid. He was scrubbing the bloodstains with a brush and mopping up the excess water with a rag, muttering darkly to himself.

Vince was already working on the door. Clint stocked the boat with an extra of everything: pipes, fittings, nails, screws, bolts, all kinds of tools, and even such things as window fasteners and hinges and extra doorknobs and locks. When Clint hit the door with his shoulder, it had bent the hinges and the doorplate was shattered. Clint went to help him.

Roberty came in with Marvel's cocoa. She took a sip of it and smiled tremulously at him. "Not too hot. Thank you, Rob."

"Welcome, Marv," he said affectionately. Then he went and joined Ezra, down on his knees scrubbing.

After about half an hour Clint and Vince had the door repaired and the new doorknob and lock replaced. Clint put the new key into the lock and said, "Keep it locked from now on, Jeanne. I swear to you that he's never coming back. But it'll make you feel safer."

Jeanne murmured, "Clint? Clint, do you think—is he—"

"He's not dead," Clint rasped. "Unfortunately. I saw where the bullet hit him, I honestly did, Jeanne. His shoulder's probably all busted up, but he's going to be fine. Now I'm going to help Ezra and Roberty. You two just sit here and relax. Jeanne, another little shot of that brandy wouldn't hurt you a bit, you're still as pale as a ghost."

He went out to help them, for Vince was already starting on one of the steps, where Roberty and Ezra were scrubbing. "Thet varmint's blood must be thinner'n water, he's done made a mess ever step of his sorry way," Ezra grunted.

"Rotgut thins your blood," Clint said with disgust. "I'm surprised his wasn't whiskey-colored."

Ezra was right, there were blood spatters on almost every step, across the cargo deck, and down the gangplank. Clint did catch himself glancing at where he'd thrown him down, for it was a lot of blood. But of course, he'd seen when he threw out the mattress that Bettencourt was gone. Clint said, "Roberty, I need you to do a favor for me.

Go burn that mattress and all of that stuff. You've scrubbed enough, I'll take over."

With a look of fierce joy on his face, Roberty said, "Yes, sir!" and hurried into the engine room to get coal oil and matches.

They had been working for about an hour when four shadowy men appeared at the gangplank. Three of them hung back, while one came forward into the lantern-lit deck. Vince, Ezra, and Clint were all down on their hands and knees, scrubbing. When Clint saw him, he slowly got to his feet.

He was a tall, rangy man with a slouch hat shading his features. He was dressed in dark clothing. Around his waist was a cartridge belt lined with bullets, and at his side was a holster with the handle of a six-gun sticking out of it. A five-pointed silver star was on his chest. He looked up at Clint. "Are you Clint Hardin?"

"Yes, sir."

"I'm Deputy Sheriff Elias Fields. Clint Hardin, I'm placing you under arrest for the attempted murder of Max Bettencourt."

CHAPTER TWENTY-ONE

Jeanne spent a completely sleepless night. She couldn't even bring herself to get into her nightclothes, she just threw herself down on the bed beside Marvel and laid there in misery, the side of her face pounding and her lips stinging. The sheriff had told them that no one could go to the jail with Clint, and that he would be arraigned at nine o'clock in the morning. The only sensible thing Jeanne did that eternal dark night was to decide to go to Nathaniel Deshler's office and try to retain him for Clint's defense. She didn't have any idea if he even practiced criminal law, but she knew that he would help her and Clint. If he couldn't take the case, she was confident that he would know a good lawyer that would.

Just as dawn was breaking Jeanne got up and decided to go to the galley and make herself some coffee. Ezra, Vince, and Roberty were already up, with coffee and tea already made and breakfast almost finished. She sat down wearily on one of the stools, with Leo's head in her lap, and allowed them to wait on her. After a cup of good strong coffee she felt her mind clear somewhat, and was able to eat the fluffy cheese omelet that Ezra had made for her. "I'm going to Nathaniel Deshler's office first thing," she told them. "I don't even know what time his office opens, but I'm going to leave at seven o'clock just in case."

"Miss Jeanne, please allow me to accompany you," Vince said formally. "Clint's like a brother to me, he has been all of our lives. I want to do something to help him."

"I would appreciate your company very much, Vince," Jeanne said warmly. "As far as I'm concerned, we're all like family."

"Miss Jeanne," Ezra said with some difficulty, "I cain't tell you how sorry I am this has happened to you. I'd give anything if I woulda knowed that maggot was aboard. I'm telling you I woulda shot him dead and niver been sorry for it."

All of them had been giving her appalled looks; when Roberty first saw her, tears had come into his eyes though he had quickly dashed them away. Jeanne hadn't looked in the mirror and she realized now that her injuries must be very shocking. She said quietly, "I know that all of you feel guilty. But don't. I certainly don't, and Clint is completely guiltless too. I know—knew Max, and it never occurred to me that he would do something like this. He is the only one who should feel guilty. And—and—" she lightly touched her face, "it looks worse than it feels, I assure you." She rose and said, "Would you heat me some water, Ezra? And when that's ready, please bring Marvel some breakfast."

Jeanne felt better after taking a nice warm bath. Already the morning was like early autumn, cool and damp. She decided to wear her dark blue skirt and black winter shawl with a sky-blue bonnet she had bought, trimmed with black silk rosettes and jetbeads. Now she was glad of the bonnet's deep brim that hid her bruised face.

As she and Vince were leaving the *Helena Rose*, Jeanne was bemused to see Nathaniel Deshler just arriving at the gangplank. He looked as trim and dapper as always, his mustache and beard short and perfectly trimmed, in a gray striped frock coat and maroon waistcoat. He came forward to bow to Jeanne. "Mrs. Bettencourt, how glad I am that I managed to get here early enough to catch you. Good morning, ma'am."

"Good morning, Mr. Deshler," Jeanne managed to say. "Vince, I have the honor of introducing you to Mr. Nathaniel Deshler, Esquire. Mr. Deshler, this is my friend, Vincent Norville."

They exchanged handshakes and Jeanne said, "Mr. Deshler, I'm so surprised to see you. Vince and I were just on our way to your office."

"Good," he said, eyeing Jeanne's face with narrowed, sharp gray eyes. "I assume it was to engage my services, and that is exactly why I'm here, to offer them. I consider it an honor to act as Mr. Hardin's defense attorney."

The three of them went up to Jeanne's cabin, and Roberty brought them coffee and tea. "Ah, I do love black tea," Deshler said with satisfaction. "Now, I know you're wondering how it is that I'm here. As it happens, Sheriff John Latimore is a close friend of mine. The sheriff's office works very closely with my firm. We get the notices of arrest every morning. When I saw that Mr. Hardin had been arrested, I immediately went to the jail and offered my services. I'm glad to say that he engaged me."

"I was going to ask you," Jeanne said. "But I was under the impression that you weren't exactly a criminal lawyer."

He gave her a small neat smile. "I rarely take any criminal clients any more. But I made an exception in this case, since I am acquainted with Mr. Hardin and with you, Mrs. Bettencourt. And please don't worry. Even though it's been many years since I've defended a client with these charges, I assure you I will do my utmost to defend Mr. Hardin. I'm actually a very good lawyer."

"Clint knew that for sure," Vince said firmly. "He told me all about you, Mr. Deshler. He had you checked out up, down, and around when this thing with the *Helena Rose* came up, and he said you've got a fine reputation as a smart, honest man. So what exactly are the charges against him?"

"Assault and battery of Maxwell Bettencourt, and the attempted murder of Maxwell Bettencourt."

"That's tripe!" Vince said heatedly. "That swine was assaulting Jeanne! Clint was only protecting her, and Bettencourt pulled a gun on him and it went off before Clint could take it away from him!"

"I know that, sir," Deshler said quietly. Then he turned his intense gaze on Jeanne. "I can tell you now, Mrs. Bettencourt, that you could very easily have Max Bettencourt charged with assault and battery. The evidence is plain to see."

Jeanne considered for long moments. "I—he is my husband, Mr. Deshler. Would it make any difference if I did charge him? Would it help Clint at all?"

Deshler looked pained. "I'm sorry to say, ma'am, that even if he is found guilty, the only punishment he is likely to receive would be a token fine. As far as it helping Mr. Hardin's case, the reality of it is that Bettencourt's hearing would likely be long after Mr. Hardin's trial is already over, so of course it would be no use to us at all."

Jeanne looked crestfallen. "Max knew this. It's hopeless, isn't it?"

"Not at all," Deshler said crisply. "I have every assurance that Mr. Hardin will be found not guilty of any charges."

"But how?" Jeanne cried.

In a highly uncharacteristic gesture for him, he reached across the table and took Jeanne's hand. "Mrs. Bettencourt, I want you to trust me. I know what I'm doing. Even though I don't know all of the circumstances of the case yet, I do know this: Clinton Hardin is innocent. And I'm going to prove it."

Deshler went with Jeanne and Vince to the arraignment. The district courtroom was grand, indeed. It held two hundred people on the ground floor, and seventy in the gallery. The benches, twenty on each side, were of walnut. The walls were painted a dark gold, and solemn portraits of presidents, congressmen, and judges lined them. At the front was the high dais, the judge's seat, of gleaming mahogany. To the left was the witness stand, on the right was the court clerk's desk. In front of the railing were two long tables, one for the prosecution and one for the defendant. It was an austere and dark and solemn room, and people's voices rang hollowly up to the thirty-foot-high ceiling.

About twenty people, mostly women, but with a couple of jaunty-looking young men, were scattered around. Deshler seated Jeanne and Vince on the front bench, then said, "I'm going to go to Mr. Hardin. Wait for me until after he's arraigned, please."

The judge came in, and one by one the prisoners were brought in. Two toughs were charged with public drunkenness and disturbing the peace, and then they brought Clint in. He glanced at Jeanne and Vince, and smiled as if he hadn't a care in the world. He looked well, too, considering. He wasn't pale, he was clean, and he stood straight and tall. Jeanne longed to rush to him, to at least talk to him, but Deshler had warned them that this arraignment would only take a minute or two at most, and that Clint wouldn't be allowed to speak to them. Still, Jeanne had insisted that she had to at least see him.

The judge read the charges and asked, "How do you plead, Mr. Hardin?"

"Not guilty," he said firmly.

"So entered," the judge said. "Mr. Deshler, you are representing Mr. Hardin?"

"Yes, sir."

"I'd like to set his trial date for next Monday, the tenth. Is that agreeable to you?"

"Yes, Judge Poynter. Thank you, sir."

Immediately after the arraignment Deshler insisted that Jeanne see a doctor. "But I don't need a doctor," Jeanne argued. "I know it looks horrible, but really it doesn't hurt that badly. I know nothing's broken, my teeth aren't loose or anything."

Deshler said, "I told you that charging your husband with assault and battery wouldn't do us much good. What I didn't say was that the fact that he assaulted you and battered you will indeed help. I want a doctor to be able to attest to it. I know a good man, a well-respected man that has a reputation for being forthright and honest. Now don't tell him the whole story, Mrs. Bettencourt. Just answer his questions."

He took her to an obviously very successful Dr. Augustus Hightower, whose office looked more like a governor's office than a doctor's clinic. He looked familiar to Jeanne, and finally she recalled that he was one of the Calvary Choristers. He must know Clint, and Jeanne knew that if he knew Clint at all, he would know that he was innocent.

The next week was extremely stressful for Jeanne. The newspapers had gotten word of the sensational story, and they came to the *Helena Rose* every single day to shout

out questions at anyone that showed their face aboard the boat. Sometimes they were people that looked like ordinary citizens, men dressed in frock coats, well-dressed women, couples who came to goggle at the boat and talk among themselves. Every day for a week some article in the *Memphis Appeal* appeared concerning her, the female riverboat pilot, or the *Helena Rose*, or Clint, entailing his careeer as a master machinist and playing up sensational stories of his astonishing voice.

All parties had been warned not to publicly discuss the case at all, but that didn't stop Max Bettencourt. He gave interviews to all and sundry, bragging about his service in the United States Army and bemoaning the horrors and terrors of being "a prisoner" of the Sikhs. Several articles were written about him, all of them sympathetic. Max Bettencourt was smooth and slyly clever and wholly believable.

The district attorney's office sent two investigators, attorneys who were actually deputized to the sheriff but who wore plain clothes. They crawled all over the boat, and even drew pictures of it, the outside and every single room on the inside. In Jeanne's room they included diagrams of every stick of furniture, every whatnot set around, including Marvel's dollhouse, and even measured the room to the inch.

They questioned every person, and Jeanne balked when they wanted to question Marvel alone. "I won't allow it," she said stiffly. "Unless you have some kind of order from a judge, I will not allow it."

One of them, a coolly professional older man, said, "Mrs. Bettencourt, she is an eyewitness. She may be summoned to testify. I promise you that we will be perfectly courteous to the little girl. Wouldn't it be better if she were exposed to questioning now, without you at her side?"

Jeanne asked Marvel about it. "It's okay, Mama. I can just tell them what happened, I'm not scared." Jeanne relented.

They talked to her for what seemed like a long time to Jeanne. When they came out of the cabin the detective said, "She's a very smart, observant child."

"I'm so proud of you, little girl," she told Marvel. "You're so grown up, and so smart. I'm very, very proud that you're my daughter."

In a small voice, Marvel said, "Thank you, Mama. I didn't mind talking to them, they were nice. But if I had to tell it in court, would my daddy be there?"

Jeanne hugged her hard. "You won't have to tell it in court, my darling. I promise."

No women were allowed to visit the jail, but they did allow Vince to see Clint. He told Jeanne that Clint was cheerful and confident, and that the most complaining he did was that he couldn't take a bath. "But don't they give him water for sponge baths?" she asked.

"Yeah, but he's like some kinda otter when it comes to dunking," Vince answered. "He's got a bathtub in his cabin. I know you didn't know that. Sometimes it takes him hours to heat up enough water for it, but he doesn't care. He's like a drunkard, only with bathing instead of drinking."

Vince also took paper and pen to Clint, and he wrote Jeanne a note every single day. He never was romantic, for he knew that in spite of what had happened, she still felt in her heart that she was married to Max Bettencourt and she would always be mindful of it. His quick notes were always lighthearted, with some encouraging words for her and Marvel.

The three best things that have ever happened in my life are this: That the Lord loves me and saved me. That I met you, Jeanne. That I met you, Marvel. I love you both very

*much. No matter what happens, I will love you
always. One day we'll all be together, a family.
Never doubt it.*

On Friday before the trial on Monday, Nate Deshler
came to the *Helena Rose* with his clerk. "You remember
Mr. Beebe, Mrs. Bettencourt. He's here to document for
me, because I'm going to be conducting my own little
investigation and I don't want to be distracted by trying to
make notes. Mr. Beebe is conversant with the case, and I
have full confidence in him and his discretion."

"Mr. Deshler, I do trust you implicitly," Jeanne assured
him. "Mr. Beebe, you are welcome here. Thank you so
much for helping us."

Deshler went over the boat, but he showed little interest in anything except Jeanne's bedroom. "This is what I
want us to do," he told Jeanne and Vince. "We are going to
act out that night, exactly as it happened, as closely as possible to the real events."

"I want to be Clint," Vince said, grinning.

"Very well," Deshler said with amusement. "Mr. Beebe
will be happy to act as Maxwell Bettencourt."

Mr. Beebe was five feet, five inches tall, with a round
prim face and thick spectacles teetering on the end of a
long thin nose. He rolled his eyes at Deshler's suggestion,
but he gamely took part in the pantomime.

Marvel went through her part, explaining in her high little voice what Max had said to her, and how he had yanked
her to the door and thrown her out. "No, Mr. Beebe," she
said patiently. "You have to grab my arm this way. We'll
play like you yank it hard."

Jeanne started out doing very well, but it became
extremely hard for her to even say out loud what Max had
done to her. Deshler, sitting by the door in one of Jeanne's
desk chairs, said firmly, "Mrs. Bettencourt, I want you to be

very clear about these events. Clear and detailed. I must insist."

"Yes, sir," she gulped, and looked at Beebe helplessly.

He said with feeling, "I'm sorry, Mrs. Bettencourt, but it really is very important."

"All right. Then—" she took Beebe's right hand, lifted it, and said, "He hit me across the face with the back of his hand. And I fell." She went on, relating everything about those awful few minutes.

Vince acted the part of Clint heroically. Ezra and Vince and Roberty and even Leo duly played out their parts, with a continual dire mutterings from Ezra.

Deshler had Vince take Beebe down the stairs, just as Clint had done to Bettencourt, though perhaps not quite as roughly, and he allowed no one to follow them, since Clint and Bettencourt at that time had been alone.

When all the players had returned, he asked, "I want to be perfectly clear about this. The only persons who actually witnessed the shooting were Mrs. Bettencourt, Marvel, Mr. Hardin, and Bettencourt, correct?"

Vince replied, "I followed Clint after we heard Marvel screaming, but he's a lot faster than I am. By the time I got here it was all over but the cryin'." Roberty and Ezra both regretfully told him that by the time they got to Jeanne's cabin Clint was already dragging Max out the door.

Deshler nodded. "This is very important. Did anyone see the gun?" They all looked at each other, then shook their heads mutely. "Ah, the weapon, the weapon," Deshler murmured. "This mysterious, invisible weapon. Very well. Now, what happened when Mr. Hardin returned to the room?"

He made them all go through everything, from Clint stripping Jeanne's bed, Ezra's activities in the galley and attending to Jeanne, from Vince and Clint repairing the door, from all of them scrubbing, and Roberty burning the mattress and bedclothes. He insisted on knowing every single detail, no matter how small, from the time Max had entered Jeanne's room until the deputies had come to arrest Clint.

After that was over he sat down with them all at Jeanne's dining table. Even Leo was allowed to attend, and he laid his head on Jeanne's lap even though they weren't eating. The dog had been especially attentive to Jeanne since that night.

"I'm going to interview each of you separately after we talk," Deshler said. "But first I want to talk to all of you. Normally a defense lawyer will guide his witnesses, he will teach them exactly what to say and how to say it. I do have some suggestions for you, and I'll discuss that when I talk to each of you alone. But just for the record I want to tell you this: you must tell me the absolute, honest, perfect truth about *everything.* Even if you don't understand why I'm asking some question, I want you all to promise me now that you'll tell me the truth."

They all agreed. Deshler went on, "I believe you all are truthful people, anyway, but it helps us all, me included, to say it out loud. Now the only other thing I want to tell you is how you can best help Mr. Hardin with his defense." He gave them one of his rare smiles. "This is most unusual advice for a criminal defense attorney to be giving. My advice to you is this: tell the truth. If the prosecutor comes up with something that you wish he didn't know, don't try to cover. Just answer his questions honestly. Don't volunteer any information; when possible, just answer, 'Yes, sir' and 'No, sir.'" Any sensible man or woman can tell that you, and Mr. Hardin, are honest people. And that is going to be Mr. Hardin's best defense of all."

Ezra scowled. "Thet's all fine and good, Lawyer Deshler, but me and Vinnie here has been called up by the prostecuter's office fer the prostecution! Now I ain't gonna lie, but I've a mind not to answer their fool questions a-tall!"

Jeanne was shocked; she had no idea. She assumed that they hadn't told her so she wouldn't worry.

"I know you have," Deshler said soothingly. "And if you simply refuse to answer the prosecutor's questions, they will put you in jail until you agree to testify. Even if you decide never to answer the questions, then you'll die in jail. And, Mr. Givens, please trust me, and take my advice about your testimony. Answer their questions, and tell the truth. I guarantee you that will help Mr. Hardin much more than you rotting in jail for contempt."

"Well, I got me some contempt, all right," Ezra grunted. "But I b'lieve you, Lawyer Deshler. I'll answer their tomfool questions, and make 'em wish they woulda left me alone."

Then Deshler interviewed Ezra, Vince, and Roberty alone. He returned to Jeanne's room and said, "Mrs. Bettencourt, my client Mr. Hardin has directed me that under no circumstances am I going to be allowed to summon Marvel to testify. At first I argued with him, but now that I've seen what I've seen today, and talked to Mr. Givens and Mr. Norville at length, I must say that I don't think that Marvel's testimony will be crucial to Mr. Hardin's defense."

Jeanne asked hesitantly, "You don't think that the prosecutor's office may summon her?"

"I doubt it. In my opinion, she would be a very credible witness for the defense, not the prosecution. The prosecutor is a very intelligent man, and from her statement that she gave to his investigators, and their opinion of her, he's going to realize that Marvel could do some serious damage to the way people perceive Mr. Bettencourt." He added wryly, "That's why I would really like to call her for

Mr. Hardin's defense. But I cannot, since he's forbidden me to. And ma'am, I would never do such a thing unless you agreed. I hope you know that."

"I do," Jeanne said with overwhelming relief. "Thank you, Mr. Deshler."

"You're welcome, ma'am. Now, let me explain something to you about Cyrus Jameson, the district attorney. I know him very well. He's somewhat older than I, I would imagine he's about in his mid-fifties. He's a fair man, but he's strict. He got elected because he is a no-nonsense law-and-order man, and the major reason he won his election is because he promised to clean up the docks, it's sort of his mission. He works very hard, and harshly prosecutes all violent crimes committed on the docks. And I have to say that he is very old-fashioned about women. He believes that their place is in the home, by their husband's side, caring for the children, and never airing their opinions or views in public."

Jeanne sighed. "He's going to think that I'm a loose, cheap, tawdry woman. But then I suppose that most people do."

"That's possible. You are unorthodox, Mrs. Bettencourt. When a person differs in the slightest from the norm—particularly women—people have a tendency to believe the worst. But you knew, did you not, when you decided to pilot the *Helena Rose*, that you would be subject to all kinds of gossip about you and your character?"

"Yes, I did."

"And when you decided to pilot the *Helena Rose*, did you feel that it was the right thing to do?"

"Yes, I do. I still do. I believe it was a gift from God, for both me and Marvel."

"And your character. Have you done anything at all unladylike, or as you said, loose, cheap, or tawdry?"

"No, I have not."

"Are you and Clint Hardin lovers?"

Jeanne drew in a sharp breath. "What? No! That is—I— we love each other, we're betrothed. I mean, we were until I found out that Max is alive. But no, we are not intimate, at all!"

Deshler nodded knowingly. "Get it out of your system. You're going to be asked that question in front of a lot of people, Mrs. Bettencourt. Do not react as you've done just now. Please remember what I told you. Answer the question, tell the truth, but never volunteer information to the prosecutor. When Cy Jameson asks you, in whatever form, if you and Mr. Hardin are physically intimate, say, 'No, we are not and never have been.' You have no obligation at all, either legal or moral, to offer or volunteer information of any kind. I wanted you to comprehend that completely, that's why I was so impertinent."

"Mr. Deshler, you couldn't be impertinent if you had a tutor to teach you," Jeanne said gratefully. "I'm beginning to understand that 'tell the truth' sounds very simple, but it's really not, in a court of law. I promise you I will think about it more until the trial."

"Good. Now, there is one more thing that I must tell you, Mrs. Bettencourt." He hesitated for a moment, then seemed to make up his mind and went on, "I had a telegram from George Masters. He offered to engage me for Mr. Hardin's defense. And he requested that I call him as a character witness."

Jeanne was so shocked that her mouth actually opened a bit. "I had forgotten completely about poor George! Oh, I am awful! But he offered to pay for *Clint's* defense? They weren't—exactly—good friends. And he offered to be a character witness for Clint? He hardly knows him!"

"I refused his offer of payment, of course, as Mr. Hardin had already engaged me," Deshler answered. "It was, I must say, extremely charitable of Mr. Masters, under the circumstances. Oh, yes, I do know the circumstances, Mrs. Bettencourt. George Masters has been a friend of mine for many years. And I was obliged to tell him that it would do far more harm than good for him to act as a character witness."

"Harm?" Jeanne said with confusion.

"Yes. Because you see, Mr. Masters offered to be a character witness for you, Mrs. Bettencourt. He understands, as perhaps you do not, that you will be on trial, and will be judged in the court of public opinion, just as surely as Mr. Hardin will."

CHAPTER TWENTY-TWO

On Monday morning, the day of Clint's trial, Jeanne's face was almost back to normal. The swelling had gone down both on her cheek and mouth. The only evidence left was a faint yellow spot on her right cheekbone, and a very small cut remained on her lip. She was relieved. It was going to be hard enough to be seen in public—in fact, to be a public spectacle—without her face looking all beat up. Perhaps it was vanity, but somehow it made her feel less like hiding.

Shannon Byrne, a sassy, redheaded Irish lass, watched Jeanne searching her face in the mirror. "You're as pretty as a spring day, Miss Jeanne. A little pale, but oh how I wish I had that face! And your hair. Mine looks like a house afire."

Jeanne had been planning to ask Mrs. O'Dwyer to babysit Marvel during the trial, but she had found out that Mr. Deshler had called her as a witness, for some reason. Deshler hadn't told her much about Clint's defense, explaining to her that her obvious innocence and lack of inside knowledge would be a plus. She didn't understand that, but she believed him. So Vince had suggested that Shannon Byrne, the wife of his and Clint's close friend, Duffy Byrne, would make an excellent babysitter. Shannon was twenty years old, lively and cheery, and she was seven months pregnant. She had promised that Marvel could feel the baby next time he or she kicked, and Marvel had been delighted.

Roberty had begged Jeanne to let him attend the trial. At first she had refused, for she knew that some of the testimony would be graphic. But Roberty was so upset, so anxious to help, that finally she had changed her mind and gave him her permission to attend. Living on his own, he already had seen much worse things anyway. And it was sad but true, Jeanne realized. It was different from Marvel; Roberty was a boy.

Finally it was time, and Jeanne finished dressing in her brand-new outfit. Mr. Deshler had asked what clothing she would be wearing to the trial, and she had shown him her maroon skirt and capelet and bonnet and her skirts and blouses. He had advised her to buy another dress similar to the maroon, only not quite so dour. She'd bought a moss-green dress, the skirt with three flounces, and it had long full sleeves, the cuffs trimmed with white lace. The capelet was earth brown with green and white piping. She'd bought a brown bonnet trimmed with green satin ivy leaves and white and peach-colored rosettes. With satisfaction she reflected that she looked as Mr. Deshler had said, "ladylike and not too rich, not too poor, not too frilly, not too plain."

She went downstairs and she, Vince, Ezra, and Roberty left for the courthouse. A crowd of people were gathered on the docks at the *Helena Rose*, and Jeanne was very grateful to Nathaniel Deshler for sending his carriage for them. Journalists shouted out, "Captain Jeanne! Give us a smile, will you? You gonna tell us all your secrets in court? How are you and Clint the Flint doing? Have you seen him since he got arrested? C'mon, give us something we can print, Cap'n Jeanne!"

"Clint the Flint?" Jeanne asked after they got into the carriage.

"Clint the Flint Fist is his whole name," Vince said. "And I think Bettencourt got off real lucky, the little squealin' pig. I've seen Clint do a whole lot worse to a man than getting a little scratch on his shoulder."

All around the courthouse were horses, buggies, carts, and carriages, and a huge crowd of people. The deputies cleared them away from the walk up to the steps. As Jeanne alighted from the carriage she saw with a sinking heart that most of them looked at her with expressions of disdain. There were a lot of women, many with their husbands, and the looks they gave her were much more sour than the men. For the most part they were silent, and for Jeanne, walking with Vince, it was like running a gauntlet. She kept her eyes straight ahead. There were murmurings and whisperings, and she distinctly heard one woman say, "You can see she's a tramp." Jeanne didn't know it, but behind her Roberty stuck out his tongue and made a horrible face at the woman.

At the double doors to the courtroom a deputy said, "Mrs. Bettencourt, we're keeping the courtroom clear until all of the witnesses arrive. You all will be seated on the front bench, just behind the defendant's table."

They went into the courtroom. Two clerks were sitting at the court officers' table, and two bailiffs stood in front of two doors behind the judge's dais. Two more bailiffs stood at the entrance doors. Mrs. O'Dwyer was sitting on the first bench, along with another lady that Jeanne didn't know. On the second bench behind sat the Gayoso housekeeper,

Mrs. Wiedemann, and Dr. Augustus Hightower with a stiff, proud-looking woman that Jeanne assumed must be his wife.

Jeanne sat by Mrs. O'Dwyer, with Roberty, Vince, and Ezra on her left. Jeanne had just started greeting Mrs. O'Dwyer when there was a stir outside in the foyer. Evidently Max had arrived, and he was shouting answers to questions at the crowd. With dread, Jeanne sat staring straight ahead until he got to the prosecutor's table. His left arm and chest were heavily bandaged, his sky-blue velvet frock coat hanging by one shoulder. His face looked pale and drawn, but his blue eyes were bright and he still was an attractive man. He was accompanied by a short, bowlegged man with thinning dark hair and a raggedy black mustache. Bettencourt looked straight at Jeanne and gave her a big shark's grin. Jeanne looked away.

Then the bailiffs opened the doors and let the crowd in. It was like a stampede of cattle. The bailiffs kept calling, "Stop shoving, people! Stop that pushing, or you'll be heading outside instead of inside!"

From the entrance hall, on both sides, the hammering of people running up the stairs to the gallery thundered throughout the building. As the crowds settled down, Jeanne had no desire to look behind, but she could see people in the gallery. It was interesting, she thought, that the middle-class and Quality must be sitting in the courtroom, for every person in the gallery appeared to be the lower classes: roustabouts and their wives, tradesmen, charwomen, shop clerks, maids, and several very flashy women who obviously didn't have what might be called regular employment.

The door opened behind the dais, and the district attorney, Cyrus Jameson, came in and went to sit with Max. He was a big barrel-chested, round-gutted, imposing man with a shiny bald pate with a black fringe of hair and large, round dark eyes. He turned to look at Jeanne and nodded politely to her.

Then Nathaniel Deshler came in, followed by Clint. There was a distinct murmur from the crowd. Clint's hands weren't bound, and Jeanne saw that he was wearing a plain black frock coat, a gray waistcoat, and a white shirt with a black string tie. He looked amazingly handsome, towering over the average-sized Deshler, his shoulders broad and ruler-straight, his hair black and glossy, his features tanned and rugged. He smiled at Jeanne and the others as unselfconsciously as if they were on the deck of the *Helena Rose*. When he took his seat he was right in front of Jeanne.

From the gallery above one woman's high-pitched nasal voice was heard clearly. "Ooh, ain't he just dee-licious!" Laughter sounded, and also male grumbles.

The jury came in, and as Jeanne knew they would be, twelve men "good and true"—all of them average-looking men, farmers, shopkeepers, clerks, tradesmen. All of them stared at Clint, but not as long as they stared at Jeanne. She met their gazes equably, and in good time turned to look straight ahead.

After a few more minutes the bailiff stood in front of the dais and shouted, "Oyez, oyez, oyez! All rise for the Honorable Judge Eugene Poynter, presiding over the Phillips County Criminal Court, State of Tennessee!" The distinct rumble of two hundred seventy persons rising to their feet sounded, and Judge Poynter entered the courtroom.

He was of average height and build, but he had a distinguished look, with beautiful thick wavy silver-white hair, a wide brow, and hawk-like blue eyes. He was wearing a simple but beautifully tailored suit, and took his seat above them all with easy patrician grace. The bailiff said, "All be seated. Court is now in session."

Judge Poynter read the particulars of the charges against Clint, which carefully outlined the relationships between Clinton Hardin, Maxwell Bettencourt, and Jeanne Bettencourt. Then he asked formally, "Mr. Jameson, is the prosecution ready?"

"Yes, sir."

"Mr. Deshler, is the defense ready?"

"Yes, sir."

"Mr. Jameson, you may make your opening statement."

Cy Jameson rose, walked assuredly to the jury box, and rested his well-manicured hand on the railing in front of them. As he talked he turned alternately to address the jury and the courtroom. He was a charismatic man, and an expert public speaker.

"Your Honor, gentlemen of the jury, and ladies and gentlemen in the courtroom, good morning. This is a simple case. Some of the time lines of events in the lives of the participants may be unusual, but the events of the night that Mr. Bettencourt was shot are all clear and factual and easily understood."

He frowned darkly, and with dismay Jeanne saw at least ten of the male jurors frown right along with him, as if they were mirroring him. Jameson continued, "A soldier, an honorable, oft-promoted, decorated soldier returns from a terrible war. His first and only thoughts are to see his beloved wife, whom he had left with sorrow but with promises between them of undying love and faithfulness. He is as eager as a man can be to rejoin his family, his wife and the child that he has never seen. He finds them, and is overjoyed at the thought of reuniting with them. It's been long lonely years that they've been parted.

"When he visits his wife, full of loving anticipation and joy, he finds only sorrow. She cruelly spurns him, and not only that; she has completely turned his daughter, his only flesh-and-blood, against him. And even worse, he finds that she's living in sin with another man. That man is Clinton Hardin. Mr. Bettencourt comes to understand that his wife and Mr. Hardin are so greedy that they have no intention of letting Mr. Bettencourt reclaim his wife, for they had no wish to share their love nest, a profitable steamboat called the *Helena Rose*, with him.

"The tragic ending to this story is that Mr. Bettencourt visits his wife, and Mr. Hardin, his wife's lover, finds them together and tries to murder him. It is only by the grace of God that Mr. Bettencourt is alive today. But you will find, gentlemen, that the act that caused his wound has nothing to do with grace, or God. Mr. Clinton Hardin shot Maxwell Bettencourt because of jealousy over a woman, and because of money. He is guilty, and I know that you will find him guilty."

Jeanne's hands were shaking when Jameson finished, and her cheeks felt as though they were close to hot flames. She dropped her head, grateful for her bonnet. She saw a small hand reach over and touch hers, then squeeze it gently. Roberty whispered, "Don't be sad, Miss Jeanne."

The judge said, "Mr. Deshler, you may make your opening statement for the defense."

Nate Deshler rose and straightened his waistcoat. He made a complete contrast to Cy Jameson, but it was not unflattering to him. He was stately and dignified and naturally soft-spoken. When he raised his voice to be heard, it didn't sound bombastic, his voice and air were dignified and confident and sure.

"Good morning, Your Honor, gentlemen of the jury, and ladies and gentlemen.

"My esteemed opponent, Mr. Jameson, said that this case was simple. It is not. This case is far from simple. Mr. Bettencourt's story is that a jealous, greedy lover came in when he was visiting his wife and shot him. None of these things are true.

"First of all, there is a grave question that must be settled during the course of this case. Is Mr. Maxwell Bettencourt truly the lawful husband of Jeanne Langer Bettencourt, with all the rights and privileges of a husband? That is not a simple question, and it has no simple answer. I contend that Mr. Bettencourt was not, in all particulars, Jeanne Bettencourt's true husband. When you comprehend this, you will see that it dramatically changes the picture of the scene on that night. In fact, you will see that Clint Hardin shouldn't be on trial for assault here today. Max Bettencourt should be.

"Secondly, Mr. Clint Hardin and Mrs. Jeanne Bettencourt are not now, and never have been, lovers. They have never been physically intimate. This will be illustrated to you so that you will have no doubts.

"Thirdly, Mr. Clint Hardin is neither jealous, nor greedy. His sole motive for his actions was to defend Mrs. Bettencourt from a brutal attack.

"And that brings me to my last point. Mr. Clint Hardin did not shoot Mr. Max Bettencourt. And I will prove it."

This grave and sure pronouncement by Deshler had a hubbub of a response from the courtroom. Deshler sat back down and Jeanne read Clint's lips as he leaned over and said, "Well done, sir. Thank you."

Judge Poynter said, "Mr. Jameson, you may proceed."

"Thank you, Your Honor. For my first witness I call Mr. Maxwell Bettencourt."

Max rose and went to the witness chair. The same young nasal woman's voice floated on the air: "He's right purty too. Don't she nab the fine ones, though?" This time the laughter was loud and raucous.

Judge Poynter was not amused. He pounded his gavel once, hard. "I will have order in my court! All you people be quiet. Especially you, young lady!" His gaze swept the gallery, which fell utterly silent. As soon as he looked away the girl peeped, "Yessir, Yer Honor." Again the laughter, shorter and much quieter this time.

Judge Poynter looked as grave as death, but he merely said, "Proceed, Mr. Jameson."

Cy Jameson stood by the witness box, to the right of Max, so that Max could see the jury and the entire courtroom clearly. He made a good, credible witness, speaking to the men in the jury box, gesturing with manly grace, looking out over the crowd, occasionally making eye contact with a listener whose face showed sympathy.

Jameson said, "Mr. Bettencourt, what I want you to do is to tell your story to the court, as simply and honestly as you have told me. I will guide you with questions, but I want you to feel free to give full and complete answers. Please begin by telling us of your life in the United States Army."

Max told about how he had lied about his age at sixteen, telling the army that he was eighteen, because he was so anxious to serve his country. He had served in the Indian Territories for seven of the eight years of his career, earning two decorations for bravery, and field promotions until he reached the rank of captain in the artillery. "Then, in 1846, I was assigned to Fort Smith, Arkansas. That was when I met Miss Jeanne Langer."

Jameson said, "Tell us about your courtship of Miss Langer."

"I fell in love with her the first time I saw her," he said quietly, apparently so poignantly. "She was beautiful. She still is. Anyway, she was young then, only sixteen, but she was a polished, intelligent, sweet, bright young woman. The first time I ever set eyes on her she was on the deck of her father's riverboat, the *Pearl*. She had flowers in her hair, and she was wearing a bright yellow dress, and she looked like sunshine in spring. I wrangled an introduction to her father, the captain and pilot of the boat. Then I made friends with Miss Langer. I went slowly, because she was innocent and pure, and I was older and had certainly seen more of the world. But over time I showed her how much I loved her, and she fell in love with me. Because of her youth, her parents wanted us to wait to be married, and we were engaged for a year and a half. I didn't mind. I loved her so much that I would have waited all my life for her, if she'd wanted me to. But she didn't. We married when she was seventeen."

"Now please tell us something of your marriage, your life together, and how it came about that you went to war," Jameson said encouragingly.

"I resigned from the army just before Jeanne and I married, and I went to Memphis to get a job. I found work at the Victory Ironworks and Armory, as an artillery specialist and gunsmith. It was hard at first, because my army pay wasn't enough that I had much saved back, and though my pay at the ironworks was better, it would take awhile for me to be able to support us in some comfort. But Jeanne's father was very generous with us, and gave us some money to help us get started. We got a small upstairs two-room apartment in Memphis, and I worked hard. We were very happy. Jeanne was young, but she was a joyful, loving wife, and I adored her more and more every day. We were ecstatic when we found out that Jeanne was expecting our first child."

Here he sighed and looked deeply regretful. "I'm afraid that I found the civilian life very difficult, however. From the time I was just a small child I wanted to join the army, and I loved that adventurous, exciting life. I admit that I missed it. I'm afraid that at heart I am a true soldier."

"True, and brave, a warrior," Cy Jameson intoned. "And is that why you left Mrs. Bettencourt, to return to the military life?"

"Oh, no," Max said, appalled. "I would never have left her for such a selfish reason. No, it was all because I found out that if I joined the Sikh Army in what was called the Anglo-Sikh War, to train their artillery, I could earn a fortune. I was told that the maharajah would pay trained artillerists four hundred dollars a month! At the armory I was making *five hundred dollars a year!* When I told Jeanne this, she was hesitant, but then she saw that I could work overseas for only six months and earn over two thousand dollars. When she realized how much that would help us, she encouraged me to join. We believed that I would be gone, at most, for only eight months, a month's travel each way—paid by the maharajah, you understand—and six months spent training the Sikh artillery. It seemed like a dream come true, especially for a young couple just starting a family. Jeanne and I were devastated at being parted, but we both believed it was for the best. We promised each other, as when we had taken our solemn wedding vows, to love, honor, and cherish the other, unless death should part us."

Dreamy sighs were audible from several ladies in the courtroom. Cy Jameson paused for effect, then said in a low, sympathetic voice, "But, Mr. Bettencourt, all of your dreams for this venture turned into a nightmare, did they not?"

"It was a nightmare from the first day I set foot in that godforsaken land," Max said grimly. "We had been deceived by the maharajah's emissaries. When we arrived to join the army, we virtually became prisoners. We were kept under armed guard night and day. Our living quarters were worse than prison cells. For the first two months, we received not one rupee in pay. Only after I made a plea to our colonel on behalf of all of us American and British soldiers that were trapped there, did we begin to receive a hundred rupees a month, which was about twelve dollars in American money. It was a pittance, for we were half-starved, we had no uniforms provided, and their only concession for our living accommodations was a single crude tent for the thirteen of us.

"They are a cruel, sly, and sophisticated people. We were given chits each month, IOUs if you will, from the maharajah, showing that he owed us the balance, basically three hundred and eighty-eight dollars, each month and would be paid this balance at the end of our service. Of course, we all knew that we would never be paid that money," he said bitterly.

"I was half crazy when I found out I wouldn't be able to send money to Jeanne and our unborn child," he continued dramatically. "And it was even worse, for me, when I found out that we had no access to any mail at all. I wrote Jeanne long letters, full of love and begging her forgiveness for my stupidity. But none of them could ever be mailed.

"And of course, we were also deceived when we were told that we could enlist in the *Khalsa*—the Sikh Army— for any period we chose. I had enlisted for six months; I ended up a virtual prisoner there for six years. The Sikhs lost the war, and I had to flee the country secretly to avoid being executed. I came home with no glory, no honorable satisfaction as that of a soldier who knows he has done his job well, and certainly with no money. All I had left were the clothes on my back—and my family."

From here on out Max's story closely followed Cy Jameson's opening statement. He spoke movingly of his joy at finding Jeanne and Marvel, and of his devastation when she spurned him. He even teared up, and wiped his eyes. "All I wanted was my loving Jeanne, and to show my daughter how much I had missed her and loved her," he said in a ragged voice. "Jeanne grievously wounded my heart, and then that brute tried to shoot me in the heart. He dragged me off the boat and threw me down in the mud, wounded and bleeding. He threw his gun in the river and then he snarled at me, "You're a dead man, Bettencourt, and no one on this earth will know or care who killed you. Now get out of my sight!"

Max was smooth, and articulate, and emotional in a manly way. He was a magnificent liar. Very slight murmurs of sympathy punctuated his testimony, and the men's glances at the back of Jeanne's head grew more disdainful, and the women's stares became full of disgust. Jeanne kept her eyes glued on Max every moment. Her eyes grew wider, her expression more and more astonished and shocked with every passing moment. She wasn't aware of the stares of the crowd behind her. And she wasn't aware that the gentlemen jurors watched her carefully. Her honest shock was glaringly apparent. Some of them had noticed that though Max spoke skillfully to the crowd in general, he had not once looked directly at either Jeanne nor Clint. Some jurors began to look at Max Bettencourt with a more critical eye.

"Thank you, Mr. Bettencourt, I know how difficult this is for you," Cy Jameson said fervently, and took his seat.

"Mr. Deshler, are you ready to cross-examine?" Judge Poynter asked.

"Yes, Your Honor, thank you." He rose and stood to Max's side, his feet wide apart in a confident stance, his hands behind his back. His tone was exquisitely polite. "Mr. Bettencourt, can you produce any corroborating witnesses that know of your experiences in the Punjab?"

"No, sir. As I said, I was forced to flee the country secretly, and I made my way out alone. I don't know anything about my comrades."

"No documentation? No papers at all?"

"No, sir."

"And so we have only your word concerning each event, each circumstance, of those six years you were away?"

"Well, yes, I suppose so, sir. But I'm not lying, I have no reason to lie. I've told you the honest truth!"

"Please just answer my questions, Mr. Bettencourt. Unlike Mr. Jameson, I don't wish you to *embroider* your story in any way," Deshler said calmly, allowing the implication to sink in as he paced a step, then returned to his former place.

"Let's go back further, then, and talk about May of 1849, when you left your pregnant wife to go fight for the Sikhs. You testified that the maharajah paid your travel expenses?"

"Yes, sir."

"Then why, sir, did you take the last penny out of your wife's banking account and leave her penniless and destitute while you merrily went off to gain fame and glory?" Deshler suddenly barked.

"But—but no, that was our money! It was mine just as much as it was hers! And I had to have some money to travel on. The Sikhs paid for ship's passage, but that didn't include anything like food and—and—supplies!" Abruptly he calmed down and said reasonably, "And I told you, Jeanne encouraged me to go. She didn't want me to go halfway across the world with no money, she's not like that. At least, she wasn't like that back then."

"Mr. Kurt Langer, Mrs. Bettencourt's father, gave her two hundred dollars upon her marriage to you, isn't that right?" Deshler said.

"That was her dowry! It was *our* money!"

"It was put into a banking account at Memphis Bank and Trust in the name of Max and Jeanne Bettencourt, correct?"

"Yes! Both of us!"

"During the year of 1848, the sum of fifty dollars was withdrawn from that bank account in small increments. Each time any monies were withdrawn, the withdrawal slip was signed by both you and Mrs. Bettencourt, since the account was in both of your names. Is that correct?"

"Yes, but—"

"Yes, or no, Mr. Bettencourt. Now, I have a fair certified bank copy of a withdrawal made on May 10, 1849, for the sum of $151.21, which closed out the account. Please tell the court who signed this withdrawal slip." He flung the piece of paper in Max's face.

A scowl crossed his smooth features as he barely glanced at it. "I did, and I had every right to do it. I needed that money!"

Deshler snatched the paper back. "One hundred fifty-one dollars and thirty-two cents," Deshler repeated in outrage. "You deserted your wife and unborn child, and you couldn't even leave them a dollar and thirty-two cents!"

Jameson jumped up and thundered, "I object, Your Honor! My esteemed opponent is not asking the witness a question, he's testifying himself!"

Judge Poynter opened his mouth, but Nate Deshler said smoothly, "I beg your pardon, Your Honor, gentlemen of the jury. I am finished questioning this witness at this time, though I do reserve the right to call him again if I absolutely must listen to his drivel."

"Mr. Deshler," Judge Poynter said ominously, "you are pushing me, and I don't like it."

"I am so sorry, Your Honor," Deshler said lightly, and resumed his seat.

"I'm warning you, be careful, Nate," Judge Poynter warned him. "Now, Mr. Jameson, will you call your next witness?"

"I call Dr. Ernest Slattery." The man who trotted up to the witness stand was the short shabby man that had come into the courtroom with Max. He was sworn in, and Jameson said, "Dr. Slattery, please tell us where you reside and practice medicine, and of the events of the night of September 2."

He stroked his mustache with his forefinger, a habitual gesture that made the scanty black growth look greasy and limp. "My office is on Front Street, and I live above it. About nine o'clock that night a roustabout came running upstairs and banged on the door, screaming fit to wake the dead. They'd brought a man who had been shot in the chest, and was dying. I hurried downstairs and the two roustabouts brought Mr. Bettencourt into my office.

"His shirt and coat were covered with blood, and I thought for sure he would die before I could examine him," he said sadly. "And he was moaning fit to rend your heart. 'All I wanted was to talk to her,' says he. 'I just wanted to see her, my own sweet wife, my darling daughter! Oh, how I wish, before I die, that I could kiss her sweet lips one last time!' And such as that."

"Mr. Bettencourt believed he was mortally wounded," Jameson said gravely. "But he was not, of course."

"No, sir. I found upon my examination that he had been shot in the chest, but it was somewhat above his heart. It was a through-and-through wound. That means that the bullet entered his chest and came out behind. I stopped the two wounds bleeding, and then bandaged him up. After I made sure he understood that he was going to be all right, I told him that he ought to have the villain that shot him arrested. He was pretty tired, and in a lot of pain, and it seemed like he didn't much care about anything, he was so grieved. But he finally agreed, and I had the roustabouts go fetch the sheriffs."

"Thank you, Dr. Slattery," Jameson said and resumed his seat.

"Your witness, Mr. Deshler," Judge Poynter said.

Deshler asked, "Dr. Slattery, during all of Mr. Bettencourt's long lament, did he tell you that he had been shot with a .22?"

Slattery blurted out, "Yes. I mean, I guess he did. No, I'm not sure. I figured it was a .22, because the diameter of the entry wound was small."

"Again, Dr. Slattery. Did Mr. Bettencourt tell you he was shot by a .22?"

"Uh—I can't remember."

"That's unfortunate, it's extremely important, and the fact that you can't remember makes you a very poor witness, Dr Slattery. Are you certain that you have absolutely no recollection of how you knew that the wound was made by a .22?"

"I was busy attending Mr. Bettencourt. I just can't remember that one little thing," he snapped.

"Very well. Now, about the wound itself. Please tell the court the exact point of entry and exit of the bullet."

He sniffed and replied haughtily, "It entered between the fourth and fifth left ribs, nicked the posterior fourth rib, then exited through the scapula."

"Show us, please. Just point to it on your body."

He sighed with exaggerated impatience. "It hit him here," he said, pointing high on the left of his chest. And I can't reach all the way around to point, Mr. Deshler, but it came out back here." Vaguely he waved toward the back of his left shoulder.

"Thank you, Dr. Slattery. That is all for now."

Jeanne had trouble analyzing this witness's testimony. In the first place, it was extremely distracting, the way he twitched and twiddled with his mustache. But she had noticed one thing. The doctor wore a heavy square-cut ruby ring set in gold on his right middle finger. Jeanne knew that it had been the ring Max had worn on his left pinky.

The next witness the prosecutor called was Deputy Sheriff Elias Fields, the tall, coolly professional deputy that had placed Clint under arrest. He told the court who he was, and that he was the arresting officer.

Jameson said, "Deputy Fields, you reported to Dr. Slattery's office to take Max Bettencourt's statement on the night of September 2, correct?"

"Yes, sir."

"And what was Mr. Bettencourt's statement?"

"He told me that he was visiting his wife, and that a man named Mr. Clinton Hardin had shot him, intending to kill him. He told me that I could find Mr. Hardin on the steamboat *Helena Rose*."

"Mr. Bettencourt's statement was that short and spare? He didn't say anything else?"

"Yes, he said quite a bit more."

With exaggerated patience Jameson asked, "Then would you please tell the court what Mr. Bettencourt said?"

Blank-faced the deputy replied, "I can't repeat it word for word, Mr. Jameson, but I'll try to be as clear as I can. He said that he loved Jeanne with all his heart, and he loved Marvel with all his heart, and all he was trying to do was come back to his dear love and his sweet daughter, and Clint Hardin that villain, and some other descriptive words I won't repeat, that was doing things to his wife that I won't repeat, tried to murder him, and he wanted Mr. Hardin arrested and hanged and dead as a dog."

"Yes, thank you," Jameson said hurriedly. "When you went to the *Helena Rose*, you did find Clint Hardin there, and you did place him under arrest. Did Mr. Hardin protest at his arrest?"

"No, sir."

"Did he say anything at all in his own defense? Did he protest his innocence?"

"No, sir."

Jameson nodded with satisfaction. "Please tell us what you saw when you arrived on the *Helena Rose*, Deputy."

"I first saw a young boy burning something, a big bonfire, at the foot of the gangplank. I boarded the boat, and I saw Mr. Norville and Mr. Givens down on their hands and knees, scrubbing the main cargo deck. Mr. Hardin was down on his hands and knees scrubbing the top of the landing stage."

"And you arrested Mr. Hardin at that time, and he was taken away by three other deputies, and you remained behind on the *Helena Rose* to question the other two men and the boy, correct?"

"Yes, sir."

"And what was the nature of your questioning, and the result?"

"I asked Mr. Norville what they were doing. Both he and Mr. Givens said that they were cleaning up Mr. Bettencourt's blood from the boat. I then observed that there was a trail of blood still remaining down the gangplank. Then I questioned Roberty, the young boy who was tending the fire. He told me that he was burning Mrs. Bettencourt's mattress, sheets, quilts, and pillows because Mr. Bettencourt had bled on them. He said that no one, especially 'Captain Jeanne', wanted any reminder that Max Bettencourt had ever been on that boat."

"They were systematically destroying the evidence that Mr. Hardin had, for all they knew, murdered Max Bettencourt," Jameson intoned.

"Objection," Deshler said mildly. "Mr. Jameson is not questioning the witness, he is testifying, Your Honor."

"Objection sustained."

Jameson lifted his head and said quietly, "I need ask no further questions of this witness."

Judge Poynter said, "Your witness, Mr. Deshler."

Deshler rose. "I have no questions for this witness, Your Honor."

"Very well. Mr. Jameson?"

"I call for my next witness, Mr. Vincent Norville."

Vince sauntered up to the witness stand, swore to tell the truth, sat down in the witness chair, and stared up at Cy Jameson as suspiciously as if he were a cheating poker player. "Clint didn't shoot that fool," he said loudly.

Judge Poynter pounded his gavel angrily, and Jameson shouted, "I object!"

"He's your witness, Cy, you can't object," Judge Poynter rasped. "Everyone simmer down! I won't have this silly hullaballooing in my courtroom!" He pounded his gavel twice more.

When the laughter quieted down Jameson said, "Your Honor, this man is a very reluctant witness. I'm going to beg your indulgence if I am forced to question him in a more leading manner, with more assumption than is conventional."

"I'm fully cognizant of the situation, Mr. Jameson, and you may question the witness as you see fit, within the bounds of the rule of law. Mr. Norville, you will answer the questions put to you, and that is all. Another outburst like that one and I'll slap you in jail for contempt."

"Yes, sir," Vince said blandly.

"Now, Mr. Norville. You've been friends with Mr. Hardin for a long time, haven't you?" Jameson asked.

"Yes, sir."

"You know him very well, as well as anyone?"

"Yes, sir."

"And so," Jameson said heavily, "you know that he is a violent, brutal man, correct?"

"No, sir."

"He has beaten men severely. Eleven men, in fact. In the last fight he had, he almost blinded a man, did he not?"

"No, sir."

"He's a fighter, isn't he? He participates in brutal bare-knuckle fistfights, vicious knock-down free-for-all brawls, doesn't he?"

"He is an athlete in the sport of fistic competition. He is an expert pugilist."

"That's simply a sly way of saying he's a savage fighter, isn't it?"

"No, sir."

Jameson was clearly frustrated, so he moved on. "Mr. Norville, Mr. Hardin is well-known as what is called a 'ladies' man.' Has he—"

"Your Honor, I must object," Deshler said. "Mr. Jameson is stating pure gossip as fact, and his phrasing in no way poses a question to the witness."

Judge Poynter frowned. "Mr. Jameson, I will allow you some leeway with this witness, but you must submit questions to him. Objection sustained."

Jameson sighed heavily and asked, "Mr. Norville, have you ever talked with Mr. Hardin about his lady friends?"

"No, sir."

"That is not a satisfactory answer, sir. Remember, you are

sworn to tell the whole truth. Have you ever, in your entire life, talked to Clint Hardin about ladies?"

"Well, why didn't you ask me that in the first place? Yes, sir."

"Mr. Hardin has talked to you about ladies of his acquaintance?"

"Yes, sir."

"Mr. Hardin has told you about his relationships with ladies of his acquaintance?"

"No, sir."

"Mr. Norville! I must insist that you tell this court the truth, and stop lying! If you and Mr. Hardin have had conversations about ladies, he must have told you of his relationships to them, isn't that correct, Mr. Norville?" Jameson almost shouted.

"No, sir. See, all Clint ever says about any ladies is compliments about them, in general," Vince said expansively. "He says this lady is nice, that one is sweet, the other one has pretty eyes, over there, she has great teeth. Things like that. He never, not one time, has ever said one single word to me about his personal relationships to any ladies at all."

Jameson looked honestly aghast. "You've been friends with Mr. Hardin since childhood, and your sworn testimony is that he has never told you about his lady friends. Are you certain that you want that recorded as your testimony, sworn to truth with your hand on the Bible, in front of this judge and this jury and these people?"

"Yes, sir," Vince said confidently.

"Very well," Jameson said darkly. "Now, Mr. Norville, did you see Clint Hardin shoot Max Bettencourt?"

"I already told you, Clint didn't shoot Bettencourt," Vince said impudently.

"Answer the question, Mr. Norville!"

"No sir, I did not see *the shooting*. But Clint couldn't have shot Bettencourt anyway."

"Since you weren't there, how can you possibly swear to that?" Jameson demanded angrily.

"Because Clint Hardin doesn't know the upside from the downside of a gun. He's never had anything to do with them. He's never carried a gun in his life, never owned one, wouldn't have one if you gave it to him."

"Mr. Norville, according to the law your assertion is meaningless, because one cannot prove a negative," Jameson said with superiority. "What do you say to that?"

Vince shrugged carelessly. "Then prove a positive, Mr. Lawyer. You prove he had a gun that night."

"Your Honor, I'm through with this witness," Jameson said with disdain.

"Mr. Deshler?" Judge Poynter asked.

"Your Honor, I don't wish to question this witness at this time. However, I would like the opportunity to recall him if necessary."

"So noted."

The next witness, who was also pointed out to be an unwilling prosecutorial witness, was Ezra Givens. He sat in the witness chair, his arms crossed, and glared at Jameson.

"Mr. Givens, you live on the riverboat *Helena Rose*, with Mrs. Jeanne Bettencourt, Mr. Clinton Hardin, Mr. Vince Norville, Marvel Bettencourt, and Roberty, is that correct?" he asked.

"Yes, sir."

Jameson obviously didn't want to get into a quagmire as he did with Vince Norville, so he asked Ezra blunt, pointed questions. "You saw Mr. Clint Hardin and Mrs. Jeanne Bettencourt kissing, didn't you?"

Ezra's eyes narrowed. "Yes, sir," he bit off.

"In fact, you saw them in a passionate embrace, didn't you?"

"No, sir."

"But they were kissing, and had their arms around each other, and so it was an embrace, was it not?"

"I don't got no idear where their arms was. I only saw 'em for a second, and I tuck off 'cause it weren't none of my bidness," he said sourly.

"But you have seen them, many times, show physical affection?"

"Thet there question don't make no sense, and I ain't a-gonna answer it."

"Oh, come now, Mr. Givens. You're a grown man, you know perfectly well what I mean. I insist that you answer the question."

"I ruffle up Roberty's hair sometimes, 'cause I care about the boy. Is that what you mean? No, I ain't never seed Clint nor Miss Jeanne mess up one 'nother's hair."

Giggles and titters sounded throughout the courtroom, but it only took a stern look from Judge Poynter to stifle it quickly.

"Just—never mind, let the record show that the witness has seen Mr. Hardin and Mrs. Bettencourt kiss. Now, with Your Honor's indulgence, I'm going to bring out a diagram and ask Mr. Givens to explain it to us."

A bailiff brought out a three-legged easel and set a large square white board on it. It was the floor plan of the Texas deck of the *Helena Rose*. He set it up so that the jury, and the entire courtroom, could see it.

"Now, Mr. Givens, will you please go to the drawing, and point out each room, and tell us what each room is, what it is used for, and who inhabits each room?"

Ezra turned to look up at Judge Poynter. "Why do I have to do all that silly fol-de-rol, Judge? Any idiot can look at that there pitcher, and read what it says."

"Mr. Givens, you live on the boat, so you are considered an expert in this matter. Please just do as Mr. Jameson asks."

Ezra rose and went to the easel. As if he were speaking to a roomful of non-English speakers, he enunciated slowly, "This here is the cargo area on the Texas deck. That's where the cargo inhabits.

"This here is the galley, even though some fool printed 'kitchen' on it. At differin' and sundry times, me and Roberty and Mr. Vince Norville and Marvel Bettencourt and Captain Jeanne Bettencourt and Mr. Clint Hardin inhabits this here galley.

"Now over here is the crew quarters. This nice little pitcher here is my bunk. This nice little square here is Mr. Vince Norville's bunk. This nice little square here is Roberty's bunk. This nice little square here is nobody's bunk.

"This here is Captain Jeanne's cabin. Her and Marvel inhabits it.

"And this here is Clint Hardin's cabin. He inhabits here. Now here—" he stabbed a gnarled forefinger—"and here— and here—and here—is where Leo inhabits from time to time."

"Who's Leo?" Judge Poynter blurted out.

"He's our dog. He's been knowed to inhabit lotsa places on that boat. I jist figgered since all you folks is so nosy 'bout where we all place our bodies all the time, you'd best know about Leo too."

This time even Judge Poynter cracked a wintry smile. "Very well, Mr. Givens. Thank you for your expert information."

Ezra resumed his seat. Jameson, whose mouth had twitched also, regained his severe countenance. "Mr. Givens, the reason I wanted to make the arrangements on the *Helena Rose* is so that I can ask you this question: Mrs. Bettencourt's and Mr. Hardin's cabins are very close to each other, aren't they?"

"They's acrost a six-foot, three-inch-wide hall from each other."

"It would be very easy for either Mrs. Bettencourt or Mr. Hardin to slip into the other's cabin for romantic reasons, wouldn't it?"

"Me 'n you is closer than them cabins, so it would be very easy fer me to punch your face, Lawyer Jameeson," Ezra snarled.

Judge Poynter said, "Mr. Givens, you know very well that is unacceptable. Please answer the question."

"No, it wouldn't be easy a-tall for either Cap'n Jeanne nor Clint to slip around shameful," he said sturdily. "There's yer answer."

Jameson demanded, "Have you ever seen Mrs. Bettencourt either entering, or leaving, or inside Mr. Hardin's cabin?"

"No, siree!"

"Have you ever seen Mr. Hardin entering, or leaving, or inside Mrs. Bettencourt's cabin?"

"On the night of September 2, I saw Mr. Hardin inside it, then leave it, then enter it and be inside it, and then leave it," he answered precisely.

"Did you see Mr. Hardin shoot Mr. Bettencourt?"

"No, sir. I didn't git there in time, or I woulda shot Mr. Lyin' Maxwell Bettencourt my own self. But Mr. Clint Hardin didn't shoot that fool, he done shot his own dumb self with his own gun, and that there is my swore-on-the-Bible-truth testimony, Mr. Lawyer Jameeson!"

"Judge Poynter—" Jameson pleaded.

"Yes, yes, Mr. Jameson. Strike Mr. Given's last sentence from the record, Mr. Evans," he told one of the busily writing clerks. "Do you have any further questions for this witness, Mr. Jameson?"

"I certainly do not, Your Honor."

"Mr. Deshler?"

"No questions at this time, with option to recall, Your Honor."

Judge Poynter said, "It's almost noon. I'm going to adjourn this court for two hours. All concerned parties will report back here at two o'clock." He struck his gavel and left.

Jeanne was thinking that perhaps some good had been done by Vince's and Ezra's stout testimonies. Uneasily, she told herself that it seemed that the men of the jury were all paying strict attention to everyone and everything, and surely they would see Max as the evil liar that he was.

But as the bailiffs escorted her and Vince, Ezra and Roberty out of the courtroom first, she saw that the looks directed her way were just as dark and hostile as when she had first entered the court. The court of public opinion may have been amused by Vince and Ezra, but Jeanne and Clint were still in deep trouble.

CHAPTER TWENTY-THREE

"Oyez, oyez, oyez! All rise for the Honorable Judge Eugene Poynter, presiding over the Phillips County Criminal Court, State of Tennessee!"

Nathaniel Deshler called his first defense witness, Mrs. Herman Wiedemann. Immediately Cyrus Jameson rose to his feet. "Judge Poynter, I wish to enter a formal protest against the first four defense witnesses that my esteemed colleague has called. They were not present when Mr. Bettencourt was shot, they have no knowledge of the events of that night, they can offer no relevant expert testimonials of any matter with a bearing on this case."

Deshler responded, "Judge Poynter, the prosecution has defamed my client's character, and the character of Mrs. Jeanne Bettencourt. They have offered no proof, no corroborating testimony whatsoever, of the grave moral offenses attributed to them. However, I am able, through these witnesses, to offer testimony that disputes Mr. Bettencourt's charges regarding their moral fiber and, therefore, their motives for this alleged crime."

Judge Poynter nodded. "I'll allow these witnesses' testimony. Proceed."

Mrs. Wiedemann sternly affirmed that Jeanne was an honest, hardworking, conscientious Christian lady of high moral standing. She was such an austere, rigid woman that no one in the courtroom could doubt that if she knew of any failing of Jeanne's, either as an employee or as a woman, she would not hesitate to denounce her. Jameson didn't even attempt to cross-examine her.

Mrs. O'Dwyer was a cheerful, thin woman with a lined, weary, but kind face. Having lived in the same house with Jeanne for four years, she stoutly asserted that Jeanne had never, not once, been seen in the company of any man in their home. She stressed Jeanne's and even Marvel's charity, as they shared wood, household goods, food, and even money, with the O'Dwyers.

She said proudly, "Once my husband, who's a deckhand on the *William Crawford*, got his foot almost broke in two. That Old Mock's cart broke down whilst they was unloading his pitiful sticks of wood, I swear he'd bring his logs down to the docks in paper bags if he thought it'd cost him a penny less. Anyways, there's Mr. O'Dwyer home, with two of his toes broke and his foot swelt up like a fat ham, and he missed a whole twelve-day turnaround 'cause of it. We lacked two dollars for the rent that month, and what did Jeanne do? She loaned us the money to help us pay! *Two whole dollars!*"

Cy Jameson had no questions for this eager defense witness either.

Next, Deshler set on his repair of Clint's character. He called old L. F. Warner, whom Clint had been apprenticed to since he was twelve years old. He was almost seventy, wrinkled and walking slowly with a cane. He told the court movingly of how Clint, even as a young boy, had been scrupulously honest, and had worked as hard as two full-grown men.

"Not once in his life has Clint ever asked me for one blessed thing. He never complained about the hard work. In fact, through the years he's thanked me, over and over again, for being so kind to him." The old man wiped a tear away from his eyes. "It got to where he was almost like a son to me, and I'm as proud of him as any father ever could be."

Sighing, Jameson said, "I have no questions for this witness, Your Honor."

Clint's landlady, Mrs. Archibald Bowlin, was a short, round little woman with childlike bright blue eyes and chubby pink cheeks. She wore a very obvious blonde wig of fat ringlets underneath her bonnet, with a few airy wisps of gray floating about her cherubic face. She was sworn in and gave her residence as Bowlin's Boardinghouse on Adams Avenue.

Deshler established that she was Clint's landlady until he moved onto the *Helena Rose*, and then said, "Please tell the court of how you came to know Mr. Clint Hardin, and in your own words, what kind of man he is."

"Oh, Mr. Hardin came to my boardinghouse when he was but sixteen years old," she said, fanning herself vigorously with a violently purple silk fan. "But even then he was such a fine young gentleman! So tall, so handsome, so charming! Such fine manners, so respectful he always was. And mind you, he paid his rent on time every single month of those six or so years. He loves my cooking, and always brags on it and thanks me, which is a great deal more than I can say for most of my boarders, with all their nattering and complaining.

"Now I must say that Clint wasn't above asking me for little extra tidbits every now and then," she continued her gossipy chatter, "in particular, he loves my raspberry sponge cake. He always asked for a second piece of my raspberry sponge cake, and sometimes he'd ask the next day if there was any left, the sly thing, and I have to admit that I spoiled him somewhat, with cakes and cookies and sometimes we'd even have our own little tea, if he was in of an afternoon."

"And what about Mr. Hardin's social life? Did he ever introduce you to any lady friends?"

"No, he did not, though I don't mind my boarders having callers, or bringing young ladies, if they *are* ladies, to introduce me to them. I pick and choose my boarders, Mr. Deshler, and I only take in respectable, clean people. Oh, yes! I must tell you that Mr. Hardin is the cleanest man, the cleanest *person* I ever have known. He was in the kitchen all hours heating up my big copper pot for water for washing, I've never seen—"

"Yes, Mrs. Bowlin, thank you, I believe we understand your observance of Mr. Hardin's personal habits," Deshler said with amusement. "So, you never met Mr. Hardin's friends?"

"Of course I've met Mr. Hardin's friends," she said indignantly. "Haven't I known that scoundrel Vinnie Norville as long as I've known Mr. Hardin? And Duffy Byrne, and Eddie Long, and, oh, there are about half a dozen young men that Mr. Hardin introduced me to over the years. But no ladies, oh, no."

"In view of your strict Christian morals, Mrs. Bowlin, do you think it possible that Mr. Hardin could not introduce you to his lady friends, because they might not be the clean respectable persons that you might countenance?"

She stopped fanning and summoned up a surprising amount of dignity in her answer. "I think that Mr. Hardin is a discreet man that keeps himself to himself, for the most part. But in the six years I've known him, I have found him to be a kind, honest, hardworking man. And he has always, without fail, shown the utmost gentlemanly respect to me."

"Thank you, Mrs. Bowlin. Now I am going to ask you some questions, not as Mr. Hardin's landlady, but as a lady who owns a boardinghouse. How many boarders do you have at this time?"

"Four rooms I let out," she answered. "Right now I have three gentlemen and one lady."

"I see. May I assume that the four boarders' rooms are in close proximity to each other?"

She looked puzzled. "You mean, are they close together? Why, yes. It's my upstairs, you see, what used to be, until poor Mr. Bowlin passed on, the master bedroom and three other bedrooms. Two on one side of the hall and two on the other."

Deshler said carelessly, "So the lady must be across the hall from a gentleman?"

"Well, yes."

"So naturally this lady and the gentleman across the hall from her are lovers?"

Mrs. Bowlin's eyes grew as big as china plates. "What! No, sir, no sir, not in my house, not under my roof! And Miss Carew wouldn't—what kind of terrible question is that, sir? How dare you?"

"I apologize, Mrs. Bowlin, it is quite a shocking thing to assume that just because two unrelated people live under the same roof they must, in fact, be lovers. Yes, Judge, I know, I'll stop testifying. I have no more questions for this witness."

"Neither do I," Jameson said grumpily without even rising.

Dr. Augustus Hightower was called to the stand, and he clinically described Jeanne's injuries, and affirmed that they were consistent with a blow from a strong person.

Jameson asked him, "Dr. Hightower, is it possible that Mrs. Bettencourt might have received this small injury in any other way than from a blow?"

"It is possible, but highly unlikely."

"But couldn't she have accidentally just bruised her face in a fall?" Jameson persisted.

Icily, Hightower replied, "The cheekbone is a curve, Mr. Jameson. Mrs. Bettencourt's cheek was contused, and her lip was abraded. If she sustained these two injuries in a fall, then she must have bounced."

Jameson, looking chastised, gave up.

"Judge Poynter, at this time I wish to recall Mr. Maxwell Bettencourt," Deshler said.

Max came up to the witness box, and the judge reminded him that he was still under oath.

Deshler crisply asked, "Mr. Bettencourt, when you went to the *Helena Rose* on the night of September 2, and went up to the Texas deck to Mrs. Bettencourt's cabin, did you knock?"

"What?" he asked, startled.

"Did you knock on the door, and announce yourself, and ask for permission to enter?"

"Why—why, no! She's my wife! We've been married for eight years! I am her husband! Her home is my home!"

This time Deshler didn't instruct him to simply answer the question; he seemed content to let Max bluster on.

"So although you had not seen Mrs. Bettencourt for six years, you thought it permissible to just break into her bedroom?"

"I didn't break in! And—and I had seen her the day before, she knew I was here and I wasn't dead and I am her husband, I have a perfect right to be in her bedroom."

"Did you lock the door behind you?"

"No! I know Jeanne says that I did, but she's lying. I never did any such thing."

"Did you grab your daughter by the arm, call her a brat, haul her bodily out into the hallway, and then lock the bedroom door?"

Bettencourt had regained his composure, and he answered with apparent deep regret, "That is not at all what happened, sir. All I wanted to do was talk to Jeanne, try to win back her love. But she had so corrupted my sweet daughter's mind against me, that Marvel panicked and kept interrupting so that it was simply impossible for me to be able to speak to Jeanne at all. I took Marvel's hand, and explained to her that we were adults, and we needed to talk about grown-up things, and we needed to talk privately." He sighed deeply. "Marvel has been thoroughly spoiled, and certainly she's not likely to obey me. I'm sure that she's said that I treated her more roughly than I actually did. I certainly did not 'grab' her nor 'haul' her. And again, sir, I never locked that bedroom door at any time."

Like rapid-fire, as soon as Max finished Deshler asked, "Did you hit Mrs. Bettencourt?"

"No! I—I didn't even know that she had a bruise on her face until I heard that doctor's testimony!" He visibly calmed himself, then went on, "While I was trying to talk to Jeanne, she flew at me. I don't know if she was going to try to scratch me or hit me or what. I naturally tried to defend myself, and we struggled. Jeanne is strong for a woman. Somehow she fell, and that must have been how she bruised her face."

"When Clint Hardin came into the room, where was Mrs. Bettencourt?"

"She was sitting on the bed when that animal came bursting into the room like a mad dog," Max said darkly. "By that time I had calmed her down somewhat, and we were just going to sit down and talk, as we used to."

"What exactly did Mr. Hardin do when he came into the room?"

"He charged right at me like a maddened bull. He drew very close, and then I saw a small gun in his hand. I realized later, since I am an expert on firearms, that from the diameter of the gun barrel it must be a .22 caliber or even smaller, and those guns are only accurate at a distance, at best, of six to ten feet. He aimed that gun right at my heart and he knew he would have to be close for his shot to be accurate. And then he shot me, an unarmed man, in cold blood."

"And so, to sum up your narration of the events of that night, Mrs. Bettencourt is lying, your daughter is lying, and Clint Hardin is lying, is that correct?"

"Well, yes."

"How tall are you?"

"What?"

"How tall are you?"

"I'm—uh—six feet tall."

"Do bullets travel in a straight line?"

"What?"

"Since you are an expert on firearms, I am asking you if bullets travel in a straight line."

"What—that's a stupid question! Of course they travel in a straight line!"

Deshler turned to Judge Poynter. "At this time, Judge Poynter, I would like to make a demonstration to the courtroom. I request that Mr. Bettencourt stand out here, in front of the witness box, and I request that Dr. Ernest Slattery assist me."

"Objection, Your Honor! This is a court of law, not a theater! My client has no obligation whatsoever to assist the defense!"

Judge Poynter pursed his lips, then asked Deshler, "Is the point of the demonstration vital to an understanding of this case?"

"Your Honor, it is absolutely crucial. The point must be visibly, not verbally, illustrated."

"Then I'm going to allow it. Dr. Slattery, please come forward, remembering that you are still under oath."

"At this time I would like to introduce into evidence my set of fountain pens, Your Honor," Deshler said, bringing up a velvet box to show first to the judge, then to the clerks. He walked over to the jury box and walked slowly down, allowing the men to clearly see the two slim silver pens in the blue velvet case.

Judge Poynter looked interested, Cy Jameson looked puzzled, and Max Bettencourt looked enraged. But he said nothing, and merely stood tall and stiffly in front of the witness box.

Deshler said, "Mr. Bettencourt, please turn to face the jury box."

As if he were on parade, Max made a concise right turn.

Deshler continued, "Now, Dr. Slattery, please come over here and stand at Mr. Bettencourt's left side, facing him. Thank you. Now I want you to take these two fountain pens. With one, I want you to point straight to the entry wound on Mr. Bettencourt's shoulder. With the other, I want you to point to the exit wound."

His lip curling, the doctor placed one fountain pen against Max's shoulder and one fountain pen on the back. Carefully Deshler reached up and tipped the front pen at an angle until it pointed downward toward the floor. Then he lifted the back pen until it pointed to the ceiling.

He came around and looked up at Max Bettencourt. "My client is six feet, two inches tall, Mr. Bettencourt. So I assume that he was on his knees when he shot you?"

The courtroom erupted in a loud babble. Judge Poynter pounded his gavel, but with much less force than previously. It took a long time for the courtroom to quiet down to low sibilant constant whispering.

Max started to angrily resume his seat at the prosecution table, but Deshler said, "Sir, I am not finished questioning you." Max returned to the witness chair.

Deshler very slowly moved to stand in front of him, his back to the courtroom. He leaned on the railing and, for the first time, raised his voice in righteous indignation. "Isn't it true that you, Max Bettencourt, sneaked onto the *Helena Rose* in the dead of night, went into Jeanne Bettencourt's bedroom, threw your daughter out bodily, and beat Mrs. Bettencourt so that you could rape her?"

"She's my wife! She belongs to me! I have a right to do whatever I want to her!" Max snarled, jumping to his feet, his smooth face scarlet with rage.

Deshler turned and said quietly, "I have no more questions for him, Your Honor."

Jameson then re-examined Max, trying to mitigate some of the damage done. He elicited more declarations of love and loyalty to Jeanne, and his longing to know his only daughter, so that he could love her as a father should, and so on and so on. Jeanne thought that Jameson sounded not half-hearted, but rather automatic, as if he were painstakingly performing a bothersome chore.

Then it was time for Jeanne to testify. Her heart was beating like a timpani, and her hands were icy. But her gaze was direct, her expression calm, her voice quiet and sure.

First Deshler asked her about her marriage to Max, and Jeanne explained how they had begun as what she thought was a happy couple, but soon Max was cruelly and often crudely describing his liaisons with other women. She told of how he was often gone for two or three days at a time, and in April of 1849 he left for ten days. When he returned he told her that he had been in New Orleans with one of his army comrades meeting with emissaries of the Maharajah Ranjit Singh, and of his plans to join the *Khalsa* and leave for the Punjab in two weeks.

"And did you encourage him in these plans?"

"No, sir. Even though we were—estranged—I was five months expectant with his child. I didn't want him to desert us, of course not."

"Did you and Mr. Bettencourt agree that he should take the money out of your joint banking account?"

"No, sir. He never mentioned it to me, and he was so confident of all of the money he would make from the Sikhs that somehow it just never occurred to me that he would leave me absolutely penniless. I know that he knew that my parents would take care of me, of course, but at the time he left my parents had been killed in an accident, and I—"

Max jumped up and shouted, "Jeanne, darling, I didn't know that! Of course I never would have left if I had known!"

Judge Poynter pounded his gavel and said even more harshly than he'd admonished the flighty girl in the gallery, "Sir! I will have no more such *theatrics* in my courtroom! If you say one more word I will have the bailiffs remove you and take you to jail immediately!"

Smirking, Max said, "Yes, sir, Your Honor," and sat down.

"Continue, Mr. Deshler. There will be no more such melodramatic outbursts from Mr. Bettencourt," Judge Poynter said.

Deshler picked up a paper from his table and said, "Mrs. Bettencourt, I have here a death certificate issued by the Clerk of Court on February 8 of this year. It states that Maxwell Bettencourt, husband of Jeanne Langer Bettencourt, is declared dead *in absentia*. Will you explain this document to the court, please?"

"Yes, sir. I found out that if a spouse has been missing for a period of five years, and can reasonably be assumed to be dead, the surviving spouse can attest such to the court, and then the person is legally declared to be dead. Mr. Bettencourt had been missing for more than five years, and he had been fighting in a war, and I finally decided that it was best to have him legally declared deceased."

"Why did you feel that it was best, Mrs. Bettencourt?"

"I knew, I had known for years that he was dead. What else could I possibly think? But there was no grave, no marker, nothing tangible for me to hold on to, to make it real. Somehow I felt that it was better both for Marvel and for me to establish his death as a fact."

"In your mind, you honestly and completely believed yourself to be a widow?"

"Yes, sir."

"In your mind you believed that your marriage to Max Bettencourt had been dissolved in every sense, legally, morally, and spiritually?"

"Yes, sir."

"Did you believe that in the eyes of God you were no longer bound to Max Bettencourt?"

"I am a Christian, sir, and though I fail miserably sometimes, I try to seek the Lord's will and His counsel in all things that truly matter in this life. In my heart I believed that there was no longer any bond between me and Max Bettencourt, according to the will of God."

Deshler paused; the courtroom was utterly silent.

Then he led Jeanne through the night Max had come to the *Helena Rose*. Jeanne was able to keep her countenance steady all throughout the painful ordeal. She made it clear that Max had violently laid hands on Marvel, that he had brutally assaulted her, and he had made his intent to rape her very clear. Then she told of Clint suddenly charging into the room, the struggle that ensued, and that after Max had been shot Clint had clearly seen that he had received a wound in the shoulder. She spoke movingly of how bitterly poignant the scene was, of the men down on their hands and knees, scrubbing away the taint of Max Bettencourt from her life.

She concluded, "I know that the oath of marriage I took is for life, so in my mind I know that I am Maxwell Bettencourt's wife. I made a promise before God, and I must keep that promise, and not marry again while Max is living. But that is my sole and only obligation to him. My promise is all that's left."

Jameson cross-examined Jeanne, and tried every tactic to get her to change her story, to trip her up, to trap her. But she remained calm and steadfast, and he was unable to alter her testimony in any way. She was surprised that he didn't question her about Clint at all. What she didn't realize was that she had come across as so honorable, so chaste and pure in heart, that he felt that to insult her would only do more damage to Maxwell Bettencourt's case.

Then Deshler called Clint to the stand. He stood, his head held high, and marched confidently to the witness stand. He appeared to be perfectly relaxed and utterly fearless. Briefly, Deshler got him to relate how he had met Jeanne, his half ownership of the *Helena Rose*, and the nature of the business partnership he and Jeanne had.

Deshler said, "Mr. Hardin, I want you to describe now, in your own words, the events of the night of September 2."

"Vince and I were returning to the *Rose* from town. It was about eight o'clock in the evening. When we reached the boat, I saw Marvel up at the top of the steps on the Texas deck, and she screamed, "Mr. Clint! He's hurting Mama!" So I ran as fast as I could to Mrs. Bettencourt's cabin, heard her shouting, found the door locked, and I rammed it open." He went on to describe the scene perfectly, of a man assaulting a woman. He made it clear that under any circumstances at all he would have intervened to protect the lady, whoever she was. He stressed that he had no gun, had never in fact owned or carried a gun, and that Max Bettencourt had pulled the gun on him.

"I just saw a flash of silver, and I knew it was a gun, so I grabbed his hand. That little pistol didn't have a—uh—thing, the round piece of metal in front of the trigger—I don't know what it's called?"

"A trigger guard, I believe," Deshler said, his gray eyes alight.

"Yeah, a trigger guard. So as soon as I grabbed Bettencourt's hand it just went off. But until then, I had no control at all over the gun. I never touched the trigger."

Deshler went on to lead him through the rest of the sequence of events. Clint articulately and passionately explained that he wanted to cleanse the boat of all of Max's blood, not to hide any evidence, but for Jeanne's and Marvel's sake. "As far as I was concerned, that man is as close to pure evil as it's possible to be. I didn't want Mrs. Bettencourt, or Marvel, to have one bit of his filth in their home," he growled.

"Mr. Hardin, are you and Mrs. Bettencourt lovers?" Deshler asked.

Clint answered soberly, "Have we engaged in the physical act of love ordained by God between a husband and wife? No. Never. Mrs. Bettencourt would never consent to such a thing, because she's a virtuous woman. And now, thanks to the Lord Jesus Christ, neither would I."

He paused, and a small joyful smile flitted across his face. "But I want to tell you this. I love Jeanne Bettencourt with all my heart, to the depths of my soul. I would gladly give my life for her, and if I am convicted of this crime, I will happily take any punishment this court sees fit to give me. In the eyes of God I am guiltless. I am so proud, and so thankful to Him, that I was able to protect her. That's all I want from this life, to protect Jeanne and love her until the end of my days."

THE JURY DELIBERATED FOR an hour and eight minutes.

The foreman, a rawboned farmer, stood straight and tall. "We find the defendant not guilty on all charges."

Jeanne pushed past Vince and Ezra, ran around the defense table, and threw herself into Clint's arms. He lifted her up high. She looked down at him and through her tears said, "Thank you."

He set her down on her feet and whispered in her ear, "This is the last time I'll say it, my darling. I love you now and forever."

He released her then, and Jeanne turned to Nate Deshler. She said simply, "Thank you for saving my life."

He took her hand and briefly pressed his lips to it, then smiled at her and turned away.

VINCE, EZRA, AND ROBERTY went to Anderton's Grocery and practically bought out the store. It took all three of them, their arms full of packages, to bring everything back to the *Helena Rose*. They had a twenty-five-pound ham, a smoked joint of beef, six pounds of barbecued pork, three different kinds of cheeses, lettuce, tomatoes, cucumbers, carrots, radishes, green onions, apples, pears, oranges, bananas, grapes, plums, candies, bonbons, and two gallons of sparkling cider. That night there was a lavish party in Captain Jeanne's cabin on the *Helena Rose*.

"Ezra, I couldn't believe you said, right to a judge's face, that you would have shot Bettencourt yourself!" Vince said merrily.

"Dadblamed right, too. And you'll take note, Mr. Smarty-britches, thet I didn't git arrested for it, neither," Ezra retorted.

Roberty grinned devilishly. "How'd that happen?"

Everyone laughed, and Ezra went on, "Anyways, I'm of a mind afore the trial was over thet Judge Poynter mighta wished I woulda had the chance."

"I wouldn't be a bit surprised, Ezra," Jeanne agreed. She was sitting in her chair, with Leo's head in her lap. He gazed up at her adoringly, though it might have had something to do with the fact that she had a bonbon in her hand. "Mr. Jameson came up to me before I could get out of the courtroom door and begged me to have Max charged with assault and battery. He swore that he would have him thrown in prison. I refused, of course. I hope I never have to see that man again as long as I live."

"Mr. Deshler told me that Jameson told Bettencourt to get out of Memphis and never show his face here again," Clint said with satisfaction. "Bettencourt made Jameson look like a fool, and I have the impression that that's not a good thing to do to Cyrus Jameson."

"So do you think that my daddy isn't going to come see us again, Mama?" Marvel asked hopefully.

She was sitting on the floor in front of her dollhouse, sharing a bowl of grapes with Mrs. Topp and Avaymaria. Clint hurried to her, picked her up, and whirled her around in circles. "Don't you worry, little girl. You and your mama will never have to see him again, not as long as I'm breathin'."

"Not as long as I'm breathin', either," Roberty put in, seated cross-legged by Marvel. "If I see him, I'm not climbing no stepladder, I'll throw the ladder at his ugly face!"

"He is ugly, isn't he," Marvel, returned to the earth, said complacently. Clint and Jeanne exchanged amused glances.

His brow furrowed, Vince said, "You know, there is one thing that I don't get. How come Jameson didn't tackle Jeanne about George Masters? You know, that might not have looked so good. Surely Jameson knew about him, all those toffs run and play together."

Clint looked positively smug. "Jameson did know about him. They're friends, actually. But Bettencourt didn't know about him, there was nothing in his statements or anything said at the trial about him, so Jameson wasn't under any obligation whatsoever to put him forward, since he didn't have anything to do with that night."

Jeanne said slowly, "I think I should tell you all this. Mr. Masters offered to pay for Clint's defense. And he offered to be a character witness for me. It would have been very scandalous and embarrassing for him to be involved, of course. I didn't realize . . . that he cared so much."

"He did," Clint said somberly. "I saw. I knew. But who wouldn't care for you and Marvel, Captain Jeanne?"

Murmurs of agreement came from Vince, Ezra, and Roberty. Then Vince said, "I just have one last question I gotta ask you, Clint."

"What's that?"

Vince grinned boyishly. "Whatever happened to *gentlemen never tell?*"

LATE THAT NIGHT, BY mutual agreement, Clint and Jeanne met down on the main deck, standing on the starboard side that faced the river. It was a cool, clean-feeling sort of night, with a low yellow harvest moon and an ivory veil over the stars. They leaned on the railing without touching each other.

"Jeanne, I promised that I wouldn't burden you with any more declarations, and I won't," Clint said. "But I do want to tell you this. Before I really knew about my exact feelings toward you, I cared a lot about you and Marvel. I like you both, I enjoy your company. And we have a great business partnership. I—I just want to say that I hope you'll let me stay on the *Helena Rose*. It'll be hard, I know, for me, at least, but I don't think it will be any harder than being parted from you. But if you tell me that you feel it's not right or proper, then I'll be glad to go."

Jeanne turned to lean back against the rail. "One thing this trial showed me is that no matter how it appears to the rest of the world, I know that it was God's will that you and I, together, inherited the *Helena Rose*. It has always been right and proper for us to make her our home, and it still is.

"When I realized that I was in love with you, Clint, I thought that you didn't feel for me in that way. But I did know that you loved me and Marvel, and I treasured that love. Even though I knew how difficult it would be for me, I determined that I would never let you know how I truly felt about you. It was that important to me, to keep your friendship. And it's that important to me now. Please stay with me, Clint. This is the last time that I'll say this: I know in my heart that you are my partner, and forever you will be."

CHAPTER TWENTY-FOUR

At dusk the little hamlet of Helena, Arkansas, pretty much shut down. No cargo was loaded on the riverboats. The docks were deserted. The only lights on the riverfront came from the occasional lanterns lit on the steamboats overnighting there. Even the saloons and brothels, always mindful of the wrath of the Anti-Gambling Society and the Temperance Society and the strict sheriff, kept their festivities down to a subdued mumble.

On this misty September night, there were only three steamboats docked for an overnight stay at Helena. One of them was the *Helena Rose*. Several bright lanterns shone through her sparkling windows, casting a golden glow around her. Voices could be heard from her, and children's laughter. The sound of a lively fiddle drifted playfully on the air. Finally the music stopped, and the steamboat grew quiet. Two figures, one slender lady and a tall broad-shouldered man, came out to stand at the railing of the lower deck. They talked quietly, the man's voice a rich baritone murmur, the lady's voice a soft airy soprano.

Max Bettencourt stepped out of the black alley, his shoulders hunched, his chin jutting forward belligerently. He walked toward the *Helena Rose*, his gait a silent stamping march. As he neared the boat, he kept up his deliberate pace and slowly raised his right arm straight out, chest-high. In his hand he held a Colt .38 caliber nickel-plated revolver. The long thick silvery barrel glinted menacingly in the uncertain light.

Clint and Jeanne heard a gunshot. Instantly Clint pushed Jeanne to the ground and threw himself on top of her.

"Miz Langer? Mr. Hardin? Are you two all right?" Cautiously, Clint raised his head, then helped Jeanne to her feet. By the prone figure of Max Bettencourt stood Sheriff Hank Burnett, holding a gun, with grimy wisps of smoke rising from the barrel.

When he saw Jeanne and Clint standing there unharmed, he shook his head and looked down at Max Bettencourt. Then he said regretfully, "The rule is: no guns."

ON THE DAY THAT Marvel Bettencourt turned eight years old, her mama married Clint Hardin. It was a crisp, cold December 5, and the snow had turned Helena, Arkansas, into a Christmas greeting card village. The couple was married in the picturesque First Baptist Church, a small square clapboard building painted white, with a modest steeple and the front door painted bright green. The church was full. Sheriff Hank Burnett gave the bride away.

Clint and Jeanne chose to use the old Episcopal wedding vows.

I, Jeanne Langer Bettencourt, take thee, Clinton Hardin, to be my wedded husband, to have and to hold from this day forward, for better, for worse; for richer, for poorer; in sickness and in health; to love, cherish, and to obey, till death us do part, according to God's holy ordinance; and thereto I give thee my troth.

Clint held a plain gold band and took Jeanne's left hand.

With this ring I thee wed, with my body I thee worship, and with all my worldly goods I thee endow: In the name of the Father, and of the Son, and of the Holy Ghost. Amen.

And then he added softly, "I am my beloved's, and my beloved is mine."